SELECTIONS FROM LONGMAN WORLD HISTORY

PRIMARY SOURCES AND CASE STUDIES

Volume 1

George F. Jewsbury

Centre d'Études du Monde Russe
École des Hautes Études en Sciences Sociales

Longman

New York San Francisco Boston
London Toronto Sydney Tokyo Singapore Madrid
Mexico City Munich Paris Cape Town Hong Kong Montreal

Vice President/Publisher: Priscilla McGeehon
Acquisitions Editor: Erika Gutierrez
Executive Marketing Manager: Sue Westmoreland
Project Coordination, Text Design, and
    Electronic Page Makeup: Pre-Press Company, Inc.
Cover Design Manager: Wendy Fredericks
Cover Designer: David G. Bartow
Cover Photographs: *Background:* relief sculpture on a Hindu temple, © Steve Estvanik/
Corbis RF; *Counterclockwise from top left:* Head of Constantine, 330 C.E., Palazzo dei
Conservatori, © Corbis RF; African sculpture depicting a female, © Danile Calilung/
Corbis RF; Detail of Dome of the Rock, © Corbis/RF; travel photo © David
Lorenz Winston/Brand X Pictures/PictureQuest; Longman World History website
logo, Janette Afsharian
Senior Print Buyer: Dennis Para
Printer and Binder: Hamilton Printing Co.
Cover Printer: Lehigh Press, Inc.

Library of Congress Cataloging-in-Publication Data
Selections from Longman world history—primary sources and case studies
/[edited by] George Jewsbury.
    v. cm.
Selected from the website "Longman world history—primary sources and
case studies" http://longmanworldhistory.com.
Includes bibliographical references.
  ISBN 0-321-09847-1 (v.1)
  1. World history—Sources. I. Jewsbury, George F. II. Longman world
history—primary sources and case studies.
  D20.S4142002
  909—dc21

                            2002034008

Please visit our website at http://www.ablongman.com

ISBN 0-321-09847-1

10 9 8 7 6 5 4 3 2 1—HT—05 04 03 02

Contents

CHAPTER 4   CLASSICAL CHINA: 2100 B.C.E.
TO 220 C.E.   42

CHAPTER 5   THE EMERGENCE OF CLASSICAL
WESTERN CIVILIZATION   57

Topic and Theme Contents

Preface

"The historical sense involves a perception, not only of the pastness of the past, but of its presence."

T.S. ELIOT

By not only studying the works of the historians but also the documents which make up their foundations, students gain a deeper understanding of the past and its meanings for the present. By reading primary documents, students gain direct access to the identities of the world's peoples expressed through their religious practices, oral traditions, literatures, and governmental archives. These documents are the touchstones of who our global neighbors are, where they come from, and where they—and we—are going.

This reader grew out of *Longman World History—Primary Sources and Case Studies*, *http://longmanworldhistory.com*, a Web site composed of primary sources, maps, images, and global comparative case studies. This book, as does the site, encourages students to analyze the themes, issues, and complexities of world history in a meaningful, exciting, and informative way. While the Web site contains an enormous database of material for professors and students, it is understood that in certain cases, a printed book is sometimes useful where Internet access is limited. Thus the idea for this print reader was born. *Selections from Longman World History* is in essence the best of that wonderful site.

Selections from Longman World History helps readers handle the evidence of these documents "scientifically," as they advance their understanding as to why events have occurred. Unlike physical scientists, who can verify their hypotheses under controlled conditions in a laboratory, those who study history have to pay special attention to the uniqueness of documents because each event takes place at a particular time and at a particular place. Historians analyze documents with the same objective attitude employed by scientists examining natural phenomena. This scientific spirit requires historians to deal with the documents according to established rules of historical analysis, to recognize biases and to make conclusions as the evidence seems to warrant. The documents here have been subjected to the demands of *external criticism*—they are genuine as sources. It is up to the reader to take the next stage, *internal criticism*, to see what the documents' meanings and implications are.

SELECTIONS AND ORGANIZATION

The documents in this reader were carefully chosen to give a balance among the social, cultural, economic, political, and military aspects of each era. They also represent an attempt to provide global coverage—giving equal treatment to the Americas, Africa and the Middle East, Asia, and Europe.

To ensure a book of manageable length, difficult choices had to be made when selecting material to include from the Web site. The reader includes such selections as excerpts from The Holy Qur'an, Lady Murasaki Shikibu's Diary, and Martin Luther's *Sermon at the Castle Pleissenburg*. There were many wonderful selections and case studies that I simply could not include because of space limitations. In order to offer the best of both worlds, print and technology, each copy of *Selections from Longman World History* contains a free twelve-month subscription to the Web site. As we have become more comfortable and familiar with technology we realize that it is best to integrate the two forms of media to create a seamless flow that is accessible to all. Throughout the chapters, readers will find marginal icons that point students to key images and maps related to the sources at hand. The end of chapter material also includes an extensive list of pertinent Web links for students interested in further research. Because there were many selections that did not fit in this printed reader, the Web links section of each chapter begins with a link to the accompanying Web site with suggestions for other readings and case studies available online for that chapter.

There are many ways in which a reader can be organized and just as many ways that professors go about incorporating this type of material into their classes. In the case of this reader, the documents are arranged chronologically, for ease of use, and by region. There is also a table of contents included that references the documents according to topic and theme. Finally, should professors desire to organize the material around the chapters of their Longman World History survey textbook, the Web site provides a correlation for each book on the Longman list. This can be found on the Web site's home page.

FEATURES AND PEDAGOGICAL AIDS

Selections from Longman World History contains a number of pedagogical aids to promote student learning, provide a basis for unfamiliar information, and develop students' analytical skills.

- Marginal icons link students directly to photos and interactive and static maps found on the Longman World History Web site.

- Comparative Case Studies—At the end of each chronological part, there is an accompanying case study that introduces a topic and asks students to examine multiple primary sources related to it. These activities encourage students to act as historians and think analytically. Each case study is prefaced by its own introduction and is well suited to be the nucleus of class discussion or the basis for a project. The case study ends with a set of thought-provoking questions that encourage students' deeper analysis. An excellent example is the case study entitled "Battlefields to Courtrooms: Conflict and Agency in the Americas," which has students examine The Second Letter of Hernan Cortéz to King Charles V of Spain (1519) and *The New Laws of the Indies for the Good Treatment and Preservation of the Indians* (1542). This case study urges the student to consider the issues and debate surounding the treatment of Indians in the New World.

- Each chapter and document is accompanied by introductory information giving students enough context and background to begin interpreting the written or visual source.

- Footnotes with definitions of potentially unfamiliar words can be found throughout the book.

- Each document is concluded by a set of Analysis and Review Questions prompting students to think closely about the readings.

■ Each chapter ends with a number of Selected Weblinks, carefully chosen for their educational value, that offer students at least one direction for further research. A list of other documents and case studies found on the Web site can also be found in this section.

SUPPLEMENTS

The Instructor's Manual to accompany Longman World History is a comprehensive resource that guides instructors through the basics of logging on to the site and suggests how to relate the primary sources to the students. Introductions explain the basic navigation and pedagogical aspects of the site, and in-depth analysis of each chapter, topics for class discussion, and key questions for each source are also provided.

ACKNOWLEDGMENTS

As the general editor for this reader, I would like to thank the many historians, known for their fine classroom work and scholarship, who contributed to the product as a whole: Wayne Ackerson, Salisbury University; Eric Bobo, Hinds Community College; Wade G. Dudley, East Carolina University; James Halverson, Judson College; David L. Ruffley, United States Air Force Academy; Denise Le Blanc Scifres, Hinds Community College; Deborah Schmitt, United States Airforce Adacemy; John VanderLippe, State University of New York at New Paltz; Bryan E. Vizzini, West Texas A&M University; Pingchao Zhu, University of Idaho. This book is dedicated to their students and all who seek to know the past through the words of those who lived, worked, brought up families, and struggled to maintain their communities.

Much appreciation also goes to the fine people at Longman whose creativity and hard work brought this project to life: my acquisitions editor, Erika Gutierrez, Lisa Pinto, Nancy Crochiere, Beth Strauss, Patrick McCarthy, Doug Tebay, Marie Iacobellis, and Charles Annis.

Last of all, thank you to the reviewers who have been so enthusiastic about *Longman World History—Primary Sources and Case Studies* from the very beginning and who graciously offered their suggestions about selections, usability, features, and pedagogy: Richard H. Bradford, West Virginia University Institute of Technology; Pingchao Zhu, University of Idaho; Wade G. Dudley, East Carolina University; Aran S. MacKinnon, State University of West Georgia; Robert Chisholm, Columbia Basin College; Jon Lee, San Antonio College; Eric Bobo, Hinds Community College; Jessica Sheetz-Nguyen, Oklahoma City Community College; David Flaten, Plymouth State College; Richard Baldwin, Gulf Coast Community College; J. Lee Annis, Montgomery College; Richard S. Williams, Washington State University; Jim Halverson, Judson College; Kenneth A. Osgood, Florida Atlantic University; John A. Nichols, Slippery Rock University; Norman D. Love, El Paso Community College; Oscar Schmiege, Alliant International University; Clifford F. Wargelin, Georgetown College; Jennifer Hevelone-Harper, Gordon College; Deborah Gerish, Emporia State University.

George F. Jewsbury

CHAPTER 1

From Human Origins to the Neolithic Revolution to the First Cities

Millions of years ago, a new species, the *homo sapien,* appeared on earth. *Homo sapiens* were the ancestors of modern humans, and their survival was not guaranteed. These protohumans lacked the sharp teeth, rending claws, tremendous speed, and thick pelts of the creatures that preyed on them. But the advantages possessed by the new species far outweighed those disadvantages. They stood erect, allowing them to spot their enemies over a longer distance. They possessed opposable thumbs capable of creating and using tools far more powerful than tooth and claw. They learned to work as a group—a band, a clan, a society—finding a strength in numbers that offset the weakness of the individual. Most importantly, this species had evolved a brain capable of reasoning, of combining disparate pieces of data to reach a new and unique conclusion. And as they grew in numbers, eventually spreading across the face of their world, their minds grappled with the same difficult questions that still trouble their descendants: *Who am I? Why do I exist? What awaits beyond the veil of death?*

In evaluating how humans have dealt with these and so many other questions, historians rely on the written word, primary source documents in particular. Writing, however, did not appear until the end of the Neolithic Age, roughly 5,500 years ago, and the language of some of these early cultures still cannot be translated today. Thus, the study of early preliterate peoples belongs to the realm of archaeology—the study of past cultures through examination and interpretation of surviving material artifacts. Chapter 1 uses selected images of such artifacts to explore the long journey of prehistoric humans.

THE LONG JOURNEY

About the Document

Human ancestors first appeared on the plains of Africa some 28 million years ago. These hominids,° also referred to as prehumans, began the long journey across land masses and through time that eventually resulted in modern humans. As ages passed, new species of hominids developed. Those that survived were taller and more upright in posture than the earlier hominids. They possessed larger brains capable of storing a tremendous quantity of data. They proved adept at combining their ability to reason with their flexible fingers and opposable thumbs, developing tools that allowed these early humans to dominate other species. By roughly 2000 B.C.E., the hand of *homo sapiens* had been felt throughout the inhabitable portions of the world.

*Map 1.1
The spread of
human populations*

The Document

Figure 1.1a

Between 3.5 and 5 million years ago, an adult hominid and a child made these footprints near Laetoli, Tanzania. Perhaps they were travelers on the long journey that would eventually spread the descendants of their species around the globe.

hominids: The family of primates that includes humans; usually refers to the evolving humans of the ancient African plains. Figure 1.1b illustrates not only the long journey from early hominid to *Homo sapien*, but also provides an artist's conception of the changing human form, a form that came to rely more and more on tools for its survival.

Figure 1.1b

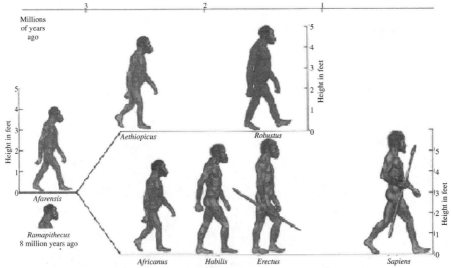

The chart not only illustrates the long journey from early hominid to *Homo sapien*, but also provides an artist's conception of the changing human form, a form that came to rely more and more on tools for its survival.

Analysis and Review Questions

1. Is it significant that the hominid footprints are those of an adult and a child? Why?
2. What forces led to the human evolution illustrated in Figure 1.1b?
3. Are those forces still at work? Will another million years of evolution find our physical and mental abilities significantly changed?
4. Most religions have creation myths or stories. How can we relate these to the concept of evolution?

A NEED TO REMEMBER

About the Document

Though their societies were preliterate, Paleolithic peoples seemed to possess some need to remember and record the world around them in great detail. Working with simple pigments, such as carbon, lime, and various colored clays, or even with a sharp stone, early humans left a remarkably detailed vista of their world. From the walls of caves leap the elk, horses, mammoths, and bison whose flesh sustained and whose skin clothed those distant peoples, as well as the predators that they feared—the cave bear, the lion, and the panther. The details are amazing: a horse depicted in springtime, his molting fur quite obvious; a herd of elk in full leap, perhaps fleeing from the very hunter who so carefully etched and colored them. Along with this visual record of the past, archaeologists often find what may well have been the signatures of these early artists—the carefully made print of a human hand.

By the late Neolithic Age, human societies often settled in permanent sites. Sometimes the walls of their homes exhibited paintings, while their pottery featured designs or etchings from their daily lives. Simple glyphs, the precursors of a written language, adorned more than rocks and walls and cups, for with the invention of tattoos the human body found a canvas in itself.

The Document

Figure 1.2a

This drawing of a horse, dated to 13,000 B.C.E., can be found in the Lascaux Cave in France. The horse appears to be molting—shedding its winter fur as summer approaches. Such details vividly illustrate Paleolithic peoples' awareness of and interest in the natural cycles of life.

Figure 1.2b

Opposable thumbs and flexible fingers gave early humans the ability to build and use tools. Where humans trod, those hands left marks of their passing; in this case, an artist from 13,000 B.C.E. placed his or her hand print among the marvelous drawings at Lascaux, France. Was it the artist's signature? Or was it merely an acknowledgment of the importance of the hand to the survival of the artist's people?

Analysis and Review Questions

1. Why would early humans have drawn pictures primarily of animals?
2. Why would primitive humans have invented tattoos?
3. What value does the survival of primitive art have for us?
4. What is the significance of the deliberate print of a human hand (such as that in Figure 1.2b)?

EARLY ART: RELIGION AND WORSHIP?

About the Document

The ability to communicate among themselves probably developed rapidly among early humans. Survival of the group demanded relatively complex planning and direction. Coupled with an increasing capacity to reason and a growing store of knowledge, at some point verbal communication reached beyond a survival skill. It would have been then that humans first addressed a troubling series of questions: Who am I? Why do I exist? Where do I go when this brief existence ends? I create my tools, but who created the world in which I live? Why? Why? Why?

There were, and sometimes still are, no easy answers to many of those questions. But the lack of final answers did not stop prehistoric humans from applying their knowledge, reason, and logic to provide their own answers. Paintings of half animal, half human creatures suggest the growth of humanity from bestial beginnings—the triumph of reason over animal nature. The observation of the human birth process is mimicked by numerous statues with exaggerated female reproductive organs—perhaps the "Earth Mother"° from whence sprang the first

Figure 1.3a

The Aphrodite of Willendorf, dated to 25,000 B.C.E., is typical of the multitude of carvings and statues found throughout Europe and Asia that are collectively known as "Earth Mothers." Symbols of fertility and the Earth Goddess cult, they also reflect the importance of women in early human societies.

"*Earth Mother*": Stylized representations of a pregnant female existed in many prehistoric societies; this led to the theory that an Earth Goddess, or Earth Mother, the creator and sustainer of the human race, existed at the center of many early religions.

humans. Graves containing bodies carefully placed and surrounded by useful artifacts, reflect the idea that the cycle of life did not necessarily end with death. And glyphs° carved by Neolithic people on flat stones emphasize a belief in cycles of life, death, and new life.

The Document

Figure 1.3b

The petroglyphs on this wall depict a battle, and they date from the Bronze Age around 1800–750 B.C.E. Are these strangely misshapen figures—winged humans and demonic apparitions—the gods of a lost culture? Are they an attempt by a forgotten priest to convey the message of creation, or, perhaps, a warning of how the world will end?

Analysis and Review Questions

1. Describe the Aphrodite of Willendorf. Why would primitive humans have attached religious significance to a figurine of a woman?
2. Referring to the artifacts in this document, speculate on the relation between religion and objects of veneration.
3. Why would religion have increased in importance among primitive humans?
4. One of the ways in which archaeologists learn about primitive humans is through the examination of burial sites. Briefly discuss the ethics of such investigations.

---

glyphs: A stylized symbol; when found in prehistoric societies it is often viewed as a precursor to modern writing.

REDEFINING SELF—FROM TRIBE TO VILLAGE TO CITY

About the Document

Paleolithic peoples lived a nomadic life, ever following their sources of food. During the Mesolithic Age,° roughly 12,000 to 8000 B.C.E., humans domesticated animals—dogs and sheep—and the first farming communities arose. In the Neolithic Age, farming and domestication of animals increased. Humans began to settle in small agricultural villages where they produced an abundance of food. By the end of the Neolithic Age, when conditions proved especially favorable, sedentary societies and a food surplus led to the creation of cities. Therein lived farmers as well as specialists such as stonemasons, carpenters, and doctors who traded their labor for surplus food. An expanding population crowded into a relatively small area required a government to allocate resources and to provide protection from internal and external threats. Trade routes developed between cities, and another class of non-farmers, merchants, became wealthy by managing the exchange of local food surpluses and unique resources for those of distant locales.

Map 1.2
The Spread of
Agriculture

The early settlements had a number of things in common. They were built near water, necessary for intensive agriculture as well as providing alternative food sources. Most were walled for security; buildings clustered close within the walls. They were built of local materials, commonly stone, brick, or wood. Thanks in part to the specialization of their dwellers, urban sites became repositories of knowledge—knowledge that expanded as trade between cities developed, then increased.

The Document

Figure 1.4a

An exterior view of late Neolithic (1500 B.C.E.) houses at Skara Brae in the Orkney Islands reveals thick walls built of locally quarried stone. Though a relatively small settlement, Skara Brae was typical of the Neolithic communities that, when circumstances favored, eventually developed into ancient cities. Note that the town was located near the sea, a ready source of protein for its inhabitants.

Mesolithic Age: 10,000 to 8000 B.C.E.; from the Greek words for "middle" and "stone"; transitional period in which stone age man first learned to domesticate animals and began to develop agriculture.

In the expanding cities the first written languages appeared, as accurate record-keeping became necessary for increasingly complex trade, government, and religion. Classes of people arose who did not spend every moment laboring for sustenance. Their luxury time allowed art and philosophy to formalize and flourish. Most importantly, the rise of urban sites caused a critical shift in the manner in which Neolithic humans defined themselves. Their primary allegiance shifted from the nomadic group—tribe or clan—to the city, a fixed geographic point. That subtle shift in self-perception enabled the rise of city states, nation states, and empires.

Figure 1.4b

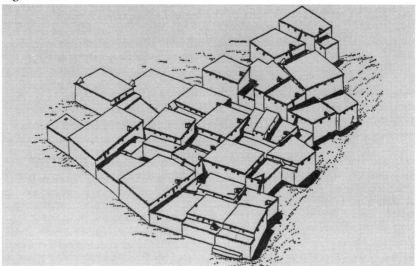

Çatal Hüyük, a Neolithic settlement in modern Turkey, contained the oldest map yet discovered (6200 B.C.E.). Above the settlement towered a volcano, Hassan Dag, and from its slopes the villagers quarried obsidian, which they shaped into tools and ornaments for trade. Also, the nutrient-rich terraces at the base of the volcano would have been highly productive for primitive farmers. This artist's conception of Çatal Hüyük, prepared from the map and archeological finds, depicts the village as it may have been in 6200 B.C.E. Individual homes were entered via ladders from the roofs. Many of the rooms in the village seem to have been used for ceremonial or religious purposes (perhaps not surprising when one realizes that these people lived at the base of an active volcano!), and the settlement's dead were buried beneath the floors of their homes, perhaps as a form of ancestor worship.

Analysis and Review Questions

1. Why did Neolithic villages differ in construction?
2. After examining Figures 1.4a and 1.4b, identify some similarities between Skara Brae and Çatal Hüyük. Why would local maps have been of importance to Neolithic humans?
3. Why is the increasing urbanization during the Neolithic Age of critical importance to the development of later civilizations?

WEB LINKS

Selections from Longman World History—Primary Sources and Case Studies

http://longmanworldhistory.com
The following additional readings and case studies can be found on the Web site.
Document 1.2, The Toolmaker
Document 1.6, A Visitor from the Neolithic Age—The Iceman
Case Study 1.1, The Development of Tools—A Question of Survival
Case Study 1.2, The Development of Religion in Primitive Cultures
Case Study 1.3, The Neolithic Village

Paleolithic Tools

http://citd.scar.utoronto.ca/antd15/wall/mulitmed.html
Excellent discussion of stone age tools and their development.

Evolution

http://www.talkorigins.org
A forum for the examination of scientific evolution.

Paleolithic Art

http://www.subtlemoon.com/paleo/
An excellent overview of ancient art, tools, and tool making.

General Archaeology

http://www.archaeology.org
A journal of archaeology featuring articles pertaining to prehistoric studies.

Prehistoric Humans

http://www.archaeologyinfo.com/evolution.htm
A well-illustrated approach to early humans and their evolution.

http://www.indiana.edu/~origins/
A multi-disciplinary approach to the study of early humans.

The Iceman, South Tyrol Museum of Archaeology

http://iceman.it
Features detailed and up-to-date material covering the Iceman.

The Chauvet Cave

http://www.culture.fr/culture/arcnat/chauvet/en/
An extensive presentation of the prehistoric art of the Chauvet Cave.

PHOTO CREDITS

Photo credit: SPL/Photo Researchers
Photo credit: Reprinted from Life Introduction to Biology, *3rd ed., by Beck, Liem & Simpson* ©

CHAPTER 2

The Ancient Near East

As people in what is known today as the Middle East began to establish villages and small towns between 8000 B.C.E. and 5000 B.C.E., society became more complex. More political functions appeared, as people became more settled. The arts began to emerge, and writing became essential to the central authority's administrative power. Eventually, large urban centers appeared, and the period around 2500 B.C.E. is known as one of the great periods of urbanization in the West, as cities such as Ur, Uruk, Babylon, Memphis, and others blossomed.

Despite the fact that we often lump a large number of societies together into "Mesopotamia" or the "ancient Near East," the area held great diversity. In Egypt, a unique religion and a divine monarchy emerged by 3100 B.C.E., while cities such as Memphis and, later, Thebes grew. In Asia Minor (modern-day Turkey), Egypt's great rival, the Hittite Empire, was a dominant military force. In Palestine, the Hebrews, bearers of a truly monotheistic religion, settled after centuries of wandering. These different peoples may have had their own ways of life, but they shared many of the same concerns and fears about life—a fact substantiated in the documentary evidence.

SUFFERING EXPLAINED

About the Document

Among the early Near Eastern peoples were the Babylonians and the Hebrews. The Babylonian kingdom reached its height between 2000 and 1600 B.C.E., borrowing heavily (as all contemporary societies in this region did) from the Sumerians who had dominated before them. The Babylonians became the ancient world's most accomplished mathematicians, and government scribes worked diligently to preserve earlier learning and scholarship. Conversely, the Hebrews developed little in the way of art, military achievement, or science, but created a monotheistic religion based on ethics and morality. Hebrew law was also a direct offshoot of their religion.

Despite the fact that the Babylonians were polytheists with a religion that placed much less emphasis on morality and ethical behavior, and the fact that the Hebrews were strict believers in one god, the assorted religious beliefs in the region influenced one another. No matter what the religious beliefs, the basic human concerns remain the same. Both of the following documents address the issue of human suffering. The first is a Babylonian tale, the "Poem of the Righteous Sufferer," written from the point of view of a worshiper. The poem is similar to an earlier Sumerian version, but dates from the high point of Babylonian influence. The second selection is the Old Testament story of Job, thought to have been written around 700 B.C.E. Each document attempts to confront the issue of human suffering in its own way.

The Document

FROM "POEM OF THE RIGHTEOUS SUFFERER"

"What Strange Conditions Everywhere!"

My god has forsaken me and disappeared,
My goddess has failed me and keeps at a distance.
The benevolent angel who walked beside me has departed,
My protecting spirit has taken to flight, and is seeking someone else.
My strength is gone; my appearance has become gloomy;
My dignity has flown away, my protection made off. . . .
The king, the flesh of the gods, the sun of his peoples,
His heart is enraged with me, and cannot be appeased.
The courtiers plot hostile action against me,
They assemble themselves and give utterance to impious words. . . .
They combine against me in slander and lies.
My lordly mouth have they held as with reins,
So that I, whose lips used to prate, have become like a mute.
My sonorous shout is reduced to silence,
My lofty head is bowed down to the ground,
Dread has enfeebled my robust heart. . . .
If I walk the street, ears are pricked;
If I enter the palace, eyes blink.
My city frowns on me as an enemy;
Indeed my land is savage and hostile.
My friend has become foe,
My companion has become a wretch and a devil. . . .
As I turn round, it is terrible, it is terrible;
My ill luck has increased, and I do not find the right.
I called to my god, but he did not show his face,
I prayed to my goddess, but she did not raise her head.
The diviner with his inspection has not got to the root of the matter,
Nor has the dream priest with his libation elucidated my case.
I sought the favour of the zaqiqu-spirit, but he did not enlighten me;
And the incantation priest with his ritual did not appease the divine wrath against me.
What strange conditions everywhere!
When I look behind, there is persecution, trouble.

"Prayer Was Discretion, Sacrifice My Rule"

Like one who has not made libations to his god,
Nor invoked his goddess at table,
Does not engage in prostration, nor takes cognizance of bowing down;
From whose mouth supplication and prayer is lacking,
Who has done nothing on holy days, and despised sabbaths,
Who in his negligence has despised the gods' rites,
Has not taught his people reverence and worship,
But has eaten his food without invoking his god,
And abandoned his goddess by not bringing a flour offering,
Like one who has grown torpid and forgotten his lord,
Has frivolously sworn a solemn oath by his god, like such a one do I appear.
For myself, I gave attention to supplication and prayer:
To me prayer was discretion, sacrifice my rule.
The day for reverencing the god was a joy to my heart;
The day of the goddess's procession was profit and gain to me.
The king's prayer—that was my joy,
And the accompanying music became a delight for me.
I instructed my land to keep the god's rites,
And provoked my people to value the goddess's name.
I made praise for the king like a god's,
And taught the populace reverence for the palace.
I wish I knew that these things were pleasing to one's god!

"Who Knows the Will of the Gods?"

What is proper to oneself is an offence to one's god,
What in one's own heart seems despicable is proper to one's god.
Who knows the will of the gods in heaven?
Who understands the plans of the underworld gods?
Where have mortals learnt the way of a god?
He who was alive yesterday is dead today.
For a minute he was dejected, suddenly he is exuberant.
One moment people are singing in exaltation,
Another they groan like professional mourners.
Their condition changes like opening and shutting the legs.
When starving they become like corpses,
When replete they vie with the gods.
In prosperity they speak of scaling heaven,
Under adversity they complain of going down to hell.
I am appalled at these things; I do not understand their significance. . . .

Conclusion: *"Marduk° Restored Me"*

The Lord took hold of me,
The Lord set me on my feet,
The Lord gave me life,
He rescued me from the pit,

---

marduk: The most important god in the Babylonian pantheon, known for his wisdom
and compassion for humanity.

He summoned me from destruction,
[...] he pulled me from the Hubur river,
[...] he took my hand....
Marduk, he restored me....
The Babylonians saw how Marduk restores to life,
And all quarters extolled his greatness: ...
Mortals, as many as there are, give praise to Marduk!

FROM *THE BOOK OF JOB*

"Let the Day Perish Wherein I Was Born"

Let the day perish wherein I was born, and the night in which it was said, There is a man child conceived. Let that day be darkness; let not God regard it from above, neither let the light shine upon it. . . .

Why died I not from the womb? why did I not give up the ghost when I came out of the belly? . . . For now should I have laid still and been quiet, I should have slept; then had I been at rest; There the wicked cease from troubling; and there the weary be at rest. . . .

Wherefore is light given to him that is in misery, and life unto the bitter in soul; Which long for death, but it cometh not; and dig for it more than for hid treasures; Which rejoice exceedingly, and are glad, when they can find the grave? Why is light given to a man whose way is hid, and whom God hath hedged in? . . .

"I Am Full of Confusion"

My soul is weary of my life; I will leave my complaint upon myself; I will speak in the bitterness of my soul. . . .

If I be wicked, woe unto me; and if I be righteous, yet will I not lift up my head. I am full of confusion; therefore see thou mine affliction; For it increaseth. Thou huntest me as a fierce lion: and again thou showest thyself marvelous upon me. . . .

Are not my days few? cease then, and let me alone, that I may take comfort a little, Before I go whence I shall not return, even to the land of darkness and the shadow of death, without any order, and where the light is darkness. . . .

Man that is born of a woman is of few days, and full of trouble. He cometh forth like a flower, and is cut down: he fleeth also as a shadow, and continueth not. . . .

For there is hope of a tree, if it be cut down, that it will sprout again, and that the tender branch thereof will not cease. . . . But man dieth, and wasteth away: yea, man giveth up the ghost, and where is he? As the waters fail from the sea, and the flood decayeth and drieth up; So man lieth down, and riseth not: till the heavens be no more, they shall not awake, nor be raised out of their sleep.

If a man die, shall he live again? all the days of my appointed time will I wait, till my change come. . . . The waters wear the stones: thou washest away the things which grow out of the dust of the earth; and thou destroyest the hope of man.

"Oh That I Knew Where I Might Find Him!"

Even today is my complaint bitter: my stroke is heavier than my groaning. Oh that I knew where I might find him! that I might come even to his seat! I would order my cause before him, and fill my mouth with my arguments. . . .

Behold, I go forward, but he is not there; and backward, but I cannot perceive him: On the left hand, where he doth work, but I cannot behold him: he hideth on the right hand, that I cannot see him. . . .

Why, seeing times are not hidden from the Almighty, do they that know him not see his days? Some remove the landmarks; they violently take away flocks, and feed thereof. They drive away the ass of the fatherless, they take the widow's ox for a pledge. They turn the needy out of the way: the poor of the earth hide themselves together. . . .

Men groan from out of the city, and the soul of the wounded crieth out: yet God layeth not folly to them. They are of those that rebel against the light; they know not the ways thereof, nor abide in the paths thereof. . . . And if it be not so now, who will make me a liar, and make my speech nothing worth? . . .

"The Lord Answered Job"

Then the Lord answered Job out of the whirlwind, and said, Who is this that darkeneth counsel by words without knowledge? Gird up now thy loins like a man; for I will demand of thee, and answer thou me.

Where wast thou when I laid the foundations of the earth? declare, if thou hast understanding. Who hath laid the measures thereof, if thou knowest? or who hath stretched the line upon it? Whereupon are the foundations thereof fastened? or who laid the corner stone thereof; when the morning stars sang together, and all the sons of God shouted for joy? . . .

Hast thou entered into the springs of the sea? or hast thou walked in the search of the depth? Have the gates of death been opened unto thee? or hast thou seen the doors of the shadow of death? Hast thou perceived the breadth of the earth? declare if thou knowest it all. . . .

Shall he that contendeth with the Almighty instruct him? he that reproveth God, let him answer it. . . .

"Job Answered the Lord and Said, I Repent"

Then Job answered the Lord, and said, I know thou canst do every thing, and that no thought can be hidden from thee. Who is he that hideth counsel without knowledge? therefore have I uttered that I understood not; things too wonderful for me, which I knew not. . . . I have heard of thee by the hearing of the ear; but now mine eye seeth thee; Wherefore I abhor myself, and repent in dust and ashes. . . . So the Lord blessed the latter end of Job more than his beginning: for he had fourteen thousand sheep, and six thousand camels, and a thousand yoke of oxen, and a thousand she asses. He had also seven sons and three daughters. . . . And in all the land were no women found so fair as the daughters of Job: and their father gave them inheritance among their brethren. After this lived Job a hundred and forty years, and saw his sons, and his sons' sons, even four generations. So Job died, being old and full of days.

Analysis and Review Questions

1. In the "Poem of the Righteous Sufferer," does Marduk eventually help the worshiper?
2. Is Job finally helped by God?
3. List some similarities between the two selections.
4. Would you say that the worshiper in the first selection is pious and dedicated to his religion?
5. Why do you think these two selections are so similar?

ELDERS' ADVICE TO THEIR SUCCESSORS

About the Document

The ancient Egyptians, unlike most people in Mesopotamia, did not create heroic tales like the *Epic of Gilgamesh*. They did, however, produce an abundance of other writings. The Egyptians left extensive religious writings, mostly contained in collections we call the "Books of the Dead" because they were frequently found on tomb walls. They also left to posterity numerous treaties, deeds, legal documents, and other official documentation.

One form of text that survives is the "instruction." This was a document of advice written by an elder to his son or successor, by priests to future priests, by government officials to lesser administrators, and by pharaohs to their heirs. The first document was written during Egypt's First Intermediate Period, a period of chaos lasting from around 2250 B.C.E. until 2052 B.C.E. The author is supposedly Wahkare, pharaoh and father of Merikare, who became the next ruler. The second document was written about 2450 B.C.E. and found in a tomb from the period known as the Old Kingdom. The author is the vizier (chief advisor) Ptah-hotep, who is writing to his son. Both sources help us understand the prevalent values and attitudes in different periods of Egyptian history.

The Document

THE INSTRUCTION FOR KING MERIKARE

If thou findest a man . . . whose adherents are many in total, and he is gracious in the sight of his partisans, and he is excitable, a talker—remove him, kill him, wipe out his memory, destroy his faction, banish the memory of him and of his adherents who love him. The contentious man is a disturbance to citizens: he produces two factions among the youth. If thou findest that the citizens adhere to him, denounce him in the presence of the court, and remove him. He is also a traitor. A talker is an exciter of a city. Divert the multitude and suppress its heat.

Be a craftsman in speech, so that thou mayest be strong, for the tongue is a sword to a man, and speech is more valorous than any fighting. No one can circumvent the skillful of heart. They who know his wisdom do not attack him, and no misfortune occurs where he is. Truth comes to him fully brewed, in accordance with the sayings of the ancestors.

Copy thy fathers and thy ancestors. Behold, their words remain in writing. Open, that thou mayest read and copy their wisdom. Thus the skilled man becomes learned. Be not evil: patience is good. Make thy memorial to last through the love of thee. God will be praised as thy reward, praises because of thy goodness and prayers for thy health.

Respect the noble and make thy people to prosper. Establish thy boundaries and thy frontier-patrol. It is good to act for the future. Advance thy great men, so that they may carry out thy laws. He who is rich does not show partiality in his own house. He is a possessor of property who has no wants. But the poor man does not speak according to what is right for him. It is of no avail to say: "Would that I had!" Great is a great man when his great men are great. Valiant is the king possessed of courtiers; august is he who is rich in his nobles.

Mayest thou speak justice in thy own house, that the great ones who are on earth may fear thee. Uprightness of heart is fitting for the lord. It is the forepart of the house that inspires respect in the back. Do justice whilst thou endurest upon earth. Be on thy guard against punishing wrongfully. Do not slaughter: it is not of advantage to thee. But thou shouldst punish with beatings and with arrests. Do not kill a man when thou knowest his good qualities, one with whom thou once didst sing the writings.

Foster thy younger generation, that the residence city may love thee, and increase thy adherents with recruits. Behold, thy citizenry is full of new growing boys. It is twenty years that the younger generation is happy flowing its heart, and then recruits come forth anew. Make thy officials great, advance thy soldiers, increase thy younger generation of thy following, provided with property, endowed with fields, and rewarded with cattle.

Do not distinguish the son of a man [of birth and position] from a poor man, but take to thyself a man because of the work of his hands. Protect thy frontier and build thy fortresses, for troops are of advantage to their lord.

Make the offering-table flourish, increase the loaves, and add to the daily offerings. It is an advantage to him who does it. The god is aware of him who works for him. Let thy statues be transported into a distant country. It is a goodly office, the kingship. It has no son and no brother, made to endure on its monuments. But it is one king who promotes another. A man works for him who was before him, through a desire that what he has done may be maintained by someone else coming after him. Act for the god, that he may act similarly for thee, with oblations which make the offering-table flourish and with a carved inscription—that is what bears witness to thy name. The god is aware of him who acts for him.

Behold, I have spoken to thee the profitable matters of my very belly. Mayest thou act on what is established before thy face.

THE INSTRUCTION OF PTAH-HOTEP

Preface: Royal Approval

The mayor and vizier° Ptah-hotep said: "O king, my lord, years come on, old age is here, decrepitude arrives, weakness is renewed. . . . Let it be commanded of your servant to make a staff of old age: let my son be set in my place. Let me tell him the sayings of those who obeyed, the conduct of them of old, of them who listened to the gods."

Said the majesty of this god [the king]: "Instruct him in the sayings of the past. . . . Speak to him, for no one is born wise."

Title and Aim

Beginning of the maxims of good words spoken by the . . . mayor and vizier, Ptah-hotep, teaching the ignorant to know according to the standard of good words, expounding the profit to him who shall listen to it, and the injury to him who shall transgress it. He said to his son:

Intellectual Snobbery

Be not arrogant because of your knowledge, and be not puffed up because you are a learned man. Take counsel with the ignorant as with the learned, for the limits of art

vizier: The pharaoh's chief advisor.

cannot be reached, and no artist is perfect in his skills. Good speech is more hidden than the precious greenstone, and yet it is found among slave girls at the millstones.

Leadership and "Maat"

If you are a leader, commanding the conduct of many, seek out every good aim, so that your policy may be without error. A great thing is truth [*maat*], enduring and surviving; it has not been upset since the time of Osiris. He who departs from its laws is punished.

Conduct as a Guest at the Table

If you are a guest at the table of one who is greater than you, take what he offers as it is set before you. Fix your gaze upon what is before you, and pierce not your host with many glances, for it is an abomination to force your attention upon him. Speak not to him until he calls, for no one knows what may be offensive; speak when he addresses you, for then your words will give satisfaction. Laugh when he laughs; that will please him, and then whatever you do will please him. . . .

Patience with Suppliants (Subordinates)

If you are a leader be kind in hearing the speech of a suppliant. Treat him not roughly until he has unburdened himself of what he was minded to tell you.

Relations with Women

If you wish to prolong friendship in a house into which you enter as master, brother or friend, or any place that you enter, beware of approaching the women. No place in which that is done prospers. There is no wisdom in it. A thousand men are turned aside from their own good because of a little moment, like a dream, by tasting which death is reached. . . . He who fails because of lusting after women, no plan of his will succeed.

Greed

If you want your conduct to be good, free from every evil, then beware of greed. It is an evil and incurable sickness. No man can live with it; it causes divisions between fathers and mothers, and between brothers of the same mother; it parts wife and husband; it is a gathering of every evil, a bag of everything hateful.

Marriage

If you are prosperous you should establish a household and love your wife as is fitting. Fill her belly and clothe her back. Oil is the tonic for her body. Make her heart glad as long as you live. She is a profitable field for her lord. . . .

Obedience to a Superior

Bend your back to him who is over you, your superior in the administration; then your house will endure by reason of its property, and your reward will come in due season. Wretched is he who opposes his superior, for one lives only so long as he is gracious.

Exhortation to Listen

If you listen to my sayings, then all your affairs will go forward. They are precious; their memory goes on in the speech of men because of their excellence. If each saying is carried on, they will never perish in this land.

If the son of a man accepts what his father says, no plan of his will fail. Failure follows him who does not listen. He who hears is established; he who is a fool is crushed.

A son who hears is a follower of Horus: there is good for him who listens. When he reaches old age and attains honor, he tells the like to his children, renewing the teaching of his father. Every man teaches as he has acted. He speaks to his children so that they may speak to their children.

Conclusion

May you succeed me, may your body be sound, may the king be well pleased with all that is done, and may you spend many years of life! It is no small thing that I have done on earth; I have spent one hundred and ten years of life, which the king gave me, and with rewards greater than those of the ancestors, by doing right for the king until death.

Analysis and Review Questions

1. Are there any religious recommendations in King Merikare's instructions?
2. What does the author of Merikare's instructions mean by saying, "Be a craftsman in speech, so that thou mayest be strong"?
3. Is there any military advice given by Merikare?
4. Are there any similarities in advice between the two documents?
5. What advice does Ptah-hotep give about dealing with one's superiors?

NEAR EASTERN LAW CODES

Map 2.1 (interactive) Empires of the Ancient Near East

About the Document

Centered in southern Turkey, the Hittite Empire first emerged around 2000 B.C.E. and reached its height in the period between 1370 and 1180 B.C.E. A successful military empire, it gathered tribute from several neighboring kingdoms and was powerful enough to limit Egypt's northern expansion during the height of Egypt's military power, the New Kingdom. Because of its military focus, the Hittite Empire was a great borrower of its neighbors' cultural achievements. It is no surprise, then, that there are similarities between its law codes and those of other Near Eastern societies.

The Hittites may well have been influenced by the law code of the Eshnunna. The kingdom, which shares the name of its major city, was located in modern-day Iraq, stretching north from Babylon. Eshnunna flourished between 2000 and 1700 B.C.E., and it was conquered by the Babylonians as that people were establishing their empire. Their law code, not quite as comprehensive as that of the conqueror Hammurabi, predates that more complete legal code by several hundred years.

The Document

THE HITTITE LAW CODE

7: If anyone blinds a free man or knocks out his teeth, he would formerly give 1 mina° of silver, now he shall give 20 shekels of silver and pledge his estate as security.

---

mina: An ancient coin worth 500 shekels (a more common coin).

8: If anyone blinds a male or female slave or knocks out his/her teeth, he shall give 10 shekels of silver and pledge his estate as security.

10: If anyone batters a man so that he falls ill, he shall *take care* of him. He shall give a man in his stead who can look after his house until he recovers. When he recovers, he shall give him 6 shekels of silver, and he shall also pay the physician's fee.

11: If anyone breaks a free man's hand or foot, he shall give him 20 shekels of silver and pledge his estate as security.

12: If anyone breaks the hand or foot of a male or a female slave, he shall give 10 shekels of silver and pledge his estate as security.

13: If anyone bites off a free man's nose, he shall give 1 mina of silver and pledge his estate as security.

14: If anyone bites off the nose of a male or female slave, he shall give 30 shekels of silver and pledge his estate as security.

15: If anyone mutilates a free man's ear, he shall give 15 shekels of silver and pledge his estate as security.

16: If anyone mutilates the ear of a male or female slave, he shall give 6 shekels of silver.

17: If anyone causes a free woman to miscarry, he shall give 20 shekels of silver.

18: If anyone causes a slave-woman to miscarry, if (it is) the 10th month, he shall give 5 shekels of silver.

Later version of 18: If anyone causes a slave-girl to miscarry, he shall give 10 shekels of silver.

22: If a slave runs away and anyone brings him back—if he seizes him in the vicinity, he shall give him shoes; if on this side of the river, he shall give him 2 shekels of silver; if on the other side of the river, he shall give him 3 shekels of silver.

24: If a male or female slave runs away, the man at whose hearth his master finds him/her, shall give a man's wages for 1 year (namely) x shekels of silver, but a woman's wages for 1 year, (namely) x shekels of silver. . . .

87: If anyone strikes the dog of a herdsman so that it dies, he shall give 20 shekels of silver and pledge his estate as security.

88: If anyone strikes the dog of a dog fancier so that it dies, he shall give 12 shekels of silver and pledge his estate as security.

89: If anyone strikes an *ordinary* dog so that it dies, he shall give 1 shekel of silver.

90: If a dog devours pig's lard and the owner of the lard finds him out, he may kill it and recover the lard from its stomach. There will be no compensation. . . .

146: If anyone buys a house or a village or a garden or a pasture and the other man goes and beats him up and demands a purchasing price over and above the (first) price, he is a felon and he shall give 1 mina of silver. [The purchaser] will pay the first price.

147: If anyone buys an unskilled man, and another (man) beats him up, he is a felon and he shall give 5 shekels of silver.

189: If a man violates his own mother, it is a capital crime. If a man violates his daughter, it is a capital crime. If a man violates his son, it is a capital crime.

190: . . . If a man violates his stepmother, there shall be no punishment. (But) if his father is living, it is a capital crime. . . .

192: If a man's wife dies (and) he marries his wife's sister, there shall be no punishment.

194: If a free man cohabits with (several) slave-girls, sisters and their mother, there shall be no punishment. If blood-relations sleep with (the same) free woman, there shall be no punishment. If father and son sleep with (the same) slave-girl or harlot, there shall be no punishment.

195: If however a man sleeps with the wife of his brother while his brother is living, it is a capital crime. If a man has a free woman (in marriage) and then lies also with her daughter, it is a capital crime. If a man has the daughter in marriage and then lies also with her mother or her sister, it is a capital crime.

197: If a man seizes a woman in the mountains, it is the man's crime and he will be killed. But if he seizes her in (her) house, it is the woman's crime and the woman shall be killed. If the husband finds them, he may kill them, there shall be no punishment for him.

THE LAW CODE OF ESHNUNNA

10: The hire for a donkey is 1 seah of barley, and the wages for its driver are 1 seah of barley. He shall drive it the whole day.

11: The wages of a hired man are 1 shekel of silver; his provender is 1 pan of barley. He shall work for one month.

20: If a man gives a loan . . . expressing the value of the silver in barley, he shall at harvest time receive the barley and its interest, 1 pan (and) 4 seah per kor.

21: If a man gives silver (as a loan) *at face value*, he shall receive the silver and its interest, one-sixth (of a shekel) and [6 grain] per shekel.

26: If a man gives bride-money for a(nother) man's daughter, but another man seizes her forcibly without asking the permission of her father and her mother and deprives her of her virginity, it is a capital offence and he shall die.

27: If a man takes a(nother) man's daughter without asking the permission of her father and her mother and concludes no formal marriage contract with her father and her mother, even though she may live in his house for a year, she is not a housewife.

28: *On the other hand*, if he concludes a formal contract with her father and her mother and cohabits with her, she is a housewife. When she is caught with a(nother) man, she shall die, she shall not get away alive.

29: If a man has been made prisoner during a raid or an invasion or (if) he has been carried off forcibly and [stayed in] a foreign [count]ry for a [long] time, (and if) another man has taken his wife and she has born him a son—when he returns, he shall [get] his wife back.

30: If a man hates his town and his lord and becomes a fugitive, (and if) another man takes his wife—when he returns, he shall have no right to claim his wife.

31: If a man deprives another man's slave-girl of her virginity, he shall pay one-third of a mina of silver; the slave-girl remains the property of her owner.

40: If a man buys a slave, a slave-girl, an ox or any other valuable good but cannot (legally) establish the seller, he is a thief.

42: If a man bites the nose of a(nother) man and severs it, he shall pay 1 mina of silver. (For) an eye (he shall pay) 1 mina of silver; (for) a tooth one-half mina; (for) an ear one-half mina; (for) a slap in the face 10 shekels of silver.

43: If a man severs a(nother) man's finger, he shall pay two-thirds of a mina of silver.

53: If an ox gores an(other) ox and causes (its) death, both ox owners shall divide (among themselves) the price of the live ox and also the equivalent of the dead ox.

54: If an ox is known to gore habitually and the authorities have brought the fact to the knowledge of its owner, but he does not have his ox *dehorned*, it gores a man and causes (his) death, then the owner of the ox shall pay two-thirds of a mina of silver.

55: If it gores a slave and causes (his) death, he shall pay 15 shekels of silver.

56: If a dog is vicious and the authorities have brought the fact to the knowledge of its owner, (if nevertheless) he does not keep it in, it bites a man and causes (his) death, then the owner of the dog shall pay two-thirds of a mina of silver.

57: If it bites a slave and causes (its) death, he shall pay 15 shekels of silver.

58: If a wall is threatening to fall and the authorities have brought the fact to the knowledge of its owner, (if nevertheless) he does not strengthen his wall, the wall collapses and causes a free man's death, then it is a capital offence; jurisdiction of the king.

Analysis and Review Questions

1. According to Hittite law, are slaves protected at all from abuse?
2. Are there any protections for animals in either document?
3. Is Hittite law "fair"? Why or why not?
4. In the two excerpts, are there any similarities about assault?
5. Is there anything we might consider "consumer protection" in either document?

Map 2.2
The Eastern
Mediterranean

DARIUS THE GREAT: RULER OF PERSIA

About the Document

King Darius the Great ruled Persia from 522 to 486 B.C.E. Like all Persian kings, he ruled with absolute authority. However, he held himself responsible to the god Ahuramazda, and he was therefore obligated to rule in a responsible and ethical manner. Indeed, the Persian Empire was the first to govern many different racial groups while attempting to maintain equal rights for all peoples. Darius would not interfere with local customs as long as his subjects paid their taxes and kept the peace.

The inscription below was created to assure the Persian people that their king was both powerful and honorable.

The Document

A great god is Ahuramazda who created this excellent work which one sees; who created happiness for man; who bestowed wisdom and energy upon Darius the king. Says Darius the king: by the favor of Ahuramazda I am of such a kind that I am a friend to what is right, I am no friend to what is wrong. It is not my wish that to the weak is done wrong because of the mighty, it is not my wish that the weak is hurt because of the mighty, that the mighty is hurt because of the weak. What is right, that is my wish. I am no friend of the man who is a follower of the lie. I am not hot-tempered. When I feel anger rising, I keep that under control by my thinking power. I control firmly my impulses. The man who co-operates, him do I reward according to his co-operation. He who does harm, him I punish according to the damage. It is not my wish that a man does harm, it is certainly not my wish that a man if he causes damage be not punished. What a man says against a man, that does not convince me, until I have heard testimony from both parties. What a man does or performs according to his powers, satisfies me, therewith I am satisfied and it gives me great pleasure and I am very satisfied and I give much to faithful men.

I am trained with both hands and feet. As a horseman I am a good horseman. As a bowman I am a good bowman, both afoot and on horseback. As a spearman I am a good spearman, both afoot and on horseback. And the skills which Ahuramazda has bestowed upon me, and I have had the strength to use them, by the favour of Ahuramazda, what has been done by me, I have done with these skills which Ahuramazda has bestowed upon me.

Analysis and Review Questions

1. According to the document, what strengths does Darius have as a ruler?
2. What qualities does Darius reward in his subjects?
3. How does Darius show himself to be fair and impartial in adjudicating disputes?
4. Why does Darius repeatedly give credit to Ahuramazda for his strengths?
5. Based on this inscription, how important was the physical and military prowess of the king?

WEB LINKS

http://longmanworldhistory.com
The following additional readings and case studies can be found on the Web site.
Document 2.2, Two accounts of an Egyptian Famine.
Document 2.4, Hammurabi's Law Code
Document 6.7, Slaves in Roman Law
Document 14.8, Louis XIV Writes to His Son
Case Study 2.1, Law in the Ancient Near East
Case Study 2.2, Slavery in Antiquity
Case Study 2.3, Preparing Rulers of Different Centuries.

http://www.escape.com/~farras/ancient.html
Excellent visuals and documents enable one to take a "trip back in time" to Egypt or Mesopotamia.

http://www.reallyuseful.com/joseph
The official Web site of Andrew Lloyd Webber's musical *Joseph and the Amazing Technicolor Dreamcoat*, which remains quite true to the original Biblical tale.

http://www.mfa.org/egypt/explore_ancient_egypt/index.html
Site of the Museum of Fine Arts in Boston, this includes slide shows of such topics as daily life, mummies, and archaeology.

http://www.ancientegypt.co.uk/menu.html
A beautiful site spotlighting gods and goddesses, Egyptian life, and so on, based on items held by one of the world's great museums, the British Museum.

http://pubpages.unh.edu/~cbsiren/hittite-ref.html
An excellent resource on the Hittite Empire.

CHAPTER 3

Classical India: Harappan Civilization to the Gupta Empire

Geography provided the essential settings for the first civilizations and none so greatly as those that arose on the Indian subcontinent. This landmass (almost worthy of designation as a continent in its own right) was protected on two sides by the sea and on its third side by mountainous terrain. The climate favored agriculture, and on the fertile flood plain of the Indus River, the Harappan civilization flourished from 2500 to roughly 1700 B.C.E.

However, mountains have passes, and seas can serve as roads as well as moats; thus, around 1500 B.C.E., a semibarbaric people calling themselves "Aryans" ("the noble people") began a violent migration onto the subcontinent. Though they destroyed the Harappans, the Aryans in time developed their own civilization and extended it throughout most of modern India. Central to their culture was their religion, in which they worshiped a pantheon with sacrifices and hymns of praise. These verses of praise, or "rics," were later collected into the *Rig-Veda* (*Veda* translates as "knowledge"), the oldest Indo-European text. Other Vedic literature followed; in fact, 1500–600 B.C.E. is designated the Vedic Age.

Aryan beliefs of the Vedic Age led to the first major Indian religion, Hinduism. The *Upanishads*, codified around 600 B.C.E., added elements of mysticism and the concept of the transmigration of souls. But religion would never be a unifier for India—shortly after 600 B.C.E., two additional religions, Jainism and Buddhism, developed and gained followers on the subcontinent.

In 326 B.C.E., Alexander the Great invaded northwestern India. Alexander died shortly thereafter, and his empire collapsed after his death (the Hellenistic successors were driven from most of India by 305 B.C.E.); however, he opened contact between Greco-Roman Europe and the subcontinent. The flow of trade and ideas would never completely cease after that invasion; in fact, Rome would open a regular trade route with India in 1 B.C.E.

Alexander's invasion stimulated the rise of Chandragupta Maurya. In 321 B.C.E., Chandragupta seized control of the state of Magadha in the Ganges Valley. During the remainder of his brilliant life, he expanded his holdings into northern India, establishing an empire and the Mauryan Dynasty in the process. His heirs would add all but the southern tip of the subcontinent to the empire before its collapse in 185 B.C.E. to a revolt led by Hindu priests. Though this empire had both good organization and a professional military, its reliance on an extensive secret police force marks the oppression its rulers imposed on their subjects.

With the revolt against the Mauryans, the empire collapsed into numerous small states, often at war with each other. The lack of unity allowed two waves of invaders, Bactrian Greeks and Kushans, to establish themselves in India. Both cultures left their imprint on the already diverse peoples of the subcontinent, but neither could establish lasting dominance. Only in 320 C.E. did a new dynasty, the Guptas, arise to provide a period of stability for India.

This chapter explores key writings from the three great religions of classical India: Hinduism, Jainism, and Buddhism. It also allows the reader to consider the impact of this diverse Indian culture on one specific portion of society—women.

HINDU CREATION MYTH AND THE CASTE SYSTEM

About the Document

The Aryan invasion of the subcontinent around 1500 B.C.E. brought with it a new religion that featured a pantheon of gods that the Aryans worshiped through ritualism and with burnt sacrifices. Over the next thousand years, the religion matured, probably incorporating some elements of Harappan theology and certainly establishing a rigid social structure. Centuries later, Europeans would dub this five-tiered social structure "the caste system."

To understand the future development of India and Hinduism, one must recognize and understand the caste system. The caste system became a central element of both Hindu theology and Indian society. The *brahman*, or priest class, followed by the *kshatriya*, or warrior class, and the *vaishya*, or merchant class, were at the top of Indian society. The bulk of India's population was *shudra*, the class of peasants and artisans. A fifth element of that society, one not even acknowledged in religious writings but certainly existing, were the *pariahs*, or untouchables. These menials labored at jobs considered demeaning or taboo for the four classes.

Around 500 B.C.E., Indians began to record their extensive oral religious traditions in what has become known as the Vedic literature. The oldest of the four *Vedas* is the *Rig-Veda*, and it is there that the Hindu creation myth and the basis for the caste system can be found. Another glimpse of the origins of the Hindu caste system can be seen in *The Law of Manu*, written around 200 C.E., viewed as a guide to proper behavior for Hindus. Selections from both texts are included below.

Map 3.1
Classical India

The Document

FROM THE RIG-VEDA

> Thousand-headed Purusha, thousand-eyed, thousand-footed he, having pervaded the earth on all sides, still extends ten fingers beyond it.
> Purusha alone is all this whatever has been and whatever is going to be. Further, he is the lord of immortality and also of what grows on account of food.

Image 3.1
*Statue of India,
God of War*

Such is his greatness; greater, indeed, than this is Purusha. All creatures constitute but one quarter of him, his three-quarters are the immortal in the heaven.

With his three-quarters did Purusha rise up; one-quarter of him again remains here. With it did he variously spread out on all sides over what eats and what eats not. From him was Virâj born, from Virâj evolved Purusha. He, being born, projected himself behind the earth as also before it.

When the gods performed the sacrifice with Purusha as the oblation,° then the spring was its clarified butter, the summer the sacrificial fuel, and the autumn the oblation. The sacrificial victim, namely, Purusha, born at the very beginning, they sprinkled with sacred water upon the sacrificial grass. With him as oblation the gods performed the sacrifice, and also the Sâdhyas [a class of semidivine beings] and the rishis [ancient seers].

From that wholly offered sacrificial oblation were born the verses and the sacred chants; from it were born the meters; the sacrificial formula was born from it.

From it horses were born and also those animals who have double rows [i.e., upper and lower] of teeth; cows were born from it, from it were born goats and sheep.

When they divided Purusha, in how many different portions did they arrange him? What became of his mouth, what of his two arms? What were his two thighs and his two feet called?

His mouth became the brahman; his two arms were made into the râjanya; his two thighs the vaishyas; from his two feet the shûdra was born.

The moon was born from the mind, from the eye the sun was born; from the mouth Indra° and Agni,° from the breath the wind was born.

From the navel was the atmosphere created, from the head the heaven issued forth; from the two feet was born the earth and the quarters [the cardinal directions] from the ear. Thus did they fashion the worlds.

Seven were the enclosing sticks in this sacrifice, thrice seven were the fire-sticks made, when the gods, performing the sacrifice, bound down Purusha, the sacrificial victim.

With this sacrificial oblation did the gods offer the sacrifice. These were the first norms [dharma] of sacrifice. These greatnesses reached to the sky wherein live the ancient Sadhyas and gods.

FROM *THE LAW OF MANU*

But in the beginning he assigned their several names, actions, and conditions (created beings), even according to the words of the Veda.

He, the Lord, also created the class of the gods, who are endowed with life, and whose nature is action; and the subtile class of the Sâdhyas, and the eternal sacrifice.

But from fire, wind, and the sun he drew forth the threefold eternal Verda, called Rik, Yaius, and Sâman, for the due performance of the sacrifice.

Time and the divisions of time, the lunar mansions and the planets, the rivers, the oceans, the mountains, plains, and uneven ground,

Austerity, speech, pleasure, desire, and anger, this whole creation he likewise produced, as he desired to call these beings into existence.

Whatever he assigned to each at the (first) creation, noxiousness or harmlessness, gentleness or ferocity, virtue or sin, truth or falsehood, that clung (afterwards) spontaneously to it.

---

oblation: Offering made to a deity.
Indra: Chief of the Vedic gods, god of rain and thunder.
Agni: Hindu god of fire.

As at the change of the seasons each season of its own accord assumes its distinctive marks, even so corporeal beings (resume in new births) their (appointed) course of action.

But for the sake of the prosperity of the worlds, he created the Brahman, the Kshatriya, the Vaishya, and the Shûdra to proceed from his mouth, his arms, his thighs and his feet.

To Brahmans he assigned teaching and studying (the Veda), sacrificing for their own benefit and for others, giving and accepting (of alms).

The Kshatriya he commanded to protect the people, to bestow gifts, to offer sacrifices, to study (the Veda), and to abstain from attaching himself to sensual pleasures.

The Vaishya to tend cattle, to bestow gifts, to offer sacrifices, to study (the Veda), to trade, to lend money, and to cultivate land.

One occupation only the lord prescribed to the Shûdra, to serve meekly even these (other) three castes.

Analysis and Review Questions

1. In your own words, describe the Hindu creation myth. Why are creation myths important?
2. The word "sacrifice" appears several times in the first passage. What could this tell us about Hinduism?
3. Describe the Hindu caste system as given in the two passages.
4. What suggests that the caste system will be integral to Hindu society?
5. Compare caste to your society.

TRANSMIGRATION OF SOULS IN THE *UPANISHADS*

About the Document

The development of a religion is a slow and continuous process. Thus it was with Hinduism. The whole of the Vedic literature consisted of four *Vedas,* several commentaries on the *Vedas,* and various philosophical investigations collected in the *Upanishads.* The *Upanishads* were critical to the development of modern Hinduism. They explored and explained the mystical aspects of the religion; most important, they addressed the nature of the human soul—the part of us that transcends the physical body.

One of the most important concepts examined in the *Upanishads* is the transmigration of souls, a process of death and rebirth that lasts until the individual human soul attains a level of absolute purity. At that point, individuality is surrendered and the soul becomes one with *Brahman,* a state of existence associated with the chief god of the Hindu pantheon (*Brahma*) but usually treated as a state of absolute perfection instead of an ascension to the godhead. Rebirth is tied directly to the caste system and the concept of good *karma*—the obeying of *dharma,* or religious law. At each level of Hindu castes, *dharma* assumes increasing strictness. When a soul is reborn, good *karma* in its past existence allows its new physical body to be that of a higher caste. This progression eventually allows every soul the opportunity to transcend human existence and reach *Brahman.*

The Document

The Self at Death

Just as a heavily loaded cart moves creaking, even so the self in the body mounted by the self of intelligence moves creaking, when one is breathing with difficulty (i.e., when one is about to expire).

When this (body) gets to thinness, whether he gets to thinness through old age or disease, just as a mango or a fig or a fruit of the peepul tree releases itself from its bond (gets detached from its stalk), even so this person frees himself from these limbs and returns again as he came to the place from which he started back to (new) life.

Just as for a king who is coming, policemen, magistrates, chariot drivers, leaders of the village wait for him with food, drink and lodgings, saying, "here he comes, here he comes," even so for him who knows this, all beings wait for him saying, "here comes Brahman, here he approaches."

The Soul of the Unreleased After Death

When this self gets to weakness, gets to confusedness, as it were, then the breaths gather round him. He takes to himself those particles of light and descends into the heart. When the person in the eye turns away, then he becomes non-knowing of forms.

He is becoming one, he does not see, they say; he is becoming one, he does not smell, they say; he is becoming one, he does not taste, they say; he is becoming one, he does not speak, they say; he is becoming one, he does not hear, they say; he is becoming one, he does not think, they say; he is becoming one, he does not touch, they say; he is becoming one, he does not know, they say. The point of his heart becomes lighted up and by that light the self departs either though the eye or through the head or through other apertures of the body. And when he thus departs, life departs after it. And when life thus departs, all the vital breaths depart after it. He becomes one with intelligence. What has intelligence departs with him. His knowledge and his work take hold of him as also his past experience.

Just as a leech (or caterpillar) when it has come to the end of a blade of grass, after having made another approach (to another blade) draws itself together towards it, so does this self, after having thrown away this body, and dispelled ignorance, after having another approach (to another body) draw itself together (for making the transition to another body).

And as a goldsmith, taking a piece of gold turns it into another, newer and more beautiful shape, even so does this self, after having thrown away this body and dispelled its ignorance, make unto himself another, newer and more beautiful shape like that of the fathers or of the *gandharvas,* or of the gods or of *Praja-pati* or of *Brahma* or of other beings.

That self is, indeed, Brahman, consisting of (or identified with) the understanding, mind, life, sight, hearing, earth, water, air, ether, light and no light, desire and absence of desire, anger and absence of anger, righteousness and absence of righteousness and all things. That is what is meant by saying, (it) consists of this (what is perceived), consists of that (what is inferred). According as one acts, according as one behaves, so does he become. The doer of good becomes good, the doer of evil becomes evil. One becomes virtuous by virtuous action, bad by bad action. Others, however, say that a person consists of desires. As is his desire so is his will; and is his will, so is the deed he does, whatever deed he does, that he attains.

On this there is the following verse: "The object to which the mind is attached, the subtle self goes together with the deed, being attached to it alone. Exhausting the results of whatever works he did in this world he comes again from that world, to this world for (fresh) work." This (is for) the man who desires. But the man who does not desire, he who is without desire, who is freed from desire, whose desire is satisfied, whose desire is the self; his breaths do not depart. Being *Brahman* he goes to *Brahman.*

On this there is the following verse: "When all the desires that dwell in the heart are cast away, then does the mortal become immortal, then he attains *Brahman* here (in this very body)." Just as the slough of a snake lies on an anthill, dead, cast off, even so lies this body. But this disembodied, immortal life is *Brahman* only, is light indeed. Your Majesty. "I give you, Venerable Sir, a thousand cows," said Janaka (King) of Videha.

Desire the Cause of Rebirth

He knows that supreme abode of *Brahman,* wherein founded, the world shines brightly. The wise men, who, free from desires, worship the Person, pass beyond the seed (of rebirth).

He who entertains desires, thinking of them, is born (again) here and there on account of his desires. But of him who has his desire fully satisfied, who is a perfected soul, all his desires vanish even here (on earth).

This self cannot be attained by instruction nor by intellectual power nor even through much hearing. He is to be attained by the one whom (the self) chooses. To such a one the self reveals his own nature.

This self cannot be attained by one without strength nor through heedlessness nor through austerity without an aim. But he who strives by these means, if he is a knower, this self of his enters the abode of *Brahman.*

The Nature of Liberation

Having attained Him, the seers (who are) satisfied with their knowledge (who are) perfected souls, free from passion, tranquil, having attained the omnipresent (self) on all sides, those wise, with concentrated minds, enter into the All itself.

The ascetics who have ascertained well the meaning of the Vedanta knowledge, who have purified their natures through the path of renunciation, they (dwelling) in the worlds of Brahma, at the end of time, being one with the immortal, are all liberated.

Gone are the fifteen parts to their (respective) supports (the elements) and all the gods (the sense organs) into their corresponding deities. One's deeds and the self, consisting of understanding, all become one in the Supreme Immutable Being.

Just as the flowing rivers disappear in the ocean casting off name and shape, even so the knower, freed from name and shape, attains to the divine person, higher than the high.

Analysis and Review Questions

1. What is the central theme of these passages from the *Upanishads?*
2. Discuss the concept of "desire" and its relationship to rebirth.
3. Discuss the concept of *Brahman.*

4. Compare the concept of *Brahman* to descriptions of "heaven" in other religions with which you are familiar.

5. What does the concept of transmigration of souls reveal about the human need for religions?

JAINISM: SELECTIONS FROM *THE BOOK OF SERMONS* AND *THE BOOK OF GOOD CONDUCT*

About the Document

During the sixth century B.C.E., two new religious movements arose in India, Buddhism and Jainism. Buddhism would spread through Asia, while Jainism remained primarily within the subcontinent. This does not denigrate the importance of Jainism, as several princes and key administrators throughout Indian history held to its tenets. And of all the world's religious movements, Jainism is the one most exclusively devoted to the value of life.

For the Jainist, all things are alive and have a soul. This includes stones, water, sand, and air, as well as animals and plants. These souls are infinite in number, and each is unique. To destroy life, whether through intent or accident, results in bad *karma* (a concept borrowed, to some degree, from Hinduism), and the higher the form of life one destroys, the more bad *karma* one accrues. Avoiding this *karma* is central to the transmigration of the soul, and a soul can never escape the cycle of life and death until it manages to rid itself of its *karma*. When a soul at last manages to escape the material cycles, it rises to the top of the universe and continues its individual existence in eternal bliss.

Forty-five texts compose the Jain religious canon. Though all of these stem from the teachings of the Great Hero, Mahavira (the chief prophet of Jainism), the first were not written until some two hundred years after his death, and the process of consideration and discussion continued through the fifth century C.E. The selected passage stresses both the definition of life and the value placed on life by Jainism.

The Document

FROM *THE BOOK OF SERMONS*

One should know what binds the soul, and knowing, break free from bondage.
What bondage did the Hero declare, and what knowledge did he teach to remove it?
He who grasps at even a little, whether living or lifeless, or consents to another doing so, will never be freed from sorrow.
If a man kills living things, or slays by the hand of another, or consents to another slaying, his sin goes on increasing.
The man who cares for his kin and companions is a fool who suffers much, for their numbers are ever increasing.
All his wealth and relations cannot save him from sorrow.
Only if he knows the nature of life, will he get rid of karma.

FROM *THE BOOK OF GOOD CONDUCT*

Earth is afflicted and wretched, it is hard to teach, it has no discrimination. Unenlightened men, who suffer from the effects of past deeds, cause great pain in a world full of pain already, for in earth souls are individually embodied. If, thinking to gain praise, honor, or respect, or to achieve a good rebirth, or to win salvation, or to escape pain, a man sins against earth or causes or permits others to do so, he will not gain joy or wisdom. Injury to the earth is like striking, cutting, maiming, or killing a blind man. Knowing this a man should not sin against earth or cause or permit others to do so. He who understands the nature of sin against earth is called a true sage who understands karma.

And there are many souls embodied in water. Truly water is alive. He who injures the lives in water does not understand the nature of sin or renounce it. Knowing this, a man should not sin against water, or cause or permit others to do so. He who understands the nature of sin against water is called a true sage who understands karma.

By wicked or careless acts one may destroy fire-beings and, moreover, harm other beings by means of fire. For there are creatures living in earth, grass, leaves, wood, cowdung, or dustheaps, and jumping creatures which fall into a fire if they come near it. If touched by fire, they shrivel up, lose their senses, and die. He who understands the nature of sin in respect of fire is called a true sage who understands karma.

And just as it is the nature of a man to be born and grow old, so is it the nature of a plant to be born and grow old. One is endowed with reason, and so is the other; one is sick, if injured, and so is the other; one grows larger, and so does the other; one changes with time, and so does the other. He who understands the nature of sin against plants is called a true sage who understands karma.

All beings with two, three, four, or five senses, in fact all creation, know individually pleasure and displeasure, pain, terror, and sorrow. All are full of fears, which come from all directions. And yet there exist people who would cause greater pain to them. Some kill animals for sacrifice, some for their skin, flesh, blood, feathers, teeth, or tusks; some kill them intentionally and some unintentionally; some kill because they have been previously injured by them, and some because they expect to be injured. He who harms animals has not understood or renounced deeds of sin. He who understands the nature of sin against animals is called a true sage who understands karma.

A man who is averse from harming even the wind knows the sorrow of all things living. He who knows what is bad for himself knows what is bad for others, and he who knows what is bad for others knows what is bad for himself. This reciprocity should always be borne in mind. Those whose minds are at peace and who are free from passions do not desire to live [at the expense of others]. He who understands the nature of sin against wind is called a true sage who understands karma.

In short he who understands the nature of sin in respect of all the six types of living beings is called a true sage who understands karma.

Analysis and Review Questions

1. In the first passage, to what does the term "bondage" refer?

2. In both passages, the term "karma" is used. Define this term as it relates to Jainism.

3. Jainists define the degree of life in a thing by the number of senses that it possesses. Why would the Jains have tied the concept of life directly to the five senses?

4. Discuss what these passages reveal about the nature of Jainism.

5. How difficult would it be for you to live as a Jainist?

Image 3.2
Buddhist
Religious Site

BUDDHA'S *SERMON AT BENARES* AND *THE EDICTS OF ASHOKA*

About the Document

Few people have placed their imprint so emphatically on history as Siddhartha Gautama. Born to the *kshatriya* caste in the mid-sixth century B.C.E., he enjoyed an early life of privilege denied to the masses of India. But at some point, perhaps in what is today called a mid-life crisis, he experienced disenchantment with Hinduism and the answers that it offered to society as a whole. In travel and meditation, Gautama discovered enlightenment. He preached, and those who listened often became his disciples. Ever increasing in numbers, they called him Gautama Buddha (from the Indian word *bodhi*, or wisdom), and they spread the religious philosophy of Buddhism around the world.

Buddhism borrowed key elements from Hinduism. It accepted the transmigration of souls and the role of *karma* in rebirth, as well as the importance of nonviolence and asceticism in the *karmic* cycle. *Nirvana*, the ultimate state of grace to be achieved by a soul, resembled *Brahman*, involving the ultimate extinction of self and immersion in what the Buddha called the "Great World Soul." At the same time, Buddhism directly challenged several key Hindu concepts. It denied the individuality of the soul, instead viewing it as a distinct portion of a group soul. It viewed the material world as an illusion, a transitory state above which the soul must rise to achieve *nirvana*. Only by escaping the pain and misery, joy and lust of materiality could one reach completeness. Most important, the Buddha rejected both the caste system and the pantheon of Hindu gods. He also forbade his followers to worship him as a god, thus making Buddhism a religious philosophy rather than a religion in the strictest sense of the term.

The selection below is from the Buddha's first sermon, and it contains the cornerstone doctrine of Buddhism, the Four Noble Truths. The second selection examines the practical applications of Buddhist principles by the third emperor of the Mauryan Empire, Ashoka. During his reign, Ashoka caused thousands of stone pillars to be raised throughout the empire. Some commemorated the life of Buddha, but many featured edicts issued by Ashoka or celebrated events from his reign. The second selection features a number of those edicts.

The Document

FROM BUDDHA'S *SERMON AT BENARES*

1. *The Truth Concerning Misery*

And how, O priests, does a priest live, as respects the elements of being, observant of the elements of being in the four noble truths?

Whenever, O priest, a priest knows the truth concerning misery, knows the truth concerning the origin of misery, knows the truth concerning the cessation of misery, knows the truth concerning the path leading to the cessation of misery.
And what, O priests, is the noble truth of misery?
Birth is misery; old age is misery; disease is misery; death is misery; sorrow, lamentation, misery, grief, and despair are misery; to wish for what one cannot have is misery; in short, all the five attachment-groups are misery.
This, O priests, is called the noble truth of misery.

2. The Truth of the Origin of Misery

And what, O priests, is the noble truth of the origin of misery?
It is desire leading to rebirth, joining itself to pleasure and passion, and finding delight in every existence—desire, namely, for sensual pleasure, desire for permanent existence, desire for transitory existence.
But where, O priests, does this desire spring up and grow? Where does it settle and take root?
Where anything is delightful and agreeable to men, there desire springs up and grows, there it settles and takes root.
And what is delightful and agreeable to men, where desire springs up and grows, where it settles and takes root?
The eye is delightful and agreeable to men; there desire springs up and grows, there it settles and takes root.
The ear, the nose, the tongue, the body, the mind is delightful and agreeable to men; there desire springs up and grows, there it settles and takes root.
The Six Objects of Sense.
Forms, sounds, odors, tastes, things tangible, ideas are delightful and agreeable to men; there desire springs up and grows, there it settles and takes root.
The Six Consciousnesses.
Eye-consciousness, ear-consciousness, nose-consciousness, tongue-consciousness, body-consciousness, mind-consciousness is delightful and agreeable to men; there desire springs up and grows, there it settles and takes root.
The Six Contacts.
Contact of the eye, ear, nose, tongue, body, mind is delightful and agreeable to men; there desire springs up and grows, there it settles and takes root.
The Six Sensations.
Sensation produced by contact of the eye, ear, nose, tongue, body, mind is delightful and agreeable to men; there desire springs up and grows, there it settles and takes root.
The Six Perceptions.
Perception of forms, sounds, odors, tastes, things tangible, ideas is delightful and agreeable to men; there desire springs up and grows, there it settles and takes root.
The Six Thinkings.
Thinking on forms, sounds, odors, tastes, things tangible, ideas is delightful and agreeable to men; there desire springs up and grows, there it settles and takes root.
The Six Desires.
Desire for forms, sounds, odors, tastes, things tangible, ideas is delightful and agreeable to men; there desire springs up and grows, there it settles and takes root.
The Six Reasonings.
Reasoning on forms, sounds, odors, tastes, things tangible, ideas is delightful and agreeable to men; there desire springs up and grows, there it settles and takes root.

The Six Reflections.

Reflection on forms, sounds, odors, tastes, things tangible, ideas is delightful and agreeable to men; there desire springs up and grows, there it settles and takes root. This, O priests, is called the noble truth of the origin of misery.

3. The Truth of the Cessation of Misery

And what, O priests, is the noble truth of the cessation of misery?

It is the complete fading out and cessation of this desire, a giving up, a losing hold, a relinquishment, and a nonadhesion.

But where, O priests, does this desire wane and disappear? Where is it broken up and destroyed?

Where anything is delightful and agreeable to men; there desire wanes and disappears, there it is broken up and destroyed.

And what is delightful and agreeable to men, where desire wanes and disappears, where it is broken up and destroyed?

The eye is delightful and agreeable to men; there desire wanes and disappears, there it is broken up and destroyed.

[Similarly respecting the other organs of sense, the six objects of sense, the six consciousnesses, the six contacts, the six sensations, the six perceptions, the six thinkings, the six desires, the six reasonings, and the six reflections.]

This, O priests, is called the noble truth of the cessation of misery.

4. The Truth of the Path Leading to the Cessation of Misery

And what, O priests, is the noble truth to the path leading to the cessation of misery?

It is this noble eightfold path, to wit, right belief, right resolve, right speech, right behavior, right occupation, right effort, right contemplation, right concentration.

And what, O priests, is right belief?

The knowledge of misery, O priests, the knowledge of the origin of misery, the knowledge of the cessation of misery, and the knowledge of the path leading to the cessation of misery, this, O priests, is called "right belief."

And what, O priests, is right resolve?

The resolve to renounce sensual pleasures, the resolve to have malice towards none, and the resolve to harm no living creature, this, O priests, is called "right resolve."

And what, O priests, is right speech?

To abstain from falsehood, to abstain from backbiting, to abstain from harsh language, and to abstain from frivolous talk, this, O priests, is called "right speech."

And what, O priests, is right behavior?

To abstain from destroying life, to abstain from taking that which is not given one, and to abstain from immorality, this, O priests, is called "right behavior."

And what, O priests, is right occupation?

Whenever, O priests, a noble disciple, quitting a wrong occupation, gets his livelihood by a right occupation, this, O priests, is called "right occupation."

And what, O priests, is right effort?

Whenever, O priests, a priest purposes, makes an effort, heroically endeavors, applies his mind, and exerts himself that evil and demeritorious qualities not yet arisen may not arise; purposes, makes an effort, heroically endeavors, applies his mind, and exerts himself that evil and demeritorious qualities already arisen may be abandoned; purposes, makes an effort, heroically endeavors, applies his mind, and exerts himself that meritorious qualities not yet arisen may arise; purposes, makes an effort, heroically endeavors, applies his mind, and exerts himself for the preservation, retention, growth, increase, development, and perfection of meritorious qualities already arisen, this, O priest, is called "right effort." And what, O priests, is right contemplation?

Whenever, O priests, a priest lives, as respects the body, observant of the body, strenuous, conscious, contemplative, and has rid himself of lust and grief; as respects sensations, observant of sensations, strenuous, conscious, contemplative, and has rid himself of lust and grief; as respects the mind, observant of the mind, strenuous, conscious, contemplative, and has rid himself of lust and grief; as respects the elements of being, observant of the elements of being, strenuous, conscious, contemplative, and has rid himself of lust and grief, this, O priests, is called "right contemplation."

And what, O priests, is right concentration?

Whenever, O priests, a priest, having isolated himself from sensual pleasures, having isolated himself from demeritorious traits, and still exercising reasoning, still exercising reflection, enters upon the first trance which is produced by isolation and characterized by joy and happiness; when, through the subsidence of reasoning and reflection, and still retaining joy and happiness, he enters upon the second trance, which is an interior tranquilization and intentness of the thoughts, and is produced by concentration; when, through the paling of joy, indifferent, contemplative, conscious, and in the experience of bodily happiness—that state which eminent men describe when they say, "Indifferent, contemplative, and living happily" he enters upon the third trance; when, through the abandonment of happiness, through the abandonment of misery, through the disappearance of all antecedent gladness and grief, he enters upon the fourth trance, which has neither misery nor happiness, but is contemplation as refined by indifference, this, O priests, is called "right concentration."

This, O priests, is called the noble truth of the path leading to the cessation of misery.

FROM *THE EDICTS OF ASHOKA*

When the king, Beloved of the Gods and of Gracious Mien, had been consecrated eight years Kalinga was conquered, 150,000 people were deported, 100,000 were killed, and many times that number died. But after the conquest of Kalinga, the Beloved of the Gods began to follow Righteousness (Dharma), to love Righteousness, and to give instruction in Righteousness. Now the Beloved of the Gods regrets the conquest of Kalinga, for when an independent country is conquered people are killed, they die, or are deported, and that the Beloved of the Gods finds very painful and grievous. And this he finds even more grievous—that all the inhabitants—brahmans, ascetics, and other sectarians, and householders who are obedient to superiors, parents, and elders, who treat friends, acquaintances, companions, relatives, slaves, and servants with respect, and are firm in their faith—all suffer violence, murder, and separation from their loved ones. Even those who are fortunate enough not to have lost those near and dear to them are afflicted at the misfortunes of friends, acquaintances, companions, and relatives. The participation of all men in common suffering is grievous to the Beloved of the Gods. Moreover there is no land, except that of the Greeks, where groups of brahmans and ascetics are not found, or where men are not members of one sect or another. So now, even if the number of those killed and captured in the conquest of Kalinga had been a hundred or a thousand times less, it would be grievous to the Beloved of the Gods. The Beloved of the Gods will forgive as far as he can, and he even conciliates the forest tribes of his dominions; but he warns them that there is power even in the remorse of the Beloved of Gods, and he tells them to reform, lest they be killed.

For all beings the Beloved of the Gods desires security, self-control, calm of mind, and gentleness. The Beloved of the Gods considers that the greatest victory is the victory of Righteousness; and this he has won here (in India) and even five hundred leagues beyond his frontiers in the realm of the Greek king Antiochus, and beyond the Antiochus among the four kings Ptolemy, Antigonus, Magas, and Alexander. Even where the envoys of the Beloved of the Gods have not been sent men hear of the way in which he follows and teaches Righteousness, and they too follow it and will follow it. Thus he achieves a universal conquest, and conquest always gives a feeling of pleasure; yet it is but a slight pleasure, for the Beloved of the Gods only looks on that which concerns the next life as of great importance.

I have had this inscription of Righteousness engraved that all my sons and grandsons may not seek to gain new victories, that in whatever victories they may gain they may prefer forgiveness and light punishment, that they may consider the only [valid] victory the victory of Righteousness, which is of value both in this world and the next, and that all their pleasure may be in Righteousness.

. . .

Thus speaks Ashoka, the Beloved of the Gods. For two and a half years I have been an open follower of the Buddha, though at first I did not make much progress. But for more than a year now I have drawn closer to the [Buddhist] Order, and have made much progress. In India the gods who formerly did not mix with men now do so. This is the result of effort, and may be obtained not only by the great, but even by the small, through effort thus they may even easily win heaven.

Father and mother should be obeyed, teachers should be obeyed; pity should be felt for all creatures. These virtues of Righteousness should be practiced. This is an ancient rule, conducive to long life. It is good to give, but there is no gift, no service, like the gift of Righteousness. So friends, relatives, and companions should preach it on all occasions. This is duty; this is right; by this heaven may be gained—and what is more important than to gain heaven?

. . .

Here no animal is to be killed for sacrifice, and no festivals are to be held, for the king finds much evil in festivals, except for certain festivals which he considers good.

Formerly in the Beloved of the God's kitchen several hundred thousands of animals were killed daily for food; but now at the time of writing only three are killed—two peacocks and a deer, though the deer not regularly. Even these three animals will not be killed in the future.

. . .

I am not satisfied simply with hard work or carrying out the affairs of state, for I consider my work to be the welfare of the whole world, of which hard work and the carrying out of affairs are merely the basis. There is no better deed than to work for the welfare of the whole world, and all my efforts are made that I may clear my debt to all beings. I make them happy here and now that they may attain heaven in the life to come. But it is difficult without great effort.

. . .

By order of the Beloved of the Gods. Addressed to the officer in charge of Tosali. Let us win the affection of all men. All men are my children, and as I wish all welfare and happiness in this world and the next for my own children, so do I wish it for all men. But you do not realize what this entails; here and there an officer may understand in part, but not entirely.

Often a man is imprisoned and tortured unjustly, and then he is liberated for no [apparent] reason. Many other people suffer also [as a result of this injustice]. Therefore it is desirable that you should practice impartiality, but it cannot be attained if you are inclined to habits of jealousy, irritability, harshness, hastiness, obstinacy, laziness, or lassitude. I desire you not to have these habits. The basis of all this is the constant avoidance of irritability and hastiness in your business.

This inscription has been engraved in order that the officials of the city should always see to it that no one is ever imprisoned or tortured without good cause. To ensure this I shall send out every five years on a tour of inspection officers who are not fierce or harsh. The prince at Ujjain shall do the same not more than every three years, and likewise at Taxila.

. . .

My governors are placed in charge of hundreds of thousands of people. Under my authority they have power to judge and to punish, that they calmly and fearlessly carry out their duties, and that they may bring welfare and happiness to the people of the provinces and be of help to them. They will know what brings joy and what brings sorrow, and, conformably to Righteousness, they will instruct the people of the provinces that they may be happy in this world and the next. And as when one entrusts a child to a skilled nurse one is confident that she will care for it well, so have I appointed my governors for the welfare and happiness of the people. That they may fearlessly carry out their duties I have given them power to judge and to inflict punishment on their own initiative. I wish that there should be uniformity of justice and punishment.

. . .

In the past kings went out on pleasure trips and indulged in hunting and similar amusements. But the Beloved of the Gods ten years after his consecration set out on the journey to Enlightenment. Now when he goes on tour he interviews and gives gifts to brahmans and ascetics; he interviews and gives money to the aged; he interviews the people of the provinces, and instructs and questions them on Righteousness; and the pleasure which the Beloved of the Gods derives therefrom is as good as a second revenue.

. . .

The Beloved of the Gods honors members of all sects, whether ascetics or house-holders, by gifts and various honors. But he does not consider gifts and honors as important as the furtherance of the essential message of all sects. This essential message varies from sect to sect, but it has one common basis, that one should so control one's tongue as not to honor one's own sect or disparage another's on the wrong occasions; for on certain occasions one should do so only mildly, and indeed on other occasions one should honor other men's sects. By doing this one strengthens one's own sect and helps the others, while by doing otherwise one harms one's own sect and does a dis-service to the others. Whoever honors his own sect and disparages another man's, whether from blind loyalty or with the intention of showing his own sect in a favor-able light, does his own sect the greatest possible harm. Concord is best, with each hearing and respecting the other's teachings. It is the wish of the Beloved of the Gods that members of all sects should be learned and should teach virtue. Many officials are busied in this matter and the result is the progress of my own sect and the illumination of Righteousness.

Analysis and Review Questions

1. According to Buddha, what is "misery"?
2. According to Buddha, why do humans live in misery?
3. According to Buddha, how can humans escape misery?
4. What does Ashoka mean when he uses the term "righteousness"?
5. Did Buddhism make Ashoka a "godly" king? Why or why not?

CAST(E)AWAYS? WOMEN IN CLASSICAL INDIA

About the Document

Gender relations and the societal conditions experienced by women became topics of intense study and debate in the second half of the twentieth century. Central to that study are the place of religion and its impact on the experience of women throughout history. Hindu beliefs, as expressed in the Vedic literature, placed the Indian woman in a thoroughly subservient position within the caste system. Her entire life was circumscribed by rigid laws, and even in death she could not guarantee escape from domination by men.

The Law of Manu offers one of the clearest statements of *dharma* as its re-lates to Hindu women. Jainism and Buddhism offered little in the way of im-proving the lot of Indian women, though the Buddha reluctantly agreed to ac-cept female nuns among his followers. In striking contrast to the strictures related by the scribe Manu are the second and third selections included below: poems by two Buddhist nuns, Mutta and Sumangalamata. Though still treated as second-class citizens, the two women revel in the freedom of their unique social position.

The Document

FROM *THE LAW OF MANU*

By a girl, by a young woman, or even by an aged one, nothing must be done independently, even in her own house.

In childhood a female must be subject to her father, in youth to her husband, when her lord is dead to her sons; a woman must never be independent.

She must not seek to separate herself from her father, husband, or sons; by leaving them she would make both (her own and her husband's) families contemptible.

She must always be cheerful, clever in (the management of her) household affairs, careful in cleaning her utensils, and economical in expenditure.

Him to whom her father may give her, or her brother with the father's permission, she shall obey as long as he lives, and when he is dead, she must not insult (his memory).

For the sake of procuring good fortune to (brides), the recitation of benedictory texts and the sacrifice to the Lord of creatures are used at weddings; (but) the betrothal (by the father or guardian) is the cause of (the husband's) dominion (over his wife).

The husband who wedded her with sacred texts, always gives happiness to his wife, both in season and out of season, in this world and in the next.

Though destitute of virtue, or seeking pleasure (elsewhere), or devoid of good qualities (yet) a husband must be constantly worshipped as a god by a faithful wife.

No sacrifice, no vow, no fast must be performed by women apart (from their husbands); if a wife obeys her husband, she will for that (reason alone) be exalted in heaven.

A faithful wife, who desires to dwell (after death) with her husband, must never do anything that might displease him who took her hand, whether he be alive or dead.

At her pleasure let her emaciate her body by (living on) pure flowers, roots, and fruit; but she must never even mention the name of another man after her husband has died.

Until death let her be patient (of hardships), self-controlled, and chaste, and strive (to fulfil) that most excellent duty which (is prescribed) for wives who have one husband only.

Many thousands of Brahmans who were chaste from their youth, have gone to heaven without continuing their race.

A virtuous wife who after the death of her husband constantly remains chaste, reaches heaven, though she have no son, just like those chaste men.

But a woman who from a desire to have offspring violates her duty towards her (deceased) husband, brings on herself disgrace in this world, and loses her place with her husband (in heaven).

Offspring begotten by another man is here not (considered lawful), nor (does offspring begotten) on another man's wife (belong to the begetter), nor is a second husband anywhere prescribed for virtuous women.

She who cohabits with a man of higher caste, forsaking her own husband who belongs to a lower one, will become contemptible in this world, and is called a remarried woman.

By violating her duty towards her husband, a wife is disgraced in this world, (after death) she enters the womb of a jackal, and is tormented by diseases (the punishment of) her sin.

She who, controlling her thoughts, words, and deeds, never slights her lord, resides (after death) with her husband (in heaven), and is called a virtuous (wife).

In reward of such conduct, a female who controls her thoughts, speech, and actions, gains in this (life) highest renown, and in the next (world) a place near her husband.

POEMS FROM TWO BUDDHIST NUNS

Mutta

So free am I, so gloriously free,
Free from three petty things—
From mortar, from pestle and from my twisted lord,
Freed from rebirth and death I am,
And all that has held me down
Is hurled away.

Sumangalamata

A woman well set free! How free I am,
How wonderfully free, from kitchen drudgery.
Free from the harsh grip of hunger,
And from empty cooking pots,
Free too of that unscrupulous man,
The weaver of sunshades.
Calm now, and serene I am,
All lust and hatred purged.
To the shade of the spreading trees I go
And contemplate my happiness.

Analysis and Review Questions

1. According to Manu, what are the primary duties of a Hindu woman?
2. Picture yourself as a woman living under Hindu *dharma*. What are some of the key words that you would use to describe that life?
3. What rules or beliefs served to keep women in a subservient position?
4. Can you understand the sentiments revealed by the nuns? Why or why not?
5. What part do you think religion has played in gender relations throughout history?

WEB LINKS

http://longmanworldhistory.com

The following additional case studies can be found on the Web site.

Case Study 3.1 Hinduism and the Mauryan Empire
Case Study 3.2 Buddhism and the Mauryan Empire
Case Study 3.3 Kautilya and Machiavelli: Political Theorists Extraordinaire

http://www.hp.uab.edu/image_archive/udg/
A collection of annotated images from the Mauryan Empire.

http://www.harappa.com/
Excellent site for material artifacts from the Harappan culture.

http://www.geocities.com/Athens/Academy/5185/2-2women.html
Women in ancient India.

CHAPTER 4

Classical China: 2100 B.C.E. to 220 C.E.

Although Classical China is held to have existed between 2100 B.C.E. and 220 C.E, important historical evidence—oracle bones—suggests Chinese civilization flourished two millennia earlier. The oracle bones, known in Chinese as *jia gu wen*, are either tortoise shells (*jia*) or ox shoulder blades (*gu*) with scripted texts *(wen)*. The first oracle bone was discovered in 1889 in An Yang County, the capital of the Shang Dynasty (1600–1100 B.C.E.), and so far nearly 100,000 pieces have been unearthed. It is believed that the original function of the oracle bone scripts was for fortune telling. The scripted bones were thrown into fire, and the priests read the crack signs from the bones and told fortunes. The inscriptions on the oracle bones represent the earliest form of the Chinese written language. Unlike most of the languages in the world, the Chinese language has never evolved from its original pictographic and ideographic structure into alphabetic or syllabic form. Historians and archaeologists continue to work on this historical evidence to enhance their understanding of pre-dynastic China.

From its first legendary Xia Dynasty (2100 B.C.E.) to the Han Dynasty (220 C.E.), China underwent a series of important changes that gave it the centralized government and sophisticated philosophy that would dominate the society for the next two millennia. Among these important changes, early Chinese writings like those discovered on oracle bones evolved to become a standardized language system that has continued into contemporary time. China's political system went from kingship (up to the Zhou Dynasty) to emperorship (beginning with the Qin Dynasty under the rule of the First Emperor).

*Map 4.1
(Interactive)
Classical China*

Three major philosophies, Confucianism, Daoism, and Legalism, emerged during the Warring States period, all searching for solutions to deal with the chaos. Confucianism emphasized the fundamental principle of human relationships for creating an orderly society, and Daoism, turning away from political engagements, looked to natural harmony. Legalism, on the other hand, emphasized strong government control and the use of force to keep social order. While the First Emperor of the Qin Dynasty adopted Legalism to unify the country, the early Han emperors tried Daoism briefly, only to give way to Confucianism, which was to become a dominant force in both China's political and social systems. Chronologically, the Han Dynasty roughly corresponds to the heyday of the Roman Empire.

CONFUCIANISM: GOVERNMENT AND THE SUPERIOR MAN

About the Document

Confucius was a scholar who lived between ca. 551 and 479 B.C.E. During this time, China experienced political decentralization and social instability as a result of rivalry among difference princes. In his search for restoration of social order, Confucius argued that this chaotic situation was due to the breakdown of China's social foundation, which was based on the principle of proper relationships. According to Confucius, the key relationships included those between ruler and subject, father and son, husband and wife, elder brother and younger brother, and friend and friend. Only by fixing these relationships could China regain peace and order. The ideas of Confucius, however, were not well accepted by the ruling class of his time, and he spent the rest of his lifetime teaching.

After Confucius, China sank into an even worse period known as the Warring States (475–221 B.C.E.). Confucius did not leave any written works, but his disciples recorded and further enriched his ideas by putting together—in a rather unsystematic way—a collection of his teachings and arguments. These *Analects*, which describe what we commonly know as Confucianism, would reshape the Chinese way of thinking in the millennia to come. The ideas of Confucius on good government and proper relationships in the society are clearly reflected in the following arguments.

Image 4.1
An Inscribed
Oracle Bone

The Document

Filial Piety

Zi, you asked what filial piety° was. The Master said, "The filial piety of now-a-days means the support of one's parents. But dogs and horses likewise are able to do something in the way of support—without reverence, what is there to distinguish the one support giver from the other?"

The Master said, "In serving his parents, a son may remonstrate with them, but gently; when he sees that they do not incline to follow his advice, he shows an increased degree of reverence, but does not abandon his purpose; and should they punish him, he does not allow himself to murmur."

Mang I asked what filial piety was. The Master said, "It is not being disobedient." Soon after, as Fan Chih was driving him, the Master told him, saying, "Mang Sun asked

---

filial piety: Dutiful respect for parents.

me what filial piety was, and I answered him, 'not being disobedient.'" Fan Chih said, "What did you mean?" The Master replied, "That parents, when alive, should be served according to propriety; that, when dead, they should be buried according to propriety; and that they should be sacrificed to according to propriety."

Propriety

The Master said, "Respectfulness, without the rules of propriety,° becomes laborious bustle; carefulness, without the rules of propriety, becomes timidity; boldness, without the rules of propriety, becomes insubordination; straightforwardness, without the rules of propriety, becomes rudeness."

Ideal Government

The Master said, "When rulers love to observe the rules of propriety, the people respond readily to the calls on them for service."

The Master said, "If the people be led by laws, and uniformity sought to be given them by punishments, they will try to avoid the punishment, but have no sense of shame.

"If they be led by virtue, and uniformity sought to be given them by the rules of propriety, they will have the sense of shame, and moreover will become good."

The Master said, "He who exercises government by means of his virtue may be compared to the north polar star, which keeps its place and all the stars turn towards it."

The duke Ai asked, saying, "What should be done in order to secure the submission of the people?" Confucius replied, "Advance the upright and set aside the crooked, then the people will submit. Advance the crooked and set aside the upright, then the people will not submit."

Ji Kang asked how to cause the people to reverence their ruler, to be faithful to him, and to go on to serve themselves to virtue. The Master said, "Let him preside over them with gravity—then they will reverence him. Let him be filial and kind to all—then they will be faithful to him. Let him advance the good and teach the incompetent—then they will eagerly seek to be virtuous."

Ji Kang asked Confucius about government. Confucius replied, "To govern means to rectify. If you lead on the people with correctness, who will dare not to be correct?"

. . .

The Master said, "If a minister makes his own conduct correct, what difficulty will he have in assisting in government? If he cannot rectify himself, what has he to do with rectifying others?"

The Master said, "If good men were to govern a country in succession for a hundred years, they would be able to transform the violently bad, and dispense with capital punishments." True indeed is this saying!

The Superior Man

Confucius said, "There are three things of which the superior man stands in awe. He stands in awe of the ordinances of Heaven. He stands in awe of great men. He stands in awe of the words of sages.

---

propriety: Conformity to proper behavior.

"The mean man does not know the ordinances of Heaven, and consequently does not stand in awe of them. He is disrespectful to great men. He makes sport of the words of sages."

Zi Gong asked what constituted the superior man. The Master said, "He acts before he speaks, and afterward speaks according to his actions."

The Master said, "The mind of the superior man is conversant with righteousness; the mind of the mean man is conversant with gain."

The Master said, "If the will be set on virtue, there will be no practice of wickedness."

The Master said, "Riches and honors are what men desire. If it cannot be obtained in the proper way, they should not be held. Poverty and meanness are what men dislike. If it cannot be obtained in the proper way, they should not be avoided.

"If a superior man abandons virtue, how can he fulfill the requirements of that name?

"The superior man does not, even for the space of a single meal, act contrary to virtue. In moments of haste, he cleaves to it. In seasons of danger, he cleaves to it."

The Master said, "By nature, men are nearly alike; by practice, they get to be wide apart."

. . .

The Master said, "By extensively studying all learning, and keeping himself under the restraint of the rules of propriety, one may thus likewise not err from what is right."

. . .

The Master said, "The accomplished scholar is not a utensil.°

Spirits

The subjects on which the Master did not talk, were extraordinary things, feats of strength, disorder, and spiritual beings.

. . .

Ji Lu asked about serving the spirits of the dead. The Master said, "While you are not able to serve men, how can you serve their spirits?"

Ji Lu added, "I venture to ask about death?" He was answered, "While you do not know life, how can you know about death?"

Analysis and Review Questions

1. Summarize Confucius's idea of an ideal government.
2. What should be the major qualities of a superior man, according to Confucius?
3. Why does Confucius consider *propriety* important for individuals and family, as well as the state?
4. From this document, what can be seen as the major themes in Confucianism?
5. Why was the Warring States period so important for the development of Confucianism?

---

utensil: An instrument or tool.

DAOISM: THE CLASSIC OF THE WAY AND VIRTUE

About the Document

Daoism was associated with a legendary scholar, Lao Zi, who was believed to be a contemporary of Confucius. Lao Zi's view of restoring peace in the face of China's collapsing social order was quite different from that of Confucius. According to Lao Zi, the proper way to escape from war and political entanglement is to retreat into seclusion and embrace the harmony of nature. Through this contemplation of nature, one could become attuned to the Dao ("the way" in Chinese). Daoist views on government and human relationships were also different from those of Confucius. Daoism suggests a less active role for the government and more freedom for the people. Because of this retreatist attitude toward politics and society, Daoism gradually evolved into a popular religion absorbing its rites and organizational forms from Buddhism and local superstitions.

Map 4.2
The Shang
Kingdom

The Document

The Way

The Dao that can be trodden is not the enduring and unchanging Dao. The name that can be named is not the enduring and unchanging name.

Conceived of as having no name, it is the Originator of heaven and earth; conceived of as having a name, it is the Mother of all things.

. . .

The Dao produces all things and nourishes them; it produces them and does not claim them as its own; it does all, and yet does not boast of it; it presides over all, and yet does not control them. This is what is called "The mysterious quality" of the Dao.

When the Great Dao ceased to be observed, benevolence and righteousness came into vogue.

Then appeared wisdom and shrewdness, and there ensued great hypocrisy.

Man takes his law from the Earth; the Earth takes its law from Heaven; Heaven takes its law from the Dao. The law of the Dao is its being what it is.

All-pervading is the Great Dao! It may be found on the left hand and on the right.

All things depend on it for their production, which it gives to them, not one refusing obedience to it. When its work is accomplished, it does not claim the name of having done it. It clothes all things as with a garment, and makes no assumption of being their lord—it may be named in the smallest things; . . . it may be named in the greatest things.

. . .

He who has in himself abundantly the attributes of the Dao is like an infant.

. . .

The Dao in its regular course does nothing, for the sake of doing it, and so there is nothing which it does not do.

The Wise Person

When we renounce learning we have no troubles.

. . .

If we could renounce our sageness and discard our wisdom, it would be better for the people a hundredfold. If we could renounce our benevolence and discard our righteousness, the people would again become filial and kindly. If we could renounce our artful contrivances and discard our scheming for gain, there would be no thieves nor robbers.

. . .

The sage manages affairs without doing anything, and conveys his instructions without the use of speech.

. . .

Therefore the sage holds in his embrace the one thing of humility, and manifests it to all the world. He is free from self-display, and therefore he shines; from self-assertion, and therefore he is distinguished; from self-boasting, and therefore his merit is acknowledged; from self-complacency, and therefore he acquires superiority. It is because he is thus free from striving that therefore no one in the world is able to strive with him.

. . .

When gold and jade fill the hall, their possessor cannot keep them safe. When wealth and honors lead to arrogance, this brings its evil on itself. When the work is done, and one's name is becoming distinguished, to withdraw into obscurity is the way of Heaven.

The Ideal Government

A state may be ruled by measures of correction; weapons of war may be used with crafty dexterity; but the kingdom is made one's own only by freedom from action and purpose.

How do I know that it is so? By these facts: In the kingdom the multiplication of prohibitive enactments increases the poverty of the people; the more implements to add to their profit that the people have, the greater disorder is there in the state and clan; the more acts of crafty dexterity that men possess, the more do strange contrivances appear; the more display there is of legislation, the more thieves and robbers there are.

Therefore a sage has said, "I will do nothing, and the people will be transformed of themselves; I will be fond of keeping still, and the people will of themselves become correct. I will take no trouble about it, and the people will of themselves become rich; I will manifest no ambition, and the people will of themselves attain to the primitive simplicity."

Not to value and employ men of superior ability is the way to keep the people from rivalry among themselves; not to prize articles which are difficult to procure is the way to keep them from becoming thieves; not to show them what is likely to excite their desires is the way to keep their minds from disorder.

Therefore the sage, in the exercise of his government, empties their minds, fills their bellies, weakens their wills, and strengthens their bones.

He constantly tries to keep them without knowledge and without desire, and where there are those who have knowledge, to keep them from presuming to act on it. When there is this abstinence from action, good order is universal.

Analysis and Review Questions

1. What is the Way in Daoist interpretation?
2. How does Daoism portray the relationship between people and nature? Why is harmony between man and nature important?
3. What is the Daoist view of "good order"?
4. What kind of people in China's classical society were likely to be attracted by Daoist teaching?
5. How different is the Daoist idea of an ideal government from that of Confucianism?

LEGALISM: THE WAY OF THE STATE

About the Document

Legalism, like Confucianism and Daoism, emerged during the Warring States period (475–221 B.C.E.). Initially social philosophies, all three attempted to search for solutions to end political chaos and social instability. While Confucianism emphasized the fundamental principle of human relationships for a centralized government and social order, Daoism offered passage away from political engagement by embracing natural harmony. Legalism, on the other hand, emphasized the importance of strong government control and the use of force to keep social order.

Han Feizi (ca. 233 B.C.E.), originally a Confucian scholar in training, was a key figure in the development of the Legalist school of political philosophy. Like other Legalists, he advocated absolute power for China's rulers in order to promote the strength and wealth of the state. A ruler had no obligations toward the welfare of his subjects according to Legalist thought; his main responsibility was to use harsh punishments to strictly enforce the state's laws.

Legalism reached its apex in the synthesis of Han Feizi's writings, which not only influenced Qin Shihuang's court politics, but also contributed to classic Chinese thought. The following selections represent Han Feizi's major Legalist views on government.

The Document

Having Regulations

No country is permanently strong. Nor is any country permanently weak. If conformers to law are strong, the country is strong; if conformers to law are weak, the country is weak . . .

Any ruler able to expel private crookedness and uphold public law, finds the people safe and the state in order; and any ruler able to expunge private action and act on public law, finds his army strong and his enemy weak. So, find out men following the discipline of laws and regulations, and place them above the body of officials. Then the sovereign cannot be deceived by anybody with fraud and falsehood . . .

Therefore, the intelligent sovereign makes the law select men and makes no arbitrary promotion himself. He makes the law measure merits and makes no arbitrary regulation himself. In consequence, able men cannot be obscured, bad characters cannot be disguised; falsely praised fellows cannot be advanced, wrongly defamed people cannot be degraded . . .

To govern the state by law is to praise the right and blame the wrong. The law does not fawn on the noble . . .

Whatever the law applies to, the wise cannot reject nor can the brave defy. Punishment for fault never skips ministers, reward for good never misses commoners. Therefore, to correct the faults of the high, to rebuke the vices of the low, to suppress disorders, to decide against mistakes, to subdue the arrogant, to straighten the crooked, and to unify the folkways of the masses, nothing could match the law. To warn the officials and overawe the people, to rebuke obscenity and danger, and to forbid falsehood and deceit, nothing could match penalty. If penalty is severe, the noble cannot discriminate against the humble. If law is definite, the superiors are esteemed and not violated. If the superiors are not violated, the sovereign will become strong and able to maintain the proper course of government. Such was the reason why the early kings esteemed Legalism and handed it down to posterity. Should the lord of men discard law and practice selfishness, high and low would have no distinction.

The Two Handles

The means whereby the intelligent ruler controls his ministers are two handles only. The two handles are chastisement and commendation. What are meant by chastisement and commendation? To inflict death or torture upon culprits, is called chastisement; to bestow encouragements or rewards on men of merit, is called commendation.

Ministers are afraid of censure and punishment but fond of encouragement and reward. Therefore, if the lord of men uses the handles of chastisement and commendation, all ministers will dread his severity and turn to his liberality. The villainous ministers of the age are different. To men they hate they would by securing the handle of chastisement from the sovereign ascribe crimes; on men they love they would by securing the handle of commendation from the sovereign bestow rewards. Now supposing the lord of men placed the authority of punishment and the profit of reward not in his hands but let the ministers administer the affairs of reward and punishment instead, then everybody in the country would fear the ministers and slight the ruler, and turn to the ministers and away from the ruler. This is the calamity of the ruler's loss of the handles of chastisement and commendation.

Analysis and Review Questions

1. According to Legalist teaching, what is the most important factor in keeping a country strong?
2. What is the role of "the two handles" in government?
3. What does the statement "to govern the state by law is to praise the right and blame the wrong" tell you about the nature of a Legalist government?
4. Legalist teaching is closely tied to the use of law in governing. What is the merit, if any, in Legalist teaching?
5. What are the major differences between Confucianist and Legalist philosophies with regard to governing?

SIMA QIAN ON QIN SHIHUANG

*Image 4.2
Qin Shihuang's
Terra Cotta
Soldiers*

About the Document

Sima Qian (145–86 B.C.E.) was the son of the Grand Historian of China and as-sumed that title himself in the imperial court of the Han Dynasty in 107 C.E. He is most famous for writing a monumental work on Chinese history known as *Shi Ji, The Records of the Grand Historian. Shi Ji* consists of 130 chapters in five volumes. In it, Sima Qian presents biographies of the Chinese rulers from the first leg-endary Yellow Emperor to the emperor of his time, as well as well-known feudal families and famous men. He also treats various subjects such as ritual practice, music, and general history. *Shi Ji* is considered to be the greatest history writing of Classical China, and Sima Qian is considered the greatest historian of all time. Sima Qian's portrait of the Qin Shihuang was the most vivid and truthful record in understanding both the Qin Dynasty and its ruler.

The document that follows includes excerpts from Sima Qian's *Biography of Qin Shihuang* on two major events: the First Emperor's ascension of China's sa-cred mountains and his erecting of stone monuments. Erecting stones was a common imperial practice in order to record a ruler's accomplishments with the blessing of heaven. On Mount Tai, according to Sima Qian, the inscribed stone monument praises the greatness, virtue, and hard work of the First Emperor. In the second inscription, Sima Qian gives a long list of the First Emperor's accom-plishments in bringing unification and peace to the country. As a court historian, Sima Qian's major task was to eulogize the rulers and record historical events ac-cording to the best interests of the government.

Qin Shihuang, however, remains a controversial figure in Chinese history. Most contemporary Chinese historians would disagree with Sima Qian's assess-ment of him. They saw the First Emperor as a merciless ruler with few credited achievements. Yes, Qin Shihuang unified China, but he also sent millions of forced laborers to their deaths during the construction of the Great Wall. Yes, Qin Shihuang standardized language, weight, and measures, but he also buried alive hundreds of Confucian scholars who disagreed with his Legalist rule. Although biased, the selections that follow give us important insight into the role and achievements of the First Emperor.

Qin Shihuang, the First Emperor of the Qin Dynasty (221–207 B.C.E.), was the first ruler in Chinese history to take the title of emperor. Hence, he is best known as the First Emperor of China. The rule of the First Emperor was a critical historical period that transformed both China's politics and society.

Born Zhao Cheng, the First Emperor was raised in a time of political chaos af-ter the fall of the Zhou Dynasty (770–256 B.C.E.) when numerous warring states fought for central leadership. Qin Shihuang's father was the king of Qin state. While a hostage in Zhao state, the Qin king fell for a concubine who later gave birth to a son to be named Zhao Cheng. When Zhao Cheng was 13, the Qin king died, and the son succeeded the throne. War among states went on for an-other 36 years until the new Qin king was able to defeat all other rivals and unify the country in 210 B.C.E.

In defining his title, the new king decided to adopt a new appellation: *Huangdi*, or the Emperor, a title implying supremacy over the previous kings. He also took the title *Yingzheng*, meaning "winning the throne." The emperor issued an edict that read: "We are Shi Huangdi, the First Sovereign Emperor, and our successors shall be known as the Second Emperor, Third Emperor and so on for generations without end." Having done this, the new ruler of a unified China ascended the imperial throne with a new name, Qin Shihuang. While *Qin* represents the original name of state, *Shi* means the first or number one.

Qin Shihuang is remembered for many deeds, both great and terrible, during his rather short rule of only 11 years. He unified a once war-torn China. He standardized the Chinese writing system as well as the monetary system and weights and measures. He consolidated his rule by enforcing Legalism, which emphasized strong government control and severe punishment to those who disobeyed. To achieve that goal, he not only forbade Confucian teaching, which promoted the good nature of human beings and a benevolent ruler, but also persecuted Confucius scholars by burying many alive. He established a formidable army to defend an expanding empire. For over two millennia, his name has been closely associated with another marvelous human accomplishment: the Great Wall of China. In order to establish a stronger fortress against the increasing barbarian threat from the north, Qin ordered his minions to connect many sections of existing walls and add an extension along China's northern border. He built a majestic mausoleum and buried a grand terra cotta army with him on his death. The excavation of his underground palace has become one of the greatest archaeological discoveries of our time. Today, Qin Shihuang's tomb is still standing, sealed, five miles west of the terra cotta army pits.

Qin Shihuang's espousal of Legalist policies in governing his empire led to civil revolt and probably the fall of his short-lived dynasty. Ironically, the failure of Legalism in Qin Shihuang's government and society eventually gave rise to the dominant position of Confucianism in Chinese civilization thereafter. Qin Shihuang left behind him a growing empire, soon to be both powerful and expansive.

The Document

The emperor ascended Mount Tai,° erected a stone monument and offered sacrifice to Heaven. The sacrifice to the Earth was offered at Mount Liangfu. And a stone monument was erected with this inscription:

The Sovereign Emperor came to the throne, made decrees and laws which
    all his subjects heeded;
In his twenty-sixth year the land was unified, all obeyed his rule;
He inspected the black-headed people in distant parts, ascended Mount
    Tai and viewed the eastern extremity;
His obedient subjects remember his achievements, trace them from the
    start and celebrate his virtue.

Mount Tai: One of the three major holy mountains in China: it represents the power of heaven and earth, according to Chinese mythology.

Beneath his wide sway all things find their place, all is decreed by law;
Great and manifest, his virtue is handed down to ages yet to come, to be
    followed without change.
The sage emperor who has pacified all under heaven is tireless in his rule;
He rises early, goes to sleep late, makes lasting benefits and offers wise
    instructions;
Wide spread his teachings, all far and near is well ordered according to his
    will;
High and low are set apart, men and women observe the proprieties, fulfill
    their different tasks;
Public and private affairs are clearly distinguished; peace reigned and will
    endure till a future age;
His influence knows no end, his will obeyed and his orders will remain
    through eternity.

The emperor had a tower built on Mount Langya and a stone inscription set up to
praise the power of Qin and make clear his will. The inscription read:

A new age is inaugurated by the Emperor;
Rules and measures are rectified,
The myriad things set in order,
Human affairs are made clear
And there is harmony between fathers and sons.
The Emperor in his sagacity, benevolence and justice
Has made all laws and principles manifest.
He set forth to pacify the east,
To inspect officers and men;
This great task accomplished
He visited the coast.
Great are the Emperor's achievements,
Men attend diligently to basic tasks,
Farming is encouraged, secondary pursuit discouraged,
All the common people prosper;
All men under the sky
Toil with a single purpose;
Tools and measures are made uniform,
The written script is standardized;
Wherever the sun and moon shine,
Wherever one can go by boat or by carriage,
Men carry out their orders
And satisfy their desires;
For our Emperor in accordance with the time
Has regulated local customs,
Made waterways and divided up the land.
Caring for the common people,
He works day and night without rest;
He defines the laws, leaving nothing in doubt,
Making known what is forbidden.
The local officials have their duties,
Administration is smoothly carried out,
All is done correctly, all according to plan.
The Emperor in his wisdom

Inspects all four quarters of his realm;
High and low, noble and humble,
None dare overshoot the mark;
No evil or impropriety is allowed,
All strive to be good men and true,
And exert themselves in tasks great and small;
None dares to idle or ignore his duties,
But in far-off, remote places
Serious and decorous administrators
Work steadily, just and loyal.
Great is the virtue of our Emperor
Who pacifies all four corners of the earth,
Who punishes traitors, roots out evil men,
And with profitable measures brings prosperity.
Tasks are done at the proper season,
All things flourish and grow;
The common people know peace
And have laid aside weapons and armor;
Kinsmen care for each other,
There are no robbers or thieves;
Men delight in his rule,
All understanding the law and discipline.
The universe entire
Is our Emperor's realm,
Extending west to the Desert,
South to where the houses face north,
East to the East Ocean,
North to beyond Dahsia;
Wherever human life is found,
All acknowledge his suzerainty,°
His achievements surpass those of the Five Emperors,
His kindness reaches even the beasts of the field;
All creatures benefit from his virtue,
All live in peace at home.

Analysis and Review Questions

1. According to Sima Qian, what are the major achievements of the First Emperor?
2. In your view, how important are the achievements of the First Emperor to the development of Chinese civilization? How important are they to the development of other civilizations?
3. What kind of ruler was the First Emperor in Sima Qian's opinion?
4. What was the Chinese view of an empire?
5. What are the similarities between the rules of China's First Emperor and those of Hammurabi?

suzerainty: The position of power of a reigning sovereign.

LI SI AND THE LEGALIST POLICIES OF QIN SHIHUANG

About the Document

Qin Shihuang's policy was guided by the doctrine of Legalism, which emphasized tight government control and severe punishment of the opposition. The First Emperor relied on the wisdom of his Grand Counselor, Li Si (280–208 B.C.E.), who was a staunch advocate of Legalism. Like Han Feizi, Li Si originally was a Confucian scholar in training. He admired the power of the First Emperor and believed that force was "Qin's strength to found a single empire and unify the world." To a large extent, Li Si's views on government became the policies of the First Emperor. Ironically, Li Si was later imprisoned and executed in 208 B.C.E. by the son of the First Emperor, who did not like men with political ambition.

At one imperial banquet, Chunyu Yueh, a Confucian scholar, challenged the First Emperor's policy of departing from traditional values by saying: "I have yet to hear of anything able to endure that was not based on ancient precedents." Yueh pointed out that an empire's lack of popular support would be hard to survive. In response to this criticism, Li Si gave the reply below.

Image 4.3
The Great Wall

The Document

The Five Emperors did not emulate each other nor did the Three Dynasties adopt each other's ways, yet all had good government. This is no paradox, because times had changed. Now Your Majesty has built up this great empire to endure for generations without end. Naturally this passes the comprehension of a foolish pedant.° Chunyu Yueh spoke about the Three Dynasties, but they are hardly worth taking as examples. In times gone by different barons fought among themselves and gathered wandering scholars. Today, however, the empire is at peace, all laws and order come from one single source, the common people support themselves by farming and handicrafts, while students study the laws and prohibitions.

Now these scholars learn only from the old, not from the new, and use their learning to oppose our rule and confuse the black-headed people. As prime minister I must speak out on pain of death. In former times when the world, torn by chaos and disorder, could not be united, different states arose and argued from the past to condemn the present, using empty rhetoric to cover up and confuse the real issues, and employing their learning to oppose what was established by authority. Now Your Majesty has conquered the whole world, distinguished between black and white, seen unified standards. Yet these opinionated scholars get together to slander the laws and judge each new decree according to their own school of thought, opposing it secretly in their hearts while discussing it openly in the streets. They brag to the sovereign to win fame, put forward strange arguments to gain distinction, and incite the mob to spread rumors. If this is not prohibited, the sovereign's prestige will suffer and factions will be formed among his subjects. Far better put a stop to it!

pedant: Person who overemphasizes or adheres rigidly to rules.

I humbly propose that all historical records but those of Chin be burned. If anyone who is not a court scholar dares to keep the ancient songs, historical records or writings of the hundred schools, these should be confiscated and burned by the provincial governor and army commander. Those who in conversation dare to quote the old songs and records should be publicly executed; those who use old precedents to oppose the new order should have their families wiped out; and officers who know of such cases but fail to report them should be punished in the same way.

If thirty days after the issuing of this order the owners of these books have still not had them destroyed, they should have their face tattooed and be condemned to hard labor at the Great Wall. The only books which need not be destroyed are those dealing with medicine, divination, and agriculture. Those who want to study the law can learn it from the officers. The emperor sanctioned this proposal.

Analysis and Review Questions

1. What is Li Si's response to the criticism of the "opinionated scholars," and what is his suggestion to control them?
2. What is the main point of scholar Chunyu Yueh's comments on Qin Shihuang's policy?
3. Li Si says that "... those scholars learn only from the old, not from the new, and use their learning to oppose our rule." What does "old" and "new" mean in Li Si's opinion?
4. Why are rules and laws important to keep social order, according to Li Si?
5. Given the fact that the First Emperor unified China by adopting Legalist policy, what were the points from Legalism that were appealing at that time?

WEB LINKS

Selections from Longman World History—Primary Sources and Case Studies

http://longmanworldhistory.com
The following additional readings and case studies can be found on the Web site.
Document 2.6, Darius the Great: Ruler of Persia
Document 4.1, An Inscribed Oracle Bone
Document 6.6, Augustus on His Accomplishments
Case Study 4.1, Two Great Emperors: East vs. West
Case Study 4.2, Absolute Rule: The Emperor and the King

On Qin Shihuang

http://library.thinkquest.org/12255/library/dynasty/qin.html
Thinkquest library site on Xiang Qi, the ancient art of Chinese chess. Information about history, art, and religions of China through a site organized into a virtual museum, temple, and library.

http://academic.brooklyn.cuny.edu/core9/phalsall/texts/ssuma1.html
Two biographical excerpts from Sima Qian's *Records of the Grand Historian of China*, plus Sima Qian's writing about his castration and decision not to commit suicide.

http://academic.brooklyn.cuny.edu/core9/phalsall/texts/ssuma2.html
More from *the Records of the Grand Historian of China* by Sima Qian. This excerpt concerns the Legalist policies of the Qin.

On the Terra Cotta Soldiers

http://members.aol.com/h2oskineil/travel/page10c.htm
Contains photos and a history of the creation of the terra cotta army.

http://www.nfb.ca/FMT/E/MSN/19/19805.html
Information on the movie, *The First Emperor of China.*

CHAPTER 5

The Emergence of Classical Western Civilization

Sometime around 800 B.C.E., Greece began to emerge from a period now known as the "Greek Dark Ages." During this period, literacy nearly vanished, and warfare was common; yet it was also the era of the author Homer, whose epic poems the *Iliad* and the *Odyssey* are considered cultural masterpieces. Greek civilization, the so-called Hellenic Age as we usually know it, began to emerge as these Dark Ages were ending. Western scholars have often credited the ancient Greeks with "creating" Western culture. It is certainly true that the Greeks promoted a leisurely lifestyle and that many values traditionally considered "Western," such as individualism, freedom, and optimism, come to us from the Greeks.

But behind the scenes of what was generally a fairly advanced civilization lurked serious problems, such as an inability to forge a lasting, effective government in the scattered Greek city-states or solve the problems of conflict between its two great rival city-states, Athens and Sparta. The conflict between these two city-states and their allies, the Peloponnesian Wars (431–404 B.C.E.) eventually led to the end of the Athenian Age, and the transfer of political power to the north, in Macedonia. There, during the fifth century, Philip and his son, Alexander, built a power base from which they expanded to control most of the known world of the time. Culturally, the Hellenic Age gave way to the Hellenistic Age, which followed Alexander's conquest of the Middle East in the 300s B.C.E.

This new epoch ushered in a period of economic and cultural (if not political) unity in the eastern Mediterranean and the Middle East. Alexander the Great is said to have founded over 70 cities during his conquest of the Middle East and Persia, and many of them bear his name. There is no disputing that, at least to some extent, one of Alexander's goals was the spread of Greek culture, of which he was a great admirer. Crucial to this was the establishment of Greek-styled cities, which could serve as centers of diffusion for Greek ideas, attitudes, and culture. The result, however, was not the spread of pure Greek culture, but rather the emergence of a new cultural synthesis, which combined elements of Greek and local cultures. The city of Alexandria, Egypt, became the center for Hellenistic culture and scholarship.

GREEK POETRY

About the Document

Greek culture is correctly remembered as varied, with notable artistic, philosophical, and literary achievements. Homer's tales remained popular throughout Greek history and after. Little is known about Homer, and it is possible that there was more than one "Homer." If there was a real Homer, he was born sometime around 800 B.C.E. on the coast of Asia Minor. Homer's stories, passed down orally for centuries, inspired other storytellers and singers.

The ancient Greeks also loved poetry, and they made use of numerous poetic styles. Most poetry was not actually read by the citizenry, but rather was read and sung by the poet or other types of traveling minstrels. Greek poetry is as varied as Greek culture; poems range from the love poetry of Sappho to the political poetry of Solon. The poets whose pieces follow include Solon, Xenophanes, Sappho, Homer, and Pindar.

Solon was a noble who rose to Athens' top political position, Archon, in 594 B.C.E. Solon is best known for his attempted reforms in the city, including efforts to level the political playing field by encouraging more popular participation in the government. Solon also made several economic reforms, was a noted poet, and wrote about Athens' political situations.

Xenophanes, who lived from 572 to 480 B.C.E., was critical of the Greek image of gods as having human weaknesses and characteristics. Rather, Xenophanes said, the gods were actually all part of one moral and ethical deity.

Sappho, who lived on the island of Lesbos and made her living as a teacher around 600 B.C.E., enjoyed unprecedented freedom for a Greek woman and was so highly regarded that she became known as "The Poetess." Her poems display Greek ideas about life and sensuality, and many were written for men as well as for women.

The poet Pindar was born around 518 B.C.E. near Thebes in Greece, and early in life he earned a reputation as a great eulogizer of victorious athletes and athletic contests. The poems included here are written to winners of boxing and chariot contests, respectively.

The Document

APOLOGIA OF HIS RULE

> Where did I fail? When did I give up goals
> for which I gathered my torn people together?
> When the judgment of time descends on me,
> call on my prime witness, Black Earth, supreme
> excellent mother of the Olympian gods,
> whose expanse was once pocked with mortgage stones,
> which I dug out to free a soil in bondage.
> Into our home, Athens, founded by the gods,
> I brought back many sold unlawfully as slaves,
> and throngs of debtors harried into exile,
> drifting about so long in foreign lands

they could no longer use our Attic tongue;
here at home men who wore the shameful brand
of slavery and suffered the hideous moods
of brutal masters—all these I freed. Fusing
justice and power into an iron weapon,
I forced through every measure I had pledged.
I wrote the laws for good and bad alike,
and gave an upright posture to our courts.

Had someone else controlled the whip of power,
a bungler, a man of greed, he would not
have held the people in. Had I agreed
to do what satisfied opponents, or else
what their enemies planned in turn for them,
our dear city would be widowed of her men.
But I put myself on guard at every side,
spinning like a wolf among a pack of dogs.

      SOLON (C.638–C.558 B.C.E.)

THE MAKING OF THE GODS

1
Man made his gods, and furnished them
with his own body, voice and garments.

2
If a horse or lion or a slow ox
had agile hands for paint and sculpture,
the horse would make his god a horse,
the ox would sculpt an ox.

3
Our gods have flat noses and black skins
say the Ethiopians. The Thracians say
our gods have red hair and hazel eyes.

      XENOPHANES (C.572–C.480 B.C.E.)

TO ANAKTORIA

Some say cavalry and others claim
infantry or a fleet of long oars
is the supreme sight on the black earth.
I say it is

the one you love. And easily proved.
Did not Helen°—who far surpassed all
mortals in beauty—desert the best
of men, her king,
and sail off to Troy and forget

Helen: According to legend, the beautiful Helen was the daughter of Zeus. Her abduction by Paris
caused the Trojan War.

her daughter and dear kinsmen? Merely
the Kyprian's gaze made her bend and led
her from her path;

these things remind me now
of Anaktoria who is far,
and I
for one

would rather see her warm supple step
and the sparkle of her face—than watch
all the dazzling chariots and armored
hoplites° of Lydia.

A PRAYER TO APHRODITE

On your dazzling throne, Aphrodite,°
sly eternal daughter of Zeus,
I beg you: do not crush me with grief,

but come to me now—as once
you heard my far cry, and yielded,
slipping from your father's house

to yoke the birds to your gold
chariot, and came. Handsome sparrows
brought you swiftly to the dark earth,

their wings whipping the middle sky.
Happy, with deathless lips, you smiled:
"What is wrong, why have you called me?

What does your mad heart desire?
Whom shall I make love you, Sappho,
who is turning her back on you?

Let her run away, soon she'll chase you;
refuse your gifts, soon she'll give them.
She will love you, though unwillingly."

Then come to me now and free me
from fearful agony. Labor
for my mad heart, and be my ally.

TO APHRODITE OF THE FLOWERS, AT KNOSSOS

Leave Krete and come to this holy temple
where the graceful grove of apple trees
circles an altar smoking with frankincense.

Here roses leave shadow on the ground
and cold springs babble through apple branches
where shuddering leaves pour down profound sleep.

In our meadow where horses graze
and wild flowers of spring blossom,

hoplites: Heavily armored foot soldiers used by most ancient Greek city states.
Aphrodite: Ancient Greek goddess of love and beauty

anise shoots fill the air with aroma.

And here, Queen Aphrodite, pour
heavenly nectar into gold cups
and fill them gracefully with sudden joy.

SAPPHO (C.620–C.565 B.C.E.)

THE EARTH MOTHER: A HOMERIC HYMN

O universal Mother, who dost keep
From everlasting thy foundations deep,
Eldest of things, Great Earth, I sing of thee!
All shapes that have their dwelling in the sea,
All things that fly, or on the ground divine
Live, move, and there are nourished—these are thine;
These from thy wealth thou dost sustain; from thee
Fair babes are born, and fruits on every tree
Hand ripe and large, revered Divinity!

The life of mortal men beneath thy sway
Is held; thy power both gives and takes away!
Happy are they whom thy mild favours nourish;
All things unstinted round them grow and flourish.
For them, endures the life-sustaining field
Its load of harvest, and their cattle yield
Large increase, and their house with wealth is filled.
Such honoured dwell in cities fair and free,
The homes of lovely women, prosperously;
Their sons exult in youth's new budding gladness,
And their fresh daughters free from care or sadness,
With bloom-inwoven dance and happy song,
On the soft flowers the meadow-grass among,
Leap round them sporting—such delights by thee
Are given, rich Power, revered Divinity.

Mother of gods, thou Wife of starry Heaven,
Farewell! be thou propitious, and be given
A happy life for this brief melody,
Nor thou nor other songs shall unremembered be.

HOMER (C.800 B.C.E.)

HAGESIDAMOS OF WESTERN LOKROI, BOYS' BOXING, 476 B.C.

Turn Sometimes men need the winds most,
at other times
waters from the sky,
rainy descendants of the cloud.
And when a man has triumphed
and put his toil behind,
it is time for melodious song
to arise, laying

the foundation of future glory,
a sworn pledge securing proud success.

Counterturn For Olympian victors, such acclaim
is laid in store
without limit, and I
am eager to tend it with my song.
For a man flourishes
in wise understanding,
as in all things,
through a god's favor.
Know now, son of Archestratos,
Hagesidamos, because of your boxing victory.

Stand I will sing, and my song will be
an added adornment
to your gold olive crown,
shining with love for Western Lokroi,
Go there
and join the revels, Muses.
By my bond,
you will not find a people indifferent to strangers
or blind to beauty, but men of keenest discernment
and courage in war.
For the crimson fox
and thunderous lion cannot change their inborn ways.

MEGAKLES OF ATHENS, CHARIOT RACE, 486 B.C.

Turn Praise of great Athens
is the noblest foundation
we can lay down as prelude
to a song honoring
a chariot victory
gained by the mighty sons of Alkmaion.
For what country will you dwell in,
what home will you inhabit,
telling all Greece it is more radiant than Athens?

Counterturn Familiar to every city is the story
of Erechtheus' townsmen
who made your temple, Apollo,
a wonder to behold
in sacred Pytho.
But five Isthmian triumphs inspire me now,
and one
flamelike in glory
At Zeus' Olympia, and two more at Kirrha.

Stand yours, Megakles, and your forefathers'.
No small joy do I feel
for this fresh success,
and yet I grieve

that envy pays back noble deeds.
This is exactly what is meant
in the saying of men:
Happiness
of abiding bloom bears
now and then a bitter fruit.

      PINDAR (C.522–C.443 B.C.E.)

Analysis and Review Questions

1. From his poem, list the changes Solon claims to have made.
2. Does Solon suggest that passing his reforms was easy or difficult?
3. What appears to be the theme of Xenophanes's poem, "The Making of the Gods"?
4. Is there any advice appropriate for modern times in Sappho's "A Prayer to Aphrodite"?
5. What do Pindar's poems tell us about the actual events the athletes competed in?

ARISTOTLE ON SLAVERY

About the Document

Slavery has existed since early times, even in a civilization as "enlightened" as that of ancient Athens. Scholars who study slavery continue to argue over the place of the slave in ancient Greek society. Generally speaking, slaves who lived in the cities were well treated; could have their own, separate jobs; and were sometimes freed for loyal service. Slaves who lived outside the cities and toiled in the mines or fields were subject to much harsher treatment and literally might be worked to death.

    Aristotle (384–322 B.C.E.) was the most noted student of the philosopher Plato and wrote extensively about the natural world. In addition, however, Aristotle wrote on many of the same subjects as his mentor: politics, government, and society in general. Aristotle provides the following insight into the position of Greek slaves in ancient Athens.

*Map 5.2
Greek and Phoenician
Colonies and Trade*

The Document

    Property is a part of the household, and the art of acquiring property a part of household management (since no kind of life, and certainly not a fulfilled life, is possible without the basic necessities); and so, just as in particular crafts the relevant tools are needed if a job is to be done, exactly the same applies to managing a household. Tools can be divided into animate and inanimate (for instance, for the helmsman of a ship, the rudder is inanimate while the look-out man is animate: since an assistant can be categorised as a "tool" as regards that particular craft). So a piece of property is, similarly, a tool needed to live; "property" is a collection of such tools, and a slave is an animate piece of property.

The word "property" is used in the same way as the word "part": a part is not simply a section of something else, but belongs to it completely, and the same is true of a piece of property. Therefore a master is simply the master of a slave, but does not belong to the slave, while the slave isn't just the slave of a master, but belongs to him completely.

It will be clear from these facts what the nature and the functions of a slave are.

A: A human being who by nature does not belong to himself but to another person—such a one is by nature a slave.

B: A human being belongs to another when he is a piece of property as well as being human.

C: A piece of property is a tool which is used to assist some activity, and which has a separate existence of its own.

(1) The principal and most essential form of property is that which is best and most central to managing a household: the human being. So the first thing to do is acquire good slaves. There are two categories of slaves: overseer and labourer. Since we can see that it is upbringing that gives young people their particular character, it is essential to educate any slaves we have bought if we intend to give them that kind of work which is appropriate to free persons [i.e. supervisory functions].

(2) In our dealings with slaves, we should not let them be insolent towards us nor allow them free rein. Those whose position is nearer to that of free men should be treated with respect, those who are labourers given more food. Since the consumption of wine makes free men behave insolently too (and in many cultures even free men abstain from it—like the Carthaginians when they go campaigning), it is clear that wine should never, or only very rarely, be given to slaves.

(3) There are three things [that concern slaves]: work, punishment and food. Having food but no work and no punishment makes a slave insolent; giving him work and punishment without food is an act of violence and debilitates him. The alternative is to give him work to do together with sufficient food. One cannot manage someone without rewarding them, and food is a slave's reward. Slaves, just like other human beings, become worse when better behaviour brings no benefits, and there are no prizes for virtue and vice.

(4) Consequently we ought to keep a watch over how our slaves behave, and make our distributions and apportion privileges according to desert, whether it is a matter of food or clothes or free time or punishment. In word and deed we must adopt the authority of a doctor when he issues his prescriptions—noting the difference that, unlike medicine, food has to be taken continuously.

(5) The races best suited for work are those which are neither extremely cowardly nor extremely courageous, since both of these are likely to cause trouble. Those who are too easily cowed cannot persevere with their work, while those who have too much courage are difficult to control.

(6) It is essential that each slave should have a clearly defined goal (*telos*). It is both just and advantageous to offer freedom as a prize—when the prize, and the period of time in which it can be attained, are clearly defined, this will make them work willingly. We should also let them have children to serve as hostages; and, as is customary in cities, we should not buy slaves of the same ethnic origins. We should also organise sacrifices and holidays, for the sake of the slaves rather than the free men—for free men get more of the things for the sake of which these practices have been instituted.

Analysis and Review Questions

1. How does Aristotle define property?
2. What are the nature and functions of a slave?
3. What needed to be done to slaves who were bought to be supervisors?
4. What does Aristotle claim is an advantageous "prize" to entice slaves with?
5. What provision for punishment is given in this selection?

THUCYDIDES ON ATHENS

About the Document

A common exercise when learning about ancient Greece is to compare the lives and cities of the Athenians and Spartans. One of the most useful primary sources is a speech that the Athenian leader Pericles gave to honor soldiers who died in a war with Sparta. Pericles, a well-respected young noble, dominated Athenian politics and society during the 460s through the 420s B.C.E. and presided over Athens when the city was at its height.

Under Pericles, Athens' developing democracy became even more fair and open to all. For the first time, poor citizens could actively participate, and the city prospered as never before. Pericles also served numerous times as a general in the early years of the Peloponnesian War between Athens and Sparta. Another general, Thucydides, wrote an accurate first-hand account of the first years of the war called the *History of the Peloponnesian War*. In the winter of 431–430 B.C.E., Pericles delivered a funeral speech to commemorate soldiers killed in the fighting, and he also praised his city.

The Document

Our constitution does not copy the laws of neighboring states; we are rather a model for others than imitators ourselves. Its administration favors the many instead of the few; this is why it is called a democracy. If we look at the laws, they afford equal justice to all in settling private differences. As for prestige, advancement in public life goes to men with reputations for ability: class considerations are not allowed to interfere with merit, nor again does poverty bar the way. If a man is able to serve the state, he is not hindered by obscure origins or poverty. The freedom we enjoy in our government extends also to our private life. There . . . we do not feel called upon to be angry with our neighbor for doing what he likes, or even to indulge in those injurious looks which cannot fail to be offensive, although they inflict no actual harm. But all this ease in our private relations does not make us lawless as citizens. . . . We obey the magistrates and the laws, particularly those for the protection of the injured, whether they are actually on the statute book, or belong to that code which, although unwritten, yet cannot be broken without acknowledged disgrace.

Further, we provide plenty of means for the mind to refresh itself from business. We celebrate games and sacrifices all the year round, and the elegance of our private establishments forms a daily source of pleasure and helps to banish our cares. Then, too, the magnitude of our city draws the produce of the world into our harbor, so that to the Athenian the products of other countries are as familiar a luxury as those of his own.

If we turn to our military policy, there also we differ from our antagonists. We throw open our city to the world, and never pass laws to exclude foreigners from any opportunity of learning or observing, although the eyes of the enemy may occasionally profit from our liberality. . . . In education, where our rivals from their very cradles seek after manliness through a very painful discipline, at Athens we live as we please, and yet are just as ready to encounter every legitimate danger.

In generosity we are equally singular, acquiring our friends by conferring, not receiving, favors. Yet, of course, the doer of the favor is the firmer friend of the two, in order by continued kindness to keep the recipient in his debt; while the debtor feels less keenly from the very consciousness that the return he makes will be a repayment, not a free gift, and it is only the Athenians who, fearless of consequences, confer their benefits not from calculations of expediency, but in the confidence of liberality.

In short, I say that as a city we are the school of Hellas;° while I doubt if the world can produce a man who is equal to so many emergencies where he has only himself to depend upon, and who is graced by so happy a versatility as the Athenian . . . For Athens alone of her contemporaries is found when tested to be greater than her reputation, and alone gives no occasion to her assailants to blush at the antagonist by whom they have been worsted, or to her subjects to question her title by merit to rule. Rather, the admiration of the present and succeeding ages will be ours, since we have not left our power without witness, but have shown it by mighty proofs; and far from needing a Homer for our panegyrist, or another poet whose verses might charm for the moment only for the impression which they gave, to melt at the touch of fact, we have forced every sea and land to be the highway of our daring, and everywhere, whether for evil or for good, have left imperishable monuments behind us. Such is the Athens for which these men, in the assertion of their resolve not to lose her, nobly fought and died; and well may every one of their survivors be ready to suffer in her cause.

If I have dwelt at some length upon the character of our country, it has been to show that our stake in the struggle is not the same as theirs who have no such blessings to lose, and also that the praise of the men over whom I am now speaking might be confirmed by definite proofs. My speech is now largely complete; for the Athens that I have celebrated is only what the heroism of these and others like them have made her, men whose fame, unlike that of most Hellenes, will be found to be only proportionate to what they deserve. And if a test of worth be wanted, it is to be found in their last scene, and this not only in the cases in which it set the final seal upon their merit, but also in those in which it gave the first intimation of their having any. For there is justice in the claim that steadfastness in his country's battles should be as a cloak to cover a man's other imperfections, since the good more than outweighed his demerits as an individual. . . . And while committing to hope the uncertainty of final success, in the business before them they thought fit to act boldly and trust in themselves. Thus choosing to die resisting, rather than to live submitting.

So died these men as became Athenians. You, their survivors, must be determined to have as unfaltering a resolution in the field, though you may pray that it may have a happier outcome. . . . You must yourselves realize the power of Athens, and feed your eyes upon her from day to day, till the love of her fills your hearts; and then when all her greatness shall break upon you, you must reflect that it was by courage, sense of duty,

---

Hellas: Greece; citizens of Hellas are known as Hellenes.

and a keen feeling of honor in action that men were enabled to win all this, and that no personal failure in an enterprise could make them consent to deprive their country of their bravery except as a sacrifice of the most serious contribution they could offer.

Take these as your model, and recognize that happiness comes from freedom and freedom comes from courage; never decline the dangers of war. For it is not the miserable who have the most reason to risk their lives; they have nothing to hope for: instead, it is they to whom continued life may bring reverses as yet unknown, and to whom a fall, if it came, would be most tremendous in its consequences.

Comfort, therefore, not condolence, is what I have to offer to the parents of the dead who may be here. Numberless are the chances to which, as they know, the life of man is subject; but fortunate indeed are they who draw their lot a death so glorious as that which has caused your mourning, and to whom life has been so exactly measured as to terminate in the happiness in which it has been passed.

My task is now finished. If deeds be in question, those who are here interred have received part of their honors already, and for the rest, their children will be brought up till manhood at the public expense: thus the state offers a valuable prize as the garland of victory in this race of valor, for the reward both of those who have fallen and their survivors. And where the rewards for merit are greatest, there the best citizens are found.

And now that you have brought to a close your lamentations for your relatives, you may depart.

Image 5.1
The Athenian
Acropolis

Analysis and Review Questions

1. Does Pericles claim Athens is a generous city?
2. Is Athens an "isolationist" city, according to Pericles?
3. Is everyone in Athens eligible to serve the city?
4. Would Pericles say that Athenians were a law-abiding people?
5. Would you call this speech a "patriotic" one?

PLUTARCH ON LIFE IN SPARTA

About the Document

The city of Sparta was Athens' great rival in Greece during the fifth century B.C.E. and after. The early Spartans quickly outgrew their original city and then conquered the surrounding peoples, forcing them into a serf-like position. Ruling over a much larger but subservient population provided numerous challenges to the Spartan government, so changes were made to Spartan politics. Between ca. 800 and 600 B.C.E., the Spartan "lawgiver," Lycurgus, is credited with establishing what amounted to a military state in Sparta. (Historians are not sure there was an actual Lycurgus, though the changes he is credited with are real.)

The Greek historian Plutarch was born near Corinth in Greece around 45 C.E., and he was a great traveler throughout the eastern Mediterranean. By nature an optimist, Plutarch is noted for his uplifting accounts and philosophical observations. Unfortunately, though he was an incredibly prolific writer, less than a third of his original writings survive, and only fragments of his most noted work, *Parallel Lives*. His work included biographical sketches of famous Greeks and Romans such as Alexander the Great, Caesar, and Cicero, as well as Lycurgus, the Spartan lawgiver.

The Document

Among the many innovations which Lycurgus made, the first and most important was his institution of a senate, or Council of Elders, which, as Plato says, by being blended with the "feverish" government of the kings, and by having an equal vote with them in matters of the highest importance, brought safety and due moderation into counsels of state. For before this the civil polity was veering and unsteady, inclining at one time to follow the kings towards tyranny,° and at another to follow the multitude towards democracy; but now, by making the power of the senate a sort of ballast for the ship of state and putting her on a steady keel, it achieved the safest and the most orderly arrangement, since the twenty-eight senators always took the side of the kings when it was a question of curbing democracy, and, on the other hand, always strengthened the people to withstand the encroachments of tyranny.

[Sparta's assemblies met between a bridge and a river.]

Between these they held their assemblies, having neither halls nor any other kind of building for the purpose. For by such things Lycurgus thought good counsel was not promoted, but rather discouraged, since the serious purposes of an assembly were rendered foolish and futile by vain thoughts, as they gazed upon statues and paintings, or scenic embellishments, or extravagantly decorated roofs of council halls. When the multitude was thus assembled, no one of them was permitted to make a motion, but the motion laid before them by the senators and kings could be accepted or rejected by the people. Afterwards, however, when the people by additions and subtractions perverted and distorted the sense of motions laid before them, Kings Polydorus and Theopompus inserted this clause into the rhetra: "But if the people should adopt a distorted motion, the senators and kings shall have power of adjournment"; that is, should not ratify the vote, but dismiss outright and dissolve the session, on the ground that it was perverting and changing the motion contrary to the best interests of the state.

A second, and a very bold political measure of Lycurgus, was his redistribution of the land. For there was a dreadful inequality in this regard, the city was heavily burdened with indigent and helpless people, and wealth was wholly concentrated in the hands of a few. Determined, therefore, to banish insolence and envy and crime and luxury, and those yet more deep-seated and afflictive diseases of the state, poverty and wealth, he persuaded his fellow-citizens to make one parcel of all their territory and divide it up anew, and to live with one another on a basis of entire uniformity and equality in the means of subsistence, seeking preeminence through virtue alone, assured that there was no other difference or inequality between man and man than that which was established by blame for base actions and praise for good ones.

Next, he undertook to divide up their movable property also, in order that every vestige of unevenness and inequality might be removed. In the first place, he withdrew all gold and silver money from currency, and ordained the use of iron money only.

---

tyranny: In ancient Greek sense, government by one who seizes power illegally.

In the next place, he banished the unnecessary and superfluous arts. And even without such banishment most of them would have departed with the old coinage, since there was no sale for their products. For the iron money could not be carried into the rest of Greece, nor had it any value there, but was rather held in ridicule. It was not possible, therefore, to buy any foreign wares or bric-à-brac; no merchant-seamen brought freight into their harbours; no rhetoric teacher set foot on Laconian° soil, no vagabond soothsayer, no keeper of harlots, no gold- or silver-smith, since there was no money there. But luxury, thus gradually deprived of that which stimulated and supported it, died away of itself.

With a view to attack luxury still more and remove the thirst for wealth, he introduced his third and most exquisite political device, namely, the institution of common messes, so that they might eat with one another in companies, of common and specified foods.

In the matter of education, which he regarded as the greatest and noblest task of the law-giver, he began at the very source, by carefully regulating marriages and births.

He made the maidens exercise their bodies in running, wrestling, casting the discus, and hurling the javelin, in order that the fruit of their wombs might have vigorous root in vigorous bodies and come to better maturity, and that they themselves might come with vigour to the fulness of their times, and struggle successfully and easily with the pangs of child-birth.

For their marriages the women were carried off by force, not when they were small and unfit for wedlock, but when they were in full bloom and wholly ripe.

[Children of Spartan citizens, especially the boys, were under the control of the city more so than under their parents.]

. . . as soon as [the boys] were seven years old, Lycurgus ordered them all to be taken by the state and enrolled in companies, where they were put under the same discipline and nurture, and so became accustomed to share one another's sports and studies.

Of reading and writing, they learned only enough to serve their turn; all the rest of their training was calculated to make them obey commands well, endure hardships, and conquer in battle. Therefore, as they grew in age, their bodily exercise was increased; their heads were close-clipped, and they were accustomed to going bare-foot, and to playing for the most part without clothes.

The training of the Spartans lasted into the years of full maturity. No man was allowed to live as he pleased, but in their city, as in a military encampment, they always had a prescribed regimen and employment in public service, considering that they belonged entirely to their country and not to themselves.

In a word, he trained his fellow-citizens to have neither the wish nor the ability to live for themselves; but like bees they were to make themselves always integral parts of the whole community, clustering together about their leader, almost beside themselves with enthusiasm and noble ambition, and to belong wholly to their country.

. . . he did not permit them to live abroad at their pleasure and wander in strange lands, assuming foreign habits and imitating the lives of peoples who were without training and lived under different forms of government. Nay more, he actually drove away from the city the multitudes which streamed in there for no useful purpose, not because he feared they might become imitators of his form of government and learn

Laconia: An area in southern Greece where Sparta is located.

useful lessons in virtue, as Thucydides says, but rather that they might not become in any wise teachers of evil. For along with strange people, strange doctrines must come in; and novel doctrines bring novel decisions, from which there must arise many feelings and resolutions which destroy the harmony of the existing political order. Therefore he thought it more necessary to keep bad manners and customs from invading and filling the city than it was to keep out infectious diseases.

Analysis and Review Questions

1. What institutions appear to have helped the two kings rule in Sparta?
2. How much power do the assemblies appear to have had?
3. Why did the assemblies meet between a bridge and a river?
4. Why did Lycurgus decree that all money was to be made out of iron?
5. What role do women seem to have played in Sparta?

PLUTARCH ON ALEXANDER THE GREAT

About the Document

The Hellenistic Age was an era of great change for the eastern Mediterranean. Ushered in by Philip of Macedon's conquest of Greece in 338 B.C.E. and lasting until Rome's takeover of Egypt in 31 B.C.E., this age saw the spread of a Greek-like culture throughout the Middle East and Egypt. This change was made possible by the empire-building of Alexander III of Macedon, or "Alexander the Great."

Alexander the Great is often cited by military historians as the greatest military figure in human history. It is certainly true that, as a general, he never lost a battle, and he overcame serious obstacles to conquer a huge empire stretching from Greece to western India in just over 10 years. As with most major historical figures, however, Alexander is still a subject of controversy. Some historians call him one of the world's great visionaries—a leader who wanted to create a unified, peaceful Greek world. Others call Alexander little more than a drunken brawler, prone to violence and excess. These scholars say that after a night of extreme revelry Alexander died in 323 B.C.E.

One of the surviving sketches written by the Greek historian Plutarch is on Alexander the Great.

The Document

It is the life of Alexander the king that I am writing in this book, and the multitude of the deeds to be treated is so great that I shall make no other preface than to entreat my readers, in case I do not tell of all the famous actions of these men, nor even speak exhaustively at all in each particular case, but in epitome for the most part, not to complain.

. . . The outward appearance of Alexander is best represented by the statues of him which Lysippus made, and it was by this artist alone that Alexander himself thought it fit that he should be modelled. For those peculiarities which many of his successors and friends afterwards tried to imitate, namely, the poise of the neck, which was bent slightly to the left, and the melting glance of his eyes, this artist has accurately observed. Appelles, however, in painting him as wielder of the thunderbolt, did not reproduce his complexion, but made it too dark and swarthy. Whereas he was of a fair colour, as they say, and his fairness passed into ruddiness on his breast particularly, and in his face. Moreover, that a very pleasant odour exhaled from his skin and that there was a fragrance about his mouth and all his flesh, so that his garments were filled with it.

But while he was still a boy his self-restraint showed itself in the fact that, although he was impetuous and violent in other matters, the pleasures of the body had little hold upon him, and he indulged in them with great moderation, while his ambition kept his spirit serious and lofty in advance of his years. For it was neither every kind of fame nor fame from every source that he courted, as Philip did, who plumed himself like a sophist on the power of his oratory, and took care to have the victories of his chariots at Olympia engraved upon his coins; nay, when those about him inquired whether he would be willing to contend in the foot-race at the Olympic games, since he was swift of foot, "Yes," said he, "if I could have kings as my contestants." And in general, too, Alexander appears to have been averse to the whole race of athletes; at any rate, though he instituted very many contests, not only for tragic poets and players on the flute and players on the lyre, but also for rhapsodists, as well as for hunting of every sort and for fighting with staves, he took no interest in offering prizes either for boxing or for the pancratium.

[Alexander's father, Philip, employed Aristotle as his son's tutor.]

Well, then, as a place where master and pupil could labour and study, he assigned them the precinct of the nymphs near Mieza, where to this day the visitor is shown the stone seats and shady walks of Aristotle. It would appear, moreover, that Alexander not only received from his master his ethical and political doctrines, but also participated in those secret and more profound teachings which philosophers designate by the special terms "acroamatic" and "epoptic" [private, oral teachings], and do not impart to many.

Moreover, in my opinion Alexander's love of the art of healing was inculcated in him by Aristotle preeminently. For he was not only fond of the theory of medicine, but actually came to the aid of his friends when they were sick, and prescribed for them certain treatments and regimens, as one can gather from his letters. He was also by nature a lover of learning and a lover of reading.

. . . Aristotle he admired at the first, and loved him, as he himself used to say, more than he did his father, for that the one had given him life, but the other had taught him a noble life; later, however, he held him in more or less of suspicion, not to the extent of doing him any harm, but his kindly attentions lacked their former ardour and affection towards him, and this was proof of estrangement. However, that eager yearning for philosophy which was imbedded in his nature and which ever grew with his growth, did not subside from his soul.

. . . To the use of wine also he was less addicted than was generally believed. The belief arose from the time which he would spend over each cup, more in talking than in drinking, always holding some long discourse, and this too when he had abundant leisure. For in the stress of affairs he was not to be detained, as other commanders were, either by wine, or sleep, or any sport, or amour, or spectacle. This is proved by his life, which, though altogether brief, he filled to overflowing with the greatest exploits.

In his times of leisure, however, after rising and sacrificing to the gods, he immediately took breakfast sitting; then, he would spend the day in hunting, or administering justice, or arranging his military affairs, or reading. If he were making a march which was not very urgent, he would practise, as he went along, either archery or mounting and dismounting from a chariot that was under way. Often, too, he would hunt foxes or birds, as may be gathered from his journals. After he had taken quarters for the night, and while he was enjoying bath or anointing, he would enquire of his chief cooks and bakers whether the arrangements for his supper were duly made. When it was late and already dark, he would begin his supper, reclining on a couch, and marvellous was his care and circumspection at table, in order that everything might be served impartially and without stint; but over the wine, as I have said, he would sit long, for conversation's sake. And although in other ways he was of all princes most agreeable in his intercourse, and endowed with every grace, at this time his boastfulness would make him unpleasant and very like a common soldier. Not only was he himself carried away into blustering, but he suffered himself to be ridden by his flatterers. These were a great annoyance to the finer spirits in the company, who desired neither to vie with the flatterers, nor yet to fall behind them in praising Alexander. The one course they thought disgraceful, the other had its perils. After the drinking was over, he would take a bath and sleep, frequently until midday; and sometimes he would actually spend the entire day in sleep.

. . . Alexander was naturally munificent, and became still more so as his wealth increased. His gifts, too, were accompanied by a kindly spirit, with which alone, to tell the truth, a giver confers a favour. . . . [A] common Macedonian was driving a mule laden with some of the royal gold, and when the beast gave out, took the load on his own shoulders and tried to carry it. The king, then, seeing the man in great distress and learning the facts of the case, said, as the man was about to lay his burden down, "Don't give out, but finish your journey by taking this load to your own tent." Furthermore, he was generally more displeased with those who would not take his gifts than with those who asked for them.

Map 5.1
The Conquests of
Alexander the Great

[The Greeks considered anyone who did not speak Greek to be a "Barbarian." Alexander and his armies obviously encountered many non-Greek speakers, but here Plutarch is probably referring to the Parthians. Parthia, a Middle Eastern kingdom, was attacked in late 330 B.C.E.]

. . . [H]e marched into Parthia, where, during a respite from fighting, he first put on the barbaric dress, [perhaps] from a desire to adapt himself to the native customs, believing that community of race and custom goes far towards softening the hearts of men. . . . At first he wore this only in intercourse with the Barbarians and with his companions at home, then people generally saw him riding forth or giving audience in this attire. The sight was offensive to the Macedonians, but they admired his other high qualities and thought they ought to yield to him in some things which made for his pleasure or his fame.

Under these circumstances, too, he adapted his own mode of life still more to the customs of the country, and tried to bring these into closer agreement with Macedonian customs, thinking that by a mixture and community of practice which produced good will, rather than by force, his authority would be kept secure while he was far away. For this reason, too, he chose out thirty thousand boys and gave orders that they should learn the Greek language and be trained to use Macedonian weapons, appointing many instructors for this work. His marriage to Roxana [from Bactria, a kingdom to the east of the Persian Empire], whom he saw in her youthful beauty taking part in a dance at a banquet, was a love affair, and yet it was thought to harmonize well with the matters which he had in hand. For the Barbarians were encouraged by the partnership into which the marriage brought them, and they were beyond measure fond of Alexander, because, most temperate of all men that he was in these matters, he would not consent to approach even the only woman who ever mastered his affections, without the sanction of law.

[By late 326 B.C.E., Alexander and his armies had conquered Persia and had crossed the Indus River Valley. After a major battle, Alexander wished to continue eastward.]

. . . [H]aving had all they could do to repulse an enemy who mustered only twenty thousand infantry and two thousand horse, they violently opposed Alexander when he insisted on crossing the river Ganges. . . . For they were told that [local] kings were awaiting them with eighty thousand horsemen, two hundred thousand footmen, eight thousand chariots, and six thousand fighting elephants.

At first, then, Alexander shut himself up in his tent from displeasure and wrath and lay there, feeling no gratitude for what he had already achieved unless he should cross the Ganges, nay, counting a retreat a confession of defeat. But his friends gave him fitting consolation, and his soldiers crowded about his door and besought him with loud cries and wailing, until at last he relented and began to break camp.

Image 5.2 Mosaic of Alexander the Great

Analysis and Review Questions

1. Does Plutarch say anything positive about Alexander, and would you characterize this account as generally positive?
2. Do you notice any negative observations in this account?
3. What kinds of leisure activities does Alexander seem to have enjoyed?
4. What reaction did the other Macedonians have when Alexander wore his "barbarian" clothes in public?
5. Is there any evidence in this selection to support those historians who argue that Alexander wished for peace and unity? If so, what is it?

WEB LINKS

Selections from Longman World History—Primary Sources and Case Studies

http://longmanworldhistory.com
The following additional readings and case studies can be found on the Web site.
Document 5.6, Descriptions of Alexandria, Egypt
Document 6.7, Slaves in Roman Law
The following case studies can be found on the Web site.
5.1 Comparing Athens and Sparta
5.2 Greek and Roman Slavery
5.3 Comparing the Ancient Cities of Athens, Sparta and Alexandria

Alexander the Great

http://wso.williams.edu:8000/~junterek/index.html
A comprehensive and witty Web site dedicated to Alexander the Great.

Alexandria, Egypt

http://www.greece.org/alexandria/
Details all sorts of things—ancient and modern—about Alexandria, Egypt.

Ancient Greece

http://wings.buffalo.edu/AandL/Maecenas/index.html
An excellent source of images from Greek and Roman Europe.

http://www.geocities.com/Athens/4752
A Web site featuring several Greek cities, including Athens, Sparta, Sikyon, Corinth, and Thebes.

http://www.museum.upenn.edu/Greek_World/Index.html
Comprehensive ancient Greek and Hellenistic site, with a focus on material culture.

CHAPTER 6

The Roman Empire

Rome began as a cluster of small villages in central Italy, but by the first century C.E., Roman power extended from the British Isles in the northwest to the Sahara in the south and to the Iranian Plateau in the east. Along with the roads, aqueducts, and theaters that can still be seen in Europe, the expansion of Rome brought with it classical Mediterranean culture. Through a combination of cruelty and efficiency, Rome enforced the longest period of peace in Western history. The combination of peace and cultural diffusion made it possible for merchants or missionaries, like the Apostle Paul, to spread goods and ideas throughout the Roman Empire.

Map 6.1
The Career of Julius Caesar

The Roman Empire has left a massive legacy to Western civilization. Almost all of classical Greek culture was preserved and passed on to European culture through the Romans. Latin, the language of Rome, lives on in the Romance languages: French, Spanish, Portuguese, Italian, and Romanian. And while the Romans prided themselves on keeping peace, a significant amount of the blood shed in European wars since then has been shed in the name of restoring the idea of the Roman Empire.

EXCERPT FROM SUETONIUS, *THE LIFE OF AUGUSTUS*

About the Document

In 30 B.C.E., Marcus Antonius, Julius Caesar's colleague and lieutenant, committed suicide, leaving Octavian, nephew and heir to Julius Caesar, as the sole ruler of Rome. Although republican institutions such as the Senate remained, increasingly authoritarian emperors would now govern Rome and its conquered territories. Octavian, now called Augustus, used his power to bring stability, prosperity, and internal peace after decades of civil disorder.

As Roman society became focused on the emperor and his household, so too did history writing. The most important work in this genre is Suetonius's *Lives of the Twelve Caesars*. Suetonius (69–135 C.E.) served as private secretary and imperial librarian to the emperor Hadrian. Unlike Plutarch, whose biographies were meant to provide moral examples, Suetonius includes both the great deeds of the emperors, as well as reports of their scandalous private behaviors. He did this for two reasons. First, his goal was not to glorify the individual emperor, but to glorify Roman power and genius in general. Second, the literate audience of his day had an appetite for juicy details of the private lives of public figures.

The Document

In military affairs he made many alterations, introducing some practices entirely new, and reviving others, which had become obsolete. He maintained the strictest discipline among the troops; and would not allow even his lieutenants the liberty to visit their wives, except reluctantly, and in the winter season only. A Roman knight having cut off the thumbs of his two young sons, to render them incapable of serving in the wars, he exposed both him and his estate to public sale. But upon observing the farmers of the revenue very greedy for the purchase, he assigned him to a freedman of his own, that he might send him into the country, and suffer him to retain his freedom. The tenth legion becoming mutinous, he disbanded it with ignominy; and did the same by some others which petulantly demanded their discharge; withholding from them the rewards usually bestowed on those who had served their stated time in the wars. The cohorts which yielded their ground in time of action, he decimated, and fed with barley. Centurions,° as well as common sentinels, who deserted their posts when on guard, he punished with death. For other misdemeanors he inflicted upon them various kinds of disgrace; such as obliging them to stand all day before the praetorium, sometimes in their tunics only, and without their belts, sometimes to carry poles ten feet long, or sods of turf.

He was advanced to public offices before the age at which he was legally qualified for them; and to some, also, of a new kind, and for life. He seized the consulship° in the twentieth year of his age, quartering his legions in a threatening manner near the city, and sending deputies to demand it for him in the name of the army. When the senate demurred, a centurion, named Cornelius, who was at the head of the chief deputation, throwing back his cloak, and shewing the hilt of his sword, had the presumption to say in the senate-house, "This will make him consul, if ye will not." His second consulship he filled nine years afterwards; his third, after the interval of only one year, and held the same office every year successively until the eleventh. From this period, although the consulship was frequently offered him, he always declined it, until, after a long interval, not less than seventeen years, he voluntarily stood for the twelfth, and two years after that, for a thirteenth; that he might successively introduce into the forum, on their entering public life, his two sons, Caius and Lucius, while he was invested with the highest office in the state.

He accepted of the tribunitian° power for life, but more than once chose a colleague in that office for ten years successively. He also had the supervision of morality and observance of the laws, for life, but without the title of censor; yet he thrice took a census of the people, the first and third time with a colleague, but the second by himself.

---

centurions: Centurions were originally leaders of Roman infantry units made up of 100 men. By the time of the early Roman Empire, the rank of centurion was the lowest commissioned rank in the Roman Army. It was also the highest rank that a soldier of low birth could reach. Thus, centurions were often men who had risen as high as they could through the ranks on account of their ability.
consulship: In the Roman Republic, executive power was shared by two men called consuls. The authority of each was limited only by the veto power of the other. Augustus wielded consular power through most of his reign, often without a second consul.
tribunitian: The Tribunes defended the rights of the lower class Romans (plebeians) against abuses by the upper class (Patricians). Augustus assumed the powers of the tribunes without holding the office. This allowed him to convene the Senate when he wanted to, acting as a man of the "people."

He twice entertained thoughts of restoring the republic; first, immediately after he had crushed Antony, remembering that he had often charged him with being the obstacle to its restoration. The second time was in consequence of a long illness, when he sent for the magistrates and the senate to his own house, and delivered them a particular account of the state of the empire. But reflecting at the same time that it would be both hazardous to himself to return to the condition of a private person, and might be dangerous to the public to have the government placed again under the control of the people, he resolved to keep it in his own hands, whether with the better event or intention, is hard to say. His good intentions he often affirmed in private discourse, and also published an edict, in which it was declared in the following terms: "May it be permitted me to have the happiness of establishing the commonwealth on a safe and sound basis, and thus enjoy the reward of which I am ambitious, that of being celebrated for moulding it into the form best adapted to present circumstances; so that, on my leaving the world, I may carry with me the hope that the foundations which I have laid for its future government, will stand firm and stable."

The city, which was not built in a manner suitable to the grandeur of the empire, and was liable to inundations of the Tiber, as well as to fires, was so much improved under his administration, that he boasted, not without reason, that he "found it of brick, but left it of marble." He also rendered it secure for the time to come against such disasters, as far as could be effected by human foresight. A great number of public buildings were erected by him, the most considerable of which were a forum, containing the temple of Mars the Avenger, the temple of Apollo on the Palatine hill, and the temple of Jupiter Tonans in the capitol. The reason of his building a new forum was the vast increase in the population, and the number of cases to be tried in the courts, for which, the two already existing not affording sufficient space, it was thought necessary to have a third. It was therefore opened for public use before the temple of Mars was completely finished; and a law was passed, that cases should be tried, and judges chosen by lot, in that place.

He corrected many ill practices, which, to the detriment of the public, had either survived the licentious habits of the late civil wars, or else originated in the long peace. Bands of robbers shewed themselves openly, completely armed, under colour of self-defence; and in different parts of the country, travellers, freemen and slaves without distinction, were forcibly carried off, and kept to work in the houses of correction. Several associations were formed under the specious name of a new college, which banded together for the perpetration of all kinds of villainy. The bandits he quelled by establishing posts of soldiers in suitable stations for the purpose; the houses of correction were subjected to a strict superintendence; all associations, those only excepted which were of ancient standing, and recognised by the laws, were dissolved. He burnt all the notes of those who had been a long time in arrear with the treasury, as being the principal source of vexatious suits and prosecutions. Places in the city claimed by the public, where the right was doubtful, he adjudged to the actual possessors. He struck out of the list of criminals the names of those over whom prosecutions had been long impending, where nothing further was intended by the informers than to gratify their own malice, by seeing their enemies humiliated; laying it down as a rule, that if any one chose to renew a prosecution, he should incur the risk of the punishment which he sought to inflict. And that crimes might not escape punishment, nor business be neglected by delay, he ordered the courts to sit during the thirty days which were spent in celebrating honorary games.

He was desirous that his friends should be great and powerful in the state, but have no exclusive privileges, or be exempt from the laws which governed others. When

Asprenas Nonius, an intimate friend of his, was tried upon a charge of administering poison at the instance of Cassius Severus, he consulted the senate for their opinion what was his duty under the circumstances: "For," said he, "I am afraid, lest, if I should stand by him the cause, I may be supposed to screen a guilty man; and if I do not, to desert and prejudge a friend." With the unanimous concurrence, therefore, of the senate, he took his seat amongst his advocates for several hours, but without giving him the benefit of speaking to character, as was usual. He likewise appeared for his clients; as on behalf of Scutarius, an old soldier of his, who brought an action for slander. He never relieved any one from prosecution but in a single instance, in the case of a man who had given information of the conspiracy of Muraena; and that he did only by prevailing upon the accuser, in open court, to drop his prosecution.

The whole body of the people, upon a sudden impulse, and with unanimous consent, offered him the title of Father of His Country. It was announced to him first at Antium, by a deputation from the people, and upon his declining the honor, they repeated their offer on his return to Rome, in a full theatre, when they were crowned with laurel. The senate soon afterwards adopted the proposal, not in the way of acclamation or decree, but by commissioning M. Messala, in an unanimous vote, to compliment him with it in the following terms: "With hearty wishes for the happiness and prosperity of yourself and your family, Caesar Augustus, (for we think we thus most effectually pray for the lasting welfare of the state), the senate, in agreement with the Roman people, salute you by the title of Father of Your Country." To this compliment Augustus replied, with tears in his eyes, in these words (for I give them exactly as I have done those of Messala): "Having now arrived at the summit of my wishes, O Conscript Fathers, what else have I to beg of the Immortal Gods, but the continuance of this your affection for me to the last moments of my life?"

In person he was handsome and graceful, through every period of his life. But he was negligent in his dress; and so careless about dressing his hair, that he usually had it done in great haste, by several barbers at a time. His beard he sometimes clipped, and sometimes shaved; and either read or wrote during the operation. His countenance, either when discoursing or silent, was so calm and serene, that a Gaul of the first rank declared amongst his friends, that he was so softened by it, as to be restrained from throwing him down a precipice, in his passage over the Alps, when he had been admitted to approach him, under pretence of conferring with him. His eyes were bright and piercing: and he was willing it should be thought that there was something of a divine vigor in them. He was likewise not a little pleased to see people, upon his looking steadfastly at them, lower their countenances, as if the sun shone in their eyes. But in his old age, he saw very imperfectly with his left eye. His teeth were thinly set, small and scaly, his hair a little curled, and inclining to a yellow color. His eyebrows met; his ears were small, and he had an aquiline nose. His complexion was betwixt brown and fair; his stature but low; though Julius Marathus, his freedman, says he was five feet and nine inches in height. This, however, was so much concealed by the just proportion of his limbs, that it was only perceivable upon comparison with some taller person standing by him.

He expired in the same room in which his father Octavius had died, when the two Sextus's, Pompey and Apuleius, were consuls, upon the fourteenth of the calends of September [the 19th August], at the ninth hour of the day, being seventy-six years of age, wanting only thirty-five days. His remains were carried by the magistrates of the municipal towns and colonies, from Nola to Bovillae, and in the night-time, because of the season of the year. During the intervals, the body lay in some basilica, or great temple, of each town. At Bovillae it was met by the Equestrian Order, who carried it to the city, and deposited it in the vestibule of his own house. The senate proceeded with so much zeal in the arrangement of his funeral, and paying honour to his memory, that, amongst several other proposals, some were for having the funeral procession made through the triumphal gate, preceded by the image of Victory which is in the senate-house, and the children of highest rank and of both sexes singing the funeral dirge. Others proposed, that on the day of the funeral, they should lay aside their gold rings, and wear rings of iron; and others, that his bones should be collected by the priests of the principal colleges.

One likewise proposed to transfer the name of August to September, because he was born in the latter, but died in the former. Another moved, that the whole period of time, from his birth to his death, should be called the Augustan age, and be inserted in the calendar under that title. But at last it was judged proper to be moderate in the honors paid to his memory. Two funeral orations were pronounced in his praise, one before the temple of Julius, by Tiberius; and the other before the rostra, under the old shops, by Drusus, Tiberius's son. The body was then carried upon the shoulders of senators into the Campus Martius, and there burnt. A man of praetorian rank affirmed upon oath, that he saw his spirit ascend from the funeral pile to heaven. The most distinguished persons of the equestrian order, bare-footed, and with their tunics loose, gathered up his relics, and deposited them in the mausoleum, which had been built in his sixth consulship between the Flaminian Way and the bank of the Tiber; at which time likewise he gave the groves and walks about it for the use of the people.

Analysis and Review Questions

1. What were Augustus's accomplishments?
2. In what ways did Augustus attempt to maintain the form of the Republic? Why did he not restore it in fact?
3. What can we infer about Roman values from the fact that Augustus had to maintain the form of Republican institutions?
4. How does Suetonius describe Augustus's rise to power? Does this seem to trouble Suetonius?
5. How did the Roman people respond to Augustus? Given the way he seized power and would not restore the Republic, what does this say about the desires of the Roman people at that time?

EXCERPT FROM *THE GOSPEL ACCORDING TO LUKE*

About the Document

At the same time that Augustus and his heirs were establishing an imperial government in Rome, religious controversies in the eastern Mediterranean province of Judea were beginning to focus on the teachings of an itinerant teacher named Jesus. For several centuries many Jews had come to believe that the coming of the Messiah (anointed one) promised in the Hebrew scriptures was imminent. The Messiah would be a descendant of David and a savior of the Jewish people. Exactly what kind of savior was open to debate. Some expected the Messiah to overthrow the Romans. Although Jesus discouraged resistance to the Romans, his followers believed him to be the Messiah. And while Jesus was executed by the Romans at the request of certain Jewish leaders, his followers claimed to have seen Jesus three days after he had been killed. His followers, called Christians, began making converts among both Jews and non-Jews. Today, more than two billion people claim to be Christian.

The Gospel According to Luke is one of many accounts of the teaching and active ministry of Jesus in the three years before he was executed and one of four to be included in the Christian scriptures (New Testament). The Gospel is actually the first part of a history of the early Christian movement. The second half, known as the Acts of the Apostles, is also included in the Christian scriptures. According to Christian tradition, Luke was a physician who traveled with the Apostle Paul. While not a modern historian, Luke was concerned with using reliable eyewitnesses and sources in composing his history. The following selection contains the Sermon on the Mount, the classic statement of Jesus' ethical teachings. It also contains passages that highlight the presence of Rome in Judea.

*Map 6.2
(Interactive) The Spread
of Christianity to 300*

The Document

Jesus' Birth in Bethlehem

2 NOW it came about in those days that a decree went out from Caesar Augustus, that a census be taken of all the inhabited earth. This was the first census taken while Quirinius was governor of Syria. And all were proceeding to register for the census, everyone to his own city. And Joseph also went up from Galilee, from the city of Nazareth, to Judea, to the city of David, which is called Bethlehem, because he was of the house and family of David, in order to register, along with Mary, who was engaged to him, and was with child. And it came about that while they were there, the days were completed for her to give birth. And she gave birth to her first-born son; and she wrapped Him in cloths, and laid Him in a manger, because there was no room for them in the inn.

Call of Levi (Matthew)

27 And after that He went out, and noticed a tax-gatherer named Levi, sitting in the tax office, and He said to him, "Follow Me." And he left everything behind, and rose and began to follow Him.

29 And Levi gave a big reception for Him in his house; and there was a great crowd of tax-gatherers and other people who were reclining at the table with them. And the Pharisees° and their scribes ran grumbling at His disciples, saying, "Why do you eat and drink with the tax-gatherers° and sinners?" And Jesus answered and said to them, "It is not those who are well who need a physician, but those who are sick. I have not come to call the righteous but sinners to repentance."

Pharisees: The Pharisees were one of several important factions among Jews during the time of Jesus. Pharisees (which means separated ones) emphasized strict adherence to the Mosaic Law as a defining characteristic of Jews. They considered other Jews who did not separate themselves from the pagan world or strictly adhere to the Law as ritually unclean or sinners.

tax-gatherers: The Roman Empire used private contractors to collect taxes. Under the contract the tax-gatherers were obliged to send a certain amount on to the provincial governor, who then sent on a fixed portion to Rome. At each phase a significant amount was kept as a way to build wealth. This system encouraged the tax-gatherers to extract as much as they could from the subject peoples.

The Beatitudes

20 And turning His gaze on His disciples, He began to say, "Blessed are you who are poor, for yours is the kingdom of God. Blessed are you who hunger now, for you shall be satisfied. Blessed are you who weep now, for you shall laugh. Blessed are you when men hate you, and ostracize you, and cast insults at you, and spurn your name as evil, for the sake of the Son of Man. Be glad in that day, and leap for joy, for behold, your reward is great in heaven; for in the same way their fathers used to treat the prophets. But woe to you who are rich, for you are receiving your comfort in full. Woe to you who are well-fed now, for you shall be hungry. Woe to you who laugh now, for you shall mourn and weep. Woe to you when all men speak well of you, for in the same way their fathers used to treat the false prophets.

27 "But I say to you who hear, love your enemies, do good to those who hate you, bless those who curse you, pray for those who mistreat you. Whoever hits you on the cheek, offer him the other also; and whoever takes away your coat, do not withhold your shirt from him either. Give to everyone who asks of you, and whoever takes away what is yours, do not demand it back. And just as you want people to treat you, treat them in the same way. And if you love those who love you, what credit is that to you? For even sinners love those who love them. And if you do good to those who do good to you, what credit is that to you? For even sinners do the same. And if you lend to those from whom you expect to receive, what credit is that to you?

"Even sinners lend to sinners, in order to receive back the same amount. But love your enemies, and do good, and lend, expecting nothing in return; and your reward will be great, and you will be sons of the Most High; for He Himself is kind to ungrateful and evil men. Be merciful, just as your Father is merciful. And do not judge and you will not be judged; and do not condemn, and you will not be condemned; pardon, and you will be pardoned. Give, and it will be given to you; good measure, pressed down, shaken together, running over, they will pour into your lap. For by your standard of measure it will be measured to you in return."

39 And He also spoke a parable to them: "A blind man cannot guide a blind man, can he? Will they not both fall into a pit? A pupil is not above his teacher; but everyone, after he has been fully trained, will be like his teacher. And why do you look at the speck that is in your brother's eye, but do not notice the log that is in your own eye? Or how can you say to your brother, 'Brother, let me take out the speck that is in your eye,' when you yourself do not see the log that is in your own eye? You hypocrite, first take the log out of your own eye, and then you will see clearly to take out the speck that is in your brother's eye. For there is no good tree which produces bad fruit; nor, on the other hand, a bad tree which produces good fruit. For each tree is known by its own fruit. For men do not gather figs from thorns, nor do they pick grapes from a briar bush. The good man out of the good treasure of his heart brings forth what is good; and the evil man out of the evil treasure brings forth what is evil; for his mouth speaks from that which fills his heart.

Builders and Foundations

46 "And why do you call Me, 'Lord, Lord,' and do not do what I say? Everyone who comes to Me, and hears My words, and acts upon them, I will show you whom he is like: he is like a man building a house, who dug deep and laid a foundation upon the rock; and when a flood rose, the torrent burst against that house and could not shake it, because it had been well built. But the one who has heard, and has not acted accordingly, is like a man who built a house upon the ground without any foundation; and the torrent burst against it and immediately it collapsed, and the ruin of that house was great."

Jesus Heals a Centurion's Servant

7 WHEN He had completed all His discourse in the hearing of the people, He went to Capernaum.

2 And a certain centurion's slave, who was highly regarded by him, was sick and about to die. And when he heard about Jesus, he sent some Jewish elders asking Him to come and save the life of his slave. And when they had come to Jesus, they earnestly entreated Him, saying, "He is worthy for You to grant this to him; for he loves our nation, and it was he who built us our synagogue." Now Jesus started on His way with them; and when He was already not far from the house, the centurion sent friends, saying to Him, "Lord, do not trouble Yourself further, for I am not worthy for You to come under my roof; for this reason I did not even consider myself worthy to come to You, but just say the word, and my servant will be healed. For I, too, am a man under authority, with soldiers under me; and I say to this one, 'Go!' and he goes; and to another, 'Come!' and he comes; and to my slave, 'Do this!' and he does it." Now when Jesus heard this, He marveled at him, and turned and said to the multitude that was following Him, "I say to you, not even in Israel have I found such great faith." And when those who had been sent returned to the house, they found the slave in good health.

Analysis and Review Questions

1. In your own words, summarize the ethical teachings of Jesus as described in this document.
2. The admonitions that Jesus gives in chapter 5:27–29 refer to how the Jews should react to mistreatment by the Romans. What does Jesus teach about responding to oppression?
3. What is the goal of life, according to Jesus? How does one achieve that goal?
4. What does this document tell us about Roman rule in Judea?
5. Two agents of Rome are mentioned in this text: Levi, a Jew who had a private contract to collect taxes on behalf of Rome, and a centurion. What do the Jewish leaders (scribes and Pharisees) think of each of these men? What does this tell us about how the Jews felt about the Romans?

EXCERPT FROM AELIUS ARISTIDES, *THE ROMAN ORATION*

About the Document

The period of Roman history between the rise of Nerva to the imperial throne in 96 C.E. and the death of the emperor Marcus Aurelius in 180 C.E. is known as the *Pax Romana* (Roman Peace), and its rulers during that time have been called the "Five Good Emperors." During this time, Rome reached the height of its military expansion and wealth. The pride and confidence of the Roman elite is clearly on display in the following document. *The Roman Oration* is one of the most important works of one of the most celebrated orators of the period. Aelius Aristides (120–189 C.E.) was a leader of the literary movement to revive the style of the Greek sophists. In *The Roman Oration*, Aelius praises the accomplishments of

Rome. His purpose was not to give an accurate account of Roman conquest and governance, but to dazzle his audience with hyperbolic eloquence. Even so, it gives us a glimpse of how Romans wished to think of themselves.

Image 6.1
Roman Aqueduct

The Document

"If one considers the vast extent of your empire he must be amazed that so small a fraction of it rules the world, but when he beholds the city and its spaciousness it is not astonishing that all the habitable world is ruled by such a capital. . . . Your possessions equal the sun's course. . . . You do not rule within fixed boundaries, nor can anyone dictate the limits of your sway. . . . Whatever any people produces can be found here, at all times and in abundance. . . . Egypt, Sicily, and the civilized part of Africa are your farms; ships are continually coming and going. . . .

"Vast as it is, your empire is more remarkable for its thoroughness than its scope: there are no dissident or rebellious enclaves. . . . The whole world prays in unison that your empire may endure forever.

"Governors sent out to cities and peoples each rule their charges, but in their relations to each other they are equally subjects. The principal difference between governors and their charges is this—they demonstrate the proper way to be a subject. So great is their reverence for the great Ruler [the emperor], who administers all things. Him they believe to know their business better than they themselves do, and hence they respect and heed him more than one would a master overseeing a task and giving orders. No one is so self-assured that he can remain unmoved upon hearing the emperor's name: he rises in prayer and adoration and utters a twofold prayer—to the gods for the Ruler, and to the Ruler for himself. And if the governors are in the least doubt concerning the justice of claims or suits of the governed, public or private, they send to the Ruler for instructions at once and await his reply, as a chorus awaits its trainer's directions. Hence the Ruler need not exhaust himself by traveling to various parts to settle matters in person. It is easy for him to abide in his place and manage the world through letters; these arrive almost as soon as written, as if borne on wings.

"But the most marvelous and admirable achievement of all, and the one deserving our fullest gratitude, is this. . . . You alone of the imperial powers of history rule over men who are free. You have not assigned this or that region to this nabob or that mogul; no people has been turned over as a domestic and bound holding—to a man not himself free. But just as citizens in an individual city might designate magistrates, so you, whose city is the whole world, appoint governors to protect and provide for the governed, as if they were elective, not to lord it over their charges. As a result, so far from disputing the office as if it were their own, governors make way for their successors readily when their term is up, and may not even await their coming. Appeals to a higher jurisdiction are as easy as appeals from parish to county. . . .

"But the most notable and praiseworthy feature of all, a thing unparalleled, is your magnanimous conception of citizenship. All of your subjects (and this implies the whole world) you have divided into two parts: the better endowed and more virile, wherever they may be, you have granted citizenship and even kinship; the rest you govern as obedient subjects. Neither the seas nor expanse of land bars citizenship; Asia and Europe are not differentiated. Careers are open to talent. . . . Rich and poor find contentment and profit in your system; there is no other way of life. Your polity is a single and all-embracing harmony. . . .

"You have not put walls around your city, as if you were hiding it or avoiding your subjects; to do so you considered ignoble and inconsistent with your principles, as if a master should show fear of his slaves. You did not overlook walls, however, but placed them round the empire, not the city. The splendid and distant walls you erected are worthy of you; to men within their circuit they are visible, but it requires a journey of months and years from the city to see them. Beyond the outermost ring of the civilized world you drew a second circle, larger in radius and easier to defend, like the outer fortifications of a city. Here you built walls and established cities in diverse parts. The cities you filled with colonists; you introduced arts and crafts and established an orderly culture. . . . Your military organization makes all others childish. Your soldiers and officers you train to prevail not only over the enemy but over themselves. The soldier lives under discipline daily, and none ever deserts the post assigned him.

"You alone are, so to speak, natural rulers. Your predecessors were masters and slaves in turn; as rulers they were counterfeits, and reversed their positions like players in a ball game. . . . You have measured out the world, bridged rivers, cut roads through mountains, filled the wastes with posting stations, introduced orderly and refined modes of life. . . .

"Be all gods and their offspring invoked to grant that this empire and this city flourish forever and never cease until stones float upon the sea and trees forbear to sprout in the springtide. May the great Ruler and his sons be preserved to administer all things well."

Analysis and Review Questions

1. What are this author's criteria for the greatness of the Roman Empire?
2. This speech reflected the opinion of the Roman elite. If you asked a member of the Roman aristocracy what the special abilities of Romans were, how would he respond?
3. The phrase "rule over men who are free" seems like a contradiction to a modern person. What does the author mean by this?
4. Pushing past the obvious exaggeration, what does this document tell us about how the Romans ruled?
5. In the modern world, most people regard imperialism as unequivocally oppressive. Based on this document, how might the Romans justify their conquests?

EXCERPT FROM SALVIAN, *THE GOVERNANCE OF GOD*

About the Document

After the reign of Marcus Aurelius, the Roman Empire was hard pressed to maintain its extensive borders. Following a series of civil wars in the third century, emperors such as Diocletian and Constantine reformed the structure of the Empire. One of the reforms divided the Empire into separate western and eastern administrative units. The eastern half would survive as the Greek-speaking Byzantine Empire until its conquest in 1453 C.E. by Ottoman Turks. The western half of the Empire, however, collapsed by the end of the fifth century and was replaced by numerous kingdoms set up by Germanic tribal warlords with the help of former Roman administrators. Identifying the reason for the disintegration of Roman power in what is now western and southern Europe is one of the longest-running controversies in the field of history. Writing amidst the collapse in 440 C.E., a Roman Christian priest named Salvian attempted to explain why nomadic tribes with no history of formal government were able to replace so easily the civilization that believed itself uniquely gifted and destined to govern the world.

*Image 6.2
Early Christian
Symbols*

The Document

What towns, as well as what municipalities and villages are there in which there are not as many tyrants as *curiales*. Perhaps they glory in this name of tyrant because it seems to be considered powerful and honored. For, almost all robbers rejoice and boast, if they are said to be more fierce than they really are. What place is there, as I have said, where the bowels of widows and orphans are not devoured by the leading men of the cities, and with them those of almost all holy men? . . . Not one of them [widows and orphans], therefore, is safe. In a manner, except for the very powerful, neither is anyone safe from the devastation of general brigandage, unless they are like the robbers themselves. To this state of affairs, indeed, to this crime has the world come that, unless one is bad, he cannot be safe. . . .

All the while, the poor are despoiled, the widows groan, the orphans are tread underfoot, so much so that many of them, and they are not of obscure birth and have received a liberal education, flee to the enemy lest they die from the pain of public persecution. They seek among the barbarians the dignity of the Roman because they cannot bear barbarous indignity among the Romans. Although these Romans differ in religion and language from the barbarians to whom they flee, and differ from them in respect to filthiness of body and clothing, nevertheless, as I have said, they prefer to bear among the barbarians a worship unlike their own rather than rampant injustice among the Romans.

Thus, far and wide, they migrate either to the Goths or to the Bagaudae, or to other barbarians everywhere in power; yet they do not repent having migrated. They prefer to live as freemen under an outward form of captivity than as captives under an appearance of liberty. Therefore, the name of Roman citizens, at one time not only greatly valued but dearly bought, is now repudiated and fled from, and it is almost considered not only base but even deserving of abhorrence.

And what can be a greater testimony of Roman wickedness than that many men, upright and noble and to whom the position of being a Roman citizen should be considered as of the highest splendor and dignity, have been driven by the cruelty of Roman wickedness to such a state of mind that they do not wish to be Romans? Hence, even those who do not flee to the barbarians are forced to be barbarians. Such is a great portion of the Spaniards and not the least portion of the Gauls, and, finally, all those throughout the whole Roman world whom Roman wickedness has compelled not to be Romans.

I am now about to speak of the Bagaudae who were despoiled, oppressed and murdered by evil and cruel judges. After they had lost the right of Roman citizenship, they also lost the honor of bearing the Roman name. We blame their misfortunes on themselves. We ascribe to them a name which signifies their downfall. We give to them a name of which we ourselves are the cause. We call them rebels. We call those outlaws whom we compelled to be criminal.

For, by what other ways did they become Bagaudae, except by our wickedness, except by the wicked ways of judges, except by the proscription and pillage of those who have turned the assessments of public taxes into the benefit of their own gain and have made the tax levies their own booty? Like wild beasts, they did not rule but devoured their subjects, and feasted not only on the spoils of men, as most robbers are wont to do, but even on their torn flesh and, as I may say, on their blood.

Thus it happened that men, strangled and killed by the robberies of judges, began to live as barbarians because they were not permitted to be Romans. They became satisfied to be what they were not, because they were not permitted to be what they were. They were compelled to defend their lives at least, because they saw that they had already completely lost their liberty. . . .

But what else can these wretched people wish for, they who suffer the incessant and even continuous destruction of public tax levies. To them there is always imminent a heavy and relentless proscription. They desert their homes, lest they be tortured in their very homes. They seek exile, lest they suffer torture. The enemy is more lenient to them than the tax collectors. This is proved by this very fact, that they flee to the enemy in order to avoid the full force of the heavy tax levy. This very tax levying, although hard and inhuman, would nevertheless be less heavy and harsh if all would bear it equally and in common. Taxation is made more shameful and burdensome because all do not bear the burden of all. They extort tribute from the poor man for the taxes of the rich, and the weaker carry the load for the stronger. There is no other reason that they cannot bear all the taxation except that the burden imposed on the wretched is greater than their resources. . . .

Therefore, in the districts taken over by the barbarians, there is one desire among all the Romans, that they should never again find it necessary to pass under Roman jurisdiction. In those regions, it is the one and general prayer of the Roman people that they be allowed to carry on the life they lead with the barbarians. And we wonder why the Goths are not conquered by our portion of the population, when the Romans prefer to live among them rather than with us. Our brothers, therefore, are not only altogether unwilling to flee to us from them, but they even cast us aside in order to flee to them.

Analysis and Review Questions

1. According to Salvian, what are the problems with Roman rule?
2. According to Salvian, what is to be gained from being ruled by the Germanic tribes rather than the Romans? What is given up?
3. Salvian describes how the idea of being "Roman" has been destroyed. What does he think being Roman should mean?
4. What does Salvian mean when he says, "They prefer to live as freemen under the outward form of captivity rather than as captives under an appearance of liberty"?
5. Given how Salvian describes the attitudes of Romans living under the rule of the Germanic tribes, is it appropriate to say that the tribes conquered Rome? From whose perspective was it a conquest?

SLAVES IN ROMAN LAW

About the Document

Slavery was a common and accepted institution in the ancient Mediterranean, practiced by virtually every civilization and society. Because of the prevalence of slaves in these societies, there were usually numerous laws governing the institution of slavery, the treatment of slaves, any rights that a slave might have, and what rights and responsibilities slave owners might have. Roman law, typically a fairly comprehensive set of codes, includes many slave laws that give us an interesting view into the past.

The first document that follows comes from an obscure legal scholar named Gaius, who, sometime in the late second century, wrote the *Institutes*, a legal textbook that became the standard law book for law students. The second document comes from a legal code ordered by the Emperor Theodosius II in 438 C.E. The Code of Theodosius was the first systematic collection of Roman laws. Each document provides insight into the position of slaves in Rome.

The Document

FROM *THE INSTITUTES**

Every community that is governed by laws and customs uses partly its own particular law and partly the law common to all mankind. Thus the Roman People in part follows its own particular system of justice and in part the common law of all mankind. We shall note what this distinction implies in particular instances at the relevant point.

- The principal distinction made by the law of persons is this, that all human beings are either free men or slaves.

- Next, some free men are free-born (*ingénue*), others freedman (*libertine*).

- The free-born are those who were free when they were born; freedmen are those who have been released from a state of slavery.

- Freedmen belong to one of three status groups: they are either Roman citizens, or Latins, or subjects (*dediticii*).

Dediticii

- The *Lex Aelia Sentia* requires that any slaves who had been put in chains as a punishment by their masters or had been branded or interrogated under torture about some crime of which they were found to be guilty; and any who had been handed over to fight as gladiators or with wild beasts, or had belonged to a troupe or gladiators or had been imprisoned; should, if the same owner or any subsequent owner manumits them, become free men of the same status as subject foreigners (*peregrini dediticii*).

- 'Subject foreigners' is the name given to those who had once fought a regular war against the Roman People, were defeated, and gave themselves up.

- We will never accept that slaves who have suffered a disgrace of this kind can become either Roman citizens or Latins (whatever the procedure or manumission and whatever their age at the time, even if they were in their masters' full ownership); we consider that they should always be held to have the status of subjects.

Citizens

- But if a slave has suffered no such disgrace, he sometimes becomes a Roman citizen when he is manumitted, and sometimes a Latin.

*Reprinted by permission of Oxford University Press from *The Institutes of Gaius*, by Francis de Zulueta, 23–27, 1946-1953.

■ A slave becomes a Roman citizen if he fulfils the following three conditions. He must be over thirty years of age; [his master must own him under very specific conditions;] and he must be set free by a just and legitimate manumission. If any of these conditions is not met, he will become a Latin.

■ A just reason for manumission exists when, for example, a man manumits in the presence of a council a natural son, daughter, brother or sister; or a child he has brought up, or his paedagogus [the slave whose job it had been to look after him as a child], or a slave whom he wants to employ as his manager, or a slave girl whom he intends to marry.

■ In the city of Rome, the council comprises five Roman senators and five equestrians; in the provinces it consists of twenty local justices who must be Roman citizens, and meets on the last day of the provincial assizes; at Rome there are certain fixed days for manumissions before a council. Slaves over thirty can in fact be manumitted at any time; so that manumissions can even take place when the Praetor or Proconsul is passing by on his way to the baths or theatre, for instance.

■ Furthermore, a slave under thirty can become a Roman citizen by manumission if he has been declared free in the Will of an insolvent master and appointed as his heir, provided that he is not excluded by another heir.

Junian Latins

■ . . . [persons who do not fulfil the conditions for full citizenship] are called 'Junian Latins': Latins because they are assimilated to the status of those Latins who lived in the ancient colonies; Junian because they received their freedom through the *Lex Junia*, since they were previously considered to have the status of slaves.

■ But the *Lex Junia* does not give them the right to make a Will themselves, or to inherit or be appointed as guardians under someone else's Will.

Digression Dediticii

■ But those who have the status of subjects cannot receive anything at all by Will, no more than any foreigner can, and according to the general opinion, they cannot make a Will themselves.

■ The lowest kind of freedom is therefore that of those whose status is that of subjects; and no statute, Senate Recommendation or Imperial Constitution gives them access to Roman citizenship.

■ They are even banned from the city of Rome or anywhere within the hundredth milestone from Rome, and any who break this law have to be sold publicly together with their property, subject to the condition that they must never serve as slaves in the city of Rome or within a hundred miles of Rome, and that they must never be manumitted; if they are manumitted, the law stipulates that they become slaves of the Roman People. All these provisions are laid down by the *Lex Aelia Sentia*.

■ But there are many ways in which Latins can become Roman citizens.

■ First of all there are the regulations laid down by the *Lex Aelia Sentia*. Anyone under thirty who has been manumitted and has become a Latin; if he marries a wife who is either a Roman citizen or a colonial Latin or a woman of the same

*Reprinted by permission of Oxford University Press from *The Institutes of Gaius*, by Francis de Zulueta, 23–27, 1946-1953.

status as himself, and this marriage was witnessed by not less than seven adult Roman citizens, and he has a son; then, when that son becomes one year old, he has the right under this law to go to the Praetor (or in a province the governor) and prove that he has married in accordance with the *Lex Aelia Sentia* and has a year-old son.

And if the magistrate to whom the case is taken declares that the facts are as stated, then both the Latin himself and his wife (if she is of the same status) and son (if he is of the same status too) must be recognised as Roman citizens.

- (I added the phrase 'if he is of the same status too' with respect to the son because if the wife of a Latin is a Roman citizen, then her son is born as a Roman citizen, in accordance with a recent Senate Recommendation proposed by the Divine Emperor Hadrian.)

- But even if the Latin dies before he has been able to establish that he has a year-old son, the mother can prove it, and if she was previously a Latin she will thus become a Roman citizen herself. Even if the son is a Roman citizen already, because he is the child of a mother who is a Roman citizen, she still ought to prove his case; for then he can become the natural heir of his father.

- What was said regarding a year-old son applies equally to a year-old daughter.

- Furthermore, under the *Lex Visellia*, anyone who has become a Latin through manumission, whether he is over or under thirty, acquires the full rights of a Roman citizen if he has completed six years' service in the *vigils* (police) at Rome. It is asserted that a Senate Recommendation was later passed granting citizenship on completion of three years' service.

[Restrictions on Manumission]

- Not everyone who wishes to manumit is legally permitted to do so.

- A manumission made with a view to defraud creditors or a patron is void; the liberation is prevented by the *Lex Aelia Sentia*.

- The same *Lex* also prevents an owner under twenty from manumitting, except by [special legal provision] and after a council has accepted that there is a just reason.

FROM *THE CODE OF THEODOSIUS*

The August Emperor Constantine, to Bassus.

If an owner has chastised a slave by beating him with sticks or whipping him or has put him into chains in order to keep him under guard, he should not stand in fear of any criminal accusation if the slave dies; and all statutes of limitations and legal interpretations are hereby set aside.

1. But he should not make excessive use of his rights; he will indeed be accused of homicide if he willingly

—kills him with a stroke of a cane or a stone;

—inflicts a lethal wound by using something which is definitely a weapon;

—orders him to be hung from a noose;

*Reprinted by permission of Oxford University Press from *The Institutes of Gaius*, by Francis de Zulueta, 23–27, 1946-1953.

—gives the shocking command that he should be thrown down from a height;

—pours a poison into him;

—mangles his body with the punishments reserved to the State, viz. by having his sides torn apart by the claws of wild beasts; or applying fire to burn his body;

—or by forcing the man's weakened limbs, running with blood and gore, to give up their life spirit as the result of torture—a form of brutality appropriate to savage barbarians.

Rome, 11 May 319 AD.

Analysis and Review Questions

1. Who were the "libertini"? What three divisions does the group have?
2. What was a "paedagogus"?
3. Do slaves who have served in the police force have any special privileges? What are they?
4. Under what conditions could a slave owner be charged with murder in the death of one of his slaves?
5. Does it seem to you that the Romans had a fairly liberal view of slavery? Do they appear to have treated slaves well, or not?

WEB LINKS

Selections from Longman World History—Primary Sources and Case Studies

http://longmanworldhistory.com
The following additional readings and case studies can be found on the Web site:
Document 6.1, Excerpt from Plutarch
Document 6.6, Augustus on His Accomplishments
Document 8.1, Fulcher of Chartes
Case Study 6.1, The Rise and Fall of Rome
Case Study 6.2, The Roman and Christian Views of the Good Life
Case Study 6.3, Warriors for Jesus

Historic Atlas Resource—Europe

http://darkwing.uoregon.edu/~atlas/europe/images.html
This site is devoted to maps, many of them interactive, and images of the Roman period.

EAWC: Ancient Rome

http://eawc.evansville.edu/ropage.htm
A comprehensive and high-quality site maintained by Evansville University. It includes images, texts, and essays about the period, external links and a search engine for ancient history material on the Web. One-stop shopping.

Internet Ancient History Sourcebook: Rome

http://www.fordham.edu/halsall/ancient/asbook09.html
A very good site maintained by one of the pioneers of academic-quality, historical content on the Web.

Rome Resources

http://www.dalton.org/groups/Rome
A comprehensive and easy-to-navigate gateway to the numerous online resources pertaining to Roman history. The maps on the site allow you to click on a region and find online resources about that region of the empire.

Maecenas: Images of Ancient Greece and Rome

http://wings.buffalo.edu/AandL/Maecenas/index.html
Over 1,660 images.

CHAPTER 7

Islamic Civilization and Culture

In 610 C.E., an Arabian merchant named Muhammad had a religious experience. While out in the desert, Muhammad heard a voice from the heavens that identified itself as the god Allah and asserted itself as the one, true God. Thus was born one of the world's most enduring religions: Islam. At first Muhammad had little success gaining converts in his home city of Mecca, and after experiencing persecution there, in 622 he undertook the *Hijrah*, or flight from Mecca to the nearby city of Medina. After this, the religion, which shares some basic doctrines with both Judaism and Christianity, grew quickly. By Muhammad's death in 632 C.E., almost all of the Arabian Peninsula had accepted Islam.

The world had never witnessed anything like the lightning-fast spread of Islam out of Arabia over the next few centuries. Islam spread into Egypt by 642, across North Africa to Tunisia by 670, and into Spain by 711. By this time, Islam had also spread eastward into Persia and India. The result was an Islamic world tied together by religion, culture, and sometimes politics. The period of the Abbasid Dynasty (750–1258 C.E.) is generally considered the golden age of traditional Islamic art, architecture, and literary achievements. This chapter focuses on this period of Islamic greatness.

Map 7.1
(Interactive)
The Spread of Islam

THE HOLY QUR'AN

About the Document

The religion of Islam was revealed to an Arabian merchant named Muhammad in 610 C.E. Within about 20 years, by the time of Muhammad's death in 632, the religion was on firm footing within the Arabian Peninsula. The next few decades would see Islam spread quickly into Egypt and North Africa, as well as into the Middle East.

Shortly after Muhammad's death in the 650s, an "official" version of God's words to Muhammad, as well as Muhammad's sayings, was written down. The Qur'an is a document much like the Judeo-Christian Old Testament, containing the mythos of the religion, as well as its basic tenets and practices. Not surprisingly, given the influence of both Judaism and Christianity (or as some scholars suggest, perhaps because the supreme God in each is actually the same being), there are many things that the three religions share in common. The following excerpt not only discusses some of the basic beliefs of Islam, but also illustrates some of the similarities between these three monotheistic religions.

Image 7.2
The Qur'an

The Document

Those unbelievers of the People of the Book°
and the idolaters wish not that any good
should be sent down upon you from your Lord;
but God singles out for His mercy whom he will;
God is of bounty abounding. . . .

Many of the People of the Book wish they might
restore you as unbelievers, after you have believed,
in the jealousy of their souls, after the truth
has become clear to them; yet do you pardon
and be forgiving, till God brings His command;
truly God is powerful over everything.
And perform the prayer, and pay the alms;
whatever good you shall forward to your souls' account,
you shall find it with God; assuredly God
sees the things you do.
And they say, "None shall enter Paradise
except that they be Jews or Christians."
Such are their fancies. Say: "Produce your
proof, if you speak truly."
Nay, but whosoever submits his will to God,
being a good-doer, his wage is with his Lord,
and no fear shall be on them, neither shall
they sorrow.

The Jews say, "The Christians stand not on
anything";
the Christians say, "The Jews stand not on
anything";
yet they recite the Book. So too the ignorant
say the like of them. God shall decide
between them on the Day of Resurrection
touching their differences.
And who does greater evil than he who bars
God's places of worship, so that His Name
be not rehearsed in them, and strives to
destroy them?
Such men might never enter them, save in
fear; for them is degradation in the present world,
and in the world to come a mighty
chastisement.

People of the Book: Jews and Christians, like the Muslims, rely on their own sacred scripture as the word of God.

To God belong the East and the West;
whithersoever you turn, there is the
Face of God;
God is All-embracing, All-knowing. . . .
Children of Israel, remember My blessing
wherewith I blessed you, and that I have
preferred you above all beings. . . .

And when his Lord tested Abraham
with certain words, and he fulfilled them.
He said, "Behold, I make you a leader
for the people." Said he, "And of my seed?"
He said, "My covenant shall not reach
the evildoers."
And when We appointed the House to be
a place of visitation for the people,
and a sanctuary,
and: "Take to yourselves Abraham's station
for a place of prayer." And We made covenant
with Abraham and Ishmael, "Purify
My House for those that shall go about it
and those that cleave to it, to those who bow
and prostrate themselves." . . .

When his Lord said to him, "Surrender,"
he said, "I have surrendered me to
the Lord of all Being."
And Abraham charged his sons with this
and Jacob likewise: My sons, God has
chosen for you the religion;
see that you die not
save in surrender."

Why, were you witnesses, when death came
to Jacob? When he said to his sons,
"What will you serve after me?" They said,
"We will serve thy God and the God of thy
fathers
Abraham, Ishmael, and Isaac, One God;
to Him we surrender."
That is a nation that has passed away;
there awaits them that they have earned,
and there awaits you that you have earned;
you shall not be questioned concerning
the things they did.

And they say, "Be Jews or Christians and
you shall be guided." Say thou: "Nay, rather
the creed of Abraham, a man of pure faith;
he was no idolater."
Say you: "We believe in God, and
in that which has been sent down on us
and sent down on Abraham, Ishmael,
Isaac and Jacob, and the Tribes,

and that which was given to Moses and Jesus
and the Prophets, of their Lord; we
make no division between any of them, and
to Him we surrender."
And if they believe in the like of that you
believe in, then they are truly guided; but if
they turn away, then they are clearly in
schism,
God will suffice you for them; He is
the All-hearing, the All-knowing;
the baptism of God; and who is there
that baptizes fairer than God?
Him we are serving.
Say: "Would you then dispute with us
concerning God, who is our Lord
and your Lord? Our deeds belong to us,
and to you belong your deeds; Him
we serve sincerely. . . . "

It is not piety, that you turn your faces
to the East and to the West.
True piety is this:
to believe in God, and the Last Day,
the angels, the Book, and the Prophets,
to give of one's substance, however cherished,
to kinsmen, and orphans,
the needy, the traveler, beggars,
and to ransom the slave,
to perform the prayer, to pay the alms.
And they who fulfill their covenant
when they have engaged in a covenant,
and endure with fortitude
misfortune, hardship, and peril,
these are they who are true in their faith,
these are the truly godfearing. . . .

O believers, prescribed for you is
the Fast, even as it was prescribed for
those that were before you—haply you
will be godfearing—
for days numbered; and if any of you
be sick, or if he be on a journey,
then a number of other days. . . .

And fight in the way of God with those
who fight with you, but aggress not: God
loves not the aggressors.
And slay them wherever you come upon them,
and expel them from where they expelled you;
persecution is more grievous than slaying.
But fight them not by the Holy Mosque
until they should fight you there;
then, if they fight you, slay them—

such is the recompense of unbelievers—
but if they give over, surely God is
All-forgiving, All-compassionate.
Fight them, till there is no persecution
and the religion is God's; then if they
give over, there shall be no enmity
save for evildoers.
The holy month for the holy month;
holy things demand retaliation.
Whoso commits aggression against you,
do you commit aggression against him
like as he has committed against you;
and fear you God, and know that God is
with the godfearing.

And expend in the way of God;
and cast not yourselves by your own hands
into destruction, but be good-doers; God
loves the good-doers.

Fulfill the Pilgrimage and the Visitation
unto God; but if you are prevented,
then such offering as may be feasible. . . .
And when you have performed your holy rites
remember God, as you remember your fathers
or yet more devoutly. . . .
God
there is no god but He, the
Living, the Everlasting.
Slumber seizes Him not, neither sleep;
to Him belongs
all that is in the heavens and the earth.
Who is there that shall intercede with Him
save by his leave?
He knows what lies before them and
what is after them,
and they comprehend not anything of
His knowledge save such as He
wills.
His Throne comprises the heavens and earth;
The preserving of them
Oppresses Him not;
He is the All-high, the All-glorious.
No compulsion is there in religion.
Rectitude has become clear from error.
So whosoever disbelieves in idols
and believes in God, has laid hold of
the most firm handle, unbreaking; God is
All-hearing, All-knowing.

God is the Protector of the believers;
He brings them forth from the shadows
into the light. . . .

Those who believe and do deeds of
righteousness,
and perform the prayer, and pay the alms—
their wage awaits them with their Lord,
and no fear shall be on them, neither shall
they sorrow. . . .

God charges no soul save to its capacity;
standing to its account is what it has earned,
and against its account what it has merited.

Our Lord,
take us not to task
if we forget, or make mistake.
Our Lord,
charge us not with a load such
as Thou didst lay upon those before us.
Our Lord,
do Thou not burden us
beyond what we have the strength to bear.
And pardon us,
and forgive us,
and have mercy on us;
Thou art our Protector.
And help us against the people
of the unbelievers.

Analysis and Review Questions

1. How are Muslims supposed to fight?
2. What is the "Pilgrimage" referred to in this excerpt?
3. Will Jews or Christians enter "Paradise" after death?
4. What sorts of good deeds should Muslims do?
5. From this excerpt, would you say that Islam is similar at all to Judaism and
   Christianity? If so, how?

A MIRROR FOR PRINCES

About the Document

In the ancient Mediterranean and the Middle East, political philosophies often
took the form of what are known as "instructions," or tracts written from a father
to his son, dispensing relevant political advice. Sometimes these were from rulers
to their heirs, but often they were from government officials to their sons. While
not technically an "instruction," the following document includes political advice
from a Persian prince to his son.

Written around 1082 C.E. by Kai Ka'us Ibn Iskander, the grandson of an important prince, *A Mirror for Princes* is also designed for consumption by the author's son. The document provides advice on all aspects of life, ranging from

how to purchase slaves, to how to raise children, to proper behavior and etiquette. In addition, it includes lengthy discussions of how rulers should govern, behave, and deal with their subjects. This advice is often in the form of stories, and thus, the following document is written as if by one of the author's ancestors, Nushirwan, to that relative's son.

The Document

THE COUNSELS OF NUSHIRWAN THE JUST TO HIS SON

Nushirwan began by saying: As long as day and night come and go, never marvel at the vicissitudes of [human] affairs. Then he said: How is it that men commit actions of which they afterwards repent, although others before them have done them and repented?

How can a man who has acquaintance with kings lay himself down to sleep free of care?

How can a man count himself happy whose life has not gone according to his desires?

Why not account that man your enemy who secretly knows his generosity to be to the detriment of mankind ?

Do not call him your friend who is the enemy of one of your well-wishers.

Form no friendship with men lacking merit, for such men are worthy neither of friendship nor of enmity.

Beware of the man who deems himself wise but is in actual fact a fool.

Do good of your own accord, thus may you be free of the [compulsion of the] lawgiver.

Speak the truth though it be bitter, and if you desire your enemy not to become possessed of your secret do not reveal it to your friend.

The great man who looks upon himself as small is indeed the great man of his age.

Do not regard as living creatures men who lack all value.

If you desire to be rich without unhappiness, let all your actions be worthy of praise.

Do not buy at any price, so that you may not be compelled to sell at any price.

Better die of hunger than be sated with the bread of ignoble men.

Place no reliance, for some fancy you may conceive, upon untrustworthy men, nor cease your reliance upon them you can trust.

Regard it as a great misfortune to stand in need of kinsmen humbler than oneself, for it is better to die in the water than to beg help of a frog.

The sinner who is a humble seeker after the next world is better than the devout but self-important man who is a seeker after this world.

There is no fool greater than he who sees a man of lowly state risen to greatness and yet continues to regard him as lowly.

There is no fault greater than for a man to lay claim to knowledge which he does not possess and then to resort to lying.

Be not misled by him that gives something which he has picked up in exchange for something not so [easily] acquired.

There is no meaner person in the world than he to whom appeal is made for help and though able to grant it refuses.

Regard him that speaks ill of you, when you are innocent, more worthy of forgiveness than him who carried the report of it to you.

He that is stricken by the misfortune of one dear to him suffers less grievously than he that hears of it and is helpless [to succour].

He that is afflicted by what his eyes behold suffers far more than he who himself suffers affliction.

Reckon any slave that is bought and sold freer than the man who is slave to his gullet.

No wise man should undertake the task of instructing him that has not been given understanding by the experience of time.

It is easier to guard a fool against anything rather than his own body.

If you desire men to speak well of you, then do you speak well of your fellow-men.

If you desire your efforts on behalf of other men not to be wasted, then do not permit others' efforts on your behalf to be wasted.

If you desire to remain free of unhappiness, be not envious.

If you do not wish to be reckoned insane, do not seek to discover the undiscoverable.

If you desire to command men's respect, then exercise justice.

If you wish not to be disillusioned, do not regard an undone task as having been done.

If you do not wish to be stricken with shame, do not remove what you have not yourself deposited; and if you desire not to be mocked behind your back, respect them that are subordinate to you.

If you wish to be saved long-lasting regret, do not indulge in the desires of your heart.

If you desire to be amongst the great, then see yourself in the mirror of other men.

If you desire to be included in the number of honourable men, give covetousness no place in your heart.

If you desire to be a man of justice, be generous as far as lies in your power towards them that are subordinate to you; and if you desire your heart never to be stricken a blow which no remedy can heal, never engage in argument with fools.

If you wish to retain men's esteem, learn how to esteem other men.

If you desire to be the most lauded of men, never reveal your secret to one who has no discretion.

If you wish to be superior to other men, be lavish of bread and salt [*i.e.* hospitable].

If you desire to be untouched by other men's disapprobation, then be ever laudatory of their works.

If you wish to remain beloved in the hearts of men and never to incur their dislike, then speak of them in the fashion that pleases them.

If you wish for effectiveness in your tongue, then restrain the rapacity of your hand.

These were the sayings of Nushirwan the Just. If you read these words, do not hold them in contempt, for there is exhaled from them the fragrance of wisdom and kingly dignity in that they are the utterances of sages and kings. Master them now while you are young: once you are old you will have no need to hear and acquire instructive counsel and wise saws, for time itself will have taught those who reach old age.

Analysis and Review Questions

1. Would you say that the advice given by Nushirwan is particular to Islamic culture only, or does it seem to apply to your own society? If so, how? If not, why not?
2. How should "lowly" people who have risen to greatness be treated?
3. According to the document, should people help and aid one another, if able?
4. What appears to be the key to remaining free of unhappiness?
5. According to Nushirwan, when should his son begin working to live up to his father's advice?

AN ARAB-SYRIAN GENTLEMAN DISCUSSES THE FRANKS

About the Document

The Crusades were a crucial series of events for both Europe and the Middle East. Scholars continue to debate exactly how much of Europe's crusading efforts were truly religious and how much were motivated by other interests. Regardless, the Crusades contributed to an expanding worldview for both Europeans and the peoples they encountered. Just as Westerners were learning about the Middle East, Middle Easterners were learning about Westerners.

In the mid-twelfth century C.E., a Syrian named Usamah Ibn-Munqidh wrote a memoir about his life and times that included discussions of his experiences with Frankish (French) Crusaders. While other parts of his memoirs address his travels throughout Egypt and Lebanon and include a section eulogizing his father, it is his portrayal of the European Crusaders for which his work is most remembered.

The Document

A Moslem cavalier survives a Frankish thrust which cuts his heart vein.—I once witnessed in an encounter between us and the Franks° one of our cavaliers, named Badi Ibn-Talll al-Qushayri, who was one of our brave men, receive in his chest, while clothed with only two pieces of garment, a lance thrust from a Frankish knight. The lance cut the vein in his chest and issued from his side. He turned back right away, but we never thought he would make his home alive. But as Allah° (worthy of admiration is he!) had predestined, he survived and his wound was healed. But for one year after that, he could not sit up in case he was lying on his back unless somebody held him by the shoulders and helped him. At last what he suffered from entirely disappeared and he reverted to his old ways of living and riding. My only comment is: How mysterious are the works of him whose will is always executed among his creatures! He giveth life and he causeth death, but he is living and dieth not. In his hand is all good, and he is over all things potent.

An artisan dies from a needle prick.—We had once with us an artisan, 'Attb by name, who was one of the most corpulent and tall of men. He entered his home one day, and as he was sitting down he leaned on his hand against a robe which happened to be near him and in which there was a needle. The needle went through the palm of his hand and he died because of it. And, by Allah, as he moaned in the lower town, his moan could be heard from the citadel on account of the bulk of his body and the volume of his voice. This man dies of a needle, whereas al-Qushayri is pierced with a lance which penetrates through his chest and issues out of his side and yet suffers no harm!

A Shayzar woman captures three Franks.—The following will serve as an illustration of women's love of adventure:

A group of Frankish pilgrims, after making the pilgrimage, returned to Rafaniyyah, which at that time belonged to them. They then left it for Afamiyah. During the night they lost their way and landed in Shayzar, which at that time had no wall. They entered the city, numbering about seven or eight hundred men, women and children. The army of Shayzar had already gone out of the town in the company of my two uncles, 'Izz-al-DIn abu-al-'Asakir Sultan and Fakhr-al-DIn abu-Kamil Shafi (may Allah's mercy rest upon their souls!), to meet two brides, whom my uncles had married, who were sisters

Franks: People of early France. "France" originally meant "Kingdom of the Franks."
Allah: The supreme being for muslims. Literally, "The God."

and belonged to the Banu-al-Sufi, the Aleppines. My father (may Allah's mercy rest upon his soul!) remained in the castle. One of our men, going out of the city at night on business, suddenly saw a Frank. He went back and got his sword, then went out and killed him. The battle cry sounded all over the town. The inhabitants went out, killed the Franks and took as booty all the women, children, silver and beasts of burden they had.

At that time there was in Shayzar a woman named Nadrah, daughter of Buzarmat, who was the wife of one of our men. This woman went out with our men, captured a Frank and introduced him into her house. She went out again, captured another Frank and brought him in. Again she went out and captured still another. Thus she had three Franks in her house. After taking as booty what they had and what suited her of their possessions, she went out and called some of her neighbors, who killed them.

During the same night my two uncles, with the army, arrived. Some of the Franks had taken to flight and were pursued by certain men from Shayzar, who killed them in the environs of the town. The horses of my uncles' army, on entering the town in the night-time, began to stumble over corpses without knowing what they were stumbling over, until one of the cavaliers dismounted and saw the corpses in the darkness. This terrified our men, for they thought the town had been raided by surprise. In fact, it was booty which Allah (exalted and majestic is he!) had delivered into the hands of our people.

Prefers to be a Frankish shoemaker's wife to life in a Moslem castle.—A number of maids taken captive from the Franks were brought into the home of my father (may Allah's mercy rest upon his soul!). The Franks (may Allah's curse be upon them!) are an accursed race, the members of which do not assimilate except with their own kin. My father saw among them a pretty maid who was in the prime of youth, and said to his housekeeper, "Introduce this woman into the bath, repair her clothing and prepare her for a journey." This she did. He then delivered the maid to a servant of his and sent her to al-AmIr Shihab-al-DIn Mlik ibn-Salim, the lord of the Castle of Ja'bar, who was a friend of his. He also wrote him a letter, saying, "We have won some booty from the Franks, from which I am sending thee a share." The maid suited Shihab-al-DIn, and he was pleased with her. He took her to himself and she bore him a boy, whom he called Badran. Badran's father named him his heir apparent, and he became of age. On his father's death, Badran became the governor of the town and its people, his mother being the real power. She entered into conspiracy with a band of men and let herself down from the castle by a rope. The band took her to Saruj, which belonged at that time to the Franks. There she married a Frankish shoemaker, while her son was the lord of the Castle of Ja'bar.

Their lack of sense.—Mysterious are the works of the Creator, the author of all things! When one comes to recount cases regarding the Franks, he cannot but glorify Allah (exalted is he!) and sanctify him, for he sees them as animals possessing the virtues of courage and fighting, but nothing else; just as animals have only the virtues of strength and carrying loads. I shall now give some instances of their doings and their curious mentality.

Newly arrived Franks are especially rough.—Everyone who is a fresh emigrant from the Frankish lands is ruder in character than those who have become acclimatized and have held long association with the Moslems.

Franks lack jealousy in sex affairs.—The Franks are void of all zeal and jealousy. One of them may be walking along with his wife. He meets another man who takes the wife by the hand and steps aside to converse with her while the husband is standing on one side waiting for his wife to conclude the conversation. If she lingers too long for him, he leaves her alone with the conversant and goes away.

Here is an illustration which I myself witnessed:

When I used to visit Nablus, I always took lodging with a man named Mu'izz, whose home was a lodging house for the Moslems. The house had windows which

Map 7.3
*Trade Routes in the
Medieval Western World*

opened to the road, and there stood opposite to it on the other side of the road a house belonging to a Frank who sold wine for the merchants. He would take some wine in a bottle and go around announcing it by shouting, "So and so, the merchant, has just opened a cask full of this wine. He who wants to buy some of it will find it in such and such a place." The Frank's pay for the announcement made would be the wine in that bottle. One day this Frank went home and found a man with his wife in the same bed. He asked him, "What could have made thee enter into my wife's room?" The man replied, "I was tired, so I went in to rest." "But how," asked he, "didst thou get into my bed?" The other replied, "I found a bed that was spread, so I slept in it." "But," said he, "my wife was sleeping together with thee!" The other replied, "Well, the bed is hers. How could I therefore have prevented her from using her own bed?" "By the truth of my religion," said the husband, "if thou shouldst do it again, thou and I would have a quarrel." Such was for the Frank the entire expression of his disapproval and the limit of his jealousy.

Map 7.4
Arabs on Horseback

Analysis and Review Questions

1. Does the author seem to favor women using their abilities or not? Why?
2. What is the character of the new arrivals from Frankish territory?
3. How diligently do the Frankish men work to keep their wives faithful, according to the author?
4. How does the author view the Franks?
5. Is there anything positive that the author recounts about the Franks?

THE RUBÁIYÁT OF OMAR KHAYYÁM

About the Document

Nearly all societies who develop writing develop forms of poetry, and even those with no writing compose poetry-like epic tales and stories that are transmitted by word-of-mouth. The themes are often similar, if not identical: heroic exploits, the activities of deities, or human issues of love or loss. In some ways, *The Rubáiyát* of Omar Khayyám includes all these themes and others.

Omar Khayyám, who was born in Persia around 1050 C.E., was a well-educated man known for his mathematical skill. He was also a noted astronomer, but he is best known in the West for his poetry. Not only is his *Rubáiyát* considered one of the masterpieces of world literature, it also gives us a glimpse into Persian life in this period. It includes oft-quoted quatrains about love.

The Document

I
Wake! For the Sun, who scatter'd into flight
The Stars before him from the Field of Night,
　　Drives Night along with them from Heav'n, and strikes
The Sultán's Turret with a Shaft of Light.

II
Before the phantom of False morning died,
Methought a Voice within the Tavern cried,

"When all the Temple is prepared within,
Why nods the drowsy Worshipper outside?"

IV
Now the New Year reviving old Desires,
The thoughtful Soul to Solitude retires,
    Where the White Hand of Moses on the Bough
Puts out, and Jesus from the Ground suspires.

VII
Come, fill the Cup, and in the fire of Spring
Your Winter-garment of Repentance fling:
    The Bird of Time has but a little way
To flutter—and the Bird is on the Wing.

VIII
Whether at Naishápúr or Babylon,
Whether the Cup with sweet or bitter run,
    The Wine of Life keeps oozing drop by drop,
The Leaves of Life keep falling one by one.

IX
Each Morn a thousand Roses brings, you say;
Yes, but where leaves the Rose of Yesterday?
And this first Summer month that brings the Rose
Shall take Jamshyd and Kaikobád away.

XI
With me along the strip of Herbage strown
That just divides the desert from the sown,
    Where name of Slave and Sultán is forgot—
And Peace to Mahmúd on his golden Throne!

XII
A Book of Verses underneath the Bough,
A Jug of Wine, a Loaf of Bread—and Thou
    Beside me singing in the Wilderness—
Oh, Wilderness were Paradise enow!

XIII
Some for the Glories of This World; and some
Sigh for the Prophet's Paradise to come;
    Ah, take the Cash, and let the Credit go,
Nor heed the rumble of a distant Drum!

XVI
The Worldly Hope men set their Hearts upon
Turns Ashes—or it prospers; and anon,
    Like Snow upon the Desert's dusty Face,
Lighting a little hour or two—is gone.

XVII
Think, in this batter'd Caravanserai
Whose Portals are alternate Night and Day,
    How Sultán after Sultán with his Pomp
Abode his destined Hour, and went his way.

XXIV

Ah, make the most of what we yet may spend,
Before we too into the Dust descend;
    Dust into Dust, and under Dust to lie
Sans Wine, sans Song, sans Singer, and—sans End!

XXV

Alike lot those who for To-day prepare,
And those that after some To-morrow stare,
    A Muezzín from the Tower of Darkness cries
"Fools! your Reward is neither Here nor There."

XXXII

There was the Door to which I found no Key;
There was the Veil through which I might not see:
    Some little talk awhile of Me and Thee
There was—and then no more of Thee and Me.

XXXVII

For I remember stopping by the way
To watch a Potter thumping his wet Clay:
    And with its all-obliterated Tongue
It murmur'd—"Gently, Brother, gently, pray!"

XXXVIII

And has not such a Story from of Old
Down Man's successive generations roll'd
    Of such a clod of saturated Earth
Cast by the Maker into Human mould?

XLII

And if the Wine you drink, the Lip you press
End in what All begins and ends in—Yes;
    Think then you are To-day what Yesterday
You were—To-morrow you shall not be less.

LV

You know, my Friends, with what a brave Carouse
I made a Second Marriage in my house;
    Divorced old barren Reason from my Bed
And took the Daughter of the Vine to Spouse.

LX

The mighty Mahmúd, Allah-breathing Lord
That all the misbelieving and black Horde
    Of Fears and Sorrows that infest the Soul
Scatters before him with his whirlwind Sword.

LXIV

Strange, is it not? that of the myriads who
Before us pass'd the door of Darkness through,
    Not one returns to tell us of the Road,
Which to discover we must travel too.

LXVI

I sent my Soul through the Invisible,
Some letter of that After-life to spell:

And by and by my Soul return'd to me,
And answer'd "I Myself am Heav'n and Hell."

LXVII
Heav'n but the Vision of fulfill'd Desire,
And Hell the Shadow from a Soul on fire,
　Cast on the Darkness into which Ourselves,
So late emerged from, shall so soon expire.

LXIX
But helpless Pieces of the Game He plays
Upon this Chequer-board of Nights and Days;
　Hither and thither moves, and checks, and slays,
And one by one back in the Closet lays.

LXXI
The Moving Finger writes; and, having writ,
Moves on: nor all your Piety nor Wit
　Shall lure it back to cancel half a Line,
Nor all your Tears wash out a Word of it.

LXXIII
With Earth's first Clay They did the Last Man knead;
And there of the Last Harvest sow'd the Seed:
　And the first Morning of Creation wrote
What the Last Dawn of Reckoning shall read.

LXXXVII
Whereat some one of the loquacious Lot—
I think a Súfi pipkin—waxing hot—
　"All this of Pot and Potter—Tell me then,
Who is the Potter, pray, and who the Pot?"

Analysis and Review Questions

1. Do there appear to be any religious aspects to this poem? If so, why do you think they are there?
2. What role does death appear to play in the poem?
3. What do you think Omar Khayyám means when he says, "took the daughter of the vine to spouse"?
4. Do any of the feelings or attitudes displayed in the poem seem appropriate for today? How?

WEB LINKS

http://longmanworldhistory.com
The following additional readings and case studies can be found on the Web site.
Document 2.3, Elders Advise to Their Successors
Document 7.4, The Sea of Precious Virtues
Case Study 7.1, "Instructions" to One's Heirs

http://www.arabiannights.org
Site presents the full texts of both the *Arabian Nights* and Omar Khayyám's *The Rubáiyát.*

http://www.islamic.org
An all-inclusive Muslim-oriented site that includes the text of the Qur'an, information on Muhammad the prophet, and an excellent discussion of the religion's main points.

http://www.islamicart.com
A beautiful Web site with numerous images of Islamic architecture, calligraphy, coins, and rugs.

KAUTILYA AND MACHIAVELLI: POLITICAL THEORISTS EXTRAORDINAIRE

Before the rise of modern nation-states, the terms "civilization" and "empire" went hand-in-hand. And at the apex of every empire sat a ruler—king or queen, emperor or empress, prince or princess. Both titles and gender changed from culture to culture and language to language, but the trappings of empire—an absolute monarch, a well-developed bureaucracy, a marriage of church and state, a tax collection system, and a professional military—were common to most such political institutions. The parallels in the great empires of history give rise to an important question: Why do some empires succeed while others, with similar institutions, fail? The answer to that question is extremely complex. Climate, geography, time, cultural divergence, cultural diversity, the capability of individual rulers, and the theory of government accepted and practiced by individual rulers are a few of the variables that must be considered if the question is to be answered. This case study addresses that last-mentioned variable.

Kautilya's *Arthashastra* is generally accepted by historians as the theory of government put in practice by Chandragupta Maurya. Obviously, the theory worked, and the Mauryan Empire became the first kingdom to span the Indian subcontinent. This case study asks the reader to compare Indian political theory of the third century B.C.E. with the theory of Niccolò Machiavelli, a sixteenth-century C.E. Italian theorist.

KAUTILYA'S *ARTHASHASTRA*

About the Document

The *Arthashastra* stresses the survival of the ruler as well as the survival of the kingdom. After viewing the selections on spies and personal security, the reader may wonder if Chandragupta was a tad paranoid, and considering the number of bodies that littered his path to empire, perhaps a degree of paranoia was justified. But how many rulers in history have experienced a premature date with death? How many modern world leaders command organizations that deal with internal and external espionage? How many of those leaders find it necessary to surround themselves with armed bodyguards? And how many of them maintain a legion of lawyers to prevent the assassination of their "good" name? Perhaps Kautilya reflected not on paranoia, but on a timeless political norm. Consider the words of Kautilya with care.

107

The Document

Chapter 10: On Spies

Advised and assisted by a tried council of officers, the ruler should proceed to institute spies.

Spies are in the guise of pseudo-student, priest, householder, trader, saint practising renunciation, classmate or colleague, desperado, poisoner and woman mendicant.

An artful person, capable of reading human nature, is a pseudo-student. Such a person should be encouraged with presents and purse and be told by the officer: "Sworn to the ruler and myself you shall inform us what wickedness you find in others."

One initiated in scripture and of pure character is a priest-spy. This spy should carry on farming, cattle culture and commerce with resources given to him. Out of the produce and profit accrued, he should encourage other priests to live with him and send them on espionage work. The other priests also should send their followers on similar errands.

A householder-spy is a farmer fallen in his profession but pure in character. This spy should do as the priest [above].

A trader-spy is a merchant in distress but generally trustworthy. This spy should carry on espionage, in addition to his profession.

A person with proper appearance and accomplishments as an ascetic is a saint-spy. He surrounds himself with followers and may settle down in the suburb of a big city and may pretend prayer and fasting in public. Trader-spies may associate with this class of spies. He may practise fortune-telling, palmistry, and pretend supernatural and magical powers by predictions. The followers will adduce proof for the predictions of their saint. He may even foretell official rewards and official changes, which the officers concerned may substantiate by reciprocating.

Rewarded by the rulers with money and titles, these five institutions of espionage should maintain the integrity of the country's officers.

Chapter 14: Administrative Councils

Deliberation in well-constituted councils precedes administrative measures. The proceedings of a council should be in camera and deliberations made top secret so that not even a bird can whisper. The ruler should be guarded against disclosure.

Whoever divulges secret deliberations should be destroyed. Such guilt can be detected by physical and attitudinal changes of ambassadors, ministers and heads.

Secrecy of proceedings in the council and guarding of officers participating in the council must be organised.

The causes of divulgence of counsels are recklessness, drink, talking in one's sleep and infatuation with women which [sic] assail councillors.

He of secretive nature or who is not regarded well will divulge council matters. Disclosure of council secrets is of advantage to persons other than the ruler and his high officers. Steps should be taken to safeguard deliberations. . . .

Chapter 20: Personal Security

The ruler should employ as his security staff only such persons as have noble and proven ancestry and are closely related to him and are well trained and loyal. No foreigners, or anonymous persons, or persons with clouded antecedents are to be employed as security staff for the ruler.

In a securely guarded chamber, the chief should supervise the ruler's food arrangements.

Special precautions are to be taken against contaminated and poisoned food. The following reveal poison: rice sending out deep blue vapour; unnaturally coloured and artificially dried-up and hard vegetables; unusually bright and dull vessels; foamy vessels; streaky soups, milk and liquor; white streaked honey; strange-tempered food; carpets and curtains stained with dark spots and threadbare; polishless and lustreless metallic vessels and gems.

The poisoner reveals himself by parched and dry mouth, hesitating talk, perspiration, tremour, yawning, evasive demeanour and nervous behaviour.

Experts in poison detection should be in attendance on the ruler. The physicians attending the ruler should satisfy themselves personally as to the purity of the drugs which they administer to the ruler. The same precaution is indicated for liquor and beverages which the ruler uses. Scrupulous cleanliness should be insisted on in persons in charge of the ruler's dress and toilet requisites. This should be ensured by seals. . . .

In any entertainment meant for the amusement of the ruler, the actors should not use weapons, fire and poison. Musical instruments and accoutrements for horses, elephants and vehicles should be secured in the palace.

The ruler should mount beasts and vehicles only after the traditional rider and driver has done so. If he has to travel in a boat, the pilot should be trustworthy and the boat itself secured to another boat. There should be a proper convoy on land or water guarding the ruler. He should swim only in rivers which are free of larger fishes and crocodiles and hunt in forests free from snakes, man-eaters and brigands.°

He should give private audience only attended by his security guards. He should receive foreign ambassadors in his full ministerial council. While reviewing his militia, the ruler should also attend in full battle uniform and be on horseback or on the back of an elephant. When he enters or exits from the capital city, the path of the ruler should be guarded by staffed officers and cleared of armed men, mendicants° and the suspicious. He should attend public performances, festivals, processions or religious gatherings accompanied by trained bodyguards. The ruler should guard his own person with the same care with which he secures the safety of those around him through espionage arrangements.

Chapter 21: Building of Villages

The ruler may form villages either on new sites or on old sites, either by shifting population from heavily populated areas in his own state or by causing population to immigrate into his state.

Viullages should consist of not less than a hundred and not more than five hundred families of cultivators of the service classes. The villages should extend from about one and a half miles to three miles each [in circumference] and should be capable of defending each other. Village boundaries may consist of rivers, hills, forests, hedges, caves, bridges and trees.

Each eight hundred villages should have a major fort. There should be a capital city for every four hundred villages, a market town for every two hundred villages, and an urban cluster for every ten villages.

brigands: Bandits.
mendicants: Beggars.

The frontiers of the state should have fortifications protected by internal guards, manning the entrances to the state. The interior of the state should be guarded by huntsmen, armed guards, forest tribes, fierce tribes and frontier men.

Those who do social service by sacrifices, the clergy, and the intellectuals should be settled in the villages on tax-free farms.

Officers, scribes, cattlemen, guards, cattle doctors, physicians, horse-trainers and news purveyors should be given life interest in lands.

Lands fit for cultivation should be given to tenants only for life. Land prepared for cultivation by tenants should not be taken away from them.

Lands not cultivated by the landholders may be confiscated and given to cultivators. Or they may be cultivated through hired labourers or traders to avoid loss to the state. If cultivators pay their taxes promptly, they may be supplied with grains, cattle and money.

The ruler should give to cultivators only such farms and concessions as will replenish the treasury and avoid denuding it.

A denuded exchequer is a grave threat to the security of the state. Only on rare occasions like settlement of new areas or in grave emergencies should tax-remissions be granted. The ruler should be benevolent to those who have conquered the crisis by remission of taxes.

He should facilitate mining operations. He should encourage manufacturers. He should help exploitation of forest wealth. He should provide amenities for cattle breeding and commerce. He should construct highways both on land and on water. He should plan markets.

He should build dikes for water either perennial or from other sources. He should assist with resources and communications those who build reservoirs or construct works of communal comfort and public parks.

All should share in corporate work, sharing the expenditure but not claiming profit.

The ruler should have suzerainty over all fishing, transport and grain trade, reservoirs and bridges.

Those who do not recognise the rights of their servants, hirelings and relatives should be made to do so.

The ruler should maintain adolescents, the aged, the diseased and the orphans. He should also provide livelihood to deserted women with prenatal care and protection for the children born to them. . . .

The ruler should abstain from taking over any area which is open to attack by enemies and wild tribes and whish is visited by frequent famines and pests. He should also abstain from extravagant sports.

He should protect cultivation from heavy taxes, slave labour and severe penalties, herds of cattle from cattle lifters, wild animals, venomous creatures and diseases.

He should clear highways of the visitation of petty officials, workmen, brigands and guards. He should not only conserve existing forests, buildings and mines, but also develop new ones.

Chapter 41: Decay, Stabilisation, and Progress of States

A state should always observe such a policy as will help it strengthen its defensive fortifications and life-lines of communications, build plantations, construct villages, and exploit the mineral and forest wealth of the country, while at the same time preventing fulfilment of similar programmes in the rival state.

Any two states hostile to each other, finding that neither has an advantage over the other in fulfilment of their respective programmes, should make peace with each other.

When any two states which are rivals expect to acquire equal possessions over the same span of time, they should keep peace with each other.

A state can indulge in armed invasion only:

Where, by invasion, it can reduce the power of an enemy without in any way reducing its own potential, by making suitable arrangements for protection of its own strategic works. . . .

Chapter 54: Restoration of Lost Balance of Power

When an invader is assailed by an alliance of his enemies, he should try to purchase the leader of the alliance with offers of gold and his own alliance and by diplomatic camouflage of the threat of treachery from the alliance of powers. He should instigate the leader of the allied enemies to break up his alliance.

The invader should also attempt to break the allied enemies' formation by setting up the leader of the alliance against the weaker of his enemies, or attempt to forge a combination of the weaker allies against their leader. He may also form a pact with the leader through intrigue, or offer of resources. When the confederation is shattered, he may form alliances with any of his former enemies.

If a state is weak in treasury or in striking power, attention should be directed to strengthen both through stabilisation of authority. Irrigational projects are a source of agricultural prosperity. Good highways should be constructed to facilitate movements of armed might and merchandise. Mines should be developed, as they supply ammunition. Forests should be conserved, as they supply material for defence, communication and vehicles. Pasture lands are the source of cattle wealth.

Thus, a state should build up its striking power through development of the exchequer, the army and wise counsel; and, till the proper time, should conduct itself as a weak power towards its neighbours, to evade conflict or envy from enemy or allied states. If the state is deficient in resources, it should acquire them from related or allied states. It should attract to itself capable men from corporations, from wild and ferocious tribes, and foreigners, and organised espionage that will damage hostile powers.

MACHIAVELLI'S *THE PRINCE*

The Document

. . . So the conclusion is: If you take control of a state, you should make a list of all the crimes you have to commit and do them all at once. That way you will not have to commit new atrocities every day, and you will be able, by not repeating your evil deeds, to reassure your subjects and to win their support by treating them well. He who acts otherwise, either out of squeamishness or out of bad judgment, has to hold a bloody knife in his hand all the time. He can never rely on his subjects, for they can never trust him, for he is always making new attacks upon them. Do all the harm you must at one and the same time, that way the full extent of it will not be noticed, and it will give least offense. One should do good, on the other hand, little by little, so people can fully appreciate it.

A ruler should, above all, behave towards his subjects in such a way that, whatever happens, whether for good or ill, he has no need to change his policies. For if you fall on evil times and are obliged to change course, you will not have time to benefit from the harm you do, and the good you do will do you no good, because people will think you have been forced to do it, and they will not be in the slightest bit grateful to you.

Chapter 9: Of the citizen-ruler

But, coming to the alternative possibility, when a private citizen becomes the ruler of his homeland, not through wickedness or some act of atrocity, but through the support of his fellow citizens, so that we may call him a citizen-ruler (remember we are discussing power acquired neither by pure strength nor mere luck—in this case one needs a lucky cunning), I would point out there are two ways to such power: the support of the populace or the favor of the elite. For in every city one finds these two opposed classes. They are at odds because the populace do not want to be ordered about or oppressed by the elite; and the elite want to order about and oppress the populace. The conflict between these two irreconcilable ambitions has in each city one of three possible consequences: rule by one man, liberty, or anarchy.

Rule by one man can be brought about either by the populace or the elite, depending on whether one or the other of these factions hopes to benefit from it. For if the elite fear they will be unable to control the populace, they begin to build up the reputation of one of their own, and they make him sole ruler in order to be able, under his protection, to achieve their objectives. The populace on the other hand, if they fear they are going to be crushed by the elite, build up the reputation of one of their number and make him sole ruler, in order that his authority may be employed in their defense. He who comes to power with the help of the elite has more difficulty in holding on to power than he who comes to power with the help of the populace, for in the former case he is surrounded by many who think of themselves as his equals, and whom he consequently cannot order about or manipulate as he might wish. He who comes to power with the support of the populace, on the other hand, has it all to himself: There is no one, or hardly anyone, around him who is not prepared to obey. In addition, one cannot honorably give the elite what they want, and one cannot do it without harming others; but this is not true with the populace, for the objectives of the populace are less immoral than those of the elite, for the latter want to oppress, and the former not to be oppressed. Thirdly, if the masses are opposed to you, you can never be secure, for there are too many of them; but the elite, since there are few of them, can be neutralized.

The worst a ruler who is opposed by the populace has to fear is that they will give him no support; but from the elite he has to fear not only lack of support, but worse, that they will attack him. For the elite have more foresight and more cunning; they act in time to protect themselves, and seek to ingratiate themselves with rivals for power. Finally, the ruler cannot get rid of the populace but must live with them; he can, however, get by perfectly well without the members of the elite, being able to make and unmake them each day, and being in a position to give them status or take it away, as he chooses.

In order to clarify the issues, let me point out there are two principal points of view from which one should consider the elite. Either they behave in a way that ties their fortunes to yours, or they do not. Those who tie themselves to you and are not rapacious, you should honor and love; those who do not tie themselves to you are to be divided into two categories. If they retain their independence through pusillanimity and because they are lacking in courage, then you should employ them, especially if they have good judgment, for you can be sure they will help you achieve success so long as things are going well for you, and you can also be confident you have nothing to fear from them if things go badly. But if they retain their independence from you out of calculation and ambition, then you can tell they are more interested in their own welfare than yours. A ruler must protect himself against such people and fear them as much as if they were publicly declared enemies, for you can be sure that, in adversity, they will help to overthrow you.

Anyone who becomes a ruler with support of the populace ought to ensure he keeps their support; which will not be difficult, for all they ask is not to be oppressed. But anyone who becomes a ruler with the support of the elite and against the wishes of the populace must above all else seek to win the populace over to his side, which will be easy to do if he protects their interests. And since people, when they are well-treated by someone whom they expected to treat them badly, feel all the more obliged to their benefactor, he will find that the populace will quickly become better inclined towards him than if he had come to power with their support. There are numerous ways the ruler can win the support of the populace. They vary so much depending on the circumstances they cannot be reduced to a formula, and, consequently, I will not go into them here. I will simply conclude by saying a ruler needs to have the support of the populace, for otherwise he has nothing to fall back on in times of adversity.

Nabis, ruler of the Spartans, survived an attack by the confederate forces of all Greece, together with an almost invincible Roman army, and successfully defended both his homeland and his own hold on power. All he needed to do, when faced with danger, was neutralize a few; but if he had had the populace opposed to him, this would have been insufficient. Do not think you can rebut my argument by citing the well-worn proverb, "Relying on the people is like building on the sand." This is quite true when a private citizen depends upon them and gives the impression he expects the populace to free him if he is seized by his enemies or by the magistrates. In such a case one can easily find oneself disappointed, as happened to the Gracchi in Rome and to Mr. Giorgio Scali in Florence. But if you are a ruler and you put your trust in the populace, if you can give commands and are capable of bold action, if you are not nonplussed by adversity, if you take other necessary precautions, and if through your own courage and your policies you keep up the morale of the populace, then you will never be let down by them, and you will discover you have built on a sound foundation.

The type of one-man rule we are discussing tends to be at risk at the moment of transition from constitutional to dictatorial government. Such rulers either give commands in their own name, or act through the officers of state. In the second case, their situation is more dangerous and less secure. For they are entirely dependent on the co-operation of those citizens who have been appointed to the offices of state, who can, particularly at times of crisis, easily deprive them of their power, either by directly opposing them or by simply failing to carry out their instructions. It is too late for the ruler once a crisis is upon him to seize dictatorial authority, for the citizens and the subjects, who are used to obeying the constituted authorities, will not, in such circumstances, obey him, and he will always have, in difficult circumstances, a shortage of people on whom he can rely. For such a ruler cannot expect things to continue as they were when there were no difficulties, when all the citizens are conscious of what the government can do for them. Then everyone flocked round, everyone promised support, everyone was willing to die for him, when there was no prospect of having to do so. But when times are tough, when the government is dependent on its citizens, then there will be few who are prepared to stand by it. One does not learn the danger of such an erosion of support from experience, as the first experience proves fatal. So a wise ruler will seek to ensure that his citizens always, no matter what the circumstances, have an interest in preserving both him and his authority. If he can do this, they will always be faithful to him.

Chapter 10: How one should measure the strength of a ruler

There is another factor one should take into account when categorizing rulers: One should ask if a ruler has enough resources to be able, if necessary, to look after himself, or whether he will always be dependent on having alliances with other rulers. In order to clarify this question, I would maintain those rulers can look after themselves who have sufficient reserves, whether of troops or of money, to be able to put together a sound army and face battle against any opponent. On the other hand, I judge those rulers to be dependent on the support of others who could not take the field against any potential enemy, but would be obliged to take shelter behind the walls of their cities and castles, and stay there. We have talked already about those who can look after themselves, and we will have more to say in due course; to those who are in the second situation, all one can do is advise them to build defenseworks and stockpile arms, and to give up all thought of holding the open ground. He who has well fortified his city and who has followed the policies towards his own subjects that I have outlined above and will describe below, can be sure his enemies will think twice before they attack him, for people are always reluctant to undertake enterprises that look as if they will be difficult, and no one thinks it will be easy to attack someone who is well-fortified and has the support of the populace.

The cities of Germany are free to do as they please. They have little surrounding territory, and obey the emperor only when they want. They fear neither him nor any other ruler in their region, for they are so well-fortified everyone thinks it will be tedious and difficult to take them. They all have appropriate moats and ramparts, and more than enough artillery. They always keep in the public stores enough food and drink, and enough firewood, to be able to hold out for a year. Moreover, in order to be able to keep the populace quiet and to guarantee tax revenues, they always keep in stock enough supplies to keep their subjects occupied for a year in those crafts that are the basis of the city's prosperity and provide employment for the bulk of the people. They also emphasize military preparedness and have numerous ordinances designed to ensure this.

A ruler, therefore, who has a well-fortified city, and who does not set out to make enemies, is not going to be attacked; and, suppose someone does attack him, his adversary will have to give up in disgrace. For political circumstances change so fast it is impossible for anyone to keep an army in the field for a year doing nothing but maintaining a siege. And if you are tempted to reply that if the people have property outside the city walls and see it burning, then they will not be able patiently to withstand a siege, and that as time goes by, and their own interests are damaged, they will forget their loyalty to their ruler; then I reply that a ruler who is strong and bold will always be able to overcome such difficulties, sometimes encouraging his subjects to think relief is at hand, sometimes terrifying them with stories of what the enemy will do to them if they concede defeat, sometimes taking appropriate action to neutralize those who seem to him to be agitators. Moreover, it is in the nature of things that the enemy will burn and pillage the countryside when they first arrive, at which time the subjects will still be feeling brave and prepared to undertake their own defense. So the ruler has little to fear, for after a few days, when the subjects are feeling less courageous, the damage will already have been done, and it will be too late to prevent it. Then they will be all the more ready to rally to their ruler, believing him to be in their debt, since they have had their houses burnt and their possessions looted for defending him. It is in men's nature to feel as obliged by the good they do to others, as by the good others do to them. So if you consider all the factors, you will see it is not difficult for a wise ruler to keep his subjects loyal during a siege, both at the beginning and as it continues, providing they are not short of food and of arms.

Let us leave to one side, then, all discussion of imaginary rulers and talk about practical realities. I maintain that all men, when people talk about them, and especially rulers, because they hold positions of authority, are described in terms of qualities that are inextricably linked to censure or to praise. So one man is described as generous, another as a miser; one is called open-handed, another tight-fisted; one man is cruel, another gentle; one untrustworthy, another reliable; one effeminate and cowardly, another bold and violent; one sympathetic, another self-important; one promiscuous, another monogamous; one straightforward, another duplicitous; one tough, another easy-going; one serious, another cheerful; one religious, another atheistical; and so on. Now I know everyone will agree that if a ruler could have all the good qualities I have listed and none of the bad ones, then this would be an excellent state of affairs. But one cannot have all the good qualities, nor always act in a praiseworthy fashion, for we do not live in an ideal world. You have to be astute enough to avoid being thought to have those evil qualities that would make it impossible for you to retain power; as for those that are compatible with holding on to power, you should avoid them if you can; but if you cannot, then you should not worry too much if people say you have them. Above all, do not be upset if you are supposed to have those vices a ruler needs if he is going to stay securely in power, for, if you think about it, you will realize there are some ways of behaving that are supposed to be virtuous, but would lead to your downfall, and others that are supposed to be wicked, but will lead to your welfare and peace of mind.

Analysis and Review Questions

1. Despite the gulp in time and cultures, what factors do Kautilya and Machiavelli find characterize strong rulers?
2. What role do "the people" play in the political process, as seen by Kautilya and Machiavelli?
3. Does either author support total and unlimited cruelty as a method of government?
4. Why do some empires succeed, and some fail?

CHAPTER 8

The West: The Middle Ages and the Crusades

The Crusades offer a unique perspective on the society and culture in the European Middle Ages and the relationship between Europe and other cultures. From the collapse of Roman power in the West in the fifth century until the eleventh century, the West was a backward and marginal region of Eurasia. Beginning in the eleventh century, however, European culture began expanding through conquest and colonization, and it began developing more sophisticated intellectual, economic, and political ideas and institutions.

The calling of the First Crusade in 1095 by Pope Urban II shows the emergence of several trends in the development of the West. The fact that European armies could operate successfully in foreign territory is evidence of new economic strength and population growth. The involvement of the papacy and royal households in organizing and leading the Crusades was part of an attempt by the Church and the upper nobility of Europe to bring greater political stability and construct more rational political structures. Finally, the Crusades spurred on the development of Western society by bringing Westerners into closer contact with the intellectual and economic resources of the more advanced Eastern cultures.

RULE OF ST. BENEDICT

About the Document

From the beginnings of Christianity, some believers attempted to live lives of radical self-denial and service, usually carried out within the context of the local church. After the legalization of Christianity, however, churches began to attract less intense, devoted members. For those who still desired a more intense religious life, the new model was the solitary holy man in the desert. When famous hermits began to gather groups of followers, rules were created for these communities.

Benedict of Nursia had become a monk after a career as a Roman soldier, and the influence of military structure and discipline is evident in his *Rule of*

St. Benedict. Written in the sixth century, it became the most important and influential rule for monastic communities in Western Christianity. Taking vows of poverty, chastity (renouncing marriage and sex), and obedience to the abbot (head of the monastery), monks lived a life revolving around scheduled, communal prayer, individual prayer and study, and manual labor. Not only did monks become the spiritual elite of the West, but, because there was a virtual monopoly on education after the fall of Roman power in the West, they dominated the intellectual and political culture of Europe for a thousand years.

The Document

What are the Instruments of Good Works.—

1. First Instrument: in the first place to love the Lord God with all one's heart, all one's soul, and all one's strength.
2. Then, one's neighbour as oneself.
3. Then not to kill.
4. Not to commit adultery.
5. Not to steal.
6. Not to covet.
7. Not to bear false witness.
8. To honour all men.
9. Not to do to another what one would not have done to oneself.
10. To deny oneself, in order to follow Christ.
11. To chastise the body.
12. Not to seek after delicate living.
13. To love fasting.
14. To relieve the poor.
15. To clothe the naked.
16. To visit the sick.
17. To bury the dead.
18. To help in affliction.
19. To console the sorrowing.
20. To keep aloof from worldly actions.
21. To prefer nothing to the love of Christ.
22. Not to gratify anger.
23. Not to harbour a desire of revenge.
24. Not to foster guile in one's heart.
25. Not to make a feigned peace.
26. Not to forsake charity.
27. Not to swear, lest perchance, one forswear oneself.
28. To utter truth from heart and mouth.
29. Not to render evil for evil.
30. To do no wrong to anyone, yea, to bear, patiently wrong done to oneself.
31. To love one's enemies.

32. Not to render cursing for cursing, but rather blessing.
33. To bear persecution for justice's sake.
34. Not to be proud.
35. Not given to wine.
36. Not a glutton.
37. Not drowsy.
38. Not slothful.
39. Not a murmurer.
40. Not a detractor.
41. To put one's hope in God.
42. To attribute any good that one sees in oneself to God and not to oneself.
43. But to recognize and always impute to oneself the evil that one does.
44. To fear the Day of Judgment.
45. To be in dread of hell.
46. To desire with all spiritual longing everlasting life.
47. To keep death daily before one's eyes.
48. To keep guard at all times over the actions of one's life.
49. To know for certain that God sees one everywhere.
50. To dash down at the feet of Christ one's evil thoughts, the instant that they come into the heart.
51. And to lay them open to one's spiritual father.
52. To keep one's mouth from evil and wicked words.
53. Not to love much speaking.
54. Not to speak vain words or such as move to laughter.
55. Not to love much or excessive laughter.
56. To listen willingly to holy reading.
57. To apply oneself frequently to prayer.
58. Daily to confess in prayer one's past sins with tears and sighs to God, and to amend them for the time to come.
59. Not to fulfill the desires of the flesh: to hate one's own will.
60. To obey in all things the commands of the Abbot, even though he himself (which God forbid) should act otherwise; being mindful of that precept of the Lord: "What they say, do ye; but what they do, do ye not."
61. Not to wish to be called holy before one is so: but first to be holy, that one may be truly so called.
62. Daily to fulfill by one's deeds the commandments of God.
63. To love chastity.
64. To hate no man.
65. Not to be jealous, nor to give way to envy.
66. Not to love strife.
67. To fly from vainglory.
68. To reverence seniors.
69. To love juniors.
70. To pray for one's enemies in the love of Christ.

71. To make peace with an adversary before the setting of the sun.
72. And never to despair of God's mercy.

Behold, these are the tools of the spiritual craft, which, if they be constantly employed day and night, and duly given back on the Day of Judgment, will gain for us from the Lord that reward which He Himself has promised—"which eye hath not seen, nor ear heard; nor hath it entered into the heart of man to conceive what God hath prepared for them that love him." And the workshop where we are to labour diligently at all these things is the cloister of the monastery, and stability in the community.

Of Obedience

The first degree of humility is obedience without delay. This becomes those who hold nothing dearer to them than Christ, and who on account of the holy servitude which they have taken upon them, and for fear of hell, and for the glory of life everlasting, as soon as anything is ordered by the superior, just as if it had been commanded by God Himself, are unable to bear delay in doing it. It is of these that the Lord says: "At the hearing of the ear he hath obeyed me." And again, to teachers he saith: "He that heareth you heareth me."

The Spirit of Silence

Let us do as says the prophet: "I said, I will take heed to my ways, that I sin not with my tongue: I have placed a watch over my mouth; I became dumb, and was silent, and held my peace even from good things." Here the prophet shows that if we ought to refrain even from good words for the sake of silence, how much more ought we to abstain from evil words, on account of the punishment due to sin!

Therefore, on account of the importance of silence, let leave to speak be seldom granted even to perfect disciples, although their conversation be good and holy and tending to edification; because it is written: "In much speaking thou shalt not avoid sin;" and elsewhere: "Death and life are in the power of the tongue." For it becomes the master to speak and to teach, but it beseems the disciple to be silent and to listen.

And, therefore, if anything has to be asked of a superior, let it be done with all humility and subjection of reverence, lest he seem to say more than is expedient.

But as for buffoonery or silly words, such as move to laughter, we utterly condemn them in every place, nor do we allow the disciple to open his mouth in such discourse.

Of Humility

The Holy Scripture cries out to us, brethren, saying: "Everyone that exalteth himself shall be humbled, and he that humbleth himself shall be exalted." In saying this, it teaches us that all exaltation is a kind of pride, against which the prophet shows himself to be on his guard when he says: "Lord, my heart is not exalted nor mine eyes lifted up: nor have I walked in great things, nor in wonders above me." Any why? "If I did not think humbly, but exalted my soul: like a child that is weaned from his mother, so wilt thou requite my soul."

Whence, brethren, if we wish to arrive at the highest point of humility and speedily to reach that heavenly exaltation to which we can only ascend by the humility of this present life, we must by our ever-ascending actions erect such a ladder as that which Jacob beheld his dream, by which the angels appeared to him descending and ascending. This descent and ascent signify nothing else than that we descend by exaltation and ascend by humility. And the ladder thus erected is our life in the world, which, if the heart be humbled, is lifted up by the Lord to heaven. The sides of the same ladder we understand to be our body and soul, in which the call of God has placed various degrees of humility or discipline, which we must ascend.

How the Monks Are to Sleep

Let them sleep each one in a separate bed, receiving bedding suitable to their manner of life, as the Abbot shall appoint.

If it be possible, let all sleep in one place; but if the number do not permit of this, let them repose by tens or twenties with the seniors who have charge of them. Let a candle burn constantly in the cell until morning.

Let them sleep clothed, and girded with belts or cords—but not with knives at their sides, lest perchance they wound themselves in their sleep—and thus be always ready, so that when the signal is given they rise without delay, and hasten each to forestall the other in going to the Work of God, yet with all gravity and modesty.

Let not the younger brethren have their beds by themselves, but among those of the seniors. And when they rise for the Work of God, let them gently encourage one another; because of the excuses of the drowsy.

Of the Daily Manual Labour

Idleness is the enemy of the soul. Therefore should the brethren be occupied at stated times in manual labour, and at other fixed hours in sacred reading.

We think, therefore, that the times for each may be disposed as follow: from Easter to the Calends of October, on coming out in the morning let them labour at whatever is necessary from the first until about the fourth hour. From the fourth hour until close upon the sixth let them apply themselves to reading. After the sixth hour, when they rise from table, let them rest on their beds in all silence; or if anyone chance to wish to read to himself, let him so read as not to disturb anyone else. Let None be said rather soon, at the middle of the eighth hour; and then let them again work at whatever has to be done until Vespers.

If, however, the needs of the place or poverty require them to labour themselves in gathering in the harvest, let them not grieve at that; for then are they truly monks when they live by the labour of their hands, as our Fathers and the Apostles did. But let all things be done in moderation for the sake of the faint-hearted.

From the Calends of October until the beginning of Lent let the brethren devote themselves to reading till the end of the second hour. At the second hour let Terce be said, after which they shall all labour at their appointed work until None. At the first signal for the hour of None all shall cease from their work, and be ready as soon as the second signal is sounded. After their meal let them occupy themselves in their reading or with the psalms.

Of the Reception of Guests

Let all guests that come be received like Christ Himself, for He will say: "I was a stranger and ye took me in." And let fitting honour be shown to all, especially, however, to such as are of the household of the faith and to pilgrims.

Analysis and Review Questions

1. In one or two sentences, describe Benedict's perfect monk.
2. What sorts of things are of most concern to Benedict in this document?
3. What does the rule imply about human nature?
4. What was the daily life of a monk like?
5. In the Middle Ages, monks were considered the ideal Christians. What would knowing this mean for a Medieval peasant or a warrior?

SUMMA DE LEGIBUS

About the Document

After the disintegration of the Carolingian Empire in the ninth century, politics in Western Europe became a matter of personal relationships between members of the warrior class. According to this arrangement, usually called feudalism, political power lay in the hands of those who could assert their strength through the ability to build fortified structures and field significant fighting forces. While a powerful warlord would have a number of soldiers who lived in his household, he also depended on "vassals" to come to his assistance in times of war. A vassal was a warrior who had sworn to submit to the authority of another, more powerful warrior. In return, the lord would provide the means for the vassal to maintain his own fighting force. This gift, called a fief, was typically a piece of land large enough to support the vassal and his men. In the twelfth and thirteenth centuries, kings and other powerful noblemen attempted to rationalize this arrangement into a legal system in order to create a more stable political structure. The following document, produced in the 1250s, is one such attempt to codify and organize the lord–vassal relationship in the northern French duchy of Normandy. It attempts to define the duties and responsibilities of lords and vassals. During this time, the kings of France kept the title and authority of Duke of Normandy to themselves.

Map 8.2
Medieval Trade Routes
and Trade Fairs

The Document

11. On the duke

1. The duke of Normandy or the prince is the one who holds the lordship [*principatum*] over the entire duchy. This dignity the lord king of France holds together with the other honors to which, with the aid of the Lord, he has been raised. From this it pertains to him to preserve the peace of the land, to correct the people by the rod of justice, and by the measure of equity to end private disputes.

Therefore, he should through the justiciars subject to him see to it that the people under his authority rejoice in the rule of justice and the tranquillity of peace. He should search out, capture, and keep in strong prisons, until they have received the wages of their crimes, robbers, thieves, arsonists, murderers, the violent deflowerers of virgins, rapers of women, committers of mayhem and other public disturbers, and others held in public infamy, who may cause damage to life or limb.

12. Concerning liege homage

1. The duke of Normandy ought to have liege homage or the loyalty of all the men of his entire province. From this they are bound to him against all men, who may live or die, to offer the assistance of their own body in counsel and in aid, and to show themselves to him inoffensive in all things, and in nothing to take the side of his adversaries.

2. He also is obligated to rule, protect, defend, and treat them according to the rights, customs, and laws of the land.

13. On fealty

1. All those living in the province are bound to do and to maintain fealty to the duke. For this they are bound to show themselves inoffensive and faithful to him in all things, and not to procure anything against his interests, nor to give counsel or aid to his manifest enemies. Whoever may be discovered to have violated this by evident cause should be reputed notorious traitors of the prince, and all their possessions shall forever remain to the prince, if for this they are convicted and condemned. For all men in Normandy are bound to observe fealty to the prince. Therefore, no one ought to receive homage or fealty from anyone else unless reserving higher fealty to the prince. This is also to be explicitly stated in receiving their fealty.

2. Between other lords and their vassals, faith ought so to be maintained that neither one of them ought to call for corporal violence or for violent blows against the person of another party. If any of them should be accused of this in court and convicted, he is bound altogether to lose his fief for violating the faith he was obligated to observe.

3. If this act should be discovered in a lord, homage should revert to his superior and dues should no longer be given, excepting what is owed the prince.

4. If, however, a vassal should be shown guilty of this, he shall be deprived of his land and right, which shall remain to the lord. It is of course understood that they will be clearly convicted of this in court, as the custom of Normandy requires.

Image 8.2
Dueling Crusaders

22. Concerning the army

1. Service in the army is to be done with arms for the benefit of the prince as it has been customary in fiefs and in towns. This service is for forty days in defense of the land and for the prince's need, when he sets forth in any expedition; those who hold fiefs or live in towns delegated for this service ought to and are bound to perform it. For all knight's fees [fiefs of a knight] instituted for the service of the duchy must fulfill this service; counties and baronies also, as well as all towns having a commune.

2. Knight's fees in the counties and baronies which were not established for the service of the duchy do not owe service in the army, but only to the lords to whom they are subjected, excepting, however, the general levy of the prince [*retrobanium*], to which all who are capable of bearing arms are bound to come without any excuse.

3. The general levy is said to occur when the duke of Normandy, in order to repel an attack of the enemy in any expedition, goes through Normandy and orders that all who are capable of wielding arms should arm themselves for his help, no matter in what sort of arms they may be found, in order to repel the enemy. However, after forty days are completed in the service of the prince, if the need of the prince should demand it, they shall remain in his service at the expense of the prince, as reason should require.

4. No one who owes this service may by any manner excuse himself from service in the army of the prince, unless by the evident impairment of his own body, and then he is bound to send a substitute who can perform for him the service which he owes.

5. At times the name of military aid is given to that monetary payment which the prince of Normandy allows his barons and knights to collect from their [subvassals] who hold from them a knight's fee or from their tenants on a knight's fee, if his barons and knights have served more than forty days. And they were not otherwise able to demand from their tenants a greater aid than that which was conceded to them by the prince of the Normans.

6. Concerning the fiefs which pertain to the duchy, if anyone should deny that any land or fief is of this sort, inquiry ought to be made through the prince or his bailiffs concerning the truth of the matter without any exception; since the service of these fiefs belongs to the duke, in any diminution of a fief not providing due service the duke may suffer damage. If it is decided that it is a knight's fee, the one holding it is bound to do that service to the prince according to the size of his possession. And this is to be understood not only concerning the fiefs of the prince, but also the fiefs of the barons which pertain to the duchy.

7. It is to be noted also that the barons hold certain fiefs assigned to the service of the duke; they were established before these baronies were granted. These types of fiefs must fulfill service with the barons; whoever does this service fulfills it at the prince's will.

8. The barons ought not to have from the other fiefs, which were not established for the service of the duchy, more than the aid conceded by the prince, as has been said. If perchance they have fiefs so constituted so that one or two, three, or four or more of them ought to provide the service of a single knight for the duke, each of them according to its size should perform and pay a portion of the service, as the barons and the knights may assign to them. Nevertheless, each of them shall be bound to relief and aid for the service of their lords. For although fiefs of this sort are considered as a single unit in regard to the duke's service, nonetheless they are many in relation to the homage owed their lord, and each of them in this respect retains the dignity of a single fief.

9. From all this it is evident that not without reason at the time of English rule it was customary in Normandy that all men holding a knight's fee were bound to possess a horse and armor and that, when they reached the age of twenty-one, they were bound to be enlisted among the knights, so that they would be found ready and prepared at the command of the prince or of their lords.

26. On tenures

1. Concerning tenures the following is to be done.
The tenure is the manner by which tenements are held from their lords.

2. Certain tenures are held through homage, others through parage, others through burgage, and others through alms.

3. Fiefs held through homage are those in which the observance of faith between the lord and his vassal is expressly promised, reserving the higher faith due to the duke of Normandy. This is received from the lord with his hands outstretched and the hands of the one making the homage placed between them; this is explained more fully in the following chapter.

4. Fiefs are held through parage when a brother or a relative receives a part of the inheritances of his ancestors, which he holds from an older relative. The older relative is in turn responsible for all the individual obligations which the portions of the fief require and which are due to its principal lords. This is made clear below.

5. By burgage are held allods and tenures established in cities which have the customs of burgesses.

6. In alms are held lands given in charity to churches.

7. Besides these, in different parts of Normandy exist fiefs held by bordage, when a cottage is given to anyone for the performance of servile labors and mean services. This holding cannot be sold or given or pledged by the one who received it in inheritance under this sort of tenure, and he does not do homage.

8. There are also held certain free tenements without homage or parage in lay fief. This situation results from an agreement made between certain persons. For example, if a person holds a fief paying twenty shillings a year, and gives half of it to a third party, that third party holds it from him and not from [the lord who] holds homage over it. The third party shall perform no homage as the total fief is considered to be held by a single homage from the lord. This kind of tenure is called voluntary, since it results from the wishes of the ones giving and receiving it and not from the necessity of inheritance.

9. It is also to be noted that certain tenures are of monetary payments, as when someone holds a rent assigned to him while the land remains to the one who holds it.

Certain tenures are of land, such as when one holds of another the fief of the land of another.

Certain tenures are of an office, such as when one holds a certain office from another, for example, holding a warren or a privilege in forests, in markets, or in other places, or holding a sergeancy, or a fine or anything else, which are held from the lords without the possession of lands.

27. On homage

1. Now homage is to be considered. Homage is the promise of keeping faith, offering no obstruction in just and necessary things but rather providing counsel and aid. It is performed by extending and joining the hands and placing them within the hands of the one receiving homage, with these words: "I become your vassal to bear for you faith against all others, reserving only the fealty owed to the duke of Normandy."

2. It is to be noted that a certain type of homage concerns a fief, another type faith and service, and another type the preservation of the peace.

3. Homage concerning a fief is performed in the manner described above.

4. Homage concerning faith and service is performed when one person receives another as his vassal who is to keep faith to him and to give him service of his own body, to fight for him if necessary, and to do other service of this sort. And if, in return for this, he gives him a pension, this shall not pass on to his heirs unless it is explicitly stated by a condition made between them. Also, if the one serving should perchance succumb while fighting for the other, the pension shall revert to the lord. It is to be understood that he shall hold for his entire life that fief which was conferred upon him by his lord, for whom, upon entering a fight, he succumbed on the field.

And this type of homage is done in the manner described above, with, however, these added words: "Reserving faith to all my other lords."

5. A homage is also sometimes performed for preserving the peace; it is called homage of payment [*paga*], because it was performed as a pledge of peace between certain persons, such as when one person pursues another for any criminal act and peace is agreed on between them, so that the one who prosecuted does homage to the other for conserving that peace. This sort of homage is received as a pledge agreed upon.

And this type of homage is performed in the manner described above with, however, these words stated and heard: "Saving the faith of all my other lords and especially for preserving the peace."

6. In homage it is also implied that the vassal be a guarantor to the lords. For the vassal is bound to provide security for his lord in any court if he should be prosecuted

for personal injury and shall appear before a justice at the assigned time. He should extend to the lord a sum equal to the rent he owes him for one year, from his movables, pledges to be paid, debts, and loans.

7. The lord has the right of judgment over all the fiefs which are held from him, whether they are held indirectly or directly.

For certain fiefs are held directly of the lords, as are those which a man holds from his lord, with no other person between them.

Those fiefs are held indirectly when some person comes between the lord and the tenant. And by this manner, all descendants hold fiefs through an older relative, and all tenants hold fiefs under a vassal who is bound by homage to the lord.

8. No one can do justice upon the fief of another unless it is held from him.

9. It should also be noted that no one may sell or pledge the land which he holds of the lord through homage without the special consent of the lord. In regard to a third part or less, many have been accustomed to sell or pledge land, since enough land remained for them in fief through which they were able to fulfill and pay fully to their lords all rights, services, jurisdictions, and offices.

Analysis and Review Questions

1. What are the rights and responsibilities of the duke?
2. What are the rights and responsibilities of the vassals of the duke of Normandy?
3. What is fealty? What is homage? How are they different?
4. Law codes portray the values of the lawgiver(s). What does this law code say about the values of its authors (lawyers working for the king of France)?
5. Law codes also tell us something about the problems a particular society is facing. What sorts of problems are being addressed in this document?

ANNA COMNENA, *THE ALEXIAD*

About the Document

Anna Comnena, the daughter of the Byzantine Emperor Alexius I, was 14 years old when the Crusaders arrived in Constantinople in 1096. After the death of her husband in 1137, she turned her extensive literary education to writing a history of her father's reign. Although Anna claimed to be writing an objective history, it is not a very reliable source for reconstructing events. Writing from memory 40 years after the event, she left many details fuzzy. The title of the work, the *Alexiad*, also gives us clues as to the purpose of the work. Anna was consciously referring to Homer's epic the *Iliad* and was trying to portray her father in heroic terms. Even so, this is one of the most important sources we have of the Crusades.

The Document

Before [the Byzantine emperor] had enjoyed even a short rest, he heard a report of the approach of innumerable Frankish armies. Now he dreaded their arrival for he knew their irresistible manner of attack, their unstable and mobile character and all the peculiar natural and concomitant characteristics which the Frank retains throughout; and he also knew that they were always agape for money, and seemed to disregard their truces readily for any reason that cropped up. For he had always heard this reported of them, and found it very true. However, he did not lose heart, but prepared himself in every way so that, when the occasion called, he would be ready for battle. And indeed the actual facts were far greater and more terrible than rumor made them. For the whole of the West and all the barbarian tribes which dwell between the further side of the Adriatic and the pillars of Heracles, had all migrated in a body and were marching into Asia through the intervening Europe, and were making the journey with all their household. . . . And they were all so zealous and eager that every highroad was full of them. And those Frankish soldiers were accompanied by an unarmed host more numerous than the sand or the stars, carrying palms and crosses on their shoulders; women and children, too, came away from their countries. And the sight of them was like many rivers streaming from all sides, and they were advancing towards us through Dacia generally with all their hosts. . . .

The incidents of the barbarians approach followed in the order I have described, and persons of intelligence could feel that they were witnessing a strange occurrence. The arrival of these multitudes did not take place at the same time nor by the same road (for how indeed could such masses starting from different places have crossed the straits of Lombardy all together?). Some first, some next, others after them and thus successively all accomplished the transit, and then marched through the continent. Each army was preceded, as we said, by an unspeakable number of locusts; and all who saw this more than once recognized them as forerunners of the Frankish armies.

. . .

But though the Emperor wished to attach himself to the Gauls and advance with them against the barbarians, yet, fearing their countless multitude, he decided to go to *Pelecanum,* in order that by camping near Nicaea he might learn what was happening to the Gauls, and also learn the undertakings of the Turks outside, as well as the conditions in the city. . . .

The august Emperor tarried about *Pelacanum* for some time, since he desired those Galliec counts who were not yet bound to him also to take the oath of loyalty. To this end, he sent a letter to Butumites, asking all the counts in common not to start upon the journey to Antioch until they had said farewell to the Emperor. If they did this, they would all be showered with new gifts by him. Bohemund was the first to prick up his ears at the mention of money and gifts. Quickly won by these words of Butumites, he strove industriously to force all the others to return to the Emperor—so greatly did cupidity move the man. The Emperor received them on their arrival at *Pelecanum* with magnificence and the greatest show of good-will. At length, when they were assembled, he addressed them thus: "You know that you have all bound yourselves to me by oath; if you do not now intend to ignore this, advise and persuade those of your number who have not yet pledged faith to take the oath." They immediately summoned the counts who had not sworn. All of these came together and took the oath.

Tancred, however, nephew of Bohemund and a youth of most independent spirit, professed that he owed faith to Bohemund alone, and would serve him even to death. Rebuked by the loud protest of those of his own fellows who stood near, and of the Emperor's retinue, besides, he turned toward the tent in which the Emperor was then dwelling—the largest and most capacious which anyone has ever seen—and, as if to make sport of them, said, "If you give me this (tent) full of money and, in addition, all the other presents which you gave all the counts, I, too, will take the oath." But Palaeologus, full of zeal for the Emperor, could not endure the mocking speech of Tancred and pushed him away with contempt. Then Tancred, very ready with his arms, sprang upon him. Seeing this, the Emperor arose hastily from his seat and stood between them. Bohemund, too, restrained the youth, saying "It is not fitting shamefully to strike the kinsman of the Emperor." Then Tancred, recognizing the disgrace of his insolence toward Palaeologus, and persuaded by the advice of Bohemund and the others, offered to take the oath himself. . . .

Analysis and Review Questions

1. Alexius had asked the pope to raise military support against the Turks. What did he get?
2. How does Anna describe the Franks?
3. What does her description of the Franks tell us about her own values and assumptions?
4. If the *Alexiad* is not an accurate account, what can we learn from it?

WEB LINKS

http://longmanworldhistory.com
The following additional readings and case studies can be found on the Web site.
Document 8.1, Fulcher of Chartres, Chronicle of the First Crusade
Document 8.3, Song of Roland
Case Study 8.1, Monks and Warriors
Case Study 8.2, Competing Visions of Knighthood
Case Study 8.3, A Byzantine's View of the Crusades

http://orb.rhodes.edu
ORB is the most important and extensive site for Medieval studies on the Web. It has excellent material on the Crusades.

http://cedar.evansville.edu~ecoleweb/
This is an exhaustive collection of documents and images pertaining to the Medieval Church, including the Crusades. It also contains helpful articles.

http://www.Fordham.edu/halsall/sbook.html
This site, together with the previous two, offers the most comprehensive and trustworthy information about the Middle Ages on the Web. The Medieval Sourcebook contains documents, maps, images, and good external links.

http://jeru.huji.ac.il/open_screen2.htm
A virtual history of Jerusalem, this site provides a Middle Eastern perspective on the Crusades.

http://www.philippe-auguste.com/uk/Index.html
An insightful glimpse into life in a Medieval town.

Map 9.2
The Byzantine Empire
Under Justinian

CHAPTER 9

Byzantium and Early Russia: The Orthodox Tradition

The notion of "separation of church and state" is a very recent and uniquely Western concept. In stark contrast to this notion stands the Orthodox tradition of intertwined political and religious authority. That tradition has made the history of the Byzantine and Russian Empires dramatically different from the Western tradition in terms of politics, culture, and society.

The documents included here highlight critical choices made by Byzantine and Russian rulers, how Orthodoxy influenced those decisions, and how those choices shaped the subsequent evolution of Orthodoxy. Also included are documents describing the transition of Orthodoxy's center of power from Byzantium to Kiev to Moscow, with all of the relevant political and religious implications of that shift. The combination of political and religious authority in the Orthodox world created a synergy—an authority greater than the sum of its parts. That synergy later took on concrete form as Russian autocracy. The legacy of that autocracy continues to shape Russian history today.

Image 9.1
Emperor Justinian

EUSEBIUS ON THE VISION AND VICTORY OF CONSTANTINE I (THE GREAT)

About the Document

Eusebius was a Christian historian who believed that Earth mirrored heaven. Therefore, God simultaneously designed the Roman Empire and the Christian Church. The "Roman Peace" of the Empire was a pale precursor to the heavenly peace of Christ.

Eusebius wrote of Constantine I's decision to adopt Christianity within the context of Constantine's conflict with Maxentius. This contest for control of Rome and the Italian peninsula in 312 C.E. culminated in Constantine's victory over Maxentius at the Milvian Bridge.

Eusebius's description must be regarded as controversial. Constantine himself never mentioned his "vision" to anyone (other than, obviously, Eusebius, who met Constantine at the Council of Nicea in 325). Whatever its historical accuracy, the vision nevertheless marks a watershed in world history. Although Constantine himself would not be baptized for many years after the "vision," he issued the Edict of Milan within one year of the battle, granting Christianity legitimate status throughout the Empire.

The Document

THE VISION OF CONSTANTINE I THE GREAT

Now, Constantine looked upon all the world as one vast body. But he observed that the head of it all, the imperial city of the Roman Empire, was oppressed by a tyrannous slavery. He had at first left the task of its protection to the rulers of the other parts of the Empire. After all, they were older than he was. But when none of these was able to provide help, when those attempting to do so were stopped in a disastrous manner, he declared that life was not worth living as long as he saw the imperial city thus afflicted. He therefore began preparations to overthrow the tyranny.

He knew well that he needed more powerful help than he could get from his army. This was on account of the evil practices and magical tricks which were so favored by the tyrant. Constantine therefore sought the help of God. Armed men and soldiers were of secondary importance when compared with God's aid, he believed, and he considered that the assistance of God was invincible and unshakable. But on which god could he depend as an ally? That was his problem. As he pondered the question, a thought occurred to him. Of his numerous imperial predecessors, those who had put their hopes in a multitude of gods and had served them with libations and sacrificial offerings were first of all deceived by flattering prophecies, by oracles promising success to them, and still had come to a bad end. None of their gods stood by them or warned them of the catastrophe about to afflict them. On the other hand, his own father, who had been the only one to follow the opposite course and denounce their error, had given honor to almighty God throughout his life and had found in Him a savior, a protector of his Empire, and the provider of all good things.

As he pondered this matter, he reflected that those who had trusted in a multitude of gods had been brought low by many forms of death. They had left neither family nor offspring, stock, name, nor memorial among men. But the God of his father had given him clear and numerous indications of His power. Constantine furthermore considered the fact that those who had earlier sought to campaign against the tyrant and had gone to battle accompanied by a great number of gods had suffered a disgraceful end. One of them shamefully retreated from an encounter without striking a blow. The other was fair game for death and was killed among his own soldiers. Constantine thought of all these things, and decided that it would be stupid to join in the empty worship of those who were no gods and to stray from truth after observing all this positive evidence. He decided that only the God of his father ought to be worshiped.

He prayed to Him, therefore. He asked Him and besought Him to say Who He was and to stretch forth a hand to him in his present situation. As he prayed in this fashion and as he earnestly gave voice to his entreaties, a most marvelous sign appeared to the Emperor from God. It would have been hard to believe if anyone else had spoken of it. But a long time later the triumphant Emperor himself described it to the writer of this work. This was when I had the honor of knowing him and of being in his company. When he told me the story, he swore to its truth. And who could refuse to believe it, especially when later evidence showed it to have been genuine?

Around noontime, when the day was already beginning to decline, he saw before him in the sky the sign of a cross of light. He said it was above the sun and it bore the inscription, "Conquer with this." The vision astounded him, as it astounded the whole army which was with him on this expedition and which also beheld the miraculous event.

He said he became disturbed. What could the vision mean? He continued to ponder and to give great thought to the question, and night came on him suddenly. When he was asleep, the Christ of God appeared to him and He brought with Him the sign which had appeared in the sky. He ordered Constantine to make a replica of this sign which he had witnessed in the sky, and he was to use it as a protection during his encounters with the enemy.

In the morning he told his friends of this extraordinary occurrence. Then he summoned those who worked with gold or precious stones, and he sat among them and described the appearance of the sign. He told them to represent it in gold and precious stones.

It was made in the following way. There was a long spear, covered with gold, and forming the shape of the Cross through having a transverse bar overlaying it. Over it all there was a wreath made of gold and precious stones. Within it was the symbol of the Savior's name, two letters to show the beginning of Christ's name. And the letter *P* was divided at the center by *X*. Later on, the Emperor adopted the habit of wearing these insignia on his helmet. . . .

The Emperor regularly used this saving symbol as a protection against every contrary and hostile power. Copies of it were carried by his command at the head of all his armies.

Constantine's Victory Over Maxentius at the Milvian Bridge

Constantine was the leading emperor in rank and dignity, and he was the first to show pity on the victims of tyranny at Rome. He prayed the God of heaven and Jesus Christ, the Savior of all, to be his allies, and with all his forces he marched to restore to the Romans their ancient liberty. Maxentius, of course, relied more upon the devices of magic than on the goodwill of his subjects. Indeed, he lacked the courage to go even beyond the city gates. Instead, he employed a numberless crowd of heavy-armed soldiers and countless legionary bands to secure every place, every region, and every city which had been enslaved by him in the neighborhood of Rome and throughout Italy. But the Emperor, who trusted in the alliance of God, attacked the first, second, and third of the tyrant's armies and easily captured them. He advanced over a great part of Italy and drew very close to Rome itself.

Forestalling the need to fight Romans on account of the tyrant, God Himself, as though using chains, dragged the tyrant far away from the gates of the city. Just as in the days of Moses himself and of the ancient godly race of Hebrews, "He cast into the sea the chariots and the host of Pharaoh, his chosen horsemen and his captains, and they sank in the Red Sea and the deep concealed them." In the same way, Maxentius, with the armed soldiers and guards who surrounded him, "sank into the depths like a stone." This happened while he was fleeing before the God-sent power of Constantine and while he was crossing the river that lay before his path. By joining the boats together, he had efficiently bridged this river, and yet by doing so he had forged an instrument of destruction for himself. . . . For the bridge over the river broke down and the passage across collapsed. At once the boats, men and all, sank into the deep, and the first to go was that most wicked man himself.

Analysis and Review Questions

1. Why did Constantine believe that he needed "more powerful help than he could get from his army," and why did he search for divine help? What advantages could the adoption of the Christian God bestow on Constantine and his army?
2. If the "whole army" also saw the miraculous vision of Constantine, why did the Emperor wait until "a long time later" to describe it to Eusebius?
3. What does the appearance to Constantine of "the Christ of God" to explain the vision say about the status and legitimacy of the Emperor?
4. Either Maxentius was "dragged" away from Rome to the Milvian bridge by "God himself," or he was "fleeing the God-sent power of Constantine." Why might this document include both of these seemingly contradictory descriptions?
5. What purposes may be served by Eusebius's comparison of Maxentius's defeat to the parting of the Red Sea in Moses' time?

Map 9.1
(Interactive)
The Rise of Moscow

VLADIMIR OF KIEV'S ACCEPTANCE OF CHRISTIANITY

About the Document

By the late tenth century, an increasingly powerful confederation of principalities developed control over the strategic trade route that ran from the Baltic Sea to Constantinople. Centered in the city of Kiev on the Dniepr River, this confederation featured a mixture of Slavic and Scandinavian cultures.

Earlier in the tenth century, the "Russes," as the people of the Kievan confederation were known, had established lively relations with Byzantium through a combination of trade, military conquest, and, occasionally, military cooperation. By the middle 980s, the Byzantine emperor faced several challenges from would-be usurpers. In the midst of this civil strife, emissaries from Kiev arrived, seeking information about the Greek faith, which had been introduced into Kievan lands but had remained just one of many faiths practiced along the Dniepr.

This document is taken from *The Russian Primary Chronicle,* compiled by Russian scholars in the eleventh and twelfth centuries.

The Document

6495 (987). Vladimir summoned together his vassals and the city elders, and said to them, "Behold, the Bulgarians came before me urging me to accept their religion. Then came the Germans and praised their own faith; and after them came the Jews. Finally the Greeks appeared, criticizing all other faiths but commending their own, and they spoke at length, telling the history of the whole world from its beginning. Their words were artful, and it was wondrous to listen and pleasant to hear them. They preach the existence of another world. 'Whoever adopts our religion and then dies shall arise and live forever. But whosoever embraces another faith, shall be consumed with fire in the next world.' What is your opinion on this subject, and what do you answer?" The vassals and the elders replied, "You know, oh Prince, that no man condemns his own possessions, but praises them instead. If you desire to make certain, you have servants at your disposal. Send them to inquire about the ritual of each and how he worships God."

Their counsel pleased the Prince and all the people, so that they chose good and wise men to the number of ten, and directed them to go first among the Bulgarians and inspect their faith. The emissaries went their way, and when they arrived at their destination they beheld the disgraceful actions of the Bulgarians and their worship in the mosque; then they returned to their own country. Vladimir then instructed them to go likewise among the Germans, and examine their faith, and finally to visit the Greeks. They thus went into Germany, and after viewing the German ceremonial, they proceeded to Tsargrad,° where they appeared before the Emperor. He inquired on what mission they had come, and they reported to him all that had occurred. When the Emperor heard their words, he rejoiced, and did them great honor on that very day.

On the morrow, the Emperor sent a message to the Patriarch to inform him that a Russian delegation had arrived to examine the Greek faith, and directed him to prepare the church and the clergy, and to array himself in his sacerdotal robes, so that the Russes might behold the glory of the God of the Greeks. When the Patriarch received these commands, he bade the clergy assemble, and they performed the customary rites. They burned incense, and the choirs sang hymns. The Emperor accompanied the Russes to the church, and placed them in a wide space, calling their attention to the beauty of the edifice, the chanting, and the offices of the archpriest and the ministry of the deacons, while he explained to them the worship of his God. The Russes were astonished and in their wonder praised the Greek ceremonial. Then the Emperors Basil and Constantine invited the envoys to their presence, and said, "Go hence to your native country," and thus dismissed them with valuable presents and great honor.

Thus they returned to their own country, and the Prince called together his vassals and the elders. Vladimir then announced the return of the envoys who had been sent out, and suggested that their report be heard. He thus commanded them to speak out before his vassals. The envoys reported, "When we journeyed among the Bulgarians, we beheld how they worship in their temple, called a mosque, while they stand ungirt. The Bulgarian bows, sits down, looks hither and thither like one possessed, and there is no happiness among them, but instead only sorrow and a dreadful stench. Their religion is not good. Then we went among the Germans, and saw them performing many ceremonies in their temples; but we beheld no glory there. Then we went on to Greece, and the Greeks led us to the edifices where they worship their God, and we knew not whether we were in heaven or on earth. For on earth there is no such splendor or such beauty, and we are at a loss how to describe it. We only know that God dwells there among men, and their service is fairer than the ceremonies of other nations. For we cannot forget that beauty. Every man, after tasting something sweet, is afterward unwilling to accept that which is bitter, and therefore we cannot dwell longer here." Then the vassals spoke and said, "If the Greek faith were evil, it would not have been adopted by your grandmother Olga, who was wiser than all other men." Vladimir then inquired where they should all accept baptism, and they replied that the decision rested with him.

After a year had passed, in 6496 (988), Vladimir marched with an armed force against Kherson, a Greek city. . . . Vladimir and his retinue entered the city, and he sent messages to the Emperors Basil and Constantine, saying, "Behold, I have captured your glorious city. I have also heard that you have an unwedded sister. Unless you give her to me to wife, I shall deal with your own city as I have Kherson." When the Emperors heard this message, they were troubled, and replied, "It is not meet for Christians to give in marriage to pagans. If you are baptized, you shall have her to wife, inherit the

Tsargrad: Constantinople.

kingdom of God, and be our companion in the faith. Unless you do so, however, we cannot give you our sister in marriage." When Vladimir learned their response, he directed the envoys of the Emperors to report to the latter that he was willing to accept baptism, having already given some study to their religion, and that the Greek faith and ritual, as described by the emissaries sent to examine it, had pleased him well. When the Emperors heard this report, they rejoiced, and persuaded their sister Anna to consent to the match. They then requested Vladimir to submit to baptism before they should send their sister to him, but Vladimir desired that the princess should herself bring priests to baptize him. . . .

*Image 9.2
Twelfth Century
Image of Christ*

By divine agency, Vladimir was suffering at that moment from a disease of the eyes, and could see nothing, being in great distress. The Princess declared to him that if he desired to be relieved of this disease, he should be baptized with all speed, otherwise it could not be cured. When Vladimir heard her message, he said, "If this proves true, then of a surety is the God of the Christians great," and gave orders that he should be baptized. The Bishop of Kherson, together with the Princess's priests, after announcing the tidings, baptized Vladimir, and as the Bishop laid his hand upon him, he straightway received his sight. Upon experiencing this miraculous cure, Vladimir glorified God, saying, "I have now perceived the one true God." When his followers beheld this miracle, many of them were also baptized.

Vladimir was baptized in the Church of St. Basil, which stands at Kherson upon a square in the center of the city, where the Khersonians trade. The palace of Vladimir stands beside this church to this day, and the palace of the Princess is behind the altar. After his baptism, Vladimir took the Princess in marriage. Those who do not know the truth say he was baptized in Kiev, while others assert this event took place in Vasiliev, while still others mention other places.

After Vladimir was baptized, the priests explained to him the tenets of the Christian faith, urging him to avoid the deceit of heretics. . . .

When the Prince arrived at his capital, he directed that the idols should be overthrown, and that some should be cut to pieces and others burned with fire. He thus ordered that Perun [the god of thunder] should be bound to a horse's tail and dragged along Borichev to the river. He appointed twelve men to beat the idol with sticks, not because he thought the wood was sensitive, but to affront the demon who had deceived man in this guise, that he might receive chastisement at the hands of men. . . . While the idol was being dragged along the stream to the Dnieper, the unbelievers wept over it, for they had not yet received holy baptism. After they had thus dragged the idol along, they cast it into the Dnieper. But Vladimir had given this injunction, "If it halts anywhere, then push it out from the bank, until it goes over the falls. Then let it loose." His command was duly obeyed. . . .

Thereafter Vladimir sent heralds throughout the whole city to proclaim that if any inhabitant, rich or poor, did not betake himself to the river, he would risk the Prince's displeasure. When the people heard these words, they wept for joy, and exclaimed in their enthusiasm, "If this were not good, the Prince and his *boyars*° would not have accepted it." On the morrow, the Prince went forth to the Dnieper with the priests of the Princess and those from Kherson, and a countless multitude assembled. They all went into the water; some stood up to their necks, others to their breasts, the younger near the bank, some of them holding children in their arms, while the adults waded farther out. The priests stood by and offered prayers. . . .

---

boyars: Nobles descended from the elite war bands serving with the king.

When the people were baptized, they returned each to his own abode. Vladimir, rejoicing that he and his subjects now knew God himself, . . . ordained that churches should be built and established where pagan idols had previously stood. He thus founded the Church of St. Basil on the hill where the idol of Perun° and the other images had been set, and where the Prince and the people had offered their sacrifices. He began to found churches and to assign priests throughout the cities, and to invite the people to accept baptism in all the cities and towns. . . .

[6502–6504 (994–996)] . . . [Vladimir] invited each beggar and poor man to come to the Prince's palace and receive whatever he needed, both food and drink, and marten skins from the treasury.

. . .

With the thought that the weak and the sick could not easily reach his palace, he arranged that wagons should be brought in, and after having them loaded with bread, meat, fish, various fruits, mead in casks, and *kvass,*° he ordered them driven out through the city. The drivers were under instruction to call out, "Where is there a poor man or a begger who cannot walk?" To such they distributed according to their necessities. . . .

While Vladimir was thus dwelling in the fear of God, the number of bandits increased, and the bishops, calling to his attention the multiplication of robbers, inquired why he did not punish them. The Prince answered that he feared the sin entailed. They replied that he was appointed of God for the chastisement of malefactors and for the practice of mercy toward the righteous, so that it was entirely fitting for him to punish a robber condignly, but only after due process of law. Vladimir accordingly abolished *wergild*° and set out to punish the brigands. The bishops and the elders then suggested that as wars were frequent, the wergild might be properly spent for the purchase of arms and horses, to which Vladimir assented. Thus Vladimir lived according to the prescriptions of his father and his grandfather. . . .

When the people heard of this [Vladimir's death on July 15, 1015], they assembled in multitudes and mourned him, the boyars as the defender of their country, the poor as their protector and benefactor. They laid him in a marble coffin and preserved the body of the blessed Prince amid their mourning.

He is the new Constantine of mighty Rome, who baptized himself and his subjects; for the Prince of Rus imitated the acts of Constantine himself. . . . Vladimir died in the orthodox faith. He effaced his sins by repentance and by almsgiving, which is better than all things else.

Analysis and Review Questions

1. What does this document say about the relationship between the Grand Prince of Kiev (Vladimir) and his closest advisors? Subsequently, what kind of relationship existed between the Grand Prince, his elite, and their subjects?

2. Why might the chronicler describe the reception of the Russian envoys by the Byzantine Emperor in so much more detail than the receptions they received in Bulgaria and Germany?

kvass: Traditional Russian fermented beer-like drink.
wergild: The value placed on the life of a murdered person to be paid to his family or lord.
Perun: The Russian pagan god of Thunder and creator of Fire.

3. Having already agreed in principle to accept the Orthodox faith, Vladimir later attacked the Byzantine city of Kherson and demanded the hand of the Emperor's sister. When the Emperor conditionally agreed, Vladimir demanded that the princess accompany priests to his baptism and subsequent wedding. What does this account demonstrate about the relative power of Kiev and Byzantium?

4. How does Vladimir demonstrate the supposed superiority of his newfound Christianity over the traditional pagan beliefs of his people?

5. The final sections of the document describe the benevolence of Vladimir toward his poorest subjects and the evolution of his position on law enforcement. How do these sections relate to the evolution of princely authority in Russia?

NESTOR-ISKANDER ON THE FALL OF CONSTANTINOPLE

About the Document

Nestor-Iskander was, insofar as we know, a Slav of Orthodox background who converted to Islam. His account of the fall of Constantinople has been preserved in Russian language sources, and it tells the story of the battle from the Byzantine perspective—that is, from inside the city. Nestor-Iskander apparently was actually present for the siege and fall of the city.

This document paints a noble picture of the Byzantine Emperor, Constantine XI. More importantly, it highlights the intimate relationship between the Byzantine ruler, the Orthodox Church, and the elite of Byzantine society.

Nestor-Iskander concludes his tale by mentioning an old Byzantine "prophecy" that held that one day a people called the *rhusios* would gain control of Constantinople. Russian sources interpreted *rhusios*, which in Greek means "red-haired," as *russkii*, which means Russian. This "prophecy" would inspire some Russians to understand that Russia would take Constantinople's place as the heir of Rome and the seat of true Christianity.

The Document

The godless [Sultan] Mohammed [II, 1451–1481], son of Murad [II, 1421–1451], who at that time ruled the Turks, took note of all the problems [that plagued Constantinople]. And, although he professed peace, he wanted to put an end to Emperor Constantine [XI, 1449–1453]. Towards that end he assembled a large army and, by land and by sea, suddenly appeared with that large force before the city [of Constantinople] and laid siege to it. [The Emperor], therefore, sent his envoys to Sultan Mohammed in order to discuss peace and past [relations]. But Mohammed did not trust them, and as soon as the envoys departed, he ordered cannons and guns to fire at the city. Others were commanded to make ready wall-scaling equipment and build assault structures. Such city inhabitants as Greek, Venetian, and Genoese [mercenaries] left because they did not want to fight the Turks. . . .

When the Emperor saw this [exodus], he ordered his nobles and high officials to assign the remaining soldiers to each sector of the city's wall, to main gates, and to windows. The entire population was mobilized and alarm bells were hoisted throughout the city. Each person was informed of his assignment and each was told to defend his country. All were organized into a fighting force to battle the Turks from city walls and no one was allowed to leave the city. They also placed cannons and guns in strategic places to defend city walls. The Emperor, the Patriarch, bishops, priests, and the entire church council, as well as a multitude of women and children, attended church service, where they prayed, cried, and lamented. . . . The Emperor frequently travelled around the city, encouraging his military leaders, soldiers, and all inhabitants, telling them to have faith, not to allow themselves to be disheartened by enemy pressure, and to trust Almighty God, their Savior and Protector. He also implored them to pray. Meanwhile, day and night, the Turks bombarded all parts of the city without stopping, and gave its defenders no time to rest.

On the fourteenth day, after they had said their heathen prayers, the Turks sounded trumpets, beat their drums, and played on all other of their musical instruments. Because of continued heavy shooting, city defenders could not stand safely on the wall. Some crouched down awaiting the attack; others fired their cannons and guns as much as they could, killing many Turks. The Patriarch, bishops, and all clergy prayed constantly, pleading for God's mercy and for [His help in] saving the city.

When the Turks surmised that they had killed all the defenders on the wall, they ordered their forces to give a loud shout [before the assault]. Some soldiers carried incendiary devices, others ladders, still others wall-destroying equipment, and the rest many other instruments of destruction. They were ordered to attack and capture the city. City defenders, too, cried out and shouted back and engaged them in a fierce battle. The Emperor toured the city, encouraging his people, promising them God's help and ordering the ringing of church bells so as to summon all the inhabitants [to defend their city]. When the Turks heard the ringing of church bells, they ordered their trumpets, flutes, and thousands of other musical instruments to sound out. And there was a great and terrible slaughter! . . .

When Mohammed saw such a multitude of his men killed, and when he was told of Emperor's bravery, he could not sleep. [On May 27, 1453] he called in his Council and informed them that he wanted to lift the siege that night, before a large [Papal] fleet arrived in the city to reinforce [its defenses]. But then there appeared an unexpected miracle of God! The anticipated [Papal] help failed to materialize. Instead, at 7:00 p.m. that evening the entire city was suddenly engulfed by a great darkness. The air suddenly thickened and, in a moaning way, it hovered above the city. Then, big black drops of rain, as large as the eye of a buffalo, began to fall. People were shocked and horrified by this unusual occurrence. Patriarch Athanasius gathered all of his clergy and members of the Imperial Council, went to the Emperor, and told him the following: "Your Illustrious Majesty! All citizens of the city believe in its vitality. But they also think that the Holy Spirit has abandoned it. Now every living creature is foretelling the demise of this city. We beseech you to leave the city. All of us will perish here. For God's sake, please leave!". . . The Emperor did not listen to them. He replied instead: "Let God's will be done!"

When he saw that the great darkness engulfed the city, the impious Mohammed called in his learned men and dignitaries and asked them to explain: "What is the meaning of the sudden darkness that descended upon the city?" And they replied: "This is an important sign portending the demise of the city."

. . . [At that moment] a Turkish military governor, whose large force was deployed on the eastern flank, attacked the Greeks. His action divided Greek forces and forced them to retreat. He even captured their standards and advanced against the Emperor.

The Emperor positioned his shield in a defensive position, knocked out [the Turk's] lance, and struck and cut off the enemy's head with his sword. When Turkish soldiers saw this they were shocked and carried away the corpse of their dead leader.

. . . When Mohammed learned about the death of his eastern military commander, he wept profusely because he admired the commander's bravery and wisdom. He also became very angry and led all of his forces to the Sublime Porte. He ordered that the Emperor's positions be bombarded with cannons and guns, being concerned that the Emperor's forces might attack him. Then, the godless [Mohammed] appeared opposite the Poloe Mesto and ordered his forces to fire cannons and guns at defenders in order to induce them to retreat. He also instructed [Turkish Admiral] Balta-Oghlu, in charge of many regiments and a select force of 3000, to capture the Emperor dead or alive.

When they noticed the determination of the godless [Mohammed], [the Byzantine] military commanders, officials, and nobles joined the battle and implored the Emperor to leave in order to escape death. He wept bitterly and told them: "Remember the words I said earlier! Do not try to protect me! I want to die with you!" and they replied: "All of us will die for God's church and for you!"

Then they escorted him to [relative] safety and many people told him to leave the city. After they pledged their allegiance to him, they lamented and cried and returned to their posts. There was fierce fighting, more vicious than all previous encounters. Many [Byzantine] military commanders, officials, and nobles perished and the few who survived went to the Emperor to report to him about the disaster. There is no way to give an accurate number of Byzantine and Turkish casualties. The select Turkish force of 3000, like wild animals, dispersed and searched all corners of the city in an effort to capture the Emperor.

The impious Mohammed then ordered all of his forces to occupy all city streets and gates in order to capture the Emperor. In his camp he retained only the Janissaries, who readied their cannons and guns in fear of a sudden attack by the Emperor. Sensing God's command, the Emperor went to the Great Church [St. Sophia], where he fell to the ground pleading for God's mercy and forgiveness for his sins. Then he bade farewell to the Patriarch, the clergy, and the Empress, bowed to those who were present and left the church. As he left the church the Emperor said: "If you want to suffer for God's church and for the Orthodox faith, then follow me!"

Then he mounted his horse and went to the Golden Gate, hoping to encounter there the godless. He was able to attract some 3000 [Byzantine] soldiers. Near the Gate they met a multitude of Turks whom they defeated. The Emperor wanted to reach the Gate but could not on account of many corpses. Then he encountered another large Turkish force and they fought till darkness. In this manner the Orthodox Emperor Constantine suffered for God's churches and for the Orthodox faith. On May 29 [1453], according to eyewitnesses, he killed more than 600 Turks with his own hand. And the saying was fulfilled. *It started with Constantine and it ended with Constantine.* . . .

City inhabitants in streets and courtyards refused to surrender to the Turks. They fought them and on that day [May 29] many died, including women and children. Others were taken into captivity. Brave soldiers stationed themselves in windows and refused to surrender and give up their posts. During daylight they ran and hid themselves in various abysses and at night they came out and fought the Turks. Others, especially women and children, threw bricks, tiles, and burning pieces of wood at them and thereby caused them great trouble.

[This form of resistance] stunned the pashas and *sanjak-beys*. Because they did not know what to do, they sent a messenger to the Sultan with the following information: "The city will not be pacified until you enter it!" He ordered that a search be made for the Emperor and the Empress. He [the Sultan] himself was afraid to enter the city and that fact troubled him greatly. He then called in [Byzantine] nobles and military commanders who had been captured in the battle and were held as war prisoners by the pashas. He gave them his resolute word and some gifts, and sent them, together with the *pashas* and *sanjak-beys*, to deliver the following message to [the defiant] city inhabitants in streets and courtyards: "All fighting must stop! There should be neither fear, nor killings nor taking people into captivity! If you disobey this order, all of you, including your wives and children, will be put to the sword!" And so it was. The fighting stopped. . . .

When he heard this the Sultan was pleased.

Then he went to the Imperial Palace. There he met a certain Serb who handed him the Emperor's [Constantine's] head. Mohammed was pleased with it and called [Byzantine] nobles and military commanders and asked them to verify whether or not the head was really Emperor's. Because they were afraid, they all said: "It is the Emperor's head!" He examined it and said: "It is clear that God is the creator of all, including emperors. Why then does everyone have to die?"

Then he sent the head to the Patriarch, instructing him to inlay it with gold and silver and to preserve it the best he knew how. The Patriarch placed it in a silver chest, gilded it, and hid it under the altar of the great church. I have heard from others that the survivors [of the battle] at the Golden Gate [where the Emperor was killed] took the Emperor's corpse that night and buried it in Galati.

. . . All of this happened as a consequence of our sins, that the godless Mohammed ascended the imperial throne. . . . Yet, those who know [history] also know that all of this was prophesied by Methodius of Patera [a third-century martyred Church Father] and by Leo the Wise [author of several prophetic works] concerning the destiny of this city. Its past has been fulfilled and so will be its future. For it is written: *"A nation of Rus, as has been prophesied in the vision of St. Daniel, will triumph. And they will inherit the traditions of the seven hills [namely, Rome], as well as its laws, and will disseminate them among five or six nations that comprise Rus, and they will implant seeds among them and will harvest many benefits."*

Analysis and Review Questions

1. What role does religion play in the outcome of the conflict, according to this source?
2. Which leader is portrayed as the better military commander, Constantine XI or Mohammed II?
3. What weapons were the most critical to the fall of the city?
4. According to Nestor-Iskander, how does Mohammed II view the Byzantine Emperor, the Orthodox Patriarch, and the other elites of Byzantine society?
5. How do the two sides view the "great darkness" that enveloped the city on 27 May 1543?

FILOFEI'S CONCEPT OF THE "THIRD ROME"

About the Document

Late in the fifteenth century, three major trends dramatically reshaped the Orthodox world. The Byzantine Empire, long in decline, fell to the Turks in 1453. In 1480, the Muscovite Grand Prince, Ivan III ("the Great"), renounced his realm's subservience to the Mongol Khan, as the empire of the Golden Horde fell into squabbling factions. At the same time, Ivan III successfully gathered the far-flung Russian principalities under Moscow's control.

These three events seemed to some the manifestation of a divine message. In about 1515, a Russian monk, Filofei, Abbott of a monastery near Pskov, developed an explanation of this "message" and submitted it to the Grand Prince of Moscow, Vasilii III. Filofei argued that Rome, the original seat of Christianity, had fallen because of corruption and heresy. Constantinople had been given over to the infidel Turks because its people had failed to practice true Christianity. Moscow, having succeeded Kiev as the center of Russian Orthodoxy, was therefore the logical successor to the first two "Romes" as the center of true Christianity. Filofei further argued that no fourth "Rome" would ever arise; thus Moscow had to carry on the true Christian faith, and the Grand Prince of Muscovy had to take on the role of Defender of the Faith.

The Document

To you who have been selected to rule, by the highest, the all-powerful and almighty hand of God, by Whose will all rulers on earth govern and Whom all great people praise and about Whom the powerful write the truth, [I address these words] to you, the illustrious sovereign, Grand Prince [of Muscovy], occupier of the high throne, the Orthodox Christian Tsar and lord of all, the administrator of all Holy Churches of God and of the Holy Universal and Apostolic Church and of the Church of the Holy Mother of God, that has made such honest and illustrious progress that it has been enabled to triumph over the Church of Rome as well as over the Church of Constantinople.

Image 9.3
Ivan the Terrible

Heresy caused the downfall of old Rome. The Turks used their axes to shatter the doors of all churches of the Second Rome, the city of Constantinople. Now [in Moscow], the new Third Rome, the Holy Ecumenical Apostolic Church of your sovereign state shines brighter than the sun in the universal Orthodox Christian faith throughout the world. Pious Tsar! Let [people of] your state know that all states of the Orthodox faith have now merged into one, your state. You are the only true Christian ruler under the sky!

Tsar! As long as you hold that position, be mindful always of God. Fear God who has bestowed so much on you. Do not rely on gold, wealth, or glory! All of that is collected here and it will remain here on earth. Tsar! Remember the Blissful who held the scepter in His hand and the imperial crown on His head and said: "Do not turn your heart to wealth that is running away from you." The wise Solomon said: "Wealth and gold are valued not when they are hidden, but when people offer help to those in need. . . ." Tsar! During your rule remember [an additional] two commandments. . . . [The first is]: Do not violate the order which was chosen by your great predecessor [Emperor] Constantine, the beatific Vladimir, the great and God-selected Iaroslav, and all other blissful and saintly [rulers] from whom you have descended. [And second]: Tsar! Do not harm the Holy churches of God and honest monasteries. [Do not expropriate] that which has been given to God in return for eternal blessing of the memory of a family. The Fifth Great and Holy Ecumenical Council issued a very strict injunction [against such action]. . . .

Now I beg you and beg you again, please remember what I have said. For God's sake, please also remember that now all [Orthodox] Christian kingdoms have merged into your tsardom. Henceforth we can expect only one kingdom to come. That kingdom is eternal. I have written this because, admiring you as I do, I have appealed and have prayed to God that He may bless you. Change your stinginess to generosity and your inclemency to kindness. Comfort those who cry and moan day and night. Protect the innocent from their tormentors.

I repeat here what I have written above. Pious Tsar! Listen and remember that all Christian kingdoms have now merged into one, your [tsardom]. Two Romes have fallen. The third stand [firm]. And there will not be a fourth. No one will replace your Christian tsardom. . . .

Analysis and Review Questions

1. Filofei admonished the Tsar to follow "an additional two commandments": not to violate the Orthodox order established by Constantine and Vladimir and not to "harm the Holy churches of God and honest monasteries." He also tells the Tsar to "change your stinginess to generosity and your inclemency to kindness." What do these admonitions say about the relationship between the Tsar and the Church during this period of consolidation of Moscow's political authority?

2. If the Tsar is the "administrator" of the Orthodox Church, why does Filofei feel the need to remind the Tsar several times to "be mindful always of God"?

3. Does Filofei really mean for Vasilii III to "let [people of] your state know that all states of the Orthodox faith have now merged into one, your state"? What purpose(s) could such a domestic emphasis serve?

4. How can Filofei call the Byzantine Emperor Constantine a "great predecessor" of Vasilii's?

5. What is it that Filofei (and the Fifth Great and Holy Ecumenical Council) forbids the Tsar to "expropriate" from the church and from "honest monasteries"?

WEB LINKS

Selections from Longman World History—Primary Sources and Case Studies

http://longmanworldhistory.com
The following additional readings and case studies can be found on the Web site.
Document 9.3, Kritovoulos on the Fall of Constantinople

Case Study 9.1, Constantine I, Vladimir and the Selection of Christianity
Case Study 9.2, Kritovoulos vs. Nestor-Iskander on the Fall of Constantinople, 1453.
Case Study 9.3, Constantine I, Vladimir's Selection of Orthodoxy, and Filofei's Theory

For Russian History in General

http://www.departments.bucknell.edu/russian/history.html
This is an exceptional Web site, perhaps the most comprehensive coverage of details of Russian history available on the Internet. Within this general site are detailed articles on many aspects of Russian history, including Orthodoxy.

http://www.russian-orthodox-church.org.ru/en.htm
This is the official Web site of the Russian Orthodox Church. While it primarily focuses on current Church leaders and positions, it does include historical material as well.

http://www.pallasart.com/ikons
This is a private Web site that demonstrates in great detail the history of ikons, the holy images of the Russian Orthodox and Byzantine Orthodox churches. It includes many beautifully detailed images of Russian Orthodox art.

For the Byzantine Empire in General

http://www.roman-empire.net/constant/constant-index.html
This is a comprehensive Web site dedicated to the Roman Empire. This particular page is a detailed history of Byzantium as the capital of the Eastern Empire. It contains many links to more specifically detailed historical articles and images.

http://www.metmuseum.org/explore/Byzantium/byzhome.html
This is a special page from the New York Metropolitan Museum of Art that highlights the museum's collection of Byzantine art and artifacts. It includes links to detailed history articles as well, but focuses primarily upon the specific exhibitions of the museum. Excellent images.

CHAPTER 10

African Societies and Kingdoms to 1500 C.E.

When much of Europe was still in the Dark Ages, there were powerful commercial empires emerging in West, East, and South Africa. These empires were built on military strength, trade, and tribute. Much of the success of these was due to the ability of Islam to bring people together regionally and, to a larger extent, internationally. Many of the primary accounts from this period are from Arab travelers who felt secure in traveling great distances because of Muslim connections across continents. Ibn Battuta was a theologian and scholar, and Leo Africanus was a famous Muslim ex-slave who was later baptized a Christian convert. When the Portuguese came into contact with African kingdoms at about 1500 C.E., they coveted the power and wealth of these kingdoms and quickly moved to conquer them.

It is evident from the travel accounts and other primary documents in this chapter that these empires were vibrant centers of trade that extended over thousands of miles. The rulers of these African empires met the challenge of kingdom-building through the same process of military conquest and consolidation that occurred in India, Persia, and China. Sundiata's *Epic of Old Mali* presents this process in a unique African way through a spellbinding tale laced with myth and facts. Studying the richness and diversity of African life before 1500 dispels the myth that Africa was isolated and less developed than other civilizations studied in world history.

*Map 10.1
(Interactive)
African Empires in
the Western Sudan*

EXCERPTS FROM *SUNDIATA: AN EPIC OF OLD MALI*

About the Document

A powerful rival to Mandingo power in the Sudan was the pagan people called Soso. In order to check the influence of the Mali Empire, the Soso king, Soumaoro, killed the 11 brothers who were heirs to the throne of Mali. There was a twelfth, Sundiata, whom they spared because he was crippled.

The story of Sundiata's rise to power reveals much of the early history of the Mandingo king and his thrilling defeat of Soumaoro in 1235. The epic of old Mali contains a fascinating description of palace intrigue in the capital city of Niani. Sundiata emerges as the central hero of the tale through magic, cunning, strength, and providence. Sundiata becomes a great king noted for his Muslim piety, wisdom, justice, and military strength. Under his reign, the Mali Empire recovers from war and returns to prosperity. Caravans of many riches traveled to Niani, and people from distant lands spoke of this great king. Sundiata is still regarded by the Mandingo as their national hero.

The oral history excerpted below is primarily the work of an obscure griot from the village of Djeliba Koro. A "griot" is a member of a hereditary caste in West Africa whose job it is to keep the oral history of the tribe or village. As explained by author D.T. Niane, at one time "griots were the counsellors of kings; they conserved the constitutions of kingdoms by memory work alone; each princely family had its griot appointed to preserve tradition; it was from among the griots that kings used to choose the tutors for young princes. In the very hierarchical society of Africa before colonization, . . . the griot appears as one of the most important of this society, because it is he who, for want of archives, records the customs, traditions and governmental principles of kings."

The Document

Soumaoro sent a detachment under his son Sosso Balla to block Sundiata's route to Tabon. Sosso Balla was about the same age as Sundiata. He promptly deployed his troops at the entrance to the mountains to oppose Sundiata's advance to Tabon. . . .

Sundiata was immovable, so the orders were given and the war drums began to beat. On his proud horse Sundiata turned to right and left in front of his troops. He entrusted the rearguard, composed of a part of the Wagadou cavalry, to his younger brother Manding Bory. Having drawn his sword, Sundiata led the charge, shouting his war cry.

The Sossos were surprised by this sudden attack for they all thought that the battle would be joined the next day. The lightning that flashes across the sky is slower, the thunderbolts less frightening and floodwaters less surprising than Sundiata swooping down on Sosso Balla and his smiths. In a trice, Sundiata was in the middle of the Sossos like a lion in the sheepfold. The Sossos, trampled under the hooves of his fiery charger, cried out. When he turned to the right the smiths of Soumaoro fell in their tens, and when he turned to the left his sword made heads fall as when someone shakes a tree of ripe fruit. The horsemen of Mema wrought a frightful slaughter and their long lances pierced flesh like a knife sunk into a paw-paw. Charging ever forwards, Sundiata looked for Sosso Balla; he caught sight of him and like a lion bounded towards the son of Soumaoro, his sword held aloft. His arm came sweeping down but at that moment a Sosso warrior came between Djata and Sosso Balla and was sliced like a calabash. Sosso Balla did not wait and disappeared from amidst his smiths. Seeing their chief in flight, the Sossos gave way and fell into a terrible rout. . . .

The news of the battle of Tabon spread like wildfire in the plains of Mali. It was known that Soumaoro was not present at the battle, but the mere fact that his troops had retreated before Sundiata sufficed to give hope to all the peoples of Mali. Soumaoro realized that from now on he would have to reckon with this young man. He got to know of the prophecies of Mali, yet he was still too confident. When Sosso Balla returned with the remnant he had managed to save at Tabon, he said to his father, "Father, he is worse than a lion; nothing can withstand him.". . .

The son of Sogolon had already decided on his plan of campaign—to beat Soumaoro, destroy Sosso and return triumphantly to Niani. He now had five army corps at his disposal. . . .

Sundiata caught sight of him and tried to cut a passage through to him. He struck to the right and struck to the left and trampled underfoot. The murderous hooves of his "Daffeké" dug into the chests of the Sossos. Soumaoro was now within spear range and Sundiata reared up his horse and hurled his weapon. It whistled away and bounced off Soumaoro's chest as off a rock and fell to the ground. Sogolon's son bent his bow but with a motion of the hand Soumaoro caught the arrow in flight and showed it to Sundiata as if to say "Look, I am invulnerable."

Furious, Sundiata snatched up his spear and with his head bent charged at Soumaoro, but as he raised his arm to strike his enemy he noticed that Soumaoro had disappeared. Manding Bory riding at his side pointed to the hill and said, "Look, brother."

Sundiata saw Soumaoro on the hill, sitting on his black-coated horse. How could he have done it, he who was only two paces from Sundiata? By what power had he spirited himself away on to the hill? The son of Sogolon stopped fighting to watch the king of Sosso. The sun was already very low and Soumaoro's smiths gave way but Sundiata did not give the order to pursue the enemy. Suddenly, Soumaoro disappeared! . . .

The battle of Neguéboria showed Djata, if he needed to be shown, that to beat the king of Sosso other weapons were necessary.

The evening of Neguéboria, Sundiata was master of the field, but he was in a gloomy mood. He went away from the field of battle with its agonized cries of the wounded, and Manding Bory and Tabon Wana watched him go. He headed for the hill where he had seen Soumaoro after his miraculous disappearance. . . .

But it was time to return to his native Mali. Sundiata assembled his army in the plain and each people provided a contingent to accompany the Mansa to Niani. . . .

Sundiata and his men had to cross the Niger in order to enter old Mali. One might have thought that all the dug-out canoes in the world had arranged to meet at the port of Ka-ba. It was the dry season and there was not much water in the river. The fishing tribe of Somono, to whom Djata had given the monopoly of the water, were bent on expressing their thanks to the son of Sogolon. They put all their dug-outs side by side across the Niger so that Sundiata's sofas could cross without wetting their feet.

When the whole army was on the other side of the river, Sundiata ordered great sacrifices. A hundred oxen and a hundred rams were sacrificed. It was thus that Sundiata thanked God on returning to Mali.

The villages of Mali gave Maghan Sundiata an unprecedented welcome. At normal times a traveller on foot can cover the distance from Ka-ba to Niani with only two halts, but Sogolon's son with his army took three days. The road to Mali from the river was flanked by a double human hedge. Flocking from every corner of Mali, all the inhabitants were resolved to see their saviour from close up. The women of Mali tried to create a sensation and they did not fail. At the entrance to each village they had carpeted the road with their multi-coloured pagnes, so that Sundiata's horse would not so much as dirty its feet on entering their village. . . .

Sundiata was leading the van. He had donned his costume of a hunter king—a plain smock, skin-tight trousers and his bow slung across his back. At his side Balla Fasséké was still wearing his festive garments gleaming with gold. Between Djata's general staff and the army Sosso Balla had been placed, amid his father's fetishes.° But his hands were no longer tied. As at Ka-ba, abuse was everywhere heaped upon him and the prisoner did not dare look up at the hostile crowd. . . .

The troops were marching along singing the "Hymn to the Bow," which the crowd took up. New songs flew from mouth to mouth. Young women offered the soldiers cool water and cola nuts. And so the triumphal march across Mali ended outside Niani, Sundiata's city.

It was a ruined town which was beginning to be rebuilt by its inhabitants. A part of the ramparts had been destroyed and the charred walls still bore the marks of the fire. From the top of the hill Djata looked on Niani, which looked like a dead city. He saw the plain of Sounkarani, and he also saw the site of the young baobab tree. The survivors of the catastrophe were standing in rows on the Mali road. The children were waving branches, a few young women were singing, but the adults were mute. . . .

With Sundiata peace and happiness entered Niani. Lovingly Sogolon's son had his native city rebuilt. He restored in the ancient style his father's old enclosure where he had grown up. People came from all the villages of Mali to settle in Niani. The walls had to be destroyed to enlarge the town, and new quarters were built for each kin group in the enormous army. . . .

After a year Sundiata held a new assembly at Niani, but this one was the assembly of dignitaries and kings of the empire. The kings and notables of all the tribes came to Niani. The kings spoke of their administration and the dignitaries talked of their kings. Fakoli, the nephew of Soumaoro, having proved himself too independent, had to flee to evade the Mansa's anger. His lands were confiscated and the taxes of Sosso were payed directly into the granaries of Niani. In this way, every year, Sundiata gathered about him all the kings and notables; so justice prevailed everywhere, for the kings were afraid of being denounced at Niani.

Djata's justice spared nobody. He followed the very word of God. He protected the weak against the strong and people would make journeys lasting several days to come and demand justice of him. Under his sun the upright man was rewarded and the wicked one punished.

In their new-found peace the villages knew prosperity again, for with Sundiata happiness had come into everyone's home. Vast fields of millet, rice, cotton, indigo and fonio surrounded the villages. Whoever worked always had something to live on. Each year long caravans carried the taxes in kind to Niani.

You could go from village to village without fearing brigands. A thief would have his right hand chopped off and if he stole again he would be put to the sword.

New villages and new towns sprang up in Mali and elsewhere. "Dyulas," or traders, became numerous and during the reign of Sundiata the world knew happiness.

There are some kings who are powerful through their military strength. Everybody trembles before them, but when they die nothing but ill is spoken of them. Others do neither good nor ill and when they die they are forgotten. Others are feared because they have power, but they know how to use it and they are loved because they love justice. Sundiata belonged to this group. He was feared, but loved as well. He was the father of Mali and gave the world peace. After him the world has not seen a greater conqueror, for he was the seventh and last conqueror. He had made the capital of an empire out of his father's village, and Niani became the navel of the earth. . . .

---

fetish: An object believed to have supernatural powers that assist those who carry them.

The griots, fine talkers that they were, used to boast of Niani and Mali saying: "If you want salt, go to Niani, for Niani is the camping place of the Sahel caravans. If you want gold, go to Niani, for Bouré, Bambougou and Wagadou work for Niani. If you want fine cloth, go to Niani, for the Mecca road passes by Niani. If you want fish, go to Niani, for it is there that the fishermen of Maouti and Djenné come to sell their catches. If you want meat, go to Niani, the country of the great hunters, and the land of the ox and the sheep. If you want to see an army, go to Niani, for it [is] there that the united forces of Mali are to be found. If you want to see a great king, go to Niani, for it is there that the son of Sogolon lives, the man with two names.". . .

After him many kings and many Mansas reigned over Mali and other towns sprang up and disappeared. Hajji Mansa Moussa, of illustrious memory, beloved of God, built houses at Mecca for pilgrims coming from Mali, but the towns which he founded have all disappeared, Karanina, Bouroun-Kouna—nothing more remains of these towns. Other kings carried Mali far beyond Djata's frontiers, for example Mansa Samanka and Fadima Moussa, but none of them came near Djata.

Maghan Sundiata was unique. In his own time no one equalled him and after him no one had the ambition to surpass him. He left his mark on Mali for all time and his taboos still guide men in their conduct.

Mali is eternal. To convince yourself of what I have said go to Mali.

Analysis and Review Questions

1. What is the role of a griot in West African societies? How important is this source for uncovering the history of the Sudanic empires? How reliable do you think oral history is to the serious historian?
2. What is the role of prophesies in the story of Sundiata? Were those predictions fulfilled?
3. How does Sundiata overcome his most hated and feared enemy on the battlefield?
4. What type of military leader was Sundiata? Why did Sundiata have a good reputation with the 12 tribes of Mali? How do the people of Mali view him today?
5. Why did Sundiata move his capital to the city of Niani? How does the griot describe Niani?

*Map 10.2
Trade Routes
in Africa*

LEO AFRICANUS' DESCRIPTION OF WEST AFRICA

About the Document

Leo Africanus was an early-sixteenth-century traveler who recorded in great detail the life of many remote African kingdoms. His work, *The History and Description of Africa and of the Notable Things Therein Contained*, was translated for the first time from Arabic into Latin in 1526. Little is actually known of the early life of Leo except that he was born in Granada and later moved to Fez, a great commercial center in the Sudan and a seat of learning containing many mosques and libraries. It was obvious to Pope Leo X, after meeting the Moorish slave, that Leo was originally from a wealthy family and educated.

Leo's account of his travels throughout the Sudan was particularly important because it described the region just when Songhai had been raised to its political and economic zenith by the conquests of Askia Muhammad (1493–1528). His accounts clearly show that regional and international trade played a dominant part in the economic life of the entire Maghrib. The rich city of Timbuktu, the large armies of the kings, the wide variety of goods sold by merchants, and the intellectual and cultural life of the Muslim inhabitants of the Songhai Empire were all described in fascinating detail. Cartographers in Europe redrew the map of Africa in light of Leo's documentary, and for two-and-a-half centuries, his travel accounts were an indispensable source of knowledge to all concerned with the study of Africa.

Map 10.1 (Interactive) African Empires in the Western Sudan

The Document

IOHN LEO HIS SEUENTH BOOKE OF THE HISTORIE OF AFRICA, AND *OF THE MEMORABLE THINGS* CONTAINED THEREIN.

Wherein he intreateth of the land of Negros, and of the confines of Egypt.

Our ancient Chroniclers of Africa, to wit, *Bichri* and *Meshudi* knew nothing of the land of Negros but onely the regions of Guechet and Cano: for in their time all other places of the land of Negros were vndiscouered. But in the yeere of the Hegeira 380, by the meanes of a certaine Mahumetan which came into Barbarie, the residue of the said land was found out, being as then inhabited by great numbers of people, which liued a brutish and sauage life, without any king, gouernour, common wealth, or knowledge of husbandrie. Clad they were in skins of beasts, neither had they any peculiar wiues: in the day time they kept their cattell; and when night came they resorted ten or twelue both men and women into one cottage together, using hairie skins instead of beds, and each man choosing his leman which he had most fancy vnto. Warre they wage against no other nation, ne yet are desirous to trauell out of their owne countrie. Some of them performe great adoration vnto the sunne rising: others, namely the people of Gualata, worship the fire: and some others, to wit, the inhabitants of Gaoga, approch (after the Egyptians manner) neerervnto the Christian faith. These Negros were first subiect vnto king *Ioseph* the founder of Maroco, and afterward vnto the fiue nations of Libya; of whom they learned the Mahumetan lawe, and diuers needfull handycrafts: a while after when the merchants of Barbarie began to resort vnto them with merchandize, they learned the Barbarian language also. But the foresaid fiue people or nations of Libya diuided this land so among themselues, that euery third part of each nation possessed one region. Howbeit the king of Tombuto° that now raigneth, called *Abuacre Izchia*, is a Negro by birth: this *Abuacre* after the decease of the former king, who was a Libyan borne, slue all his sonnes, and so vsurped the kingdome. And hauing by warres for the space of fifteene yeeres conquered many large dominions, he then concluded a league with all nations, and went on pilgrimage to Mecca, in which iournie he so consumed

Tombuto/Timbuktu: Perhaps the most famous Muslim town on the Niger River, Timbuktu was a thriving commercial center for Maghribi traders in the Sudan. It is estimated to have had a population of 25,000 when Leo Africanus visited it in about 1510. Timbuktu also became a great center of Muslim learning, and scholars from North Africa and Egypt visited the city for its universities and libraries. Doctors, judges, priests, and other learned men were maintained in Timbuktu at the king's cost.

his treasure, that he was constrained to borrow great summes of money of other princes. Moreouer the fifteene kingdomes of Negros knowen to vs, are all situate vpon the riuer of Niger, and vpon other riuers which fall thereinto. And all the land of Negros standeth betweene two vast deserts, for on the one side lieth the maine desert betweene Numidia and it, which extendeth it selfe vnto this very land: and the south side thereof adioineth vpon another desert, which stretcheth from thence to the maine Ocean: in which desert are infinite nations vnknowen to vs, both by reason of the huge distance of place, and also in regarde of the diuersitie of languages and religions. They haue no traffique at all with our people, but we haue heard oftentimes of their traffique with the inhabitants of the Ocean sea shore.

A description of the kingdome of Gualata.

This region in regarde of others is very small: for it containeth onely three great villages, with certaine granges and fields of dates. From Nun it is distant southward about three hundred, from Tombuto northward fiue hundred, and from the Ocean sea about two hundred miles. In this region the people of Libya, while they were lords of the land of Negros, ordained their chiefe princely seate: and then great store of Barbarie-merchants frequented Gualata: but afterward in the raigne of the mighty and rich prince *Heli*, the said merchants leauing Gualata, began to resort vnto Tombuto and Gago, which was the occasion that the region of Gualata grew extreme beggerly. The language of this region is called Sungai, and the inhabitants are blacke people, and most friendly vnto strangers. In my time this region was conquered by the king of Tombuto, and the prince thereof fled into the deserts, whereof the king of Tombuto hauing intelligence, and fearing least the prince would returne with all the people of the deserts, graunted him peace, conditionally that he should pay a great yeerely tribute vnto him, and so the said prince hath remained tributarie to the king of Tombuto vntill this present. The people agree in manners and fashions with the inhabitants of the next desert. Here groweth some quantitie of Mil-seed, and great store of a round & white kind of pulse, the like whereof I neuer saw in Europe; but flesh is extreme scarce among them. Both the men & the women do so couer their heads, that al their countenance is almost hidden. Here is no forme of a common wealth, nor yet any gouernours or judges, but the people lead a most miserable life.

A description of the kingdome of Ghinea.

This kingdome called by the merchants of our nation Gheneoa, by the natural inhabitants thereof Genni, and by the Portugals and other people of Europe Ghinea, standeth in the midst betweene Gualata on the north, Tombuto on the east, and the kingdome of Melli on the south. In length it containeth almost fiue hundred miles, and extendeth two hundred and fiftie miles along the riuer of Niger, and bordereth vpon the Ocean sea in the same place, where Niger falleth into the saide sea. This place exceedingly aboundeth with barlie, rice, cattell, fishes, and cotton: and their cotton they sell vnto the merchants of Barbarie, for cloth of Europe, for brazen vessels, for armour, and other such commodities. Their coine is of gold without any stampe or inscription at all: they haue certaine iron-money also, which they vse about matters of small value, some peeces whereof weigh a pound, some halfe a pound, and some one quarter of a pound. In all this kingdome there is no fruite to be found but onely dates, which are brought hither either out of Gualata or Numidia. Heere is neither towne nor castle, but a certaine great village onely, wherein the prince of Ghinea, together with his priestes, doctors, merchants, and all the principall men of the region inhabite. The walles of their houses are built of chalke, and the roofes are couered with strawe: the inhabitants are clad in blacke or blew cotton, wherewith they couer their heads also: but the priests and doctors of their law go apparelled in white cotton. This region during the three moneths of Iulie, August, and September, is yeerely enuironed with the ouerflowings of Niger in manner of an Island; all which time the merchants of Tombuto conueigh their merchandize hither in certaine Canoas or narrow boats made of one tree, which they rowe all the day long, but at night they binde them to the shore, and lodge themselues vpon the lande. This kingdome was subject in times past vnto a certaine people of Libya, and became afterward tributarie vnto king *Soni Heli*, after whom succeeded *Soni Heli Izchia*, who kept the prince of this region prisoner at Gago, where togither with a certaine nobleman, he miserably died.

Of the kingdome of Melli.

This region extending it selfe almost three hundred miles along the side of a riuer which falleth into Niger, bordereth northward vpon the region last described, southward vpon certaine deserts and drie mountaines, westward vpon huge woods and forrests stretching to the Ocean sea shore, and eastward vpon the territorie of Gago. In this kingdome there is a large and ample village containing to the number of six thousand or mo families, and called Melli, whereof the whole kingdome is so named. And here the king hath his place of residence. The region it selfe yeeldeth great abundance of corne, flesh, and cotton. Heere are many artificers and merchants in all places: and yet the king honourably entertaineth all strangers. The inhabitants are rich, and haue plentie of wares. Heere are great store of temples, priests, and professours, which professours read their lectures only in the temples, bicause they haue no colleges at all. The people of this region excell all other Negros in witte, ciuilitie, and industry; and were the first that embraced the law of Mahumet, at the same time when the vncle of Ioseph the king of Maroco was their prince, and the gouernment remained for a while vnto his posteritie: at length Izchia subdued the prince of this region, and made him his tributarie, and so oppressed him with greeuous exactions, that he was scarce able to maintaine his family.

Of the kingdome of Tombuto.

This name was in our times (as some thinke) imposed vpon this kingdome from the name of a certain towne so called, which (they say) king *Mense Suleiman* founded in the yeere of the Hegeira 610, and it is situate within twelue miles of a certaine branch of Niger, all the houses whereof are now changed into cottages built of chalke, and couered with thatch. Howbeit there is a most stately temple to be seene, the wals whereof are made of stone and lime; and a princely palace also built by a most excellent workeman of Granada. Here are many shops of artificers, and merchants, and especially of such as weaue linnen and cotton cloth. And hither do the Barbarie-merchants bring cloth of Europe. All the women of this region except maid-seruants go with their faces couered, and sell all necessarie victuals. The inhabitants, & especially strangers there residing, are exceeding rich, insomuch, that the king that now is, married both his daughters vnto two rich merchants. Here are many wels, containing most sweete water; and so often as the riuer Niger ouerfloweth, they conueigh the water thereof by certaine sluces into the towne. Corne, cattle, milke, and butter this region yeeldeth in great abundance: but salt is verie scarce here; for it is brought hither by land from Tegaza, which is fiue hundred miles distant. When I my selfe was here, I saw one camels loade of salt sold for 80. ducates. The rich king of Tombuto hath many plates and scepters of gold, some whereof weigh 1300. poundes: and he keepes a magnificent and well furnished court. When he

Image 10.1
The Catalan Map

trauelleth any whither he rideth vpon a camell, which is lead by some of his noblemen; and so he doth likewise when hee goeth to warfar, and all his souldiers ride vpon horses. Whosoeuer will speake vnto this king must first fall downe before his feete, & then taking vp earth must sprinkle it vpon his owne head & shoulders: which custom is ordinarily obserued by them that neuer saluted the king before, or come as ambassadors from other princes. He hath alwaies three thousand horsemen, and a great number of footmen that shoot poysoned arrowes, attending vpon him. They haue often skirmishes with those that refuse to pay tribute, and so many as they take, they sell vnto the merchants of Tombuto. Here are verie few horses bred, and the merchants and courtiers keepe certaine little nags which they vse to trauell vpon: but their best horses are brought out of Barbarie. And the king so soone as he heareth that any merchants are come to towne with horses, he commandeth a certaine number to be brought before him, and chusing the best horse for himselfe, he payeth a most liberall price for him. He so deadly hateth all Iewes, that he will not admit any into his citie: and whatsoeuer Barbarie merchants he vnderstandeth haue any dealings with the Iewes, he presently causeth their goods to be confiscate. Here are great store of doctors, judges, priests, and other learned men, that are bountifully maintained at the kings cost and charges. And hither are brought diuers manuscripts or written bookes out of Barbarie, which are sold for more money than any other merchandize. The coine of Tombuto is of gold without any stampe or superscription: but in matters of smal value they vse certaine shels brought hither out of the kingdome of Persia, fower hundred of which shels are worth a ducate: and sixe peeces of their golden coine with two third parts weigh an ounce. The inhabitants are people of a gentle and chereful disposition, and spend a great part of the night in singing and dancing through all the streets of the citie: they keep great store of men and women-slaues, and their towne is much in danger of fire: at my second being there halfe the town almost was burnt in fiue howers space.

Analysis and Review Questions

1. What is Leo Africanus's opinion of the people of Mali (Melli)?
2. Reading the geographic descriptions provided by Leo proved very useful to geographers of the period. What is the importance of the Niger River to kingdom-building in the Sudanic region?
3. The role of merchants is well described by this Arab traveler. What are the most important trade goods of the region? How is the trade conducted and by whom?
4. In what manner does the king of Timbuktu (Tombuto) consolidate and maintain political and economic power?
5. What is the role of Islam to kingdom-building in West Africa?

EXCERPTS FROM *A DESCRIPTION OF THE COASTS OF EAST AFRICA AND MALABAR* BY DUARTE BARBOSA

About the Document

Duarte Barbosa was a cousin of Magellan who, like the famous explorer, often worked in the employ of the Spanish government. He remained in the Indian Ocean for 16 years recording with great clarity the political, religious, ideological, military, economic, and social life of the region. His descriptions of the towns along the East African coast provide a unique view of the commercial vitality of the peoples living there at the beginning of the sixteenth century, including Africans (he calls them Gentiles), Moors (Muslims), Christians, and Indians.

Barbosa describes without apology the destruction of many Muslim towns along the coast and the slaughter of the inhabitants if they resisted. The Portuguese made these people captives and took their gold, silver, and other merchandise. His account of the Kingdom of "Benamatapa" in South Africa is one of the few descriptions we have of the great power and wealth emanating from the gold-bearing regions in the interior and how they were directly connected through trade to the coast.

The Document

Sofala

Whereon is a town of the Moors° called Sofala, close to which town the King of Portugal has a fort. These Moors established themselves there a long time ago on account of the great trade in gold which they carry on with the Gentiles of the mainland: these speak somewhat of bad Arabic (garabia), and have got a king over them, who is at present subject to the King of Portugal. And the mode of their trade is that they come by sea in small barks which they call zanbucs (sambuk), from the kingdoms of Quiloa, and Mombaza, and Melindi; and they bring much cotton cloth of many colours, and white and blue, and some of silk; and grey, and red, and yellow beads, which come to the said kingdoms in other larger ships from the great kingdom of Cambay, which merchandise these Moors buy and collect from other Moors who bring them there, and they pay for them in gold by weight, and for a price which satisfies them; and the said Moors keep them and sell these cloths to the Gentiles of the kingdom of Benamatapa who come there laden with gold, which gold they give in exchange for the before mentioned cloths without weighing, and so much in quantity that these Moors usually gain one hundred for one. They also collect a large quantity of ivory, which is found all round Sofala, which they likewise sell in the great kingdom of Cambay at five or six ducats the hundred weight, and so also some amber, which these Moors of Sofala bring them from the Vciques. They are black men, and men of colour—some speak Arabic, and the rest make use of the language of the Gentiles of the country. They wrap themselves from the waist downwards with cloths of cotton and silk, and they wear other silk cloths above named, such as cloaks and wraps for the head, and some of them wear hoods of scarlet, and of other coloured woollen stuffs and camelets, and of other silks. And their victuals are millet, and rice, and meat, and fish. . . . The Moors have now recently begun to produce much fine cotton in this country, and they weave it into white stuff because they do not know how to dye it, or because they have not got any colours; and they take the blue or coloured stuffs of Cambay and unravel them, and again weave the threads with their white thread, and in this manner they make coloured stuffs, by means of which they get much gold.

Moors: The term *Moor* refers to many tribes of the Western Sahara—some that are dark-skinned and others that are light-skinned peoples. The Moors of Morocco controlled much of the gold trade in the Maghrib with the Sudanese peoples to the south. In the Middle Ages, Moors that had moved into Spain were exiled, and they formed settlements all along the North African coast from whence they became pirates, raiding and harassing Christian shipping. Moors were generally Muslim.

Kingdom of Benamatapa

On entering within this country of Sofala, there is the kingdom of Benamatapa, which is very large and peopled by Gentiles, whom the Moors call Cafers. These are brown men, who go bare, but covered from the waist downwards, with coloured stuffs, or skins of wild animals; and the persons most in honour among them wear some of the tails of the skin behind them, which go trailing on the ground for state and show. . . . They carry swords in scabbards of wood bound with gold or other metals, and they wear them on the left hand side as we do, in sashes of coloured stuffs, which they make for this purpose with four or five knots, and their tassels hanging down, like gentlemen; and in their hands azagayes, and others carry bows and arrows: it must be mentioned that the bows are of middle size, and the iron points of the arrows are very large and well wrought. They are men of war, and some of them are merchants: their women go naked as long as they are girls, only covering their middles with cotton cloths, and when they are married and have children, they wear other cloths over their breasts.

Zinbaoch

Leaving Sofala for the interior of the country, at XV days journey from it, there is a large town of Gentiles, which is called Zinbaoch ; and it has houses of wood and straw, in which town the King of Benamatapa frequently dwells, and from there to the city of Benamatapa there are six days journey, and the road goes from Sofala, inland, towards the Cape of Good Hope. And in the said Benamatapa, which is a very large town, the king is used to make his longest residence; and it is thence that the merchants bring to Sofala the gold which they sell to the Moors without weighing it, for coloured stuffs and beads of Cambay, which are much used and valued amongst them; and the people of this city of Benamatapa say that this gold comes from still further off towards the Cape of Good Hope, from another kingdom subject to this king of Benamatapa, who is a great lord, and holds many other kings as his subjects, and many other lands, which extend far inland, both towards the Cape of Good Hope and towards Mozambich. . . .

This king constantly takes with him into the field a captain, whom they call Sono, with a great quantity of men-at-arms, and amongst them they bring six thousand women, who also bear arms and fight. With these forces he goes about subduing and pacifying whatever kings rise up or desire to revolt. The said king of Benamatapa sends, each year, many honourable persons throughout his kingdoms to all the towns and lordships, to give them new regulations, so that all may do them obeisance. . . .

Angoy

After passing this river of Zuama, at XI leagues from it, there is a town of the Moors on the sea coast, which is called Angoy, and has a king, and the Moors who live there are all merchants, and deal in gold, ivory, silk, and cotton stuffs, and beads of Cambay, the same as do those of Sofala. And the Moors bring these goods from Quiloa, and Monbaza, and Melynde, in small vessels hidden from the Portuguese ships; and they carry from there a great quantity of ivory, and much gold. And in this town of Angoy there are plenty of provisions of millet, rice, and some kinds of meat. These men are very brown and copper coloured ; they go naked from the waist upwards, and from thence downwards, they wrap themselves with cloths of cotton and silk, and wear other cloths folded after the fashion of cloaks, and some wear caps and others hoods, worked with stuffs and silks; and they speak the language belonging to the country, which is that of the Pagans, and some of them speak Arabic. These people are sometimes in obedience to the king of Portugal, and at times they throw it off, for they are a long way off from the Portuguese forts.

Mozambique Island

Mozambique . . . has a very good port, and all the Moors touch there who are sailing to Sofala, Zuama, or Anguox. Amongst these Moors there is a sheriff, who governs them, and does justice. These are of the language and customs of the Moors of Anguox, in which island the King of Portugal now holds a fort, and keeps the said Moors under his orders and government. At this island the Portuguese ships provide themselves with water and wood, fish and other kinds of provisions; and at this place they refit those ships which stand in need of repair. And from this island likewise the Portuguese fort in Sofala draws its supplies, both of Portuguese goods and of the produce of India, on account of the road being longer by the mainland. . . .

Island of Quiloa

There is another island close to the mainland, called Quiloa, in which there is a town of the Moors, built of handsome houses of stone and lime, and very lofty, with their windows like those of the Christians; in the same way it has streets, and these houses have got their terraces, and the wood worked in with the masonry, with plenty of gardens, in which there are many fruit trees and much water. This island has got a king over it, and from hence there is trade with Sofala with ships, which carry much gold, which is dispersed thence through all Arabia Felix, for henceforward all this country is thus named on account of the shore of the sea being peopled with many towns and cities of the Moors; and when the King of Portugal discovered this land, the Moors of Sofala, and Zuama, and Anguox, and Mozambique, were all under obedience to the King of Quiloa, who was a great king amongst them. And there is much gold in this town, because all the ships which go to Sofala touch at this island, both in going and coming back. These people are Moors, of a dusky colour, and some of them are black and some white; they are very well dressed with rich cloths of gold, and silk, and cotton, and the women also go very well dressed out with much gold and silver in chains and bracelets on their arms, and legs, and ears. The speech of these people is Arabic, and they have got books of the Alcoran, and honour greatly their prophet Muhamad. This King, for his great pride, and for not being willing to obey the King of Portugal, had this town taken from him by force, and in it they killed and captured many people, and the King fled from the island, in which the King of Portugal ordered a fortress to be built, and thus he holds under his command and government those who continued to dwell there.

Image 10.2
The Indian Ocean
Dhow Sailing Vessel

Island of Mombaza

A city of the Moors, called Bombaza, [is] very large and beautiful, and built of high and handsome houses of stone and whitewash, and with very good streets, in the manner of those of Quiloa. And it also had a king over it. The people are of dusky white, and brown complexions, and likewise the women, who are much adorned with silk and gold stuffs. It is a town of great trade in goods, and has a good port, where there are always many ships, both of those that sail for Sofala and those that come from Cambay and Melinde, and others which sail to the islands of Zanzibar, Manfia, and Penda, which will be spoken of further on. This Monbaza is a country well supplied with plenty of provisions. . . . The inhabitants at times are at war with the people of the continent, and at other times at peace, and trade with them, and obtain much honey and wax, and ivory. This King, for his pride and unwillingness to obey the King of Portugal, lost his city, and the Portuguese took it from him by force, and the King fled, and they killed and made captives many of his people, and the country was ravaged, and much plunder was carried off from it of gold and silver, copper, ivory, rich stuffs of gold and silk, and much other valuable merchandize.

Melinde

This town has fine houses of stone and whitewash, of several stories, with their windows and terraces, and good streets. The inhabitants are dusky and black, and go naked from the waist upwards, and from that downwards they cover themselves with cloths of cotton and silk, and others wear wraps like cloaks, and handsome caps on their heads. The trade is great which they carry on in cloth, gold, ivory, copper, quicksilver, and much other merchandise, with both Moors and Gentiles of the kingdom of Cambay, who come to their port with ships laden with cloth, which they buy in exchange for gold, ivory, and wax. Both parties find great profit in this. . . . This King and people have always been very friendly and obedient to the King of Portugal, and the Portuguese have always met with much friendship and good reception amongst them.

Penda, Manfia, and Zanzibar

Between this island of San Lorenzo and the continent, not very far from it, are three islands, which are called one Manfia, another Zanzibar, and the other Penda; these are inhabited by Moors; they are very fertile islands, with plenty of provisions. . . . They produce many sugar canes, but do not know how to make sugar. These islands have their kings. The inhabitants trade with the mainland with their provisions and fruits; they have small vessels, very loosely and badly made, without decks, and with a single mast; all their planks are sewn together with cords of reed or matting, and the sails are of palm mats. They are very feeble people, with very few and despicable weapons. In these islands they live in great luxury, and abundance; they dress in very good cloths of silk and cotton, which they buy in Mombaza of the merchants from Cambay, who reside there. Their wives adorn themselves with many jewels of gold from Sofala, and silver, in chains, ear-rings, bracelets, and ankle rings, and are dressed in silk stuffs: and they have many mosques, and hold the Alcoran of Mahomed.

Analysis and Review Questions

1. Duarte Barbosa travels around the Cape of Good Hope and reaches the southern islands off the coast of East Africa. He is very interested in the commercial activities of the east coast. What are the major products being traded at Sofala?
2. Where does the gold come from that is traded for a variety of items in Sofala?
3. What was the power of the King of Quiloa before the coming of the Portuguese? Why was the king of Quiloa destroyed by the Portuguese?
4. What is the relationship of the peoples of the three islands of Zanzibar, Mafia, and Pemba to the peoples of the interior of East Africa?
5. The East African city-states were very well off due to their commercial success. What evidence is there of the prosperity of these competing towns?

WEB LINKS

http://longmanworldhistory.com
The following additional case studies can be found on the Web site.
Case Study 10.1, Travel Accounts vs. Oral History
Case Study 10.2, Travelers' Narratives
Excellent brief descriptions of various African civilizations are provided at:
http://www.campus.northpark.edu/history/WebChron/Africa/GreatZimbabwe.html
The art of Sub-Saharan empire of Benin can be explored at:
http://www.si.edu/organiza/museums.africart/exhibits/beninsp.htm
The following are Web sites devoted to the trans-Saharan empires of Mali:
http://www.mrdowling.com/609-mansamusa.html
Africa South of the Sahara:
http://www.sul.stanford.edu/depts/ssrg/africa/guide.html
African Voices from the Smithsonian National Museum of History Site:
http://www.mnh.si.edu/africanvoices/

Pre-Columbian American Civilizations

The civilizations of Central and South America developed along much the same lines as civilizations in Europe, Africa, and Asia, but they did so alone. They moved from a hunting-gathering subsistence to farming, and, finally, to dependence on trade and a "cash crop" (maize); however, they did it without iron, without the wheel, and without the spread of knowledge that comes from contact between widely different developed groups. Between what we call the post-classical and the pre-Columbian eras, three major civilizations developed in Central and South America: the Maya, the Aztec, and the Inca. Alongside these great civilizations were village farmers and smaller groups that both invaded and were invaded, and sometimes were made into subordinate groups. Before the Europeans knew of their existence, these peoples, and many smaller tribes that lived near them, were advanced beyond anything the Europeans could have anticipated. What we have come to understand of these people speaks of their great diversity, advanced thinking, and artistic skill.

Map 11.1 (Interactive) Central and South American Civilizations

The earliest of these groups seems to be the Olmecs. The Olmecs originally lived along Mexico's Gulf Coast, but spread across southern Mexico to the Yucatán and down to Guatemala. The Olmecs were known for their huge stone sculptures of heads, carvings of jade, and vast trading network. They were a highly evolved society with well-established social classes. At the height of their civilization, the Olmecs were highly literate. Once the Olmec period waned, their influence lived on in succeeding groups. Another center of cultural growth was Teotihuacán, located in central southern Mexico. Teotihuacán was the sixth largest city in the world by 500 C.E., with an estimated population of as many as 200,000 people. It was the social and cultural center of the Valley of Mexico and the center of trade and crafts in Mexico.

One of the groups following the Olmecs was the Maya. The Maya produced what some say is the most important civilization of the time. Much is known about the Maya because their records give us a fairly complete picture of them as a people. They were artists, architects, scholars, sculptors, and scientists. The main economic activity of the Maya was agriculture, but crafts and long-distance trade were very important. Mayan goods and influence spread as far as the Atlantic coast of North America. Mayan astronomy far outdistanced astronomy in Europe. The Mayan mathematical system and system of writing were equaled by their art and architecture. They were skilled in carving, weaving, and ceramics. They were even known to file down teeth and fill the spaces with semiprecious stones.

The Maya were invaded by the Toltecs, and Mayan culture gradually merged with the more warlike and aggressive Toltec culture. This change, coupled with the nearly constant pressure of civil war between Chichén Itzá and its neighbors, finally caused the Mayan civilization to collapse, although their cultural influence lived on. There was constant invasion by different groups during this period, but none more consistent and influential than the waves of Chichimecs that came from the northern parts of Mexico. The Chichimecs did not invade everywhere at once, nor were they able to take control of every area. Some Chichimec groups largely assimilated into the conquered group, and in turn helped to fight off the new waves of invaders. Some settled into areas of their own and built cities.

One of the most important of these cities was Tula, ruled by the Toltecs. North of present-day Mexico City, it is here that recorded history of Mexico is said to have begun, with poems and stories handed down orally until finally written down some time after the Spanish invasion. Built on a hilltop (very different from previous cities, built on flat plains), Tula was the center of a vast array of neighboring states that had to pay tribute to the Toltecs. By 1000 C.E. the Toltecs had taken control of the last areas where Mayan civilization was still flourishing.

The invading Chichimecs, including the Toltecs of Tula, brought with them their religion of blood sacrifice. The gods demanded human blood for a variety of reasons, and these sacrifices took many forms. The practice of taking a beating heart and offering it to an eagle (symbol of the sun) is shown in many carvings at Tula. The Toltecs at Chichén Itzá sacrificed young girls laden with precious jewelry by throwing them into a well (really a sink hole) in hopes of better times for the entire city. Another wave of Chichimecs seems to have destroyed Chichén Itzá about 1160 C.E. Following this period, we see the rise of the last group of Chichimecs, the Aztecs. The Aztecs built their "city on a lake" on Lake Texcoco. It began on an island in the middle of the lake, but, through ingenious engineering, spread out to create a vast manmade network of land canals that became home to one of Mexico's most important cities, Tenochtitlán. Those who lived in Tenochtitlán eventually made allies—if at times unwilling allies—of those groups whose towns encircled the lake.

The Aztecs were highly literate, and many of their books have survived. They were meticulous record keepers. Ixtiuxochiti, the brother of the last native ruler of Texcoco, said of his people: "They had scribes for each branch of knowledge. Some dealt with annals, putting down in order the things which happened each year, giving the day, month, and the hour." The scribes kept the law books, and the priests recorded every religious fact, including "idolatrous doctrines, the festivals of their false gods, and their calendars."

The Inca empire was the most complex of the post-classical civilizations in the Americas. It extended 3,500 miles from Ecuador to Chile and from the Andean mountains to the Pacific coast. It contained an estimated population of at least ten million people from some 200 ethnolinguistic groups. The Incas learned to terrace the mountainsides, build roads, and engineer bridges to span the sharp valleys. They had craftsmen, carried on extended trade, and built aqueducts to carry water over long distances. They had a highly organized government that stored excess produce and other products to distribute when needed. Perhaps most fascinating, they did all this without a written language, using knotted string and oral tradition for record keeping. Archaeological records tell the story of this marvelous civilization before the coming of the Spanish.

ANONYMOUS: VICTORY OVER THE UNDERWORLD

About the Document

The Popol Vuh is a cherished work of the Maya. It is a compilation of stories that form an epic of the Mayan people. Its account of creation has been likened in some minds to an "American Bible." The author of Popol Vuh is unknown. He seems to have lived in the town of Utatlan (known later as Rotten Care and then Quiché).

The Popol Vuh is structured around the Maya's intricate use of numbers. Its pairing, tripling, and quadrupling of lines and its pairing of people form a common poetic structure. Its content assumes the traditional pattern of four successive worlds. The first three have been failures, and we are in the fourth now.

The Popol Vuh has four parts. The first shows the attempts at creating humans. This is a time of darkness, before the sun comes up, when the earth is soft and moist. The sun will come up, though, and harden the earth. The second deals with human arrogance, the third confronts death, and the fourth is the beginning of history.

Image 11.1
A Mayan Town

Part three is the most famous section of the Popol Vuh. It tells the story of overcoming the underworld. Much like *The Egyptian Book of the Dead,* the story seems to have provided an aid to the Maya on their journey through the underworld.

The Document

And now we shall name the name of the father of Hunahpu and Xbalanque. Let's drink to him, and let's just drink to the telling and accounting of the begetting of Hunahpu and Xbalanque. We shall tell just half of it, just a part of the account of their father. Here follows the account.

These are the names: One Hunahpu and Seven Hunahpu, as they are called.

And One and Seven Hunahpu went inside Dark House. And then their torch was brought, only one torch, already lit, sent by One and Seven Death,° along with a cigar for each of them, also already lit, sent by the lords. When these were brought to One and Seven Hunahpu they were cowering, here in the dark. When the bearer of their torch and cigars arrived, the torch was bright as it entered; their torch and both of their cigars were burning. The bearer spoke:

"They must be sure to return them in the morning—not finished, but just as they look now. They must return them intact, the lords say to you," they were told, and they were defeated. They finished the torch and they finished the cigars that had been brought to them.

And Xibalba is packed with tests, heaps and piles of tests.

One and Seven Death: The two lords of death in Mayan religion.

This is the first one: the Dark House, with darkness alone inside.

And the second is named Rattling House, heavy with cold inside, whistling with drafts, clattering with hail. A deep chill comes inside here.

And the third is named Jaguar House, with jaguars alone inside, jostling one another, crowding together, with gnashing teeth. They're scratching around; these jaguars are shut inside the house.

Bat House is the name of the fourth test, with bats alone inside the house, squeaking, shrieking, darting through the house. The bats are shut inside; they can't get out.

And the fifth is named Razor House, with blades alone inside. The blades are moving back and forth, ripping, slashing through the house.

These are the first tests of Xibalba,° but One and Seven Hunahpu never entered into them, except for the one named earlier, the specified test house.

And when One and Seven Hunahpu went back before One and Seven Death, they were asked:

"Where are my cigars? What of my torch? They were brought to you last night!"

"We finished them, your lordship."

"Very well. This very day, your day is finished, you will die, you will disappear, and we shall break you off. Here you will hide your faces: you are to be sacrificed!" said One and Seven Death.

And then they were sacrificed and buried. They were buried at the Place of Ball Game Sacrifice, as it is called. The head of One Hunahpu was cut off; only his body was buried with his younger brother.

"Put his head in the fork of the tree that stands by the road," said One and Seven Death.

And when his head was put in the fork of the tree, the tree bore fruit. It would not have had any fruit, had not the head of One Hunahpu been put in the fork of the tree.

This is the calabash tree, as we call it today, or "the head of One Hunahpu," as it is said.

And then One and Seven Death were amazed at the fruit of the tree. The fruit grows out everywhere, and it isn't clear where the head of One Hunahpu is; now it looks just the way the calabashes look. All the Xibalbans see this, when they come to look.

The state of the tree loomed large in their thoughts, because it came about at the same time the head of One Hunahpu was put in the fork. The Xibalbans said among themselves:

"No one is to pick the fruit, nor is anyone to go beneath the tree," they said. They restricted themselves; all of Xibalba held back.

It isn't clear which is the head of One Hunahpu; now it's exactly the same as the fruit of the tree. Calabash tree came to be its name, and much was said about it. A maiden heard about it, and here we shall tell of her arrival.

And here is the account of a maiden, the daughter of a lord named Blood Gatherer.

And this is when a maiden heard of it, the daughter of a lord. Blood Gatherer is the name of her father, and Blood Woman is the name of the maiden.

And when he heard the account of the fruit of the tree, her father retold it. And she was amazed at the account:

"I'm not acquainted with that tree they talk about. 'Its fruit is truly sweet!' they say, I hear," she said.

Next, she went all alone and arrived where the tree stood. It stood at the Place of Ball Game Sacrifice:

Xibalba: The underworld, the place of fear in the Mayan religion.

"What? Well! What's the fruit of this tree? Shouldn't this tree bear something sweet? They shouldn't die, they shouldn't be wasted. Should I pick one?" said the maiden.

And then the bone spoke; it was here in the fork of the tree:

"Why do you want a mere bone, a round thing in the branches of a tree?" said the head of One Hunahpu when it spoke to the maiden. "You don't want it," she was told.

"I do want it," said the maiden.

"Very well. Stretch out your right hand here, so I can see it," said the bone.

"Yes," said the maiden. She stretched out her right hand, up there in front of the bone.

And then the bone spit out its saliva, which landed squarely in the hand of the maiden.

And then she looked in her hand, she inspected it right away, but the bone's saliva wasn't in her hand.

"It is just a sign I have given you, my saliva, my spittle. This, my head, has nothing on it—just bone, nothing of meat. It's just the same with the head of a great lord: it's just the flesh that makes his face look good. And when he dies, people get frightened by his bones. After that, his son is like his saliva, his spittle, in his being, whether it be the son of a lord or the son of a craftsman, an orator. The father does not disappear, but goes on being fulfilled. Neither dimmed nor destroyed is the face of a lord, a warrior, craftsman, orator. Rather, he will leave his daughters and sons. So it is that I have done likewise through you. Now go up there on the face of the earth; you will not die. Keep the word. So be it," said the head of One and Seven Hunahpu—they were of one mind when they did it.

This was the word Hurricane, Newborn Thunderbolt, Raw Thunderbolt had given them. In the same way, by the time the maiden returned to her home, she had been given many instructions. Right away something was generated in her belly, from the saliva alone, and this was the generation of Hunahpu and Xbalanque.

And when the maiden got home and six months had passed, she was found out by her father. Blood Gatherer is the name of her father.

. . .

And this is the sacrifice of Hunahpu by Xbalanque. One by one his legs, his arms were spread wide. His head came off, rolled far away outside. His heart, dug out, was smothered in a leaf, and all the Xibalbans went crazy at the sight.

So now, only one of them was dancing there: Xbalanque.

"Get up!" he said, and Hunahpu came back to life. The two of them were overjoyed at this—and likewise the lords rejoiced, as if they were doing it themselves. One and Seven Death were as glad at heart as if they themselves were actually doing the dance.

And then the hearts of the lords were filled with longing, with yearning for the dance of Hunahpu and Xbalanque, so then came these words from One and Seven Death:

"Do it to us! Sacrifice us!" they said. "Sacrifice both of us!" said One and Seven Death to Hunahpu and Xbalanque.

"Very well. You ought to come back to life. After all, aren't you Death? And aren't we making you happy, along with the vassals of your domain?" they told the lords.

And this one was the first to be sacrificed: the lord at the very top, the one whose name is One Death, the ruler of Xibalba.

And with One Death dead, the next to be taken was Seven Death. They did not come back to life.

And then the Xibalbans were getting up to leave, those who had seen the lords die. They underwent heart sacrifice there, and the heart sacrifice was performed on the two lords only for the purpose of destroying them.

As soon as they had killed the one lord without bringing him back to life, the other lord had been meek and tearful before the dancers. He didn't consent, he didn't accept it:

"Take pity on me!" he said when he realized. All their vassals took the road to the great canyon, in one single mass they filled up the deep abyss. So they piled up there and gathered together, countless ants, tumbling down into the canyon, as if they were being herded there. And when they arrived, they all bent low in surrender, they arrived meek and tearful.

Such was the defeat of the rulers of Xibalba. The boys accomplished it only through wonders, only through self-transformation.

Such was the beginning of their disappearance and the denial of their worship.

Their ancient day was not a great one,
these ancient people only wanted conflict,
their ancient names are not really divine,
but fearful is the ancient evil of their faces.

They are makers of enemies, users of owls,
they are inciters to wrongs and violence,
they are masters of hidden intentions as well,
they are black and white,
masters of stupidity, masters of perplexity,
as it is said. By putting on appearances they cause dismay.

Such was the loss of their greatness and brilliance. Their domain did not return to greatness. This was accomplished by Hunahpu and Xbalanque.

Analysis and Review Questions

1. What was Xibalba? What are the five tests of Xibalba?
2. What happened when they put the head of One Hunahpu in the fork of the tree?
3. Why are One and Seven Death surprised by the head of One Hunaphu?
4. How do Hunaphu and Xbalanque trick One and Seven Death?
5. How would this section of the *Popol Vuh* give comfort to the Maya as they face death?

XICOHTENCATL, THE ELDER: "I SAY THIS"

About the Document

Xicohtencatl, the Elder, was Lord of Tizatlan. He was also a composer. What is known is that he was born in about 1425 C.E. and lived until 1522 C.E., after the arrival of the Spanish. Xicohtencatl was also a warrior. It is said he took part in important battles and conquests involving the Mexicas (Aztecs), but in the end Xicohtencatl was forced to come to an agreement making Tizatlan an ally of other chiefdoms in the lake region near Mexico-Tenochtitlán.°

Warfare for these people had very specific rules. A field needed to be marked, and the battle could not go beyond its boundaries. The battles provided an

Tenochtitlán: Aztec capital originally built on two small islands in Lake Texcoco at present-day Mexico City. The Aztec expanded the city by a process of construction that submerged reeds and other materials to build a base on which to build structures. Its "streets" were canals, and the Spanish likened it to Venice.

opportunity for sons of lords to practice warfare, but they could not attempt to gain land for chiefdoms out of the war. The captured warriors would be sacrificed to the gods.

Warfare was about the political ambitions of the combatants, and it brought out the Mexican "worldview" that they were the chosen people of Huitzelopochi, the god of war. Xicohtencatl made a decision to take advantage of the arrival of the Spanish to aid in his fight against surrounding chiefdoms. However, the Spanish were ultimately not interested in helping native groups, but in conquering them.

The Flowery Wars° tells of the past struggles of the people of Tlazcala (the wider confederacy of cities of which Tizatlan was a part). The poem speaks to the value of war in the life of Tlazcala because "flowery war" is sacred war. However, there is irony in telling the glory of wars that eventually, with the coming of the Spanish, brought doom to the people of Tlazcala.

The Document

I say this, I the lord Xicohtencatl:
Do not go forth in vain!
Take up your shield, the vessel of flowery water!
Your little bowl with a handle.
Your precious vessel, color of obsidian, stands upright,
with it, we will bring the water on our shoulders,
we will carry it there in Mexico,
from Chapolco, on the shore of the lake.
Do not go forth in vain,
my nephew, my little children, my nephews,
you, children of the water!
I make the water flow,
O Lord Cuauhtencoztli,
let us all go!

We will bring the water on our shoulders,
truly we are going to carry it!

Captain Motelchiuhtzin wants to announce it,
my friends!
He says it is not yet dawn.
We take up our burden of water:
crystal clear, precious, color of turquoise,
which moves in waves.
Thus you will come there, to the place of the vessels,
do not go forth in vain!

Nanahuatl [the god] will perhaps make noise there.
My little son!
You, leader of men, you, precious creature,
a painting with gold in the Toltec manner,
paint the precious bowl, Lord Axayacatl.

Flowery Wars: Flowery wars were considered sacred wars. They often consisted of wars between groups for political reasons. The Aztec had very specific rules of fighting.

We go together to partake,
we approach the precious waters.
They are falling, drops rain down,
there, close to the small canals.
He who carries my flowery water, Huanitzin,
now comes to give it to me,
O my uncles, Tlaxcalans, Chichimecs!
Do not go forth in vain!

The flowery war, the shield's flower,
have opened their corollas.
They resound,
the sweet-smelling flowers rain down,
Thus perhaps for this,
he came to conceal gold and silver;
for this I take the painted books.
O my little canal, with my vessel the water flows!
O my old ones!

Analysis and Review Questions

1. How does the author describe the warrior's shields?
2. What evidence do you see that war is "sacred"?
3. What references do you detect to Xicohtencatl's conversion to Christianity and baptism?
4. What references point to a war on or near Lake Texcoco, Mexico?
5. What in the poem reflects the "glory" of war?

SONG FOR ADMONISHING THOSE WHO SEEK NO HONOR IN WAR

About the Document

The *Cantares Mexicanos* is the principal collection of Aztec poetry. It was written down sometime between 1550 and 1581 C.E. The *Cantares Mexicanos* contains songs meant to be accompanied by such instruments as skin drums, slit drums, gongs, flutes, and whistles. Songs were very important in Aztec culture (as in all ancient civilizations) as ways to immortalize an event or a person.

The songs were filled with references to flowers and birds, but they were very much warrior songs. They were written and performed to instill fear in one's enemies.

In the "Song for Admonishing Those Who Seek No Honor in War," the singer is praising warriors and telling how they now lie asleep in the great beyond. He is extolling those listening to be willing to fight. "War is a glorious thing," the singer proclaims, "and if you die what of it? You will be sleeping with the gods in glory."

Map 11.2
Inca Expansion

The Document

Clever with a song, I beat my drum to wake our friends, rousing them to arrow deeds, whose never dawning hearts know nothing, whose hearts lie dead asleep in war, who praise themselves in shadows, in darkness. Not in vain do I say, "They are poor." Let them come and hear the flower dawn songs drizzling down incessantly beside the drum.

Sacred flowers of the dawn are blooming in the rainy place of flowers that belongs to him the Ever Present, the Ever Near.° The heart pleasers are laden with sunstruck dew. Come and see them: they blossom uselessly for those who are disdainful. Doesn't anybody crave them? O friends, not useless flowers are the life-colored honey flowers.

They that intoxicate one's soul with life lie only there, they blossom only there, within the city of the eagles, inside the circle, in the middle of the field, where flood and blaze are spreading, where the spirit eagle shines, the jaguar growls, and all the precious bracelet stones are scattered, all the precious noble lords dismembered, where the princes lie broken, lie shattered.

These princes are the ones who greatly crave the dawn flowers. So that all will enter in, he causes them to be desirous, he who lies within the sky, he, Ce Olintzin, ah the noble one, who makes them drizzle down, giving a gift of flower brilliance to the eagle-jaguar princes, making them drunk with the flower dew of life.

If, my friend, you think the flowers are useless that you crave here on earth, how will you acquire them, how will you create them, you that are poor, you that gaze on the princes at their flowers, at their songs? Come look: do they rouse themselves to arrow deeds for nothing? There beyond, the princes, all of them, are troupials, spirit swans, trogons, roseate swans: they live in beauty, they that know the middle of the field.

With shield flowers, with eagle-trophy flowers, the princes are rejoicing in their bravery, adorned with necklaces of pine flowers. Songs of beauty, flowers of beauty, glorify their blood-and-shoulder toil. They who have accepted flood and blaze become our Black Mountain friends, with whom we rise warlike on the great road. Offer your shield, stand up, you eagle jaguar!

Analysis and Review Questions

1. Who do you think is being referred to as "him the Ever Present, the Ever Near"?
2. Where are those who have fallen in battle?
3. How does the singer describe where the fallen are now?
4. What does the song say about war in Aztec culture?
5. How would you describe the significance of flowers and the "eagle jaguar"?
   What do you think they mean in the Aztec war culture?

ANONYMOUS: THE MIDWIFE ADDRESSES THE WOMAN WHO HAS DIED IN CHILDBIRTH

About the Document

The *Florentine Codex°* was one of several permanent records of Aztec culture. Like other codices, the *Florentine Codex* was written down by the Spanish who had Aztec elders tell them the stories of the Aztec people. It is known as the *General History of the Things of New Spain*.

Codex: A scipture, book, ancient statement in manuscript form
The Ever Present, the Ever Near: The Incan deity, Ce Olintzin.

In Aztec culture, the parents of a married couple who are expecting a child choose a midwife for the pregnant mother. After some ritualistic protests, the midwife accepts the task of delivering the child and assumes care of the expectant mother. The midwife and the woman prepare for the birth. The midwife prepares the "flower house," or birthing room. The expectant woman is urged to be like Cihuacoatl Quilaztli, source of the human race, and bring forth another human into the world. The woman is also likened to a warrior in battle.

If the woman successfully gives birth, she is addressed as a great warrior, but reminded to be humble. She should respect the Creator who gives life and takes it away. If she dies in childbirth, she is spoken of as one of the great warriors in the sky. She will become one of the women who accept the sun at midday and lead it down to the west.

Image 11.2
Aztec Warriors

In the document that follows, the midwife addresses a woman who has died in childbirth. We see that the midwife treats the woman as a god. She prays to the woman, who lies silent in death in front of her.

The Document

Precious feather, child,
Eagle woman, dear one,
Dove, daring daughter,
You have labored, you have toiled,
Your task is finished.
You came to the aid of your Mother, the noble lady, Cihuacoatl Quilaztli.
You received, raised up, and held the shield, the little buckler that she laid in your hands: she your Mother, the noble
lady, Cihuacoatl Quilaztli.
Now wake! Rise! Stand up!
Comes the daylight, the daybreak:
Dawn's house has risen crimson, it comes up standing.
The crimson swifts, the crimson swallows, sing,
And all the crimson swans are calling.
Get up, stand up! Dress yourself!
Go! Go seek the good place, the perfect place, the home of your Mother,
your Father, the Sun,
The place of happiness, joy,
Delight, rejoicing.
Go! Go follow your Mother, your Father, the Sun.
May his elder sisters bring you to him: they the exalted, the celestial women,
who always and forever know happiness, joy, delight, and rejoicing, in the company and in the presence of our
Mother, our Father, the Sun; who make him happy with their shouting.
My child, darling daughter, lady,
You spent yourself, you labored manfully:
You made yourself a victor, a warrior for Our Lord, though not without consuming all your strength; you sacrificed
yourself.
Yet you earned a compensation, a reward: a good, perfect, precious death.
By no means did you die in vain.
And are you truly dead? You have made a sacrifice. Yet how else could you have

become worthy of what you now
deserve?
You will live forever, you will be happy, you will rejoice in the company and in the
presence of our holy ones, the
exalted women. Farewell, my daughter, my child. Go be with them, join them. Let
them hold you and take you in.
May you join them as they cheer him and shout to him: our Mother, our Father,
the Sun;
And may you be with them always, whenever they go in their rejoicing.
But my little child, my daughter, my lady,
You went away and left us, you deserted us, and we are but old men and old women.
You have cast aside your mother and your father.
Was this your wish? No, you were summoned, you were called.
Yet without you, how can we survive?
How painful will it be, this hard old age?
Down what alleys or in what doorways will we perish?
Dear lady, do not forget us! Remember the hardships that we see, that we suffer,
here on earth:
The heat of the sun presses against us; also the wind, icy and cold:
This flesh, this clay of ours, is starved and trembling. And we, poor prisoners of our
stomachs! There is nothing we
can do.
Remember us, my precious daughter, O eagle woman, O lady!
You lie beyond in happiness. In the good place, the perfect place,
You live.
In the company and in the presence of our lord,
You live.
You as living flesh can see him, you as living flesh can call to him.
Pray to him for us!
Call to him for us!
This is the end,
We leave the rest to you.

Analysis and Review Questions

1. How does the midwife address the woman who has just died?
2. How does the midwife describe what it will be like in "the good place"?
3. How is the woman like a warrior?
4. How does the midwife describe life for those left behind?
5. What evidence of Aztec theology is evident in this song?

WEB LINKS

Selections from Longman World History—Primary Sources and Case Studies

http://longmanworldhistory.com
The following additional readings and case studies can be found on the Web site.

Document 11.3, Song of Tlaltecatzin
Case Study 11.1, Death in War and Childbirth in the Americas
Case Study 11.2, The Importance of War in Ancient American Culture
Case Study 11.3, The Language of Love

Aztec

http://www.ai.mit.edu/people/montalvo/Hotlist/aztec.html
This site has an Aztec calendar.

http://www.indians.org/welker/aztec.htm
General site on Aztecs.

http://windows.arc.nasa.gov/cgi-bin/tour_def/mythology/aztec_culture.html
Aztec myths.

Maya

http://www.sci.mus.mn.us/sln/ma/
The Science Museum of Minnesota presents Maya Adventure, a Web site that highlights science activities and information related to ancient and modern Mayan culture.

http://www.jaguar-sun.com/mayacities.html
General site on Maya.

Inca

http://www.raingod.com/angus/Gallery/Photos/SouthAmerica/Peru/IncaTrail/
The Inca Trail and Machu Picchu. This is an interactive site.

http://www.andes.org/bookmark.html
Links to other sites on cultures of the Andes, including Andean music, Web sites, history and archaeology, languages, geography, crafts, and political organizations.

General Mesoamerican Sites

http://www.asu.edu/lib/archives/nasg.htm
Here you can find collected scholarly files, links, resources, software, and reports relevant or interesting to Mesoamerican and pre-Columbian archaeology.

http://online.elcamino.cc.ca.us/hist1a/Pre-Columbian.htm
The peopling of the North American continent.

http://www.hurstgallery.com/exhibit/past/of_land_sea_and_sky/intro.htm
Of land, sea, and sky animals in the art of the ancient Americas.

http://www.angelfire.com/ca/humanorigins/index.html
This page supplies information on Maya, Mixtec, Zapotec, and Aztec.

http://archaeology.la.asu.edu/teo/index.htm
This site has pictures of Teotihuacán.

http://www.albany.edu/ims/papers/urbland1.html
This site has urban sites: postclassical and pre-Columbian.

http://www.cultures.com/meso_resources/meso_encyclopedia/meso_encyclopedia_home_to.html
The Encyclopedia of Mesoamerica

Other Native American Sites

http://content.lib.washington.edu/aipnw/
American Indians of the Pacific Northwest digital collection.

http://www.hist.unt.edu/09w-ar2x.htm
Links to other sites.

http://www.indigenouspeople.org/natlit/natlit.htm"
On indigenous peoples.

http://pubpages.unh.edu/%7Ecbsiren/mythold.html
Myths and legends from many places.

India and Southeast Asia: Disunity and the Arrival of Islam

I t is very difficult, especially in this early period, to speak of an "India." What we now call India was never a united, coherent kingdom or empire. The collapse of the Gupta Empire around 500 C.E. left northern India a smattering of small states and princedoms, although stronger states emerged for the first time in southern India, often supported by trade networks stretching across the Indian Ocean.

Despite the political disunity, this was a period of somewhat greater cultural and social unity than ever before. Buddhism practically vanished by 700 C.E., while Hinduism became more popular and began spreading to the southern states. By the ninth century C.E., the caste system was firmly in place in most parts of India. Nonetheless, India's political disunity provided an opening for invasion (a constant feature of Indian history, actually), and in 1192, Turko-Afghan invaders poured into northern India, establishing a new empire, the Delhi Sultanate, and introducing a new religion: Islam.

ALBERUNI ON INDIA'S HINDUS

About the Document

By 973 C.E., when the Persian traveler Abu Raihan was born, Islam held sway over all of the Middle East, North Africa, and outer regions such as Spain and Persia. The Abbasid Dynasty ruled over a religious empire that reached its height just as Europe was experiencing what are sometimes called the Dark Ages. Though we now believe Europe was not quite as "dark" (lacking in cultural and artistic development) as had been previously thought, we also know that the Islamic world was far ahead of the West in these and other areas.

Abu Raihan is often known in the West by his westernized name, Alberuni. Early in life, Alberuni gained a reputation as a scholar, writer, and scientist and served as an advisor for local princes. Around 1030 C.E., he traveled to India, and wrote with an objective observer's sensibilities about this foreign land. Writing as a Muslim, Alberuni does not hesitate to point out things he dislikes about India or its inhabitants; at the same time, however, he is quick to praise matters of which he approves.

Image 12.1
Classical Indian
Sculptures

The Document

BEFORE entering on our exposition, we must form an adequate idea of that which renders it so particularly difficult to penetrate to the essential nature of any Indian subject. . . . For the reader must always bear in mind that the Hindus entirely differ from us in every respect, many a subject appearing intricate and obscure which would be perfectly clear if there were more connection between us. The barriers which separate Muslims and Hindus rest on different causes.

First, they differ from us in everything which other nations have in common. And here we first mention the language, although the difference of language also exists between other nations. If you want to conquer this difficulty (i.e. to learn Sanskrit°), you will not find it easy, because the language is of an enormous range, both in words and inflections, something like the Arabic, calling one and the same thing by various names, . . . and using one and the same word for a variety of subjects, which, in order to be properly understood, must be distinguished from each other by various qualifying epithets. For nobody could distinguish between the various meanings of a word unless he understands the context in which it occurs, and its relation both to the following and the preceding parts of the sentence. The Hindus, like other people, boast of this enormous range of their language, whilst in reality it is a defect.

Further, the language is divided into a neglected vernacular one, only in use among the common people, and a classical one, only in use among the upper and educated classes.

Besides, some of the sounds (consonants) of which the language is composed are neither identical with the sounds of Arabic and Persian, nor resemble them in any way. Our tongue and uvula could scarcely manage to correctly pronounce them, nor our ears in hearing to distinguish them from similar sounds, nor could we transliterate them with our characters. It is very difficult, therefore, to express an Indian word in our writing.

Add to this that the Indian scribes are careless, and do not take pains to produce correct and well-collated copies. In consequence, the highest results of the author's mental development are lost by their negligence, and his book becomes already in the first or second copy so full of faults, that the text appears as something entirely new, which neither a scholar nor one familiar with the subject, whether Hindu or Muslim, could any longer understand.

Secondly, they totally differ from us in religion, as we believe in nothing in which they believe, and *vice versa*. On the whole, there is very little disputing about theological topics among themselves; at the utmost, they fight with words, but they will never stake their soul or body or their property on religious controversy. On the contrary, all their fanaticism is directed against those who do not belong to them—against all foreigners. They call them mleecha,° *i.e.* impure, and forbid having any connection with them, be it by intermarriage or any other kind of relationship, or by sitting, eating, and drinking with them, because thereby, they think, they would be polluted. They are not allowed to receive anybody who does not belong to them, even if he wished it, or was inclined to their religion. This, too, render any connection with them quite impossible, and constitutes the widest gulf between us and them.

In the third place, in all manners and usages they differ from us to such a degree as to frighten their children with us, with our dress, and our ways and customs, and as to declare us to be devil's breed, and our doings as the very opposite of all that is good and

Sanskrit: The learned language of Hinduism, much like Latin in the medieval European church.
mleecha: Untouchables.

proper. By the by, we must confess, in order to be just, that a similar depreciation of foreigners not only prevails among us and the Hindus, but is common to all nations towards each other.

There are other causes, the mentioning of which sounds like a satire—peculiarities of their national character, deeply rooted in them, but manifest to everybody. We can only say, folly is an illness for which there is no medicine, and the Hindus believe that there is no country but theirs, no nation like theirs, no kings like theirs, no religion like theirs, no science like theirs. They are haughty, foolishly vain, self-conceited, and stolid. They are by nature niggardly in communicating that which they know, and they take the greatest possible care to withhold it from men of another caste among their own people, still much more, of course, from any foreigner.

Now such is the state of things in India. I have found it very hard to work my way into the subject, although I have a great liking for it, in which respect I stand quite alone in my time, and although I do not spare either trouble or money in collecting Sanskrit books from places where I supposed they were likely to be found, and in procuring for myself, even from very remote places, Hindu scholars who understand them and are able to teach me. What scholar, however, has the same favourable opportunities of studying this subject as I have? That would be only the case with one to whom the grace of God accords, what it did not accord to me, a perfectly free disposal of his own doings and goings; for it has never fallen to my lot in my own doings and goings to be perfectly independent, nor to be invested with sufficient power to dispose and to order as I thought best. However, I thank God for that which He has bestowed upon me, and which must be considered as sufficient for the purpose.

The heathen Greeks, before the rise of Christianity, held much the same opinions as the Hindus; their educated classes thought much the same as those of the Hindus; their common people held the same idolatrous views as those of the Hindus. Therefore I like to confront the theories of the one nation with those of the other simply on account of their close relationship, not in order to correct them. For that which is not the truth (*i.e.* the true belief or monotheism) does not admit of any correction, and all heathenism, whether Greek or Indian, is in its pith and marrow one and the same belief, because it is only a deviation *from the truth*. The Greeks, however, had philosophers who, living in their country, discovered and worked out for them the elements of science, not of popular superstition, for it is the object of the upper classes to be guided by the results of science, whilst the common crowd will always be inclined to plunge into wrong-headed wrangling, as long as they are not kept down by fear of punishment. Think of Socrates when he opposed the crowd of his nation as to their idolatry and did not want to call the stars gods! At once eleven of the twelve judges of the Athenians agreed on a sentence of death, and Socrates died faithful to the truth.

The Hindus had no men of this stamp both capable and willing to bring sciences to a classical perfection. Therefore you mostly find that even the so-called scientific theorems of the Hindus are in a state of utter confusion, devoid of any logical order, and in the last instance always mixed up with the silly notions of the crowd, e.g. immense numbers, enormous spaces of time, and all kinds of religious dogmas, which the vulgar belief does not admit of being called into question. Therefore it is a prevailing practice among the Hindus *jurare in verba magistri*; and I can only compare their mathematical and astronomical literature, as far as I know it, to a mixture of pearl shells and sour dates, or of pearls and dung, or of costly crystals and common pebbles. Both kinds of things are equal in their eyes, since they cannot raise themselves to the methods of a strictly scientific deduction.

Image 12.2
Rock Temple
at Ellora

Analysis and Review Questions

1. Do you think Alberuni is appreciative of Hindu culture? Why or why not?
2. Does Alberuni believe Hindus to be egotistical or humble?
3. Why does the author compare the Greeks with the Hindus? What does he conclude?
4. What positive things does Alberuni says about India?
5. According to Alberuni, what sort of scientific skills do Hindus display?

INDIAN POETRY, 1360–1450 C.E.

About the Document

In Europe, the period from 1300 to 1450 C.E. was the time of the Renaissance, recalled as a time of great cultural and artistic development. But Europe was not the only place experiencing a cultural rebirth. India, once again in an era of relative political disunity as the Delhi Sultanate was weakening, also experienced a sort of mini–Golden Age during this time.

One of India's cultural realities—a reality which also hurt its chances for greater political unity—was its great diversity of language, both written and spoken. The learned language of Hindus was Sanskrit, though its heyday had passed by this time. Muslim scholars used Arabic, while those in Muslim governments often used Persian at court. The average person, however, was likely to use any number of other languages, ranging from Hindi to Urdu (a language combining Persian, Turkish, and Hindi) to Tamil to Kannada. Poetry, especially, was likely to be created in a variety of written languages, as the following selections show.

The poet Ratnakaravarni wrote in Kannada, one of India's oldest languages. Ratnakaravarni is well known for his folk poetry; he lived during the 1300s. The poet, scholar, and writer Vidyapati lived from around 1352 to 1448 and wrote in both Hindi and Maithili, a local dialect. Most of his poems are love poems, often written about the love of the goddess Radha for the god Krishna.

The Document

THE IDEAL MONARCH

> To the king affairs of state are as dear as affairs of spirit;
> He feasts his senses, but is master of himself.
> The king should seek worldly pleasures, but be wedded to Dharma.°
> His heart should seem to be engaged in the pursuits of life
> but be clear and unattached.
>
> Like a dancer who minds her step to the rhythm of music
> and minds her head balancing a pitcher, the king
> pursues matters of polity and high values of Dharma.

Dharma: Hindu concept of proper behavior characterized by strictly following one's caste rules.

Like a kite which plays in high heaven but is bound
to solid earth in the hands of a skilful player, a man
can indulge his body and yet be devoted to Dharma,
and there is no trickery in that.

    RATNAKARAVARNI

SONGS OF LOVE

It is the night of the rains, the damsel is tender, and it is terribly dark.
On the way, thousands of night-rangers are roaming about, and it is raining heavily.
O, Madhava, she is terrified on account of her first love.
Having gone there personally, you, please, see her (condition and then) do what
    ever (you think) proper.
On the way, there (flows) the terrible Yamuna, how will she come across?
O wise one, O sweet heart, the sentiment of sexual union, for her, is insignificant
    and worthless.
Having known all these, still you are indifferent towards the beautiful faced
    (damsel); still you do not feel ashamed!
Where has one seen, honey, itself, flowing into the bee.

First, you will decorate your hairs and besmear (sandal) paste (over your body).
    Then you will paint your unsteady eyes with collyrium.
You will go with all your limbs covered with cloth. You will remain at a distance so
    that he may become (very much)
    desirous (of meeting you).
O, damsel, first you will manifest (signs of) bashfulness, and with your side-glances
    you will arouse Cupid.
You will cover (one half of) your breasts and expose the other half. Every moment
    you will make the knot in the
    lower garment tighter.
You will show anger and then exhibit some love (for him). You will preserve the
    sentiment so that he may come
    again and again.
O damsel, what further instructions in the science of love shall I give to you? Cu
    pid himself will become the guide
    and will tell you everything.

Today I shall go for a union with Hari; how much of cravings did I have?
As soon as the superiors in the house were noticed to have fallen asleep the moon
    appeared (in the horizon).
O moon, your ways are cruel.

You got calumny° on account of such a behaviour; still you are not afraid!
The moment the face of a girl of the earth surpassed you (in beauty), vanquished,
    you went over to the sky.
Even there you fell victim (to the wrath) of Rahu. How shall I abuse you?
The creator with much effort and great zeal creates you in a month, but you are
    not allowed to live a second day as
    a consequence of that sin.

calumny: Negative attacks on others in order to ruin their reputations.

O girl, your face is very beautiful, to me it appears as if you will be accused of theft
   of the moon. Do not look at
   anybody, nor let yourself be seen by anybody; under
   the impression of the moon Rahu will devour up (your face).
Your bright eyes have become black with collyrium; they look like a sharp (arrow)
   set to a bow by a hunter.
Having gazed at you fixedly he will spread his set, and taking you for a khanjana
   bird, he will hold you up in fetters.
You have stolen the essence of the ocean (nectar) and the moon; on account of
   this Rahu is remonstrating strongly.
Where will you conceal the theft of the moon? Wherever you will hide it there it
   will be bright.

   VIDYAPATI

THE END OF YOUTH

I hide my shabby cheeks
With locks of hair,
And my grey hairs
In folds of flowers.
I paint my eyes
With black mascara.
The more I try
The more absurd I look.
My breasts loosely dangle.
My curving lines are gone.
My youth is ended
And love roams wild
In all my skin and bones.
O sadness, my sadness,
Where is my youth?

   VIDYAPATI

FIRST LOVE

Asked for her lips,
She bows her head.
She cannot bear
His hands upon her breasts.
She tightly holds
Her loosened girdle,
As flushing skin
Betrays her mounting love.
Gentle the girl,
So skilled her lover—
How will they play
The game of passion?
Her breasts in bud
Still hidden in her palms,
The crisp green plums
That change to crimson red. . . .

His nails grow eager
To set upon her breasts,
Her eyebrows curving
Like the crescent moon.
Greedy for her face, he wonders
How long can the moon
Hide within her dress.

    VIDYAPATI

FROWNS AND SMILES

When my lover comes to my courtyard,
I shall smile and move away.
Frantic, he will catch my dress,
Yet I shall not relent.
When he begs me for love,
I shall smile but not speak.
As he darts at my bodice,
I shall stop him with my hands and scolding eyes.
Distraught, the beautiful bee will seize my chin,
Suck honey from my lips,
And loot my senses.

    VIDYAPATI

Analysis and Review Questions

1. What characteristics does Ratnakaravarni recommend for the "ideal monarch"?
2. Can you relate to any of the advice given by Vidyapati in "Song of Love"? If so, how?
3. Would you say that the woman in "Frowns and Smiles" is playing "hard to get"?
4. What sort of woman is speaking in "The End of Youth"? How do you know?
5. Do the love poems here seem to be specific to ancient India, or are they "universal"?

A WORLD TRAVELER IN INDIA

About the Document

During the time of the Roman Empire, it was relatively easy for travelers to feel at home in distant parts of the Empire; there were religious similarities through Roman emperor worship, cultural connections through Greek and Latin culture, and political and economic unity. At the height of the Islamic world, during Europe's Middle Ages, similar conditions existed. Some religious unity existed in Muslim territory, merchants traveled freely between kingdoms, and a degree of cultural unity was emerging. Just as in Rome's heyday, numerous scholars and writers visited the far reaches of the territory controlled.

One of these Muslim visitors was Ibn Battuta, who was born in Morocco and lived from 1304 to 1368. A devout Muslim, Ibn Battuta traveled through Egypt

*Map 12.1
(Interactive) The
Delhi Sultanate
and Mughal India*

and the Middle East as a young man, then set off for East Asia. After visiting parts of India, he even journeyed to China. While he describes many aspects of the societies he encounters, he is primarily concerned with what Muslims were doing and how the religion functioned in faraway places. Nonetheless, his writings give us a detailed look into the places he visited. In this excerpt, he visits the capital of the Delhi Sultanate, Delhi.

The Document

On the next day we arrived at the city of Dihlí [Delhi], the metropolis of India, a vast and magnificent city, uniting beauty with strength. It is surrounded by a wall that has no equal in the world, and is the largest city in India, nay rather the largest city in the entire Muslim Orient.

The city of Delhi is made up now of four neighbouring and contiguous towns. One of them is Delhi proper, the old city built by the infidels and captured in the year 1188. The second is called Sírí, known also as the Abode of the Caliphate; this was the town given by the sultan to Ghiyath ad-Dín, the grandson of the 'Abbasid Caliph Mustansir, when he came to his court. The third is called Tughlaq Abad, after its founder, the Sultan Tughlaq, the father of the sultan of India to whose court we came. The reason why he built it was that one day he said to a former sultan "O master of the world, it were fitting that a city should be built here." The sultan replied to him in jest "When you are sultan, build it." It came about by the decree of God that he became sultan, so he built it and called it by his own name. The fourth is called Jahan Panah, and is set apart for the residence of the reigning sultan, Muhammad Shah. He was the founder of it, and it was his intention to unite these four towns within a single wall, but after building part of it he gave up the rest because of the expense required for its construction.

The cathedral mosque occupies a large area; its walls, roof, and paving are all constructed of white stones, admirably squared and firmly cemented with lead. There is no wood in it at all. It has thirteen domes of stone, its pulpit also is made of stone, and it has four courts. In the centre of the mosque is an awe-inspiring column, and nobody knows of what metal it is constructed. One of their learned men told me that it is called *Haft Júsh*, which means "seven metals," and that it is constructed from these seven. A part of this column, of a finger's breadth, has been polished, and gives out a brilliant gleam. Iron makes no impression on it. It is thirty cubits° high, and we rolled a turban round it, and the portion which encircled it measured eight cubits. At the eastern gate there are two enormous idols of brass prostrate on the ground and held by stones, and everyone entering or leaving the mosque treads on them. The site was formerly occupied by an idol temple, and was converted into a mosque on the conquest of the city. In the northern court is the minaret, which has no parallel in the lands of Islam. It is built of red stone, unlike the rest of the edifice, ornamented with sculptures, and of great height. The ball on the top is of glistening white marble and its "apples" [small balls surmounting a minaret] are of pure gold. The passage is so wide that elephants could go up by it. A person in whom I have confidence told me that when it was built he saw an elephant climbing with stones to the top. The Sultan Qutb ad-Dín wished to build one in the western court even larger, but was cut off by death when only a third of it had been completed. This minaret is one of the wonders of the world for size, and the width of its

cubit: An ancient unit of measure, generally the length from the elbow to the tip of the middle finger.

passage is such that three elephants could mount it abreast. The third of it built equals in height the whole of the other minaret we have mentioned in the northern court, though to one looking at it from below it does not seem so high because of its bulk.

Outside Delhi is a large reservoir named after the Sultan Lalmish, from which the inhabitants draw their drinking water. It is supplied by rain water, and is about two miles in length by half that breadth. In the centre there is a great pavilion built of squared stones, two stories high. When the reservoir is filled with water it can be reached only in boats, but when the water is low the people go into it. Inside it is a mosque, and at most times it is occupied by mendicants devoted to the service of God. When the water dries up at the sides of this reservoir, they sow sugar canes, cucumbers, green melons and pumpkins there. The melons and pumpkins are very sweet but of small size. Between Delhi and the Abode of the Caliphate is the private reservoir, which is larger than the other. Along its sides there are about forty pavilions, and round about it live the musicians.

The sultan's palace at Delhi is called *Dar Sara*, and contains many doors. At the first door there are a number of guardians, and beside it trumpeters and flute-players. When any amìr or person of note arrives, they sound their instruments and say "So-and-so has come, so-and-so has come." The same takes place also at the second and third doors. Outside the first door are platforms on which the executioners sit, for the custom amongst them is that when the sultan orders a man to be executed, the sentence is carried out at the door of the audience hall, and the body lies there over three nights. Between the first and second doors there is a large vestibule with platforms along both sides, on which sit those whose turn of duty it is to guard the doors. Between the second and third doors there is a large platform on which the principal naqìb [keeper of the register] sits; in front of him there is a gold mace, which he holds in his hand, and on his head he wears a jewelled tiara of gold, surmounted by peacock feathers. The second door leads to an extensive audience hall in which the people sit. At the third door there are platforms occupied by the scribes of the door. One of their customs is that none may pass through this door except those whom the sultan has prescribed, and for each person he prescribes a number of his staff to enter along with him. Whenever any person comes to this door the scribes write down "So-and-so came at the first hour" or the second, and so on, and the sultan receives a report of this after the evening prayer. Another of their customs is that anyone who absents himself from the palace for three days or more, with or without excuse, may not enter this door thereafter except by the sultan's permission. If he has an excuse of illness or otherwise he presents the sultan with a gift suitable to his rank. The third door opens into an immense audience hall called *Hazar Ustún*, which means "A thousand pillars." The pillars are of wood and support a wooden roof, admirably carved. The people sit under this, and it is in this hall that the sultan holds public audiences.

Analysis and Review Questions

1. How would you describe Ibn Battuta's impression of Delhi?
2. What sits outside of Delhi, named after the Sultan Lalmish?
3. What does the author spend more time talking about—the city's religious buildings or the city's defensive walls? Why?
4. What was named "Hazar Ustan"?
5. Where are people executed by order of the sultan?

TALES OF TEN PRINCES

About the Document

Much as Latin was long considered the "high" language of Christianity, the learned language of Hinduism is Sanskrit. Though few people could actually read it, scholars, intellectuals, and writers used it frequently in early India. One of the most well-known writers of Sanskrit literature in the early period was Dandin, who lived some time in the late 500s to early 600s C.E.

Dandin's most noted work is *Tales of the Ten Princes*, a collection of tales connected by an ongoing narrative. Focusing on the experiences of Prince Rajavahana, a Hindu prince, the tales are more secular than religious. Many of Dandin's tales tend to be sensual in nature or tend to deal with leading a virtuous life. Despite being written in a language that most Hindus could not understand, Dandin's stories provide quite a bit of detail about the lives and attitudes of common people. In this excerpt, Dandin uses his story to discuss the characteristics of the perfect wife.

The Document

"In the land of the Dravidians° is a city called Kañci. Therein dwelt the very wealthy son of a merchant, by name Saktikumara. When he was nearly eighteen he thought: 'There's no pleasure in living without a wife or with one of bad character. Now how can I find a really good one?' So, dubious of his chance of finding wedded bliss with a woman taken at the word of others, he became a fortune-teller, and roamed the land with a measure of unhusked rice tied in the skirts of his robe; and parents, taking him for an interpreter of birthmarks, showed their daughters to him. Whenever he saw a girl of his own class, whatever her birthmarks, he would say to her: 'My dear girl, can you cook me a good meal from this measure of rice?' And so, ridiculed and rejected, he wandered from house to house.

"One day in the land of the Sibis, in a city on the banks of the Kaveri,° he examined a girl who was shown to him by her nurse. She wore little jewellery, for her parents had spent their fortune, and had nothing left but their dilapidated mansion. As soon as he set eyes on her he thought: 'This girl is shapely and smooth in all her members. Not one limb is too fat or too thin, too short or too long. Her fingers are pink; her hands are marked with auspicious lines—the barleycorn, the fish, the lotus and the vase; her ankles are shapely; her feet are plump and the veins are not prominent; her thighs curve smoothly; her knees can barely be seen, for they merge into her rounded thighs; her buttocks are dimpled and round as chariot wheels; her navel is small, flat and deep; her stomach is adorned with three lines; the nipples stand out from her large breasts, which cover her whole chest; her palms are marked with signs which promise corn, wealth and sons; her nails are smooth and polished like jewels; her fingers are straight and tapering and pink; her arms curve sweetly from the shoulder, and are smoothly jointed; her slender neck is curved like a conch-shell; her lips are rounded and of even red; her pretty chin does not recede; her cheeks are round, full and firm; her eyebrows do not join above her nose, and are curved, dark and even; her nose is like a half-blown sesamum flower; her wide eyes are large and gentle and flash with three colours, black,

Dravidian: A group of people traditionally living in the south of India.
Kaveri: The principal river of South India.

white and brown; her brow is fair as the new moon; her curls are lovely as a mine of sapphires; her long ears are adorned doubly, with earrings and charming lotuses, hanging limply; her abundant hair is not brown, even at the tips, but long, smooth, glossy and fragrant. The character of such a girl cannot but correspond to her appearance, and my heart is fixed upon her, so I'll test her and marry her. For one regret after another is sure to fall on the heads of people who don't take precautions!' So, looking at her affectionately, he said, 'Dear girl, can you cook a good meal for me with this measure of rice?'

"Then the girl glanced at her old servant, who took the measure of rice from his hand and seated him on the veranda, which had been well sprinkled and swept, giving him water to cool his feet. Meanwhile the girl bruised the fragrant rice, dried it a little at a time in the sun, turned it repeatedly, and beat it with a hollow cane on a firm flat spot, very gently, so as to separate the grain without crushing the husk. Then she said to the nurse, 'Mother, goldsmiths can make good use of these husks for polishing jewellery. Take them, and, with the coppers you get for them, buy some firewood, not too green and not too dry, a small cooking pot, and two earthen dishes.'

"When this was done she put the grains of rice in a shallow wide-mouthed, round-bellied mortar, and took a long and heavy pestle of acacia-wood, its head shod with a plate of iron. . . . With skill and grace she exerted her arms, as the grains jumped up and down in the mortar. Repeatedly she stirred them and pressed them down with her fingers; then she shook the grains in a winnowing basket to remove the beard, rinsed them several times, worshipped the hearth, and placed them in water which had been five times brought to the boil. When the rice softened, bubbled and swelled, she drew the embers of the fire together, put a lid on the cooking pot, and strained off the gruel. Then she patted the rice with a ladle and scooped it out a little at a time; and when she found that it was thoroughly cooked she put the cooking pot on one side, mouth downward. Next she damped down those sticks which were not burnt through, and when the fire was quite out she sent them to the dealers to be sold as charcoal, saying, 'With the coppers that you get for them, buy as much as you can of green vegetables, ghee, curds, sesamum oil, myrobalans and tamarind.'

"When this was done she offered him a few savouries. Next she put the rice-gruel in a new dish immersed in damp sand, and cooled it with the soft breeze of a palm-leaf fan. She added a little salt, and flavoured it with the scent of the embers; she ground the myrobalans to a smooth powder, until they smelt like a lotus; and then, by the lips of the nurse, she invited him to take a bath. This he did, and when she too had bathed she gave him oil and myrobalans [as an unguent].

"After he had bathed he sat on a bench in the paved courtyard, which had been thoroughly sprinkled and swept. She stirred the gruel in the two dishes, which she set before him on a piece of pale green plantain leaf, cut from a tree in the courtyard. He drank it and felt rested and happy, relaxed in every limb. Next she gave him two ladlefuls of the boiled rice, served with a little ghee° and condiments. She served the rest of the rice with curds, three spices, and fragrant and refreshing buttermilk and gruel. He enjoyed the meal to the last mouthful.

"When he asked for a drink she poured him water in a steady stream from the spout of a new pitcher—it was fragrant with incense, and smelt of fresh trumpet-flowers and the perfume of full-blown lotuses. He put the bowl to his lips, and his eyelashes sparkled with rosy drops as cool as snow; his ears delighted in the sound of the trickling water; his rough cheeks thrilled and tingled at its pleasant contact; his nostrils opened wide at its sweet fragrance; and his tongue delighted in its lovely flavour, as he drank the

ghee: A light butter, semi-creamy.

pure water in great gulps. Then, at his nod, the girl gave him a mouthwash in another bowl. The old woman took away the remains of his meal, and he slept awhile in his ragged cloak, on the pavement plastered with fresh cowdung.

"Wholly pleased with the girl, he married her with due rites, and took her home. Later he neglected her awhile and took a mistress, but the wife treated her as a dear friend. She served her husband indefatigably, as she would a god, and never neglected her household duties; and she won the loyalty of her servants by her great kindness. In the end her husband was so enslaved by her goodness that he put the whole household in her charge, made her sole mistress of his life and person, and enjoyed the three aims of life—virtue, wealth and love. So I maintain that virtuous wives make their lords happy and virtuous."

Analysis and Review Questions

1. According to Dandin, what sorts of attributes does an ideal wife possess?
2. Which does the author seem more concerned about—the wife's moral nature or her physical appearance? Why?
3. Do domestic activities appear to be a primary concern for Indian men? Why or why not?
4. What things does the husband in this excerpt do for his wife?
5. Does this excerpt seem to paint a picture of a "typical" husband and wife relationship throughout much of history? Why or why not?

WEB LINKS

http://longmanworldhistory.com
The following additional readings and case studies can be found on the Web site.
Document 5.6, Descriptions of Alexandria, Egypt
Document 12.3, The Ideal Muslim King
Document 14.8, Louis XIV Writes to His Son
Document 14.9, Juan Luis Vives, The Office and Dutie of a Husband
Case Study 12.1, The Ideal Monarch in History
Case Study 12.2, Alexandria, Egypt and Delhi India
Case Study 12.3, The Ideal Wife

http://www.123india.com
This site portrays itself as "India's Premier Portal," with good reason. Everything from current Indian news and online India chat to Indian search engines can be found here.

http://www.humanistictexts.org/albiruni1.htm
A more complete version of Alberuni's accounts of India.

http://delhicity.net/tourist_guide/
A site that includes a history of Delhi and the Delhi Sultanate.

http://www.itihaas.com/medieval/index.html
A detailed chronology of events in medieval India.

CHAPTER 13

East Asia: Chinese Imperial Splendor and the Mongol Empire

After the Han Dynasty, China experienced a long period of disunity before the cosmopolitan Tang and Song Dynasties revitalized China's imperial brilliance for another 300 years. The consolidation of Chinese centralized government, the flourishing of Buddhism, the thriving of the famous Tang and Song poetry, and the prosperous urban culture marked the heyday of Chinese political, economic, and cultural developments between the sixth and eleventh centuries.

Map 13.1
The Mongol Empire in the Late Thirteenth Century

Meanwhile, Chinese culture continued to influence that of its neighbor, Japan. The Taikai Reforms in the seventh century and more borrowing from China throughout the Heian Period (794–1185) gave Japan a mixed culture rooted deeply in Chinese tradition. China's golden age was challenged by the nomadic Mongols from the north. From 1206, the Mongol armies led by Genghis Khan swept through Central Asia, Asia Minor, China, and Russia. In 1270, Khublai Khan, the grandson of Genghis Khan, became ruler of the Mongol Empire. He moved the capital from Karakorum in Mongolia to Beijing (Peking), where he ruled China as the emperor. He named the new dynasty Yuan, meaning "the beginning" or "the original." By 1280, the Mongol Empire stretched from the Yellow Sea to the Mediterranean.

The Mongol Empire linked Asia Minor, part of Russia, and East and Southeast Asia through its courier system and long distance trade activities. In many ways, the Mongols kept the Chinese bureaucracy, social structure, and cultural tradition almost intact, except for a short-lived suspension of the examination system. Despite the fact that the Mongols ruled China under the Yuan Dynasty, the Chinese proper remained substantially Chinese.

POEMS BY LI BAI AND DU FU

About the Document

The Tang Dynasty marked not only the heyday of Chinese political and economic developments, but also the flowering of Chinese classical poetry. Of the over 300 Tang poems, those from Li Bai and Du Fu are the most revered and well known.

Educated in both Confucian and Daoist classics, Li Bai (701–763) created a poetic style that revealed a fondness for romanticism and the wildness of nature. It was believed that Li Bai liked to drink while composing poems and that he eventually drowned himself in the lake in an attempt to catch the moon reflecting in the water.

Du Fu (712–770), who was Li Bai's contemporary, reflected in his writing the social consciousness of Confucian scholars. His poems show a deep compassion for the everyday life of ordinary people. Some of his most emotional poetry reveals his agony at the hardships of the common people and his frustration at social injustice.

Both Li Bai and Du Fu are among the most talented Chinese poets of all time. While Li Bai's "Drinking Alone Beneath the Moon" reflects his passion for nature, Du Fu's "Farewell of an Old Man" depicts the anguish of an old soldier going to war.

Image 13.1
Court Lady Yang Gufél
Ascending a Horse

The Document

DRINKING ALONE BENEATH THE MOON
(two selections)

BY LI BAI

1
A pot of wine among the flowers:
I drink alone, no kith or kin near.
I raise my cup to invite the moon to join me;
It and my shadow make a party of three.
Alas, the moon is unconcerned about drinking,
And my shadow merely follows me around.
Briefly I cavort with the moon and my shadow:
Pleasure must be sought while it is spring.
I sing and the moon goes back and forth,
I dance and my shadow falls at random.
While sober we seek pleasure in fellowship;
When drunk we go each our own way.
Then let us pledge a friendship without human ties
And meet again at the far end of the Milky Way.

2
If Heaven weren't fond of wine
Wine Star would not be found in Heaven.
If Earth weren't fond of wine
There could be no Wine Spring° on earth.
Since Heaven and Earth are fond of wine,
In Heaven being fond of wine can't be judged wrong.
Clear wine, I've heard, is compared to sages,
Also the unstrained wine spoken of as worthies.
Since I've drunk both sages and worthies
Why must I seek out the immortals?

Wine Spring: The name of a town in Gansu Province, known for its underground spring water that tastes like wine.

Three cups penetrate the Great Truth;
One gallon accords with Nature's laws.
Simply find pleasure in wine:
Speak not of it to the sober ones.

FAREWELL OF AN OLD MAN

BY DU FU

"No peace or quiet in the countryside,
Even in old age I find no rest.
My sons and grandsons lost in war,
What's the use of staying home to save my skin?"
He throws away his cane and strides out the gate;
Tears come to his old comrades-in-arms.

"I'm lucky. I still have my own teeth
Though I regret the marrow dried in my bones.
Now that I'm a soldier properly clad in armor,
I'll make a long bow to bid farewell to the magistrate.

"My dear old woman lies crying by the road,
It's late winter; her clothes are thin.
Who can be sure this won't be our final farewell—
I cannot stop worrying over her suffering in the fierce cold.
I do not expect to return from this march,
Yet her gentle urging to eat well stays with me.

"The walls at T'u-men have been fortified;
The ferry at Hsing-yuan will thwart the foe.
Conditions are different from our defeat at Yeh;
Even if I must die, there is still some time left.
Life has its partings and reunions,
Why fuss about your age; everyone must die.
But when I think back on the days of my youth
I can't help pausing—and sighing.

"The whole empire is a military camp;
Beacon fires have spread to each ridge and peak.
Corpses in piles foul fields and woods,
Blood reddens streams and plains.
If I knew where Heaven was
I wouldn't linger on this earth longer.
To leave for good this humble cottage and home
Will crush a man."

Analysis and Review Questions

1. Considering what you have read of Daoism in this text, in what aspects of Li Bai's poem can you see Daoist inspiration?
2. In what manner does Li Bai's writing present the relationship between humanity and nature?

3. What is Du Fu's view of the expansion of the Chinese Empire of his time? How does the poet express the ordinary people's response to an ever-expanding empire?
4. What are Du Fu's complaints about social injustice?
5. Theorize about what life was like for both poets.

EXCERPT FROM LADY MURASAKI SHIKIBU'S DIARY

About the Document

Murasaki Shikibu (978–c.1025) was an aristocratic woman in eleventh-century Japan. She was the author of the world famous romance *The Tale of Genji*. The fact that Lady Murasaki herself was from an aristocratic family and that the novel was about a prince's experience in the imperial court makes her work an important historical reference as well as a literary masterpiece. Lady Murasaki lived in a time period corresponding to China's Song Dynasty, when Chinese influence had spread throughout Japan in political, social, intellectual, and economic areas. During this time Japan began to depart from borrowing so heavily from China and concentrated instead on its own culture.

*Image 13.2
Japanese Court Ladies*

In addition to her description of the elegant lifestyle of the imperial family, Lady Murasaki also portrayed the Japanese upper-class women of her time as having considerable freedom to pursue their love for literature and art.

The Document

As the autumn season approaches the Tsuchimikado° becomes inexpressibly smile-giving. The tree-tops near the pond, the bushes near the stream, are dyed in varying tints whose colors grow deeper in the mellow light of evening. The murmuring sound of waters mingles all the night through with the never-ceasing recitation of sutras° which appeal more to one's heart as the breezes grow cooler.

The ladies waiting upon her honored presence are talking idly. The Queen hears them; she must find them annoying, but she conceals it calmly. Her beauty needs no words of mine to praise it, but I cannot help feeling that to be near so beautiful a queen will be the only relief from my sorrow. So in spite of my better desires [for a religious life] I am here. Nothing else dispels my grief—it is wonderful! . . .

I can see the garden from my room beside the entrance to the gallery. The air is misty, the dew is still on the leaves. The Lord Prime Minister is walking there; he orders his men to cleanse the brook. He breaks off a stalk of omenaishi [flower maiden] which is in full bloom by the south end of the bridge. He peeps in over my screen! His noble appearance embarrasses us, and I am ashamed of my morning [not yet painted and powdered] face. He says, "Your poem on this! If you delay so much the fun is gone!" and I seize the chance to run away to the writing-box, hiding my face—

Flower-maiden in bloom—
Even more beautiful for the bright dew,
Which is partial, and never favors me.

Tsuchimikado: Residence of Prime Minister Fujiwara Michnaga.
sutras: Buddhist texts.

"So prompt!" said he, smiling, and ordered a writing-box
to be brought for himself.
His answer:

The silver dew is never partial.
From her heart
The flower-maiden's beauty.

One wet and calm evening I was talking with Lady Saisho. The young Lord of the Third Rank sat with the misu° partly rolled up. He seemed maturer than his age and was very graceful. Even in light conversation such expressions as "Fair soul is rarer than fair face" come gently to his lips, covering us with confusion. It is a mistake to treat him like a young boy. He keeps his dignity among ladies, and I saw in him a much-sought-after romantic hero when once he walked off reciting to himself:

Linger in the field where flower-maidens are blooming
and your name will be tarnished with tales of gallantry.

Some such trifle as that sometimes lingers in my mind when really interesting things are soon forgotten—why? . . .

On the fifth night the Lord Prime Minister celebrated the birth. The full moon on the fifteenth day was clear and beautiful. Torches were lighted under the trees and tables were put there with rice-balls on them. Even the uncouth humble servants who were walking about chattering seemed to enhance the joyful scene. All minor officials were there burning torches, making it as bright as day. Even the attendants of the nobles, who gathered behind the rocks and under the trees, talked of nothing but the new light which had come into the world, and were smiling and seemed happy as if their own private wishes had been fulfilled. . . .

This time, as they chose only the best-looking young ladies, the rest who used to tie their hair on ordinary occasions to serve the Queen's dinner wept bitterly; it was shocking to see them. . . .

To serve at the Queen's dinner eight ladies tied their hair with white cords, and in that dress brought in Her Majesty's dining-table. The chief lady-in-waiting for that night was Miya-no-Naishi. She was brilliantly dressed with great formality, and her hair was made more charming by the white cords which enhanced her beauty. I got a side glance of her when her face was not screened by her fan. She wore a look of extreme purity. . . .

The court nobles rose from their seats and went to the steps [descending from the balcony]. His Lordship the Prime Minister and others cast dice. It was shocking to see them quarreling about paper. Some others composed poems. A lady said, "What response shall we make if some one offers to drink saki with us?" We tried to think of something.

Shijo-no-Dainagon is a man of varied accomplishments. No ladies can rival him in repartee, much less compete with him in poetry, so they were all afraid of him, but this evening he did not give a cup to any particular lady to make her compose poems. Perhaps that was because he had many things to do and it was getting late. . . .

The Great Advisor° is displeased to be received by ladies of low rank, so when he comes to the Queen's court to make some report and suitable ladies to receive him are not available, he goes away without seeing Her Majesty. Other court nobles, who

misu: A bamboo curtain to keep a person, usually a member of the royal family, from view.
The Great Advisor: Fujiwara Michitaka, the Prime Minister's brother.

often come to make reports, have each a favorite lady, and when that one is away they are displeased, and go away saying to other people that the Queen's ladies are quite unsatisfactory. . . .

Lady Izumi Shikibu° corresponds charmingly, but her behavior is improper indeed. She writes with grace and ease and with a flashing wit. There is fragrance even in her smallest words. Her poems are attractive, but they are only improvisations which drop from her mouth spontaneously. Every one of them has some interesting point, and she is acquainted with ancient literature also, but she is not like a true artist who is filled with the genuine spirit of poetry. Yet I think even she cannot presume to pass judgment on the poems of others.

The wife of the Governor of Tamba Province is called by the Queen and Prime Minister Masa Hira Emon. Though she is not of noble birth, her poems are very satisfying. She does not compose and scatter them about on every occasion, but so far as we know them, even her miscellaneous poems shame us. Those who compose poems whose loins are all but broken, yet who are infinitely self-exalted and vain, deserve our contempt and pity.

Lady Seishonagon.° A very proud person. She values herself highly, and scatters her Chinese writings all about. Yet should we study her closely, we should find that she is still imperfect. She tries to be exceptional, but naturally persons of that sort give offense. She is piling up trouble for her future. One who is too richly gifted, who indulges too much in emotion, even when she ought to be reserved, and cannot turn aside from anything she is interested in, in spite of herself will lose self-control. How can such a vain and reckless person end her days happily?

Having no excellence within myself, I have passed my days without making any special impression on anyone. Especially the fact that I have no man who will look out for my future makes me comfortless. I do not wish to bury myself in dreariness. Is it because of my worldly mind that I feel lonely? On moonlight nights in autumn, when I am hopelessly sad, I often go out on the balcony and gaze dreamily at the moon. It makes me think of days gone by. People say that it is dangerous to look at the moon in solitude, but something impels me, and sitting a little withdrawn I muse there. In the wind-cooled evening I play on the koto,° though others may not care to hear it. I fear that my playing betrays the sorrow which becomes more intense, and I become disgusted with myself—so foolish and miserable am I. . . .

A pair of big bookcases have in them all the books they can hold. In one of them are placed old poems and romances. They are the homes of worms which come frightening us when we turn the pages, so none ever wished to read them. [Perhaps her own writings, she speaks so slightingly of them.] As to the other cabinet, since the person who placed his own books [there] no hand has touched it. When I am bored to death I take out one or two of them; then my maids gather around me and say: "Your life will not be favored with old age if you do such a thing! Why do you read Chinese? Formerly even the reading of sutras was not encouraged for women." They rebuke me in the shade [i.e., behind my back]. I have heard of it and have wished to say, "It is far from certain that he who does no forbidden thing enjoys a long life," but it would be a lack of reserve to say it [to the maids]. Our deeds vary with our age and deeds vary with the individual. Some are proud [to read books], others look over old cast-away writings because they are bored with having nothing to do. It would not be becoming

---

Lady Izumi Shikibu: One of Japan's best known poets.
Lady Seishonagon: One of Lady Murasaki's contemporaries and also her rival in the literary circle.
koto: A stringed musical instrument.

for such a one to chatter away about religious thoughts, noisily shaking a rosary. I feel this, and before my women keep myself from doing what otherwise I could do easily. But after all, when I was among the ladies of the Court I did not say what I wanted to say either, for it is useless to talk with those who do not understand one and troublesome to talk with those who criticize from a feeling of superiority. Especially one-sided persons are troublesome. Few are accomplished in many arts and most cling narrowly to their own opinion.

Analysis and Review Questions

1. In what way can you see the Chinese cultural influence on the Japanese upper class?
2. What kind of life was it for the Japanese aristocratic class, according to the writing of Lady Murasaki?
3. How similar is the style in Li Bai's poetry to the poetic lines in Lady Murasaki's diary?
4. What was Lady Murasaki's vision for women?
5. In what way were the Japanese upper-class women different from the Chinese women of Confucian virtues?

MARCO POLO ON CHINESE SOCIETY UNDER THE MONGOL RULE

About the Document

Marco Polo was the son of an Italian merchant who traveled the Silk Road to Mongol China in the year 1275. A gifted linguist and master of four languages, Marco Polo was appointed by Emperor Kublai Khan as an official in the Privy Council in 1277, and for three years he was a tax inspector in Yanzhou, a city on the Grand Canal near the northeastern coast. He also visited Karakorum, the old capital of the original Mongol empire. Marco Polo stayed in Khan's court for 17 years, acquiring great wealth in gold and jewelry.

Reportedly, Marco Polo kept a detailed dairy about his travels and his experiences in China. He recalled in great detail the moment when he and other members of his family first met the Emperor Kublai Khan: "They knelt before him and made obeisance with the utmost humility. The Great Khan bade them rise and received them honorably and entertained them with good cheer. He asked many questions about their condition and how they fared after their departure . . . Then they presented the privileges and letters which the Pope had sent, with which he was greatly pleased, and handed over the holy oil, which he received with joy and prized very highly."

Marco Polo's account of his life under the Mongols and his personal experience in China's Yuan Dynasty caused both curiosity and doubts among Westerners. Many questioned the validity of his records, wondering if he had ever reached China. The controversy led to a book in 1995 entitled *Did Marco Polo Go to China?* by Frances Wood, head of Chinese Studies at the British Library. Wood argued that Marco Polo probably only went as far as Constantinople, where he gathered information on China from Arabs and Persians who returned from their China trip.

Map 13.2
(Interactive)
Chinese Empires

The Document

It is their custom that the bodies of all deceased grand khans and other great lords from the family of Chinggis Khan are carried for internment to a great mountain called Altai.° No matter where they might die, even if it is a hundred days' journey away, they nevertheless are brought here for burial. It is also their custom that, in the process of conveying the bodies of these princes, the escort party sacrifices whatever persons they happen to meet along the route, saying to them: "Depart for the next world and there serve your deceased master." They believe that all whom they kill in this manner will become his servants in the next life. They do the same with horses, killing all the best, so that the dead lord might use them in the next world. When the corpse of Mongke° Khan was transported to this mountain, the horsemen who accompanied it slew upward of 20,000 people along the way.

Now that I have begun speaking about the Tartars,° I will tell you more about them. They never remain fixed in one location. As winter approaches they move to the plains of a warmer region in order to find sufficient pasturage for their animals. In summer they inhabit cool regions in the mountains where there is water and grass and their animals are free of the annoyance of gad-flies and other biting insects. They spend two or three months progressively climbing higher and grazing as they ascend, because the grass is not sufficient in any one spot to feed their extensive herds.

Their huts, or tents, are circular and formed by covering a wooden frame with felt. These they transport on four-wheeled carts wherever they travel, since the framework is so well put together that it is light to carry. Whenever they set their huts up, the entrance always faces south. They also have excellent two-wheeled vehicles so well covered with black felt that, no matter how long it rains, rain never penetrates. These are drawn by oxen and camels and serve to carry their wives, children, and all necessary utensils and provisions.

It is the women who tend to their commercial concerns, buying and selling, and who tend to all the needs of their husbands and households. The men devote their time totally to hunting, hawking, and warfare. They have the best falcons in the world, as well as the best dogs. They subsist totally on meat and milk, eating the produce of their hunting, especially a certain small animal, somewhat like a hare, which our people call Pharaoh's rats, which are abundant on the steppes in summer. They likewise eat every manner of animal: horses, camels, even dogs, provided they are fat. They drink mare's milk, which they prepare in such a way that it has the qualities and taste of white wine. In their language they call it *kemurs*.

Their women are unexcelled in the world so far as their chastity and decency of conduct are concerned, and also in regard to their love and devotion toward their husbands. They regard marital infidelity as a vice which is not simply dishonorable but odious by its very nature. Even if there are ten or twenty women in a household, they live in harmony and highly praiseworthy concord, so that no offensive word is ever spoken. They devote full attention to their tasks and domestic duties, such as preparing the family's food, managing the servants, and caring for the children, whom they raise in common. The wives' virtues of modesty and chastity are all the more praiseworthy because the men are allowed to wed as many women as they please. The expense to the husband for his wives is not that great, but the benefit he derives from their trading and from the work in which they are constantly employed is considerable. For this reason, when he marries he pays a dowry to his wife's parents. The first wife holds the primary place in the household and is reckoned to be the husband's most legitimate wife, and this status extends to her children. Because of their unlimited number of wives, their offspring is

Altai: The Altai Mountains in eastern Mongolia.
Mongke: The same as "Menggu," the Chinese pronunciation of Mongols.
Tartars: Another name for the Mongols.

more numerous than that of any other people. When a father dies, his son may take all of his deceased father's wives, with the exception of his own mother. They also cannot marry their sisters, but upon a brother's death they may marry their sisters-in-law. Every marriage is solemnized with great ceremony.

This is what they believe. They believe in an exalted god of heaven, to whom they burn incense and offer up prayers for sound mind and body. They also worship a god called Natigay, whose image, covered with felt or other cloth, is kept in everyone's house. They associate a wife and children with this god, placing the wife on his left side and the children before him. . . . They consider Natigay as the god who presides over their earthly concerns, protecting their children, their cattle, and their grain. They show him great respect. Before eating they always take a fat portion of meat and smear the idol's mouth with it, as well as the mouths of his wife and children. Then they take some of the broth in which the meat has been cooked and pour it outside, as an offering. When this has been done they believe that their god and his family have had their proper share. The Tartars then proceed to eat and drink without further ceremony.

The rich among these people dress in gold cloth and silks and the furs of sable, ermine, and other animals. All their accouterments are expensive.

Their weapons are bows, iron maces,° and in some instances, spears. The bow, however, is the weapon at which they are the most expert, being accustomed to use it in their sports from childhood. They wear armor made from the hides of buffalo and other beasts, fire-dried and thus hard and strong.

They are brave warriors, almost to the point of desperation, placing little value on their lives, and exposing themselves without hesitation to every sort of danger. They are cruel by nature. They are capable of undergoing every manner of privation, and when it is necessary, they can live for a month on the milk of their mares and the wild animals they catch. Their horses feed on grass alone and do not require barley or other grain. The men are trained to remain on horseback for two days and two nights without dismounting, sleeping in the saddle while the horse grazes. No people on the earth can surpass them in their ability to endure hardships, and no other people shows greater patience in the face of every sort of deprivation. They are most obedient to their chiefs, and are maintained at small expense. These qualities, which are so essential to a soldier's formation, make them fit to subdue the world, which in fact they have largely done.

When one of the great Tartar chiefs goes to war, he puts himself at the head of an army of 100,000 horsemen and organizes them in the following manner. He appoints an officer to command every ten men and others to command groups of 100, 1,000, and 10,000 men respectively. Thus ten of the officers who command ten men take their orders from an officer who commands 100; ten of these captains of a 100 take their orders from an officer in charge of a 1,000; and ten of these officers take orders from one who commands 10,000. By this arrangement, each officer has to manage only ten men or ten bodies of men. . . . When the army goes into the field, a body of 200 men is sent two days' march in advance, and parties are stationed on each flank and in the rear, to prevent surprise attack.

When they are setting out on a long expedition, they carry little with them. . . . They subsist for the most part on mare's milk, as has been said. . . . Should circumstances require speed, they can ride for ten days without lighting a fire or taking a hot meal. During this time they subsist on the blood drawn from their horses, each man opening a vein and drinking the blood. They also have dried milk. . . . When setting off on an expedition, each man takes about ten pounds. Every morning they put about half a pound

mace: A club with spikes on it to break armor and other things.

of this into a leather flask, with as much water as necessary. As they ride, the motion violently shakes the contents, producing a thin porridge which they take as dinner. . . .

All that I have told you here concerns the original customs of the Tartar lords. Today, however, they are corrupted. Those who live in China have adopted the customs of the idol worshippers, and those who inhabit the eastern provinces have adopted the ways of the Muslims.

Analysis and Review Questions

1. From Marco Polo's discussion, can you tell if he himself could identify the difference between the Chinese culture and Mongol culture? Are his views positive or negative toward the Mongol rule?
2. What was women's status under the Mongols?
3. Do you get an impression from Marco Polo's accounts that, to a great extent, the Mongols changed the Chinese traditions under their control?
4. What is Marco Polo's assessment of the factors that could have contributed to the Mongol's success in governing?
5. Toward the end of his writing, what does Marco Polo imply were reasons for the fall of the Mongol Empire?

WEB LINKS

Selections from Longman World History—Primary Sources and Case Studies

Case Studies
13.1 Literary Styles in China and Japan
13.2 Women in the Imperial Courts of China and Japan

The Mongol Empire
http://www.wsu.edu/~dee/CHEMPIRE/YUAN.HTM
http://www.geocities.com/Athens/forum/2532/
http://w3.nai.net/~jroberts/mongol.htm

The Yuan Dynasty
http://campus.northpark.edu/history/WebChron/China/Yuan.html
http://www.china-on-site.com/painting/yuan/yuan.htm

Yang Guifei
http://www.span.com.au/100women/59.html
http://www.fsmitha.com/h3/h06chin.htm

Lady Murasaki Shikibu and *The Tale of Genji*
http://www.womeninworldhistory.com/heroine9.html
http://www.sla.purdue.edu/academic/fll/Japanese/JPNS280/projects/Hines.htm
http://www.i5ive.com/article.cfm/oriental_history/32683
http://www.iz2.or.jp/english/what/life.htm

COMPETING VISIONS OF KNIGHTHOOD

Comparing the models of knighthood in Fulcher's *Chronicle* and *The Song of Roland* gives us a fuller picture of the various cultural forces that shaped the warrior caste of Medieval Europe. The documents need to be read carefully, however. It would be wrong to assume that the *Chronicle* represents the Church's view and *The Song of Roland* that of the nobility. While Fulcher was a priest depicting the Crusades as a righteous holy war, he was working for and answerable to the princes whom he accompanied. Nor does *The Song of Roland* simply depict the ideals of the knights themselves. Those who committed the *Song* to writing and preserved it were priests and monks who edited ecclesiastical views into it. Finally, we should not see the Church and the nobility as totally separate. The leaders of the Church came from noble families and often had political responsibilities themselves. Even so, the two documents present some interesting contrasts.

The Document

I. The Council of Clermont

1. In the year 1095 from the Lord's Incarnation, with Henry reigning in Germany as so-called emperor, and with Philip as king in France, manifold evils were growing in all parts of Europe because of wavering faith. In Rome ruled Pope Urban II, a man distinguished in life and character, who always strove widely and actively to raise the status of the Holy Church above all things.

2. He saw that the faith of Christianity was being destroyed to excess by everybody, by the clergy° as well as by the laity.° He saw that peace was altogether discarded by the princes of the world, who were engaged in incessant warlike contention and quarreling among themselves. He saw the wealth of the land being pillaged continuously. He saw many of the vanquished, wrongfully taken prisoner and very cruelly thrown into foulest dungeons, either ransomed for a high price or, tortured by the triple torments of hunger, thirst, and cold, blotted out by a death hidden from the world. He saw holy places violated; monasteries and villas burned. He saw that no one was spared of any human suffering, and that things divine and human alike were held in derision.

clergy: Refers to priests and monks. Members of the clergy took permanent vows and were supported by the Church. Only the clergy could administer the sacraments essential to salvation or interpret scripture.
laity: All European Christians who were not members of the clergy were considered laity. They were obligated to attend religious services, but could not administer sacraments or interpret scripture.

3. He heard, too, that the interior regions of Romania,° where the Turks ruled over the Christians, had been perniciously subjected in a savage attack.

Moved by long-suffering compassion and by love of God's will, he descended the mountains to Gaul, and in Auvergne he called for a council to congregate from all sides at a suitable time at a city called Clermont. Three hundred and ten bishops and abbots, who had been advised beforehand by messengers, were present.

. . .

II. The Decree of Pope Urban in the Council

1. "Most beloved brethren," he said, "by God's permission placed over the whole world with the papal crown, I, Urban, as the messenger of divine admonition, have been compelled by an unavoidable occasion to come here to you servants of God. I desired those whom I judged to be stewards of God's ministries to be true stewards and faithful, with all hypocrisy rejected.

2. "But with temperance in reason and justice being remote, I, with divine aid, shall strive carefully to root out any crookedness or distortion which might obstruct God's law. For the Lord appointed you temporarily as stewards over His family to serve it nourishment seasoned with a modest savor. Moreover, blessed will you be if at last the Overseer find you faithful.

3. "You are also called shepherds; see that you are not occupied after the manner of mercenaries. Be true shepherds, always holding your crooks in your hands; and sleeping not, guard on every side the flock entrusted to you.

4. "For if through your carelessness or negligence, some wolf seizes a sheep, you doubtless will lose the reward prepared for you by our Lord. Nay, first most cruelly beaten by the whips of the lictors, you afterwards will be angrily cast into the keeping of a deadly place.

. . .

6. "For if because of the sloth of your management, He should find in them worms, that is, sin, straightway, He will order that they, despised, be cast into the dungheap. And because you could not make restoration for such a great loss, He will banish you, utterly condemned in judgment, from the familiarity of His love.

. . .

10. "Uphold the Church in its own ranks altogether free from all secular power. See that the tithes of all those who cultivate the earth are given faithfully to God; let them not be sold or held back.

. . .

11. "Let him who has seized a bishop be considered an outlaw. Let him who has seized or robbed monks, clerics, nuns and their servants, pilgrims, or merchants, be excommunicated.° Let the robbers and burners of homes and their accomplices, banished from the Church, be smitten with excommunication.

Romania: Fulcher is referring to the Byzantine Empire, particularly what is now Turkey.
excommunicated: Literally means to be cut off from the sacrament of communion. The Pope claimed the authority to withhold the sacraments as a form of punishment. If one were to die excommunicate, one would be eternally damned.

13. "And so by these iniquities, most beloved, you have seen the world disturbed too long; so long, as it was told to us by those reporting, that perhaps because of the weakness of your justice in some parts of your provinces, no one dares to walk in the streets with safety, lest he be kidnapped by robbers by day or thieves by night, either by force or trickery, at home or outside.

14. "Wherefore the Truce,° as it is commonly called, now for a long time established by the Holy Fathers, must be renewed. In admonition, I entreat you to adhere to it most firmly in your own bishopric. But if anyone affected by avarice or pride breaks it of his own free will, let him be excommunicated by God's authority and by the sanction of the decrees of this Holy Council."

III. The Pope's Exhortation Concerning the Expedition to Jerusalem

2. "Now that you, O sons of God, have consecrated yourselves to God to maintain peace among yourselves more vigorously and to uphold the laws of the Church faithfully, there is work to do, for you must turn the strength of your sincerity, now that you are aroused by divine correction, to another affair that concerns you and God. Hastening to the way, you must help your brothers living in the Orient, who need your aid for which they have already cried out many times.

3. "For, as most of you have been told, the Turks, a race of Persians, who have penetrated within the boundaries of Romania even to the Mediterranean to that point which they call the Arm of Saint George, in occupying more and more of the lands of the Christians, have overcome them, already victims of seven battles, and have killed and captured them, have overthrown churches, and have laid waste God's kingdom. If you permit this supinely for very long, God's faithful ones will be still further subjected.

4. "Concerning this affair, I, with suppliant prayer—not I, but the Lord—exhort you, heralds of Christ, to persuade all of whatever class, both knights and footmen, both rich and poor, in numerous edicts, to strive to help expel that wicked race from our Christian lands before it is too late.

5. "I speak to those present, I send word to those not here; moreover, Christ commands it. Remission of sins will be granted for those going thither, if they end a shackled life either on land or in crossing the sea, or in struggling against the heathen. I, being vested with that gift from God, grant this to those who go.

6. "O what a shame, if a people, so despised, degenerate, and enslaved by demons would thus overcome a people endowed with the trust of almighty God, and shining in the name of Christ! O how many evils will be imputed to you by the Lord Himself, if you do not help those who, like you, profess Christianity!

7. "Let those," he said, "who are accustomed to wage private wars wastefully even against Believers, go forth against the Infidels in a battle worthy to be undertaken now and to be finished in victory. Now, let those, who until recently existed as plunderers, be soldiers of Christ; now, let those, who formerly contended against brothers and relations, rightly fight barbarians; now, let those, who recently were hired for a few pieces of silver, win their eternal reward. Let those, who wearied themselves to the detriment of body and soul, labor for a twofold honor. Nay, more, the sorrowful here will be glad

---

Truce: The Truce of God was an attempt by the Church to reduce feudal violence in Europe. According to the Truce, engaging in violent acts on certain days or during certain times of the year would result in excommunication.

there, the poor here will be rich there, and the enemies of the Lord here will be His friends there.

. . .

IX. *The City of Constantinople and the Journey of the Pilgrims to Nicaea*

1. Oh, what an excellent and beautiful city! How many monasteries, and how many palaces there are in it, of wonderful work skilfully fashioned! How many marvelous works are to be seen in the streets and districts of the town! It is a great nuisance to recite what an opulence of all kinds of goods are found there; of gold, of silver, of many kinds of mantles, and of holy relics. In every season, merchants, in frequent sailings, bring to that place everything that man might need. Almost twenty thousand eunuchs, I judge, are kept there continuously.

2. When we had sufficiently refreshed our fatigued selves, then our leaders, after counsel, agreed upon a contract under oath with the Emperor, upon his demand. Already Lord Bohemond and Duke Godfrey, who had preceded us, had taken it. However, Count Raymond at that time refused to do so. The Count of Flanders, just as the others did, took that same oath.

3. It was necessary for all to confirm friendship with the Emperor, without whose counsel and aid we could not have completed our journey, nor could those who were to follow us on that same road. To these, then, the Emperor himself offered as many coins and silken garments as he pleased; also some horses and some money, which they needed to complete such a great journey.

4. After this was completed, we crossed the sea which they call the Arm of Saint George. We hastened then to the city of Nicaea, which Lord Bohemond, Duke Godfrey, Count Raymond, and the Count of Flanders had already surrounded in siege by the middle of May. The Oriental Turks, very keen archers and bowmen, then possessed this city. These Turks from Persia, after they had crossed the Euphrates River fifty years before, subjugated the whole land of Romania for themselves as far as the city of Nicomedia.

. . .

XXVII. *The Siege of the City of Jerusalem*

10. Then the Franks° entered the city magnificently at the noonday hour on Friday, the day of the week when Christ redeemed the whole world on the cross. With trumpets sounding and with everything in an uproar, exclaiming: "Help, God!" they vigorously pushed into the city, and straightway raised the banner on the top of the wall. All the heathen, completely terrified, changed their boldness to swift flight through the narrow streets of the quarters. The more quickly they fled, the more quickly were they put to flight.

11. Count Raymond and his men, who were bravely assailing the city in another section, did not perceive this until they saw the Saracens° jumping from the top of the wall. Seeing this, they joyfully ran to the city as quickly as they could, and helped the others pursue and kill the wicked enemy.

12. Then some, both Arabs and Ethiopians, fled into the Tower of David; others shut themselves in the Temple of the Lord and of Solomon, where in the halls a very great

Franks: Refers to Western Europeans in general. While Western Europeans were conscious of regional and ethnic distinctions such as French, Norman, German, etc., they understood themselves as different from Greek Christians and Muslims.
Saracens: European term for Muslims.

attack was made on them. Nowhere was there a place where the Saracens could escape the swordsmen.

13. On the top of Solomon's Temple, to which they had climbed in fleeing, many were shot to death with arrows and cast down headlong from the roof. Within this Temple about ten thousand were beheaded. If you had been there, your feet would have been stained up to the ankles with the blood of the slain. What more shall I tell? Not one of them was allowed to live. They did not spare the women and children.

XXVIII. *The Spoils Which the Christians Took*

1. After they had discovered the cleverness of the Saracens, it was an extraordinary thing to see our squires and poorer people split the bellies of those dead Saracens, so that they might pick out besants from their intestines, which they had swallowed down their horrible gullets while alive. After several days, they made a great heap of their bodies and burned them to ashes, and in these ashes they found the gold more easily.

2. Tancred rushed into the Temple of the Lord, and seized much of the gold and silver and precious stones. But he restored it, and returned everything or something of equal value to its holy place. I say "holy," although nothing divine was practised there at the time when the Saracens exercised their form of idolatry in religious ritual and never allowed a single Christian to enter.

3. With drawn swords, our people ran through the city;
Nor did they spare anyone, not even those pleading for mercy.
The crowd was struck to the ground, just as rotten fruit
Falls from shaken branches, and acorns from a wind-blown oak.

XXIX. *The Sojourn of the Christians in the City*

1. After this great massacre, they entered the homes of the citizens, seizing whatever they found in them. It was done systematically, so that whoever had entered the home first, whether he was rich or poor, was not to be harmed by anyone else in any way. He was to have and to hold the house or palace and whatever he had found in it entirely as his own. Since they mutually agreed to maintain this rule, many poor men became rich.

2. Then, going to the Sepulchre° of the Lord and His glorious Temple, the clerics and also the laity, singing a new song unto the Lord in a high-sounding voice of exultation, and making offerings and most humble supplications, joyously visited the Holy Place as they had so long desired to do.

3. Oh, time so longed for! Oh, time remembered among all others! Oh, deed to be preferred before all deeds! Truly longed for, since it had always been desired by all worshippers of the Catholic faith with an inward yearning of the soul. This was the place, where the Creator of all creatures, God made man, in His manifold mercy for the human race, brought the gift of spiritual rebirth. Here He was born, died, and rose. Cleansed from the contagion of the heathen inhabiting it at one time or another, so long contaminated by their superstition, it was restored to its former rank by those believing and trusting in Him.

4. And truly memorable and rightly remembered, because those things which the Lord God our Jesus Christ, as a man abiding among men on earth, practised and taught have often been recalled and repeated in doctrines. And, likewise, what the Lord wished to be fulfilled, I believe, by this people so dear, both His disciple and servant and

Sepulchre: Tomb.

predestined for this task, will resound and continue in a memorial of all the languages of the universe to the end of the ages.

THE SONG OF ROLAND

The Document

> A thousand trumpets ring out for more delight.
> Great is the noise; it reaches the French lines.
> Quoth Oliver: "I think, companion mine,
> We'll need this day with Saracens to fight."
> Roland replies: "I hope to God you're right!
> Here must we stand to serve on the King's side.
> Men for their lords great hardship must abide,
> Fierce heat and cold endure in every clime,
> Lose for his sake, if need be, skin and hide.
> Look to it now! Let each man stoutly smite!
> No shameful songs be sung for our despite!
> Paynims are wrong, Christians are in the right!
> Ill tales of me shall no man tell, say I!"

80
> Oliver's climbed upon a hilly crest,
> Looks to his right along a grassy cleft,
> And sees the Paynims and how they ride addressed.
> To his companion Roland he calls and says:
> "I see from Spain a tumult and a press—
> Many bright hauberks, and many a shining helm!
> A day of wrath, they'll make it for our French.
> Ganelon knew it, false heart and taitor fell;
> When to the Emperor he named us for this stead!"
> Quoth Roland: "Silence, Count Oliver, my friend!
> He is my stepsire, I will have no word said."

81
> Oliver's climbed a hill above the plain,
> Whence he can look on all the land of Spain,
> And see how vast the Saracen array;
> All those bright helms with gold and jewels gay,
> And all those shields, those coats of burnished mail;
> And all those lances from which the pennons wave;
> Even their squadrons defy all estimate,
> He cannot count them, their numbers are so great;
> Stout as he is, he's mightily dismayed.
> He hastens down as swiftly as he may,
> Comes to the French and tells them all his tale.

82
> Quoth Oliver: "The Paynim strength I've seen;
> Never on earth has such a hosting been:
> A hundred thousand in van ride under shield
> Their helmets laced, their hauberks all agleam
> Their spears upright, with heads of shining steel.
> You'll have such battle as ne'er was fought on field.

My lords of France, God give you strength at need!
Save you stand fast, this field we cannot keep."
The French all say: "Foul shame it were to flee!
We're yours till death; no man of us will yield."

83
Quoth Oliver: "Huge are the Paynim hordes,
And of our French the numbers seem but small.
Companion Roland, I pray you sound your horn,
That Charles may hear and fetch back all his force."
Roland replies: "Madman were I and more,
And in fair France my fame would suffer scorn.
I'll smite great strokes with Durendal my sword,
I'll dye it red high as the hilt with gore.
This pass the Paynims reached on a luckless morn;
I swear to you death is their doom therefor."

84
"Companion Roland, your Olifant now sound!
King Charles will hear and turn his armies round;
He'll succour us with all his kingly power."
Roland replies: "May never God allow
That I should cast dishonour on my house
Or on fair France bring any ill renown!
Rather will I with Durendal strike out,
With this good sword, here on my baldrick bound;
From point to hilt you'll see the blood run down.
Woe worth the Paynims that e'er they made this rout!
I pledge my faith, we'll smite them dead on ground."

85
"Companion Roland, your Olifant now blow;
Charles in the passes will hear it as he goes,
Trust me, the French will all return right so."
"Now God forbid", Roland makes answer wroth,
"That living man should say he saw me go
Blowing of horns for any Paynim foe!
Ne'er shall my kindred be put to such reproach.
When I shall stand in this great clash of hosts
I'll strike a thousand and then sev'n hundred strokes,
Blood-red the steel of Durendal shall flow.
Stout are the French, they will do battle bold,
These men of Spain shall die and have no hope."

86
Quoth Oliver: "Herein I see no blame:
I have beheld the Saracens of Spain;
They cover all the mountains and the vales,
They spread across the hillsides and the plains;
Great is the might these foreigners display,
And ours appears a very small array."
"I thirst the more", quoth Roland, "for the fray.
God and His angels forbid it now, I pray,

That e'er by me fair France should be disfamed!
I'd rather die than thus be put to shame;
If the King loves us it's for our valour's sake."

87
Roland is fierce and Oliver is wise
And both for valour may bear away the prize.
Once horsed and armed the quarrel to decide,
For dread of death the field they'll never fly.
The counts are brave, their words are stern and high.
Now the false Paynims with wondrous fury ride.
Quoth Oliver: "Look, Roland, they're in sight.
Charles is far off, and these are very nigh;
You would not sound your Olifant for pride;
Had we the Emperor we should have been all right.
To Gate of Spain turn now and lift your eyes,
See for yourself the rear-guard's woeful plight.
Who fights this day will never more see fight."
Roland replies: "Speak no such foul despite!
Curst be the breast whose heart knows cowardise!
Here in our place we'll stand and here abide:
Buffets and blows be ours to take and strike!"

88
When Roland sees that battle there must be
Leopard nor lion ne'er grew so fierce as he.
He calls the French, bids Oliver give heed:
"Sir friend and comrade, such words you shall not speak!
When the King gave us the French to serve this need
These twenty thousand he chose to do the deed;
and well he knew not one would flinch or flee.
Men must endure much hardship for their liege,
And bear for him great cold and burning heat,
Suffer sharp wounds and let their bodies bleed.
Smite with your lance and I with my good steel,
My Durendal the Emperor gave to me:
And if I die, who gets it may agree
That he who bore it, a right good knight was he."

Analysis and Review Questions

1. Does Urban appeal to any aspects of chivalry depicted in *The Song of Roland*? Does Fulcher describe the knights in ways comparable to *The Song of Roland*?

2. How are the two visions of knighthood presented in these documents different?

3. Imagine you are a squire (knight-in training) who had recently heard *The Song of Roland* and Fulcher's account of the Crusade. How would you understand knighthood and chivalry in light of both these documents?

4. How do the cultural values depicted in *The Song of Roland* help explain the brutality of the capture of Jerusalem by the Crusaders? How does the culture of violence in Europe as described in Urban's speech explain Fulcher's reaction to the sacking of Jerusalem?

CHAPTER 14

The West: The Reformation

The period in European history between 1450 and 1750 is usually referred to as the Early Modern Period. In many ways this period is more like the Middle Ages than the modern West. Even in 1750, most Europeans were illiterate, rural peasants living within traditional social and political structures. Economic productivity still depended heavily on human and animal energy. Yet the political, economic, and technological features that define western Europe today were built on the foundations laid during this period. The voyages of exploration and colonization created a new world economy with western countries at the center. The Scientific Revolution was causing many intellectuals to rethink the role and purpose of science in society. Although experimenting with different visions of royal power, both France and England developed from feudal monarchies into national monarchies, a critical step on the road to the modern nation state.

Yet it was the Protestant Reformation, with the cultural, political, and military upheaval that it spawned, that impacted the people of that time most directly. In 1517, an obscure monk and theology professor named Martin Luther proposed an academic debate on certain esoteric points of Christian doctrine. Within 40 years of this event, Europe had split into permanent and hostile religious camps. Indeed, by 1650, a significant percentage of Europeans had died in wars arising from this religious conflict.

Such a chain of events seems strange to us. That strangeness is a clue to us that something central to early modern European culture was at stake in the Reformation. Indeed, Europeans in the sixteenth century were religious to a degree that is not easily understood in our modern culture. Few Europeans of any class seriously questioned the basic teachings of the Church or the truth of the Bible. Moreover, religion permeated and gave structure to European society at that time. The social and economic centers of villages and cities were churches. Religious organizations were the primary places of socialization outside of the family. The Church administered all levels of formal education. The rulers of Europe enforced religious unity, and Church officials exercised tremendous political power. Thus, the Protestant challenge to the religious culture of the time affected every aspect of European society.

Map 14.1
Religious Diversity in
Western Europe

MARTIN LUTHER, *SERMON AT CASTLE PLEISSENBURG*

About the Document

*Image 14.1
Martin Luther*

In 1539 Martin Luther delivered a sermon at Castle Pleissenberg, in Leipzig. Twenty years before, Luther had debated Johann Eck, a papal representative, in Leipzig concerning the sale of indulgences. During this debate, Luther began to realize that his understanding of salvation was not in the mainstream of Medieval theology, which caused him to widen the focus of both his theological investigations and his criticism of the Church. Luther returned to Leipzig in 1539 to celebrate the implementation of Protestant reforms in the city. The Reformation was unsettling for many people. The conflicting claims to authority by Protestants and Roman Catholics caused many to wonder which was the true church. In an age in which almost all people believed in a god who would judge them after death, a conflict over how best to follow God cut to the heart of people's lives. Luther devoted this sermon to explaining the Protestant view of religious authority and the marks of the true church against the views of the papacy.

The Document

But when they are asked: What is the Christian church? What does it say and do? They reply: The church looks to the pope,° cardinals, and bishops. This is not true! Therefore we must look to Christ and listen to him as he describes the true Christian church in contrast to their phony shrieking. For one should and one must rather believe Christ and the apostles, that tone must speak God's Word and do as St. Peter and here the Lord Christ says: He who keeps my Word, there is my dwelling, there is the Builder, my Word must remain in it; otherwise it shall not be my house. Our papists° want to improve on this, and therefore they may be in peril. Christ says: "We will make our home with them"; there the Holy Spirit will be at work. There must be a people that loves me and keeps my commandments. Quite bluntly, this is what he wants.

Here Christ is not speaking of how the church is built, as he spoke above concerning the dwelling. But when it has been built, then the Word must certainly be there, and a Christian should listen to nothing but God's Word. Elsewhere, in worldly affairs, he hears other things, how the wicked should be punished and the good protected, and about the economy. But here in the Christian church it should be a house in which only the Word of God° resounds. Therefore let them shriek themselves crazy with their cry: church, church! Without the Word of God it is nothing. My dear Christians are steadfast confessors of the Word, in life and in death. They will not forsake this dwelling,

---

pope: The word "pope" comes from the Italian word for father. It refers to the Bishop of Rome. According to Roman Catholic teaching, the Bishop of Rome stands in the place of the Apostle Peter, who was the first leader of the Church at Rome. Using texts from the Gospels in which Jesus seems to give Peter special authority, Roman Catholics teach that the pope is the earthly leader of the Church.
papists: Derogatory name for Roman Catholics used by Protestants.
Word of God: According to Luther and other Protestants the term "Word of God," or simply "Word," could mean one of three things. First, it referred to Jesus as he is described in the Gospel of John. Second, it often referred to the Bible, since the Bible revealed the Word of God (Jesus) to humans. Finally, it could refer to the correct (to Protestants) preaching or teaching of the biblical message of salvation.

so dearly do they love this Prince. Whether in favor or not, for this they will leave country and people, boy and life. Thus we read of a Roman centurion, a martyr, who, when he was stripped of everything, said, "This I know; they cannot take away from me my Lord Christ." Therefore a Christian says: This Christ I must have, though it cost me everything else; what I cannot take with me can go; Christ alone is enough for me. Therefore all Christians should stand strong and steadfast upon the Word alone, as St. Peter says, "by the strength which God supplies" (1 Pet. 4:11).

Behold, how it all happens in weakness. Look at baptism,° it is water; where does the hallowing and the power come from? From the pope? No, it comes from God, who says, "He who believes and is baptized" (Mark 16:16). For the pope puts trust in the consecrated water. Why, pope? Who gave you the power? The ecclesia, the church? Yes, indeed, where is it written? Nowhere! Therefore the consecrated water is Satan's goblin bath (Kobelbad), which cripples, blinds, and consecrates the people without the Word. But in the church one should teach and preach nothing besides or apart from the Word of God. For the pastor who does the baptizing says: It is not I who baptize you; I am only the instrument of the Father, Son, and Holy Spirit; this is not my work.

Likewise, the blessed sacrament° is not administered by men, but rather by God's commands; we only lend our hands to it. Do you think this is an insignificant meal, which feeds not only the soul but also the mortal boy of a poor, condemned sinner for the forgiveness of sins in order that the body too may live? This is God's power, this Householder's power, not men's. So also in the absolution,° when a distressed sinner is pardoned. By what authority and command is he pardoned? Not by human command, but by God's command. Behold, here by God's power I deliver you from the kingdom of the devil and transfer you to the kingdom of God (Col. 1:13). So it is too with our prayer, which gains all things from God, not through its own power, or because it is able to do this, but because it rests in God's promise. In the world you see how hard it is to approach the Roman emperor and gain help; but a devout Christian can always come to God with a humble, believing prayer and be heard.

baptism: In the sacrament of baptism the individual is washed or sprinkled with water signifying death to sin and a new life as a Christian. In Medieval and later Roman Catholic theology, baptism is administered to infants and washes away the penalty of sin inherited from Adam and Eve, called original sin. Protestants disputed with Roman Catholics and among each other over the proper method and meaning of baptism. For all Christians, baptism is seen as a mark of membership in the universal church.

sacrament: According to Medieval theology, sacraments were the means by which God gave grace to human beings so that they might be saved. Roman Catholics recognize seven sacraments: baptism, the Lord's Supper (also called communion or the Eucharist), penance, confirmation, marriage, ordination, and last rites (extreme unction). At first, Luther retained only three (baptism, the Lord's Supper, penance), but later rejected penance. Protestants also differ from Roman Catholics over how sacraments work. Roman Catholics believe that sacraments convey divine grace whenever the ritual is performed. Protestants believe that the effectiveness of the sacrament depends on the faith of the recipient.

absolution: Absolution is part of the sacrament of penance by which sinners are forgiven for their sins. By the late Middle Ages, penance consisted of several parts. First a penitent must confess his or her sins to a priest in private. The priest had to determine whether the penitent was truly remorseful for the sins committed and resolved not to do them again. If the priest judged the penitent remorseful and committed to not sinning again, he would grant absolution. Absolution is the pronouncement of the forgiveness of sins in the name of Jesus Christ. Although forgiven, the penitent was still liable for the penalty for the sin. Thus, the priest assigned penitential acts such as charitable giving, restitution to a wronged party, or acts of self-denial like fasting. This part was called satisfaction. Much religious behavior in the late Middle Ages revolved around penitential acts of satisfaction.

. . . It is the Word which we believe—this is what makes our hearts so bold that we dare to call ourselves the children of the Father. Where does this come from? The answer is: From God, who teaches us to pray in the Lord's Prayer and puts into our hands the book of Psalms. For if we prayed without faith, this would be to curse twice over, as we learned in our nasty papistical holiness. But where there is a believing heart and that heart has before it the promise of God it quite simply and artlessly prays its "Our Father" and is heard. Outside of this church of God you may present your prayers and supplications to great lords and potentates to the best of your ability, but here you have no ability to pray except in Christ Jesus, in order that we may not boast that we are holy as they do in the papacy, who protest, of course, and say: Oh, it would be a presumption for anybody to call himself holy and fit; and yet they teach that man of himself has a "certain preparation" for prayer.

They also teach prayer according to this doctrine in their chants and say: I have prayed in despair as a poor sinner. Oh, stop that kind of praying! It would be better to drop such praying altogether if you despair. For despair ruins everything and if you go to baptism, prayer, and the sacrament without faith and in despair, you are actually mocking God. What you should quickly say, however, is this: I am certain that my dear God has so commanded and that he has assured me of the forgiveness of sins; therefore I will baptize, absolve, and pray. And immediately you will receive this treasure in your heart. It does not depend on our worthiness or unworthiness, for both of these can only make us despair. Therefore do not allow yourself by any means to be driven to despair. "Go and baptize" (Matt. 28:19), that is, baptize those who repent and are sorry for their sins. Here you hear that this is not human work; but the work of God and the Father; he is the Householder who wills to dwell here. But if we despair, then we should stay away from the sacrament and from prayer, and first learn to say: All right, it makes no difference that I am unworthy, God is truthful nevertheless, and he has most certainly promised and assured us; I'll stake my life on this.

And this we did not know under the papacy. Indeed, I, Martin Luther, for a long time could not find my way out of this papistical dream, because they were constantly blathering to me about my worthiness and unworthiness. Therefore, you young people, learn to know the church rightly.

Concerning penitence or penance we teach that it consists in the acknowledgment of sins and genuine trust in God, who forgives them all for Christ's sake. The pope, on the contrary, does nothing but scold and devise intolerable burdens; and besides he knows nothing of grace and faith, much less does he teach what the Christian church really is.

But don't you forget the main point here, namely, that God wants to make his dwelling here. Therefore, when the hand is laid upon your head and the forgiveness of sins is proclaimed to you in the words: "I absolve you from all your sins in the name of Christ," you should take hold of this Word with a sure faith and be strengthened out of the mouth of the preacher. And this is what Christ and St. Peter are saying: He, the Lord, wants to dwell in this church; the Word alone must resound in it.

In short, the church is a dwelling, in order that God may be loved and heard. Not wood or stones, not dumb animals, it should be people, who know, love, and praise God. And that you may be able to trust God with certainty in all things, including cross and suffering, you should know that it is the true church, even though it be made up of scarcely two believing persons. That's why Christ says: He who loves me keeps my Word; there I will dwell, there you have my church.

So now you must guard yourselves against the pope's church, bedaubed and bedizened with gold and pearls; for here Christ teaches us the opposite. To love God and keep his Word is not the pope's long robe and crown, nor even his decretals. There is a great difference between what God commands and what men command. Look how the pope brazenly announces—we should invoke the saints and conduct ourselves according to his human precepts. Does God's Word command this too? I still do not see it. But this I know very well, that God's Word says: I, Christ, go to the Father, and he who believes in me will be saved. For, I have suffered for him and I also give him the Holy Spirit from on high.

So the Lord Christ and the pope each have their own church, but with this mighty difference, which Christ himself, the best dialectitian (*der beste Dialecticus*), here describes, telling us what it is and where it is, namely, where his Word is purely preached. So where you hear this, there you may know that this is the true church. For where the Word of God is not present, there also are not true-believing confessors and martyrs. And if the World of God were lacking, then we would have been deceived by Christ; then he really would have betrayed us!

Oh, if we could only stake it all on Christ and mock and laugh at the pope, since Christ clearly says here, not "he who has my Word," but "he who keeps it loves me" and is also my disciple. There are many of you who have the Word, true enough, but do not keep it, and in time of trouble and trial fall away altogether and deny Christ.

It would, of course, be desirable if we could always have both: the Word and our temporal crumbs, but the good venison, peace, is very scarce in the kingdom of heaven. It's therefore something which must be recognized as a great blessing of God when there is peace among temporal lords and mutual understanding. But if not, then let them all go—goods, fame, wife, and child—if only this treasure remain with us.

I fear, however, that unfortunately there will be among us many weathercocks, false brethren, and such like weeds; and yet I am not going to be a prophet, because I must prophesy nothing but evil, and who would presume to be able to fathom it all? It will turn out all right; now we have it, let us see to it that we hold on to it. But let us be valiant against Satan, who intends to sift us like wheat (cf. Luke 22:31). For it may well be that you will have your bit of bread under a good government and then the devil will soon set a snare for you in your security and presumption, so that you will no longer trust and give place to the Word of God as much as you did before. That's why Christ says: My sheep not only hear me, they also obey and follow me (John 10:3–5); they increase in faith daily through hearing the Word of God and the right and perfect use of the blessed sacraments. There is strengthening and comfort in this church. And it is also the true church, not cowls, tonsures, and long robes, of which the Word of God knows nothing, but rather wherever two or three are gathered together (Matt. 18:20), not matter whether it be on the ocean or in the depths of the earth, if only they have before them the Word of God and believe and trust in the same, there is most certainly the real, ancient, true, apostolic church.

But we were so blinded in the papacy that, even though St. Peter tells us that "we have the prophetic word made more sure" and that we "do well to pay attention to this as to a lamp shining in a dark place" (11 Pet. 1:19), we still cannot see what a bright light we have in the gospel. Therefore we must note here once again the description of the Christian church which Christ gives us, namely, that it is a group of people who not only have his Word but also love and keep it and forsake everything for the sake of love.

. . . But Christ tells you and me something far different. He says: My church is where my Word is preached purely and is unadulterated and kept. Therefore St. Paul warns that we should flee and avoid those who would lead us away from God's Word, for if anyone defiles God's temple, which we are, God will destroy him (1 Cor. 3:17). And St. Peter also says: Take heed, if you are going to preach, then you should preach nothing but God's Word (1 Pet. 4:11), otherwise you will defile God's church.

. . . If anybody wants to teach human precepts, let him do so in secular and domestic affairs and leave the church alone. After all, the papists are really empty spewers and talkers, since Christ himself here says: He who hears my Word and keeps it, to him will I and my Father come and make our home with him. This is the end of Jerusalem and Moses; here there is to be a little band of Christ (*Heufflein Christi*), who hear God's Word and keep the same and rely upon it in every misfortune. This is my church. This Lord we shall believe, even though the pope blows his top over it.

But in these words Christ was also answering the apostle Judas, who also allowed himself to imagine that Christ would become a great secular emperor and that they, the apostles, would become great lords in the nations when he should manifest himself. But how wrong he was! Here Christ tells them straight out that his kingdom is not of this world, but that they and all believers should be that kingdom of heaven in which God the Father, Son, and Holy Spirit himself dwells. He does not install angels, emperors, kings, princes, and lords in that church. He himself wants to be the householder and be the only one to speak and act; there I will dwell, he says, and with me all believers from everlasting to everlasting.

But Judas, the good man, still cannot understand this and therefore the Holy Spirit must come and teach it to him. Of this future and this ministry, dear Christians, you will hear tomorrow, God willing. If I cannot do it, then it will be done by others who can do it better than I, though they will not admit it. Let this today serve as an introduction or the morning sermon. May the Lord help us, I cannot go on further now.

Analysis and Review Questions

1. What is the Church, according to Luther?
2. What role do activities like baptism, communion, and confession play in Luther's concept of the Church?
3. What are Luther's criticisms of the "papists" in this document?
4. If this document were the only evidence we had concerning Luther, what could we say about his religious views?
5. The contrast between faith and despair is a central theme in this document. What does Luther mean by faith? What does he mean by despair? What do his definitions have to do with the nature of the Church?

IGNATIUS LOYOLA, *RULES FOR THINKING WITH THE CHURCH*

About the Document

Image 14.2
Ignatius of Loyola

Ignatius Loyola (d. 1556) was born to a noble family in the Basque region of Spain and spent his early life as a soldier. In 1521, the same year that Luther was excommunicated, Loyola was severely injured and spent a year convalescing. Bedridden, he spent his time reading devotional literature and underwent a spiritual conversion. He renounced his inheritance and began to live as a monk.

Eventually he gathered a few followers, whom he led through his now-classic spiritual program, *The Spiritual Exercises.* In 1540 Loyola and his companions were recognized by the papacy as an official order, The Society of Jesus. Jesuits (as members of the Society came to be called) became the agents of the papacy in its efforts both to reconvert European Protestants and to convert pagans encountered by European explorers to Roman Catholicism. In this selection from *The Spiritual Exercises,* Loyola describes the proper attitude of the believer toward the teachings and practices of the Roman Catholic Church.

The Document*

1. Always to be ready to obey with mind and heart, setting aside all judgement of one's own, the true spouse of Jesus Christ, our holy mother, our infallible and orthodox mistress, the Catholic Church, whose authority is exercised over us by the hierarchy.

2. To commend the confession of sins to a priest as it is practised in the Church; the reception of the Holy Eucharist once a year, or better still every week, or at least every month, with the necessary preparation.

3. To commend to the faithful frequent and devout assistance at the holy sacrifice of the Mass, the ecclesiastical hymns, the divine office, and in general the prayers and devotions practised at stated times, whether in public in the churches or in private.

4. To have a great esteem for the religious orders, and to give the preference to celibacy or virginity over the married state.

5. To approve of the religious vows of chastity, poverty, perpetual obedience, as well as to the other works of perfection and supererogation. Let us remark in passing, that we must never engage by vow to take a state (such as marriage) that would be an impediment to one more perfect.

6. To praise relics,° the veneration and invocation of Saints: also the stations, and pious pilgrimages, indulgences, jubilees, the custom of lighting candles in the churches, and other such aids to piety and devotion.

7. To praise the use of abstinence and fasts as those of Lent, of Ember Days, of Vigils, of Friday, Saturday, and of others undertaken out of pure devotion: also voluntary mortifications, which we call penances, not merely interior, but exterior also.

8. To commend moreover the construction of churches, and ornaments; also images, to be venerated with the fullest right, for the sake of what they represent.

9. To uphold especially all the precepts of the Church, and not censure them in any manner; but, on the contrary, to defend them promptly, with reasons drawn from all sources, against those who criticize them.

10. To be eager to commend the decrees, mandates, traditions, rites and customs of the Fathers in the Faith or our superiors. As to their conduct; although there may not

---

relic: Material object held to have special powers because of its association with a saint or another holy person.

*Reprinted by permission of Oxford University Press, from *Documents of the Christian Church,* 3rd ed., Henry Bettenson, 364–67.

always be the uprightness of conduct that there ought to be, yet to attack or revile them in private or in public tends to scandal and disorder. Such attacks set the people against their princes and pastors; we must avoid such reproaches and never attack superiors before inferiors. The best course is to make private approach to those who have power to remedy the evil.

11. To value most highly the sacred teaching, both the Positive and the Scholastic, as they are commonly called.

12. It is a thing to be blamed and avoided to compare men who are living on the earth (however worthy of praise) with the Saints and Blessed, saying: This man is more learned than St. Augustine, etc.

13. That we may be altogether of the same mind and in conformity with the Church herself, if she shall have defined anything to be black which to our eyes appears to be white, we ought in like manner to pronounce it to be black. For we must undoubtedly believe, that the Spirit of our Lord Jesus Christ, and the Spirit of the Orthodox Church His Spouse, by which Spirit we are governed and directed to Salvation, is the same.

14. It must also be borne in mind, that although it be most true, that no one is saved but he that is predestinated, yet we must speak with circumspection concerning this matter, lest perchance, stressing too much the grace or predestination of God, we should seem to wish to shut out the force of free will and the merits of good works; or on the other hand, attributing to these latter more than belongs to them, we derogate meanwhile from the power of grace.

15. For the like reason we should not speak on the subject of predestination frequently; if by chance we do so speak, we ought so to temper what we say as to give the people who hear no occasion of erring and saying, 'If my salvation or damnation is already decreed, my good or evil actions are predetermined'; whence many are wont to neglect good works, and the means of salvation.

16. It also happens not unfrequently, that from immoderate, preaching and praise of faith, without distinction or explanation added, the people seize a pretext for being lazy with regard to any good works, which precede faith, or follow it when it has been formed by the bond of charity.

17. Not any more must we push to such a point when the preaching and inculcating of the grace of God, as that there may creep thence into the minds of the hearers the deadly error of denying our faculty of free will. We must speak of it as the glory of God requires that we may not raise doubts as to liberty and the efficacy of good works.

18. Although it is very praiseworthy and useful to serve God through the motive of pure charity, yet we must also recommend the fear of God; and not only filial fear, but servile fear, which is very useful and often even necessary to raise man from sin. Once risen from the state, and free from the affection of mortal sin, we may then speak of that filial fear which is truly worthy of God, and which gives and preserves the union of pure love.

*Reprinted by permission of Oxford University Press, from *Documents of the Christian Church,* 3rd ed., Henry Bettenson, 364–67.

Analysis and Review Questions

1. According to Loyola, what should a Christian's attitude be toward the Church? Toward the pope?
2. What should the Christian life look like, according to Loyola?
3. What does Loyola say about faith? In what should a Christian believe?
4. Why would Loyola advocate such radical, unquestioning obedience to the authority of the Roman Catholic Church?
5. Loyola founded the Society of Jesus (Jesuits). One mission of the Jesuits was to convert Protestants to Roman Catholicism. In many cases they were successful. Given what you know, why do you think some Protestants were attracted to Loyola's vision?

JAMES I ON THE DIVINE RIGHT OF KINGS

Map 14.2
European Population Density c. 1600

About the Document

James Stuart (James VI of Scotland, 1567–1625; James I of England, 1603–1625) was an intellectual who was rarely able to implement his ideas. He had hoped to unify England, Scotland, and Ireland, but was thwarted by both political realities and his own personal failings. He sought to ease international tensions, but his efforts to prevent the conflict that would become the Thirty Years' War were unsuccessful. The outbreak of the Thirty Years' War also destroyed his hope of brokering a European religious compromise. In addition to his duties as monarch, James I wrote on a variety of topics. His most famous work, the *True Law of a Free Monarchy*, is a classic argument for divine-right monarchy. Interestingly, although James penned this work in 1598 before he assumed the throne of England, he never tried to implement divine-right rule in England. He firmly believed that his power and authority derived solely from God but acknowledged that as king of England, he had sworn oaths to govern according to the "laws and customs of England."

The Document

THE TREW LAW OF FREE MONARCHIES: OR THE RECIPROCK AND MUTUALL DUETIE BETWIXT A FREE KING AND HIS NATURALL SUBJECTS

As there is not a thing so necessarie to be knowne by the people of any land, next the knowledge of their God, as the right knowledge of their alleageance, according to the forme of governement established among them, especially in a Monarchie (which forme of government, as resembling the Divinitie, approacheth nearest to perfection, as all the learned and wise men from the beginning have agreed upon; Unitie being the perfection of all things,) So hath the ignorance, and (which is worse) the seduced opinion of the multitude blinded by them, who thinke themselves able to teach and instruct the ignorants, procured the wracke and overthrow of sundry flourishing Commonwealths; and heaped heavy calamities, threatening utter destruction upon others. And the smiling success, that unlaw rebellions have oftentimes had against Princes in ages past (such hath bene the misery, and the iniquitie of the time) hath by way of practise strengthened many of their errour: albeit there cannot be a more deceivable argument; then to judge by the justnesse of the cause by the event thereof; as hereafter shall be proved more at length. And among others, no Common-wealth, that ever hath bene since the beginning, hath had greater need of the trew knowledge of this ground, then this our so long disordered, and distracted Common-wealth hath: the misknowledge hereof being the onely spring, from whence have flowed so many endlesse calamities, miseries, and confusions, as is better felt by many, then the cause thereof well knowne, and deepely considered. The naturall zeale therefore, that I beare to this my native countrie, with the great pittie I have to see the so-long disturbance thereof for lack of the trew knowledge of this ground (as I have said before) hath compelled me at last to breake silence, to discharge my conscience to you my deare country men herein, that knowing the ground from whence these your many endlesse troubles have proceeded, as well as ye have already too-long tasted the bitter fruites thereof, ye may by knowledge, and eschewing of the cause escape, and divert the lamentable effects that ever necessarily follow thereupon. I have chosen the onely to set downe in this short Treatise, the trew grounds of the mutuall deutie, and alleageance betwixt a free and ab-solute Monarche, and his people.

First then, I will set downe the trew grounds, whereupon I am to build, out of the Scriptures, since Monarchie is the trew paterne of Divinitie, as I have already said: next, from the fundamental Lawes of our own Kingdome, which nearest must concerne us: thirdly, from the law of Nature, by divers similitudes drawne out of the same.

By the Law of Nature the King becomes a naturall Father to all his Lieges at his Coronation: And as the Father of his fatherly duty is bound to care for the nourishing, education, and vertuous government of his children; even so is the king bound to care for all his subjects. As all the toile and paine that the father can take for his children, will be thought light and well bestowed by him, so that the effect thereof redound to their profite and weale; so ought the Prince to doe towards his people. As the kindly father ought to foresee all inconvenients and dangers that may arise towards his children, and though with the hazard of his owne person presse to prevent the same; so ought the King towards his people. As the fathers wrath and correction upon any of his children that offendeth, ought to be by a fatherly chastisement seasoned with pitie, as long as there is any hope of amendment in them; so ought the King towards any of his Lieges that offend in that measure. And shortly, as the Fathers chiefe joy ought to be in procuring his childrens welfare, rejoycing at their weale, sorrowing and pitying at their evil, to hazard for their safetie, travell for their rest, wake for their sleepe; and in a word, to thinke that his earthly felicitie and life standeth and liveth more in them, nor in himself; so ought a good Prince thinke of his people.

As to the other branch of this mutuall and reciprock band, is the duety and al-leageance that the Lieges owe to their King: the ground whereof, I take out of the words of Samuel, dited by Gods Spirit, when God had given him commandement to heare the peoples voice in choosing and annointing them a King. And because that place of Scripture being well understood, is so pertinent for our purpose, I have insert herein the very words of the Text.

10. So Samuel tolde all the wordes of the Lord unto the people that asked a King of him.

11. And he said, this shall be the maner of the King that shall raigne over you: hee will take your sonnes, and appoint them to his Charets, and to be his horsemen, and some shall runne before his Charet.

12. Also, hee will make them his captaines over thousands, and captaines over fifties, and to eare his ground, and to reape his harvest, and to make instruments of warre and the things that serve for his charets.

13. Hee will also take your daughters, and make them Apothicaries, and Cookes, and Bakers.

14. And hee will take your fields, and your vineyards, and your best Olive trees, and give them to his servants.

15. And hee will take the tenth of your seed, and of your Vineyards, and give it to his Eunuches, and to his servants.

16. And hee will take your men servants, and your maid-servants, and the chief of your young men, and your asses, and put them to his worke.

17. Hee will take the tenth of your sheepe: and ye shall be his servants.

18. And ye shall cry out at that day, because of your King, whom ye have chosen you: and the Lord God will not heare you at that day.

19. But the people would not heare the voice of Samuel, but did say: Nay, but there shall be a King over us.

20. And we also will be all like other Nations, and our King shall judge us, and goe out before us, and fight out battles.

As likewise, although I have said, a good king will frame all his actions to be according to the Law; yet is hee not bound thereto but of his good will, and for good example—giving to his subjects: For as in the law of abstaining from eating of flesh in Lenton, the king will, for examples sake, make his owne house to observe the Law; yet no man will thinke he needs to take a licence to eate flesh. And although by our Lawes, the bearing and wearing of hag-buts, and pistolets be forbidden, yet no man can find any fault in the King, for causing his traine use them in any raide upon the Borderers, or other malefactours or rebellious subjects. So as I have alreadie said, a good King, although hee be above the Law, will subject and frame his actions thereto, for examples sake to his subjects, and of his owne free-will, but not as subject or bound thereto.

And the agreement of the Law of nature in this our ground with the Lawes and constitutions of God, and man, already alleged, will by two similitudes easily appeare. The King towards his people is rightly compared to a father of children, and to a head of a body composed of divers members: For as fathers, the good Princes, and Magistrates of the people of God acknowledged themselves to their subjects. And for all other well ruled Common-wealths, the stile of Pater patriae was ever, and is commonly used to Kings. And the proper office of a King towards his Subjects, agrees very wel with the office of the head towards the body, and all members thereof: For from the head, being the seate of Judgement, proceedeth the care and foresight of guiding, and preventing all evill that may come to the body, so doeth the King for his people. As the discourse and direction flowes from the head, and the execution according thereunto belongs to the rest of the members, every one according to their office: so it is betwixt a wise Prince, and his people. As the judgement coming from the head may not onely imploy the members, every one in their owne office, as long as they are able for it; but likewise in case any of them be affected with any infirmitie must care and provide for their remedy, in-case it be curable, and if otherwise, gar cut them off for feare of infecting of the rest: even so is it betwixt the Prince, and his people. And as there is ever hope of curing any diseased member of the direction of the head, as long as it is whole; but by contrary, if it be troubled, all the members are partakers of that paine, so is it betwixt the Prince and his people.

And now first for the fathers part (whose naturally love to his children I described in the first part of this my discourse, speaking of the dutie that Kings owe to their Subjects) consider, I pray you what duetie his children owe to him, & whether upon any pretext whatsoever, it wil not be thought monstrous and unnaturall to his sons, to rise up against him, to control him at their appetite, and when they thinke good to sley him, or to cut him off, and adopt to themselves any other they please in his roome: Or can any pretence of wickedness or rigor on his part be a just excuse for his children to put hand into him? And although wee see by the course of nature, that love useth to descend more than to ascend, in case it were trew, that the father hated and wronged the children never so much, will any man, endued with the least sponke of reason, thinke it lawful for them to meet him with the line? Yea, suppose the father were furiously following his sonnes with a drawen sword, is it lawful for them to turne and strike againe, or make any resistance but by flight? I thinke surely, if there were no more but the example of bruit beasts & unreasonable creatures, it may serve well enough to qualifie and prove this my argument. We reade often the pietie that the Storkes have to their olde and decayed parents: And generally wee know, that there are many sorts of beasts and fowles, that with violence and many bloody strokes will beat and banish their yong ones from them, how soone they perceive them to be able to fend themselves; but wee never read or heard of any resistance on their part, except among the vipers; which prooves such persons, as ought to be reasonable creatures, and yet unnaturally follow this example, to be endued with their viperous nature.

And it is here likewise to be noted, that the duty and alleageance, which the people sweareth to their prince, is not bound to themselves, but likewise to their lawfull heires and posterity, the lineall to their lawfull heires and posterity, the lineall succession of crowns being begun among the people of God, and happily continued in divers Christian common-wealths: So as no objection either of heresie, or whatsoever private statute or law may free the people from their oathgiving to their king, and his succession, established by the old fundamentall lawes of the kingdom: For, as hee is their heritable over-lord, and so by birth, not by any right in the coronation, commeth to his crowne; it is a like unlawful (the crowne ever standing full) to displace him that succeedeth thereto, as to eject the former: For at the very moment of the expiring of the king reigning, the nearest and lawful heire entreth in his place: And so to refuse him, or intrude another, is not to holde out uncomming in, but to expell and put out their righteous King. And I trust at this time whole France acknowledgeth the superstitious rebellion of the liguers, who upon pretence of heresie, by force of armes held so long out, to the great desolation of their whole country, their native and righteous king from possessing of his owne crowne and naturall kingdome.

Not that by all this former discourse of mine, and Apologie for kings, I meane that whatsoever errors and intollerable abominations a sovereigne prince commit, hee ought to escape all punishment, as if thereby the world were only ordained for kings, & they without controlment to turne it upside down at their pleasure: but by the contrary, by remitting them to God (who is their onely ordinary Judge) I remit them to the sorest and sharpest school-master that can be devised for them: for the further a king is preferred by God above all other ranks & degrees of men, and the higher that his seat is above theirs, the greater is his obligation to his maker. And therfore in case he forget himselfe (his unthankfulness being in the same measure of height) the sadder and sharper will be correction be; and according to the greatnes of the height he is in, the weight of his fall wil recompense the same: for the further that any person is obliged to God, his offence becomes and growes so much the greater, then it would be in any other. Joves thunderclaps light oftner and sorer upon the high & stately oaks, then on the low and supple willow trees: and the highest bench is sliddriest to sit upon. Neither is it ever heard that any king forgets himself towards God, or in his vocation; but God with the greatnes of the plague revengeth the greatnes of his ingratitude: Neither thinke I by the force of argument of this my discourse so to perswade the people, that none will hereafter be raised up, and rebell against wicked Princes. But remitting to the justice and providence of God to stirre up such scourges as pleaseth him, for punishment of wicked kings (who made the very vermine and filthy dust of the earth to bridle the insolencie of proud Pharaoh) my onely purpose and intention in this treatise is to perswade, as farre as lieth in me, by these sure and infallible grounds, all such good Christian readers, as beare not onely the naked name of a Christian, but kith the fruites thereof in their daily forme of life, to keep their hearts and hands free from such monstrous and unnaturall rebellions, whensoever the wickednesse of a Prince shall procure the same at Gods hands: that, when it shall please God to cast such scourges of princes, and instruments of his fury in the fire, ye may stand up with cleane handes, and unspotted consciences, having prooved your selves in all your actions trew Christians toward God, and dutifull subjects towards your King, having remitted the judgement and punishment of all his wrongs to him, whom to onely of right it appertaineth.

But craving at God, and hoping that God shall continue his blessing with us, in not sending such fearefull desolation, I heartily wish our kings behaviour so to be, and continue among us, as our God in earth, and loving Father, endued with such properties as I described a King in the first part of this Treatise. And that ye (my deare countreymen, and charitable readers) may presse by all means to procure the prosperitie and welfare of your King; that as hee must on the one part thinke all his earthly felicitie and happiness grounded upon your weale, caring more for himselfe for your sake then for his owne, thinking himselfe onely ordained for your weale; such holy and happy emulation may arise betwixt him and you, as his care for your quietnes, and your care for his honor and preservation, may in all your actions daily strive together, that the Land may thinke themselves blessed with such a King, and the king may thinke himself most happy in ruling over so loving and obedient subjects.

Analysis and Review Questions

1. What are the responsibilities of a monarch to his subjects? What are the responsibilities of subjects to the monarch?
2. Are there any limits on the power of a king? What are they?
3. How does James defend divine-right monarchy?
4. What are his motives in this essay?
5. As king of England, James never tried to rule as a divine-right monarch. Does this make him a hypocrite or a realist?

LOUIS XIV WRITES TO HIS SON

About the Document

During the sixteenth and seventeenth centuries, England, for various reasons, was moving toward what we might call a "constitutional monarchy." In such a system, the power of a king or a queen is limited by a written constitution (or, in England's case, where there is no written constitution, a series of documents that serve the same general purpose as a constitution). In general, such a system tends to be more decentralized than centralized, as power is delegated to bodies such as a parliament. In contrast, France during the same period was developing, to the envy of the rest of Western Europe, a strong, centralized absolute monarchy, where the king's position was not limited in any way. Louis XIV, who ruled from 1643 to 1715, became the prototypical absolute monarch, even developing a sort of "cult of personality" around him.

Because ruling over and maintaining such a centralized system required care and attention, Louis XIV in 1661 wrote a series of memoirs to his son, the dauphin. These memoirs not only provided practical advice for the king's heir, they also provide us with insight into royal attitudes and priorities. Sadly for Louis XIV, the dauphin died before his father, and it was Louis's great-grandson who became Louis XV in 1715.

The Document

MANY REASONS, all very important, my son, have decided me, at some labour to myself, but one which I regard as forming one of my greatest concerns, to leave you these Memoirs of my reign and of my principal actions. I have never considered that kings, feeling in themselves, as they do, all paternal affection, are dispensed from the obligation common to fathers of instructing their children by example and by precept.

I have even hoped that in this purpose I might be able to be more helpful to you, and consequently to my subjects, than any one else in the world; for there cannot be men who have reigned of more talents and greater experience than I, nor who have reigned in France; and I do not fear to tell you that the higher the position the greater are the number of things which cannot be viewed or understood save by one who is occupying that position.

I have considered, too, what I have so often experienced myself—the throng who will press round you, each for his own ends, the trouble you will have in finding disinterested advice, and the entire confidence you will be able to feel in that of a father who has no other interest but your own, no ardent wish but for your greatness.

I have given, therefore, some consideration to the condition of Kings—hard and rigorous in this respect—who owe, as it were, a public account of their actions to the whole world and to all succeeding centuries, and who, nevertheless, are unable to do so to all and sundry at the time without injury to their greatest interests, and without divulging the secret reasons of their conduct.

[Louis talks briefly about his own reign.]

Two things without doubt were absolutely necessary; very hard work on my part, and a wise choice of persons capable of seconding it.

As for work, it may be, my son, that you will begin to read these Memoirs at an age when one is far more in the habit of dreading than loving it, only too happy to have escaped subjection to tutors and to have your hours regulated no longer, nor lengthy and prescribed study laid down for you.

There is something more, my son, and I hope that your own experience will never teach it to you: nothing could be more laborious to you than a great amount of idleness if you were to have the misfortune to fall into it through beginning by being disgusted with public affairs, then with pleasure, then with idleness itself, seeking everywhere fruitlessly for what can never be found, that is to say, the sweetness of repose and leisure without having the preceding fatigue and occupation.

I laid a rule on myself to work regularly twice every day, and for two or three hours each time with different persons, without counting the hours which I passed privately and alone, nor the time which I was able to give on particular occasions to any special affairs that might arise. There was no moment when I did not permit people to talk to me about them, provided that they were urgent; with the exception of foreign ministers who sometimes find too favourable moments in the familiarity allowed to them, either to obtain or to discover something, and whom one should not hear without being previously prepared.

I cannot tell you what fruit I gathered immediately I had taken this resolution. I felt myself, as it were, uplifted in thought and courage; I found myself quite another man, and with joy reproached myself for having been too long unaware of it. This first timidity, which a little self-judgment always produces and which at the beginning gave me pain, especially on occasions when I had to speak in public, disappeared in less than no time. The only thing I felt was that I was King, and born to be one. I experienced next a delicious feeling, hard to express, and which you will not know yourself except by tasting it as I have done. For you must not imagine, my son, that the affairs of State are like some obscure and thorny path of learning which may possibly have already wearied you, wherein the mind strives to raise itself with effort above its purview, more often to arrive at no conclusion, and whose utility or apparent utility is repugnant to us as much as its difficulty. The function of Kings consists principally in allowing good sense to act, which always acts naturally and without effort. What we apply ourselves to is sometimes less difficult than what we do only for our amusement. Its usefulness always follows. A King, however skilful and enlightened be his ministers, cannot put his own hand to work without its effect being seen. Success, which is agreeable in everything, even in the smallest matters, gratifies us in these as well as in the greatest, and there is no satisfaction to equal that of noting every day some progress in glorious and lofty enterprises, and in the happiness of the people which has been planned and thought out by oneself. All that is most necessary to this work is at the same time agreeable; for, in a word, my son, it is to have one's eyes open to the whole earth; to learn each hour the news concerning every province and every nation, the secrets of every court, the mood and the weaknesses of each Prince and of every foreign minister; to be well-informed on an infinite number of matters about which we are supposed to know nothing; to elicit from our subjects what they hide from us with the greatest care; to discover the most remote opinions of our own courtiers and the most hidden interests of those who come to us with quite contrary professions. I do not know of any other pleasure we would not renounce for that, even if curiosity alone gave us the opportunity.

I have dwelt on this important subject longer than I had intended, and far more for your sake than for my own; for while I am disclosing to you these methods and these alleviations attending the greatest cares of royalty I am not aware that I am likewise depreciating almost the sole merit which I can hope for in the eyes of the world. But in this matter, my son, your honour is dearer to me than my own; and if it should happen that God call you to govern before you have yet taken to this spirit of application and to public affairs of which I am speaking, the least deference you can pay to the advice of a father, to whom I make bold to say you owe much in every kind of way, is to begin to do and to continue to do for some time, even under constraint and dislike, for love of me who beg it of you, what you will do all your life from love of yourself, if once you have made a beginning.

Analysis and Review Questions

1. What do you think Louis XIV means when he writes "the function of kings consists principally in allowing good sense to act"?

2. Does Louis XIV seem arrogant, or is he simply offering experienced advice?

3. List three things Louis believes a successful ruler must do.

4. Is there anything Louis suggests *not* to do?

5. Overall, do you feel Louis gives his son good or bad advice? Why?

WEB LINKS

Selections from Longman World History—Primary Sources and Case Studies

http://longmanworldhistory.com
The following additional readings and case studies can be found on the Web site.
Document 14.3, Galileo Galilei, *Letter to the Grand Duchess Christina*
Document 14.5, English Bill of Rights
Document 14.6, Pope Boniface VIII, *Unam sanctam*
Document 14.9, Juan Luis Vives, the Office and Dutie of a Husband
Case Study 14.1, Role and Authority of the Papacy
Case Study 14.2, A Question of Trust
Case Study 14.3, God and Nature

Martin Luther

http://www.iclnet.org/pub/resources/text/wittenberg/wittenberg-home.html
Project Wittenberg is an extensive site devoted to works by and about Martin Luther. It is a good place to start.

http://www.mun.ca/rels/reform/index.html
Hans Rollman's Reformation Home Page focuses on Luther but includes resources on other Reformers and Protestant groups. It has an excellent index of links to Reformation documents on the Web and other interesting Reformation Web sites.

http://gbgm-umc.org/umw/bible/ref.html
Produced by the United Methodist Women, this site has excellent summaries of Reformation events, helpful reference materials, and good external links about the Reformation.

http://www.fordham.edu/halsall/mod/modsbook02.html
Part of Paul Halsall's *Internet Modern History Sourcebook*. It is very thorough. Other pages in the *Internet Modern History Sourcebook* have excellent resources for other aspects of the period covered in this chapter.

Ignatius Loyola and the Catholic Reformation

http://www.jesuit.org/
The official Web site of the order of Jesus.

http://campus.northpark.edu/history/WebChron/WestEurope/CatholicRef.html
Good summary of the Catholic Reformation, along with excellent links to information about Loyola and the Council of Trent.

Medieval Background

http://cedar.evansville.edu/~ecoleweb/
The Ecole Initiative is a site devoted to the History of Christianity up to 1500. It contains many documents and images produced in that period, as well as essays on various topics.

http://www.fordham.edu/halsall/sbook.html
Paul Halsall's Internet Medieval Sourcebook.

CHAPTER 15

Eastern Europe and Russia,
1450–1750

Between 1450 and 1750, Eastern Europe and Russia lagged behind Western Europe culturally, socially, and politically. These areas had been controlled by more powerful neighbors, and their pace of development and cultural outlook were affected by years of constant domination. The diverse ideas of their conquerors, both in terms of ruling methods and religion, made the cultures of Russia and Eastern Europe even more distinct from that of their Western European counterparts.

From 1450 to 1750, Europe went from the high Middle Ages through the Renaissance. The Scientific Revolution emerged to give western Europe its "rational" mind and set it on a course of secular thought. Kings and queens consolidated their power by wresting control from feudal lords and introducing the concept of absolutism. Explorers ventured off into the unknown and brought back knowledge of newly discovered lands. The countries of Europe established colonies in these faraway places to claim the riches they found there and bring them back to Europe.

NICOLAUS COPERNICUS:
ON THE REVOLUTION OF THE HEAVENLY SPHERES

About the Document

It was almost inevitable that the beginnings of modern science (the Scientific Revolution) in the sixteenth and seventeenth centuries would upset the scientific and religious status quo in Europe. The acceptance of radically new ideas about the universe was difficult for both Protestants and Catholics alike because these ideas refuted the old Ptolemaic view of an earth-centered universe, a view that fit neatly with the Bible.

A Polish canon° with a doctorate in theology, Nicolaus Copernicus was also one of the great scientific minds of the late fifteenth and early sixteenth centuries. In the preface to his work excerpted below, Copernicus tries to explain to Pope Paul III why he believes what he believes about the movement of the earth around the sun.

Image 15.1
Copernicus's Drawing of the Heliocentric Theory

The Document

I can readily imagine, Holy Father, that as soon as some people hear that in this volume, which I have written about the revolutions of the spheres of the universe, I ascribe certain motions to the terrestrial globe, they will shout that I must be immediately repudiated together with this belief. For I am not so enamored of my own opinions that I disregard what others may think of them. I am aware that a philosopher's ideas are not subject to the judgement of ordinary persons, because it is his endeavor to seek the truth in all things, to the extent permitted to human reason by God. Yet I hold that completely erroneous views should be shunned. Those who know that the consensus of many centuries has sanctioned the conception that the earth remains at rest in the middle of the heaven as its center would, I reflected, regard it as an insane pronouncement if I made the opposite assertion that the earth moves. Therefore I debated with myself for a long time whether to publish the volume which I wrote to prove the earth's motion or rather to follow the example of the Pythagoreans° and certain others, who used to transmit philosophy's secrets only to kinsmen and friends, not in writing but by word of mouth. . . . And they did so, it seems to me, not, as some suppose, because they were in some way jealous about their teachings, which would be spread around; on the contrary, they wanted the very beautiful thoughts attained by great men of deep devotion not to be ridiculed by those who are reluctant to exert themselves vigorously in any literary pursuit unless it is lucrative; or if they are stimulated to the nonacquisitive study of philosophy by the exhortation and example of others, yet because of their dullness of mind they play the same part among philosophers as drones among bees. When I weighed these considerations, the scorn which I had reason to fear on account of the novelty and unconventionality of my opinion almost induced me to abandon completely the work which I had undertaken.

But while I hesitated for a long time and even resisted, my friends [encouraged me]. . . . Foremost among them was the cardinal of Capua [a city in southern Italy], Nicholas Schönberg, renowned in every field of learning. Next to him was a man who loves me dearly, Tiedemann Giese, bishop of Chelmno [a city in northern Poland], a close student of sacred letters as well as of all good literature. For he repeatedly encouraged me and, sometimes adding reproaches, urgently requested me to publish this volume and finally permit it to appear after being buried among my papers and lying concealed not merely until the ninth year but by now the fourth period of nine years. The same conduct was recommended to me by not a few other very eminent scholars. They exhorted me no longer to refuse, on account of the fear which I felt, to make my work available for the general use of students of astronomy. The crazier my doctrine of the earth's motion now appeared to most people, the argument ran, so much the more admiration and thanks would it gain after they saw the publication of my writings

canon: A member of the clery belonging to the staff of a cathedral or of a collegiate church.
Pythagoreans: Followers of the Greek mathematician and philosopher Pythagoras.

dispel the fog of absurdity by most luminous proofs. Influenced therefore by these persuasive men and by this hope, in the end I allowed my friends to bring out an edition of the volume, as they had long besought me to do. . . .

But you [your Holiness] are rather waiting to hear from me how it occurred to me to venture to conceive any motion of the earth, against the traditional opinion of astronomers and almost against common sense. . . . [Copernicus then describes some of the problems connected with the Ptolemaic° system.]

For a long time, then, I reflected on this confusion in the astronomical traditions concerning the derivation of the motions of the universe's spheres. I began to be annoyed that the movements of the world machine, created for our sake by the best and most systematic Artisan of all [God], were not understood with greater certainty by the philosophers, who otherwise examined so precisely the most insignificant trifles of this world. For this reason I undertook the task of rereading the works of all the philosophers which I could obtain to learn whether anyone had ever proposed other motions of the universe's spheres than those expounded by the teachers of astronomy in the schools. And in fact first I found in Cicero that Hicetas supposed the earth to move. Later I also discovered in Plutarch that certain others were of this opinion. . . .

Therefore, having obtained the opportunity from these sources, I too began to consider the mobility of the earth. . . . I thought that I too would be readily permitted to ascertain whether explanations sounder than those of my predecessors could be found for the revolution of the celestial spheres on the assumption of some motion of the earth.

Having thus assumed the motions which ascribe to the earth later on in the volume, by long and intense study I finally found that if the motions of the other planets are correlated with the orbiting of the earth, and are computed for the revolution of each planet, not only do their phenomena follow therefrom but also the order and size of all the planets and spheres, and heaven itself is so linked together that in no portion of it can anything be shifted without disrupting the remaining parts and the universe as a whole. Accordingly in the arrangement of the volume too I have adopted the following order. In the first book I set forth the entire distribution of the spheres together with the motions which I attribute to the earth, so that this book contains, as it were, the general structure of the universe. Then in the remaining books I correlate the motions of the other planets and of all the spheres with the movement of the earth so that I may thereby determine to what extent the motions and appearances of the other planets and spheres can be saved if they are correlated with the earth's motions. I have no doubt that acute and learned astronomers will agree with me if, as this discipline especially requires, they are willing to examine and consider, not superficially but thoroughly, what I adduce in this volume in proof of these matters. However, in order that the educated and uneducated alike may see that I do not run away from the judgement of anybody at all, I have preferred dedicating my studies to Your Holiness rather than to anyone else. For even in this very remote corner of the earth where I live you are considered the highest authority by virtue of the loftiness of your office and your love for all literature and astronomy too. Hence by your prestige and judgement you can easily suppress calumnious attacks although, as the proverb has it, there is no remedy for a backbite.

Perhaps there will be babblers who claim to be judges of astronomy although completely ignorant of the subject and, badly distorting some passage of Scripture to their purpose, will dare to find fault with my undertaking and censure it. I disregard them

---

Ptolemaic: Referring to the ancient geographer Ptolemy, whose conception of the universe placed the earth at its center with the heavenly bodies moving around it.

even to the extent of despising their criticism as unfounded. For it is not unknown that Lactantius, otherwise an illustrious writer but hardly an astronomer, speaks quite childishly about the earth's shape, when he mocks those who declared that the earth has the form of a globe. Hence scholars need not be surprised if any such persons will likewise ridicule me. Astronomy is written for astronomers. To them my work too will seem, unless I am mistaken, to make some contribution.

Analysis and Review Questions

1. Why has Copernicus hesitated for so long before publishing his ideas on the movement of the earth? Why was he tempted to follow the example of the Pythagoreans?
2. Who encouraged Copernicus to publish his work? Why was he careful to include their names and reasons?
3. What forms the basis of Copernicus's reasoning on the movement of the earth?
4. What were the steps—the sequence of events—he formulated to bring him to his theory?
5. Why has Copernicus dedicated his work to the pope? What was his rationale?

OGIER GHISELIN DE BUSBECQ: AN AMBASSADOR'S REPORT ON THE OTTOMAN EMPIRE, 1555

About the Document

Ogier Ghiselin de Busbecq was the ambassador from the Holy Roman Empire to the court of the Ottoman Empire from 1555 to 1562. The Ottoman Turks controlled much of Eastern Europe and periodically pushed westward toward central Europe. This made them enemies of the European states. De Busbecq was given the task of using diplomatic means to put an end to the Turk raids into Europe. The years he spent in Constantinople gave de Busbecq close contact with Suleiman the Great and life at the Ottoman Court. Through his letters to a friend and his official reports, de Busbecq gives us a fascinating look into the world of the Ottoman Turks. Here was an empire the Europeans had to deal with, but whose lifestyle and customs were very different from what Europeans were accustomed to.

The Document

The Sultan's hall was crowded with people, . . . but there was not in all that great assembly a single man who owed his position to aught save valour and his merit. . . . Those who receive the highest offices from the Sultan are for the most part the sons of shepherds or herdsmen, and so far from being ashamed of their parentage, they actually glory in it, and consider it a matter of boasting that they owe nothing to the accident of birth. . . . Among the Turks, therefore, honours, high posts, and judgeships are the rewards of great ability and good service. . . . These are not our ideas, with us there is no opening left for merit; birth is the standard for everything; the prestige of birth is the sole key to advancement in the public service. . . .

When they [the Turkish army] are hard pressed . . . they take out a few spoonfuls of flour and put them into water, adding some butter, and seasoning the mess with salt and spices; these ingredients are boiled, and a large bowl of gruel is thus obtained. Of this they eat once or twice a day, according to the quantity they have, without any bread, unless they have brought some biscuit with them. In this way they are able to support themselves from their own supplies for a month, or if necessary longer. . . .

From this you will see that it is the patience, self-denial, and thrift of the Turkish soldier that enable him to face the most trying circumstances, and come safely out of the dangers that surround him. What a contrast to our men! Christian soldiers on a campaign refuse to put up with their ordinary food and call for thrushes, becaficos, and such like dainty dishes! If these are not supplied they grow mutinous and work their own ruin; and, if they are supplied, they are ruined all the same. For each man is his own worst enemy, and has no foe more deadly than his own intemperance, which is sure to kill him, if the enemy be not quick. It makes me shudder to think of what the result of a struggle between such different systems must be; one of us must prevail and the other be destroyed, at any rate we cannot both exist in safety. On their side is the vast wealth of their empire, unimpaired resources, experience and practice in arms, a veteran soldiery, an uninterrupted series of victories, readiness to endure hardships, union, order, discipline, thrift, and watchfulness. On ours are found an empty exchequer,° luxurious habits, exhausted resources, broken spirits, a raw and insubordinate soldiery, and greedy generals; there is no regard for discipline, license runs riot, the men indulge in drunkenness and debauchery, and, worst of all, the enemy are accustomed to victory, we, to defeat. Can we doubt what the result must be? . . .

Against us stands Solyman, that foe whom his own and his ancestors' exploits have made so terrible; he tramples the soil of Hungary with 200,000 horses, he is at the very gates of Austria, threatens the rest of Germany, and brings in his train all the nations that extend from our borders to those of Persia. The army he leads is equipped with the wealth of many kingdoms. Of the three regions, into which the world is divided, there is not one that does not contribute its share towards our destruction. Like a thunderbolt he strikes, shivers, and destroys everything in his way. The troops he leads are trained veterans, accustomed to his command; he fills the world with the terror of his name. Like a raging lion he is always roaring around our borders, trying to break in, now in this place, now in that.

Analysis and Review Questions

1. For those in the Sultan's service, to what do they owe their positions?
2. How does de Busbecq compare this system of service with the way the Europeans operate?
3. Compare Turkish and Christian soldiers.
4. What are the differences between the two systems in terms of wartime operations.
5. How does de Busbecq describe "Solyman"? How does he describe Solyman's strategy in war?

---

exchequer: Treasury.

ADAN OLEARIUS: A FOREIGN TRAVELER IN RUSSIA

About the Document

To Europeans, seventeenth-century Russia seemed both strange and exciting. Russia's distance from Europe and her distinct culture made it difficult for Europeans of that era to understand the Russian view of things. Few Europeans traveled to Russia, and those who did observed things that could not be interpreted accurately without an understanding of the Russian people and their culture. The result was that Europeans held very stereotypical and sometimes incorrect ideas about Russians. Because of Russia's isolation from European culture and ideas and its Mongol background, the Russians were seen as barbarians.

The most famous of the travel accounts of this era was written by a German, Adan Olearius. Olearius was sent to Russia on three diplomatic missions in the 1630s. Although his report indicates that he was well informed about Russian culture, it nevertheless gives a very unflattering view of the Russian people.

*Map 15.1
(Interactive) Russia*

The Document

The government of the Russians is what political theorists call a "dominating and despotic monarchy," where the sovereign, that is, the tsar or the grand prince who has obtained the crown by right of succession, rules the entire land alone, and all the people are his subjects, and where the nobles and princes no less than the common folk—towns-people and peasants—are his serfs and slaves, whom he rules and treats as a master treats his servants. . . .

If the Russians be considered in respect to their character, customs, and way of life, they are justly to be counted among the barbarians. . . . The vice of drunkenness is so common in this nation, among people of every station, clergy and laity, high and low, men and women, old and young, that when they are seen now and then lying about in the streets, wallowing in the mud, no attention is paid to it, as something habitual. If a cart driver comes upon such a drunken pig whom he happens to know, he shoves him onto his cart and drives him home, where he is paid his fare. No one ever refuses an opportunity to drink and to get drunk, at any time and in any place, and usually it is done with vodka. . . .

The Russians being naturally tough and born, as it were, for slavery, they must be kept under a harsh and strict yoke and must be driven to do their work with clubs and whips, which they suffer without impatience, because such is their station, and they are accustomed to it. Young and half-grown fellows sometimes come together on certain days and train themselves in fisticuffs, to accustom themselves to receiving blows, and, since habit is second nature, this makes blows given as punishment easier to bear. Each and all, they are slaves and serfs. . . .

Because of slavery and their rough and hard life, the Russians accept war readily and are well suited to it. On certain occasions, if need be, they reveal themselves as courageous and daring soldiers. . . .

Although the Russians, especially the common populace, living as slaves under a harsh yoke, can bear and endure a great deal out of love for their masters, yet if the pressure is beyond measure, then it can be said of them: "Patience, often wounded, finally turned into fury." A dangerous indignation results, turned not so much against their sovereign as against the lower authorities, especially if the people have been much oppressed by them and by their supporters and have not been protected by the higher authorities.

And once they are aroused and enraged, it is not easy to appease them. Then, disregarding all dangers that may ensue, they resort to every kind of violence and behave like mad-men. . . . They own little; most of them have no feather beds; they lie on cushions, straw, mats, or their clothes; they sleep on benches and, in winter, like the non-Germans [i.e., natives] in Livonia, upon the oven, which serves them for cooking and is flat on the top; here husband, wife, children, servants, and maids huddle together. In some houses in the countryside we saw chickens and pigs under the benches and the ovens. . . .

Russians are not used to delicate food and dainties; their daily food consists of porridge, turnips, cabbage, and cucumbers, fresh and pickled, and in Moscow mostly of big salt fish which stink badly, because of the thrifty use of salt, yet are eaten with relish. . . .

The Russians can endure extreme heat. In the bathhouse they stretch out on benches and let themselves be beaten and rubbed with bunches of birch twigs and wisps of bast° (which I could not stand); and when they are hot and red all over and so exhausted that they can bear it no longer in the bathhouse, men and women rush outdoors naked and pour cold water over their bodies; in winter they even wallow in the snow and rub their skin with it as if it were soap; then they go back into the hot bathhouse. And since bathhouses are usually near rivers and brooks, they can throw themselves straight from the hot into the cold bath. . . .

Generally noble families, even the small nobility, rear their daughters in secluded chambers, keeping them hidden from outsiders; and a bridegroom is not allowed to have a look at his bride until he receives her in the bridal chamber. Therefore some happen to be deceived, being given a misshapen and sickly one instead of a fair one, and sometimes a kinswoman or even a maidservant instead of a daughter; of which there have been examples even among the highborn. No wonder therefore that often they live together like cats and dogs and that wife-beating is so common among Russians. . . .

In the Kremlin and in the city there are a great many churches, chapels, and monasteries, both within and without the city walls, over two thousand in all. This is so because every nobleman who has some fortune has a chapel built for himself, and most of them are of stone. The stone churches are round and vaulted inside. . . . They allow neither organs nor any other musical instruments in their churches, saying: Instruments that have neither souls nor life cannot praise God. . . .

In their churches there hang many bells, sometimes five or six, the largest not over two hundred-weights. They ring these bells to summon people to church, and also when the priest during mass raises the chalice. In Moscow, because of the multitude of churches and chapels, there are several thousand bells, which during the divine service create such a clang and din that one unaccustomed to it listens in amazement.

Analysis and Review Questions

1. How does Adan Olearius describe the Russian government?
2. What prejudices does Olearius bring to his narrative?
3. Describe the Russian marriage customs. What does the author see as the consequences of these customs?
4. What assumptions does Olearius make about the Russians based purely on his observations? Speculate on what effects these observations had once they were published in Western Europe.

---

bast: A strong woody fiber used in making ropes.

Prince Mikhail Mikhailovich Shcherbatov, On the Corruption of Morals in Russia

About the Document

Russia was in many ways a closed society, shut off from Europe by geography, culture, and religion. While some Russians welcomed the Westernization begun by Peter the Great, others saw the influx of Western ideas as dangerous to Russian culture. The Russian Orthodox Church was concerned about the introduction of "false" religious thought.

Prince Shcherbatov admired Peter, but was concerned by Peter's reforms and by the result of this contact with the West. The old aristocracy felt that their place in Russian society was being undermined. The introduction of Western ideas seemed to be changing the very nature of Russian culture and undermining Russian moral values.

Shcherbatov, a scholar and historian, was given the task of editing Peter's private and public papers. This gave him direct access to Peter's "thoughts," and thus great insight into Peter himself. Shcherbatov wrote this essay late in life, and can give us a view as to the long-term effects of Peter's reforms.

The Document

Peter the Great, in imitating foreign nations, not only strove to introduce to his realm a knowledge of sciences, arts and crafts, a proper military system, trade, and the most suitable forms of legislation; he also tried to introduce the kind of sociability, social intercourse and magnificence, which he first learnt from Lefort, and which he later saw for himself. Amid essential legislative measures, the organization of troops and artillery, he paid no less attention to modifying the old customs which seemed crude to him. He ordered beards to be shaved off, he abolished the old Russian garments, and instead of long robes he compelled the men to wear German coats, and the women, instead of the "telogreya" to wear bodices, skirts, gowns and "samaras," and instead of skull-caps, to adorn their heads with fontanges and cornettes. He established various assemblies where the women, hitherto segregated from the company of men, were present with them at entertainments. . . .

The monarch himself kept to the old simplicity of morals in his dress, so that apart from plain coats and uniforms, he never wore anything costly; and it was only for the coronation of the Empress Catherine Alexeevna, his wife, that he had made a coat of blue gros-de-tours with silver-braid; they say he also had another coat, grey with gold braid, but I do not know for what great occasion this was made.

The rest was all so plain that even the poorest person would not wear it today, as can be seen from such of his clothes as have remained, and are kept in the Kunst-Kamera at the Imperial Academy of Sciences.

He disliked cuffs and did not wear them, as his portraits attest. He had no costly carriages, but usually travelled in a gig in towns, and in a chaise on a long journey.

He did not have a large number of retainers and attendants, but had orderlies, and did not even have a bodyguard, apart from a Colonel of the Guard.

However, for all his personal simplicity, he wanted his subjects to have a certain magnificence. I think that this great monarch, who did nothing without farsightedness, had it as his object to stimulate trade, industries and crafts through the magnificence and luxury of his subjects, being certain that in his lifetime excessive magnificence and voluptuousness would not enthrone themselves at the royal court. . . .

As far as his domestic life was concerned, although the monarch himself was content with the plainest food, he now introduced drinks previously unknown in Russia, which he drank in preference to other drinks; namely, instead of domestic brandy, brewed from ordinary wine—Dutch aniseed brandy which was called "state" brandy, and Hermitage and Hungarian wine, previously unknown in Russia.

His example was followed by the grandees and those who were close to the court; and indeed it was proper for them to provide these wines; for the monarch was fond of visiting his subjects, and what should a subject not do for the monarch? . . .

Closely copying him, as they were bound to do by their very rank, other leading officials of the Empire also kept open table, such as Admiral-of-the-Fleet, Count Fyodor Matveevich Apraxin, Field-Marshal-in-Chief, Count Boris Petrovich Sheremetev, the Chancellor, Count Gavrilo Ivanovich Golovkin, and the boyar, Tikhon Nikitich Streshnev, who as first ruler of the Empire during Peter the Great's absence abroad, was given estates in order to provide for such meals.

As these eminent men were copied by their inferiors, so the custom of keeping an open table was now introduced in many homes. The meals were not of the traditional kind, that is, when only household products were used; now they tried to improve the flavor of the meat and fish with foreign seasonings. And of course, in a nation in which hospitality has always been a characteristic virtue, it was not hard for the custom of these open tables to become a habit; uniting as it did the special pleasure of society and the improved flavour of the food as compared with the traditional kind, it established itself as a pleasure in its own right. . . .

With this change in the way of life, first of the leading officials of state, and then, by imitation, of the other nobles, and as expenditure reached such a point that it began to exceed income, people began to attach themselves more and more to the monarch and to the grandees, as sources of riches and rewards.

I fear someone may say that this, at any rate, was a good thing, that people began to attach themselves more and more to the monarch. No, this attachment was no blessing, for it was not so much directed to the person of the monarch as to personal ends; this attachment became not the attachment of true subjects who love their sovereign and his honour and consider everything from the point of view of the national interest, but the attachment of slaves and hirelings, who sacrifice everything for their own profit and deceive their sovereign with obsequious zeal.

Coarseness of morals decreased, but the place left by it was filled by flattery and selfishness. Hence came sycophancy, contempt for truth, beguiling of the monarch, and the other evils which reign at court to this day and which have ensconced themselves in the houses of the grandees. . . .

But despite [his] love of truth and his aversion to flattery, the monarch could not eradicate this encroaching venom. Most of those around him did not dare to contradict him in anything, but rather flattered him, praising everything he did, and never resisting his whims, while some even indulged his passions. . . .

I said that it was voluptuousness and luxury that were able to produce such an effect in men's hearts; but there were also other causes, stemming from actual institutions, which eradicated resoluteness and good behaviour.

The abolition of rights of precedence (a custom admittedly harmful to the service and the state), and the failure to replace it by any granting of rights to the noble families, extinguished thoughts of noble pride in the nobility. For it was no longer birth that was respected, but ranks and promotions and length of service. And so everyone started to strive after ranks; but since not everyone is able to perform straightforward deeds of merit, so for lack of meritorious service men began to try and worm their way up, by flattering and humouring the monarch and the grandees in every way. Then there was the introduction of regular military service under Peter the Great, whereby masters were conscripted into the ranks on the same level as their serfs. The serfs, being the first to reach officer's rank through deeds suited to men of their kind, became commanders over their masters and used to beat them with rods. The noble families were split up in the service, so that a man might never see his own kinsman.

Could virtue, then, and resolution, remain in those who from their youth had gone in fear and trembling of their commanders' rods, who could only acquire respect by acts of servility, and being each without any support from his kinsmen, remained alone, without unity or defence, liable to be subjected to violent treatment?

It is admirable that Peter the Great wished to rid religion of superstition, for indeed, superstition does not signify respect for God and his Law, but rather an affront. For to ascribe to God acts unbecoming to him is blasphemy.

In Russia, the beard was regarded as being in the image of God, and it was considered a sin to shave it off, and through this, men fell into the heresy of the Anthropomorphites.° Miracles, needlessly performed, manifestations of ikons, rarely proven, were everywhere acclaimed, attracted superstitious idolatry, and provided incomes for dissolute priests.

Peter the Great strove to do away with all this. He issued decrees, ordering beards to be shaved off, and by the Spiritual Regulation, he placed a check on false miracles and manifestations and also on unseemly gatherings at shrines set up at crossways. Knowing that God's Law exists for the preservation of the human race, and not for its needless destruction, with the blessing of the Synod and the Ecumenical patriarchs, he made it permissible to eat meat on fast-days in cases of need, and especially in the Navy where, by abstaining even from fish, the men were somewhat prone to scurvy; ordering that those who voluntarily sacrificed their lives by such abstinence, should, when they duly fell ill, be thrown into the water. All this is very good, although the latter is somewhat severe.

But when did he do this? At a time when the nation was still unenlightened, and so, by taking superstition away from an unenlightened people, he removed its very faith in God's Law. This action of Peter the Great may be compared to that of an unskilled gardener who, from a weak tree, cuts off the water-shoots which absorb its sap. If it had strong roots, then this pruning would cause it to bring forth fine, fruitful branches; but since it is weak and ailing, the cutting-off of these shoots (which, through the leaves which received the external moisture, nourished the weak tree) means that it fails to produce new fruitful branches; its wounds fail to heal over with sap, and hollows are formed which threaten to destroy the tree. Thus, the cutting-off of superstitions did harm to the most basic articles of the faith; superstition decreased, but so did faith. The servile fear of Hell disappeared, but so did love of God and his Holy Law; and morals, which for lack of other enlightenment used to be improved by faith, having lost this support began to fall into dissolution. . . .

Anthropomorphites: Those who ascribe human qualities to god(s).

And so, through the labours and solicitude of this monarch, Russia acquired fame in Europe and influence in affairs. Her troops were organized in a proper fashion, and her fleets covered the White Sea and the Baltic; with these forces she overcame her old enemies and former conquerors, the Poles and the Swedes, and acquired important provinces and sea-ports. Sciences, arts and crafts began to flourish there, trade began to enrich her, and the Russians were transformed—from bearded men to clean-shaven men, from long-robed men to short-coated men; they became more sociable, and polite spectacles became known to them.

But at the same time, true attachment to the faith began to disappear, sacraments began to fall into disrepute, resoluteness diminished, yielding place to brazen, aspiring flattery; luxury and voluptuousness laid the foundation of their power, and hence avarice was also aroused, and, to the ruin of the laws and the detriment of the citizens, began to penetrate the law-courts.

Such was the condition with regard to morals, in which Russia was left at the death of this great monarch (despite all the barriers which Peter the Great in his own person and by his example had laid down to discourage vice).

Analysis and Review Questions

1. What were the areas in which the author says Peter makes changes or "Westernizes"?
2. What societal changes does the author see?
3. How do the "magnificence and luxury" spread downward through the various ranks of people?
4. What were the problems that resulted from Peter's "Westernization"?
5. Why do Peter's ideas and reforms lead to a decline in faith?

WEB LINKS

Selections from Longman World History—Primary Sources and Case Studies

http://longmanworldhistory.com
The following additional readings and case studies can be found on the Web site.
Case Study 15.1, Two Western Views of Russia and Eastern Europe
Case Study 15.2, Reflections on the Accomplishments of Peter the Great
Case Study 15.3, The Conflict Between Science and Religion
Case Study 15.4, Lomonosov: Panegyric to the Sovereign Emperor Peter the Great.
Comparative Document 14.3, Galileo Galilei, Letter to the Grand Duchess Christina.

General History Sites

http://www.fordham.edu/halsall/mod/modsbookfull.html
Modern History Sourcebook is a collection of full-text documents that correspond with more popular reading assignments given in college classes in many areas of history.

http://www.fordham.edu/halsall/islam/islamsbook.html
Islamic History Sourcebook is a collection of full-text documents that correspond with more popular reading assignments given in college classes on Islamic history.

The Scientific Revolution

http://mars.acnet.wnec.edu/~grempel/courses/wc2/lectures/scientificrev.html
This site is a lecture on Copernicus and the Scientific Revolution.

http://www.fordham.edu/halsall/mod/modsbook09.html
This is from the *Modern History Sourcebook* and contains links on the Scientific Revolution.

Peter the Great

http://mars.acnet.wnec.edu/~grempel/courses/russia/lectures/12peter1.html
Gives a description of the personality of Peter the Great.

CHAPTER 16

Latin America, 1450–1750:
Conflicts in the Contact Zone

In the late 1400s, the Latin American contact zone became a crucible in which people from different cultures struggled for power, advantage, and control. Conflicts between Europeans and America's indigenous peoples lay at the heart of such struggles. If the conquest of the Americas had been just a war between two cultures, though, the vastly outnumbered Europeans should have suffered swift defeat. Likewise, had Europeans fully conquered, converted, and assimilated their indigenous opponents, much of the subsequent contestation by which the period is characterized would not have taken place.

The history of Latin America was as much the history of conflicts within cultures as between cultures. Conflicts between and among various Indian groups enabled small numbers of Europeans to form alliances critical to their ascent to power. For their parts, contested aims and agendas divided Europeans and provided America's indigenous peoples with substantial maneuvering room long after the conquest ended. The lines of divisiveness were many and the future anything but certain.

EXCERPTS FROM THE *ACCOUNT OF ALVA IXTLILXOCHILTL*

About the Document

Following the treaty with the Tlaxcalans, the Spaniards marched to the Aztec capital of Tenochtitlan (present site of Mexico City) where they captured the Aztec emperor, Montezuma. Subsequently, a battle took place between Cortéz's men and the Aztecs, forcing the conquistador and his men to flee the city. During the flight and ensuing battle, Montezuma was killed. His death marked a point of no return for Spaniards and Aztecs alike, though there is considerable debate over who exactly killed Montezuma. That the Aztecs and Spaniards each tried to vilify and hold the other accountable is not surprising. Excerpts from two versions—one Aztec and one Spanish—of what happened, though, demonstrate more than just finger-pointing and the inability to determine exactly what happened. They demonstrate the divisions and tensions that the Aztecs experienced even at the heart of their own empire. Moreover, they suggest that the Spaniards, in assuming Montezuma had no cause to be accountable to his people, might have allowed their own assumptions about kingship in Europe to mislead them.

Image 16.1
The Arrival of
Cortéz in Mexico

The Document

EXCERPTS FROM THE *ACCOUNT OF ALVA IXTLILXOCHITL*

Cortés turned in the direction of Tenochtitlan and entered the city of Tezcoco. He was received only by a group of knights, because the legitimate sons of King Nezahualpilli had been hidden by their servants, and the other lords were being held by the Aztecs as hostages. He entered Tenochtitlan with his army of Spaniards and allies on the day of St. John the Baptist, without being molested in any way.

The Mexicans gave them everything they needed, but when they saw that Cortés had no intention of leaving the city or of freeing their leaders, they rallied their warriors and attacked the Spaniards. This attack began on the day after Cortés entered the city and lasted for seven days.

On the third day, Motecuhzoma climbed onto the rooftop and tried to admonish his people, but they cursed him and shouted that he was a coward and a traitor to his country. They even threatened him with their weapons. It is said that an Indian killed him with a stone from his sling, but the palace servants declared that the Spaniards put him to death by stabbing him in the abdomen with their swords.

On the seventh day, the Spaniards abandoned the city along with the Tlaxcaltecas, the Huexotzincas and their other allies. They fled down the causeway that leads out to Tlacopan. But before they left, they murdered King Cacama of Tezcoco, his three sisters and two of his brothers.

There are several accounts by Indians who took part in the fighting that ensued. They tell how their warriors killed a great many of the Spaniards and their allies, and how the army took refuge on a mountain near Tlacopan and then marched to Tlaxcala.

ACCOUNT OF MONTEZUMA'S DEATH IN BERNAL DÍAZ'S *TRUE STORY OF THE CONQUEST OF MEXICO*

Here Cortés showed himself to be every inch a man, as he always was. Oh, what a fight! What a battle we had! It was something to see us dripping blood and covered with wounds, and others killed, but it pleased Our Lord that we should make our way to the place where we had kept the image of Our Lady. We did not find it, and it seems, as we learned later, Montezuma had become devoted to her and had ordered her to be cared for. We set fire to their idols and burned a good part of the room, with great help from the Tlaxcalans.

After this was done, while we were making our way back down, the priests that were in the temple and the three or four thousand Indians made us tumble six or even ten steps. There were other squadrons in the breastworks and recesses of the great *cu,* discharging so many javelins and arrows that we could not face one group or another, so we decided to return to our quarters, our towers destroyed and everybody wounded, with sixteen dead and the Indians continually pressing us. However clearly I try to tell about this battle, I can never explain it to anyone who wasn't there. We captured two of their principal priests and Cortés ordered us to take good care of them.

Many times I have seen paintings of this battle among the Mexicans and Tlaxcalans, showing how we went up the great temple, for they look upon it as a very heroic feat.

The night was spent in treating wounds and burying the dead, preparing to fight the next day, strengthening the walls they had torn down, and consulting as to how we could fight without sustaining so many casualties, but we found no solution at all. I want to tell about the curses that the followers of Narváez threw at Cortés, and how they damned him and the country and even Diego Velázquez for sending them there, when they had been peacefully settled in their homes in Cuba.

To return to our story. We decided to ask for peace so that we could leave Mexico. With dawn came many more squadrons of warriors, and when Cortés saw them, he decided to have Montezuma speak to them from a rooftop and tell them to stop the fighting and that we wished to leave his city. They say that he answered, very upset, "What more does Malinche want from me? I do not want to live, or listen to him, because of the fate he has forced on me." He would not come, and it was said too that he said that he did not want to see or hear Cortés, or listen to any more of his promises and lies.

The Mercedarian father and Cristóbal de Olid went to him, and showed him great reverence and spoke most affectionately, but Montezuma said, "I do not believe that I can do anything to end this war, for they have already elevated another lord and have decided not to let you leave here alive."

Nevertheless Montezuma stationed himself behind a battlement on a roof top with many of our soldiers to guard him and began to speak to the Mexicans in very affectionate terms, asking them to stop the war and telling them that we would leave Mexico. Many Mexican chiefs and captains, recognizing him, ordered their men to be quiet, and not to shoot stones or arrows. Four of them reached a place where they were able to talk to Montezuma, and they said, crying as they talked, "Oh, Lord, our great lord, how greatly we are afflicted by your misfortune, and that of your sons and relations! We have to let you know that we have already raised one of your kinsmen to be our lord."

They said that he was named Coadlavaca, lord of Iztapalapa. They also said that the war would have to go on to the end, for they had promised their idols not to stop until all of us were killed, and they prayed every day that he would be kept free and safe from our power. As everything would come out as they desired, they would not fail to hold him in higher regard as their lord than before, and they asked him to pardon them.

They had hardly finished this speech when there was such a shower of stones and javelins that Montezuma was hit by three stones, one on the head, another on the arm, and the third on the leg, for our men who were shielding him neglected to do so for a moment, because they saw that the attack had stopped while he was speaking with his chiefs.

They begged him to be doctored and to eat something, speaking very kindly to him, but he wouldn't, and when we least expected it they came to say that he was dead.

Cortés wept for him, and all of our captains and soldiers. There were men among us who cried as though he had been our father, and it is not surprising, considering how good he was. It was said that he had ruled for seventeen years and that he was the best king Mexico had ever had.

I have already told about the sorrow we felt when we saw that Montezuma was dead. We even thought badly about the Mercedarian father, who was always with him, for not having persuaded him to turn Christian. He gave as an excuse that he didn't think Montezuma would die from those wounds, but he did say that he should have ordered something given to stupefy him.

Finally Cortés directed that a priest and a chief among those we had imprisoned should be freed so that they could go and tell Coadlavaca and his captains that the great Montezuma was dead and that they had seen him die from the wounds his own people had caused him.

Map 16.1
European Empires
in Latin America,
1660

Analysis and Review Questions

1. How do the Aztec and Spanish versions of Montezuma's death differ?
2. To what extent do the two accounts share an assessment of Aztec divisiveness concerning their emperor?
3. What can we infer from these documents about how Aztec society was structured, and what kinds of obligations were required to maintain one's rule?
4. What are the various groups or levels that wield power in Aztec society?
5. To what extent did Aztec divisiveness aid the Spaniards in their conquest of Mexico? In what respects might such divisions have made the Spaniards' goals more difficult to attain?
6. In what ways were the Aztec society and society in Europe mirror images of one another? How were they different?

EXCERPT FROM BARTOLOMÉ DE LAS CASAS' *IN DEFENSE OF THE INDIANS*

About the Document

As Spain struggled in the mid 1500s to consolidate control over its New World possessions, a great debate erupted over the status and treatment of the Indians. At the heart of the debate lay the issue of whether Indians were civilized. An Aristotle treatise enshrined in Spanish law gave civilized peoples the right to wage war on uncivilized peoples and take them as slaves. Consequently, assessments of Indians as barbarians benefited many Spanish settlers who sought both to impose jurisdiction on the Indians and to take advantage of their labor. The Iberian scholar and theologian Juan Ines de Sepúlveda became a spokesperson for such interests.

Sepúlveda faced stiff opposition. Bartolomé de las Casas, who had served several years as a bishop in Mexico, represented the other side of the debate. Arguing that Indians were civilized, the theologian sought, on behalf of both Indians and priests outraged at the settlers' excesses, to persuade the Spanish Crown to impose stricter controls on its colonists. The debate's outcome would determine and shape Spain's policy toward *all* of its New World inhabitants.

The Document

Now if we shall have shown that among our Indians of the western and southern shores (granting that we call them barbarians and that they are barbarians) there are important kingdoms, large numbers of people who live settled lives in a society, great cities, kings, judges and laws, persons who engage in commerce, buying, selling, lending, and the other contracts of the law of nations, will it now stand proved that the Reverend Doctor Sepúlveda has spoken wrongly and viciously against peoples like these, either out of malice or ignorance of Aristotle's teaching, and, therefore, has falsely and perhaps irreparably slandered them before the entire world? From the fact that the Indians are barbarians it does not necessarily follow that they are incapable of government and have to be ruled by others, except to be taught about the Catholic faith and to be admitted to the holy sacraments. They are not ignorant, inhuman, or bestial. Rather, long before they had heard the word Spaniard they had properly organized states, wisely ordered by excellent laws, religion, and custom. They cultivated friendship and, bound together in common fellowship, lived in populous cities in which they wisely administered the affairs of both peace and war justly and equitably, truly governed by laws that at very many points surpass ours, and could have won the admiration of the sages of Athens, as I will show in the second part of this *Defense*.

Now if they are to be subjugated by war because they are ignorant of polished literature, let Sepúlveda hear Trogus Pompey:

> Nor could the Spaniards submit to the yoke of a conquered province until Caesar Augustus, after he had conquered the world, turned his victorious armies against them and organized that barbaric and wild people as a province, once he had led them by law to a more civilized way of life.

Now see how he called the Spanish people barbaric and wild. I would like to hear Sepúlveda, in his cleverness, answer this question: Does he think that the war of the Romans against the Spanish was justified in order to free them from barbarism? And this question also: Did the Spanish wage an unjust war when they vigorously defended themselves against them?

Next, I call the Spaniards who plunder that unhappy people torturers. Do you think that the Romans, once they had subjugated the wild and barbaric peoples of Spain, could with secure right divide all of you among themselves, handing over so many head of both males and females as allotments to individuals? And do you then conclude that the Romans could have stripped your rulers of their authority and consigned all of you, after you had been deprived of your liberty, to wretched labors, especially in searching for gold and silver lodes and mining and refining the metals? And if the Romans finally did that, as is evident from Diodorus, [would you not judge] that you also have the right to defend your freedom, indeed your very life, by war? Sepúlveda, would you have permitted Saint James to evangelize your own people of Córdoba in that way? For God's sake and man's faith in him, is this the way to impose the yoke of Christ on Christian men? Is this the way to remove wild barbarism from the minds of barbarians? Is it not, rather, to act like thieves, cut-throats, and cruel plunderers and to drive the gentlest of people headlong into despair? The Indian race is not that barbaric, nor are they dull witted or stupid, but they are easy to teach and very talented in learning all the liberal arts, and very ready to accept, honor, and observe the Christian religion and correct their sins (as experience has taught) once priests have introduced them to the sacred mysteries and taught them the word of God. They have been endowed with excellent conduct, and before the coming of the Spaniards, as we have said, they had political states that were well founded on beneficial laws.

From this it is clear that the basis for Sepúlveda's teaching that these people are uncivilized and ignorant is worse than false. Yet even if we were to grant that this race has no keenness of mind or artistic ability, certainly they are not, in consequence, obliged to submit themselves to those who are more intelligent and to adopt their ways, so that, if they refuse, they may be subdued by having war waged against them and be enslaved, as happens today. For men are obliged by the natural law to do many things they cannot be forced to do against their will. We are bound by the natural law to embrace virtue and imitate the uprightness of good men. No one, however, is punished for being bad unless he is guilty of rebellion. Where the Catholic faith has been preached in a Christian manner and as it ought to be, all men are bound by the natural law to accept it, yet no one is forced to accept the faith of Christ. No one is punished because he is sunk in vice, unless he is rebellious or harms the property and persons of others. No one is forced to embrace virtue and show himself as a good man. One who receives a favor is bound by the natural law to return the favor by what we call antidotal obligation. Yet no one is forced to this, nor is he punished if he omits it, according to the common interpretation of the jurists.

Analysis and Review Questions

1. On what grounds does las Casas argue that the Indians are civilized?
2. Las Casas was a master of rhetoric. How does his language in describing the Spanish settlers and their actions incline his audience to accept his bias or position? Do you think he was successful?
3. Referring to the reading, tell how important you think legal and philosophical precedents were in making a successful case before the Spanish Crown? Do you think this form of logic and argument was based on Roman precedent? Why or why not?
4. In comparing the Spaniards with the Romans, what do you think las Casas was trying to achieve?
5. How does the position of las Casas on the role of Christianity in the New World differ from that which he ascribes to Sepúlveda? What are some of the implications of this division within the Church?

Image 16.2
Spanish Mistreatment
of the Indians

Sor Juana Inéz de la Cruz, from *La Respuesta**

About the Document

Arguably one of the greatest divides in the contact zone was that between the sexes. The patriarchal nature of Spanish rule and of the Catholic Church ensured that legally, at least, women were restricted to inferior positions and to lives with few rights. This was as true of Spanish women as it was of indigenous women. Perhaps the most impressive example of gender conflict involved Sor Juana Inéz de la Cruz, a Mexican nun in the late 1600s.

A brilliant and talented scholar, Sor Juana in 1690 wrote a daring critique of an earlier Jesuit sermon. Her critique prompted the Bishop of Puebla to admonish her for overstepping herself as a woman. Sor Juana subsequently defended herself in a lengthy reply *(respuesta)* that challenged the foundations of the society in which she lived. Her 1695 response to the bishop set off a struggle that highlighted not only divisions between the sexes, but also those within the Church, and between the Church and the Spanish government, in which Sor Juana found many powerful and influential supporters.

The Document

I see many and illustrious women; some blessed with the gift of prophecy, like Abigail, others of persuasion, like Esther; others with pity, like Rehab; others with perseverance, like Anna, the mother of Samuel; and an infinite number of others, with diverse gifts and virtues.

... for all were nothing more than learned women, held, and celebrated—and venerated as well as such by antiquity. Without mentioning an infinity of other women whose names fill books. For example, I find the Egyptian Catherine, studying and influencing the wisdom of all the wise men of Egypt. I see a Gertrudis studying, writing, and teaching. And not to overlook examples close to home, I see my most holy mother Paula, learned in Hebrew, Greek, and Latin, and most able in interpreting the Scriptures. And what greater praise than, having as her chronicler a Jeronimus Maximus, that Saint scarcely found himself competent for his task, and says, with that weighty deliberation and energetic precision with which he so well expressed himself: "If all the members of my body were tongues, they still would not be sufficient to proclaim the wisdom and virtue of Paula."

The venerable Doctor Arce (by his virtue and learning a worthy teacher of the Scriptures) in his scholarly *Bibliorum* raises this question: *Is it permissible for women to dedicate themselves to the study of the Holy Scriptures, and to their interpretation?* and he offers as negative arguments the opinions of many saints, especially that of the Apostle: *Let women keep silence*

*The Spanish text for this 17th century declaration of women's intellectual freedom was discovered by Gabriel North Seymour during her Fulbright Scholarship in Mexico in 1980, following graduation from Princeton University. The English language translation by Margaret Sayers Peden was commissioned by Lime Rock Press, a small independent press in Connecticut, and was originally published in 1982 in a limited edition that included Seymour's black-and-white photographs of Sor Juana sites, under the title, "A Woman of Genius: The Intellectual Autobiography of Sor Juana Inès de la Cruz." The publication was honored at a special convocation of Mexican and American scholars at the Library of Congress. Copyright 1982 by Lime Rock Press, Inc. Reprinted by permission.

in the churches; for it is not permitted them to speak, etc. He later cites other opinions and, from the same Apostle, verses from his letter to Titus: *The aged women in like manner, in holy attire teaching well,* with interpretations by the Holy Fathers. Finally he resolves, with all prudence, that teaching publicly from a University chair, or preaching from the pulpit, is not permissible for women; but that to study, write, and teach privately not only is permissible, but most advantageous and useful. It is evident that this is not to be the case with all women, but with those to whom God may have granted special virtue and prudence, and who may be well advanced in learning, and having the essential talent and requisites for such a sacred calling. This view is indeed just, so much so that not only women, who are held to be so inept, but also men, who merely for being men believe they are wise, should be prohibited from interpreting the Sacred Word if they are not learned and virtuous and of gentle and well-inclined natures; that this is not so has been, I believe, at the root of so much sectarianism and so many heresies. For there are many who study but are ignorant, especially those who are in spirit arrogant, troubled, and proud, so eager for new interpretations of the Word (which itself rejects new interpretations) that merely for the sake of saying what no one else has said they speak a heresy, and even then are not content. Of these the Holy Spirit says: *For wisdom will not enter into a malicious soul.* To such as these more harm results from knowing than from ignorance. A wise man has said: he who does not know Latin is not a complete fool; but he who knows it is well qualified to be. And I would add that a fool may reach perfection (if ignorance may tolerate perfection) by having studied his title of philosophy and theology and by having some learning of tongues, by which he may be a fool in many sciences and languages: a great fool cannot be contained solely in his mother tongue.

For such as these, I reiterate, study is harmful, because it is as if to place a sword in the hands of a madman; which, though a most noble instrument for defense, is in his hands his own death and that of many others. So were the Divine Scriptures in the possession of the evil Pelagius and the intractable Arius, of the evil Luther, and the other heresiarchs like our own Doctor (who was neither ours nor a doctor) Cazalla. To these men, wisdom was harmful; although it is the greatest nourishment and the life of the soul; in the same way that in a stomach of sickly constitution and adulterated complexion, the finer the nourishment it receives, the more arid, fermented, and perverse are the humors it produces; thus these evil men: the more they study, the worse opinions they engender, their reason being obstructed with the very substance meant to nourish it, and they study much and digest little, exceeding the limits of the vessel of their reason. Of which the Apostle says: *For I say, by the grace that is given me, to all that are among you, not to be more wise than it behoveth to be wise, but to be wise unto sobriety, and according as God hath divided to every one the measure of faith.* And in truth, the Apostle did not direct these words to women, but to men; and that *keep silence* is intended not only for women, but for *all* incompetents. If I desire to know as much, or more, than Aristotle or Saint Augustine, and if I have not the aptitude of Saint Augustine or Aristotle, though I study more than either, not only will I not achieve learning, but I will weaken and dull the workings of my feeble reason with the disproportionateness of the goal.

Analysis and Review Questions

1. On what grounds does Sor Juana defend her right to exercise her intellect?
2. What examples does Sor Juana offer of noted and influential women? What does the variety of sources from which she draws her examples tell us of Sor Juana's education?

3. What reasons does Sor Juana give for agreeing with Doctor Arce's argument for barring women from the pulpit?

4. How does Sor Juana turn her agreement with Arce into an attack on the male-dominated society in which she lived? Do you think the Church in particular would have found Sor Juana's argument more threatening than, say, the average male Spaniard? Why or why not?

5. In her "Respuesta," Sor Juana treats intellect as a veritable weapon. To what extent do you agree with her? What examples might you provide that would support or contradict her?

Map 16.2
Spanish and Portuguese
Explorations: 1400–1600

WEB LINKS

Selections from Longman World History—Primary Sources and Case Studies

Comparative Document

Document 22.1, Catherine the Great's Constitution

http://longmanworldhistory.com
The following additional readings and case studies can be found on the Web site.
Document 16.1, *The Second Letter of Hernan Cortéz to King Charles V of Spain (1519)*
Document 16.5, *The New Laws of the Indies for the Good Treatment and Preservation of the Indians (1542)*
Case Study 16.1, Battlefields to Courtrooms: Conflict and Agency in the Americas
Case Study 16.2, Policy-making in the Americas: Subjects or Slaves?
Case Study 16.3, Challenges of Empire: The "Song" Remains the Same

Spanish Colonial Policy and the New Laws

http://www.fordham.edu/halsall/mod/1542newlawsindies.html
Brief introduction to and context for the 1542 New Laws. Includes more expansive excerpts from the New Laws.

http://www.mexconnect.com/mex_/history/jtuck/jtviceroymendoza.html
Site devoted to the colonial career of Viceroy Mendoza, the Crown bureaucrat charged with implementing and enforcing the New Laws in Mexico. Describes in detail the political backlash that forced many of the New Laws to be suspended in the New World.

The Encomienda and Its Relation to Spanish Abuses

http://muweb.millersv.edu/~columbus/papers/scott-m.html
Article-length history of the encomienda in the Americas.

The New Laws and Their Relation to the Spanish "Black Legend"

http://www.freerepublic.com/forum/a39d38e0d14db.htm
Comprehensive assessment of las Casas, the encomienda, the New Laws, and their relation to the Spanish "Black Legend" so often invoked as propaganda by Spain's enemies at home and abroad.

http://www.unl.edu/LatAmHis/RoleofChurch.html
This site deals more directly with the Church's role in unwittingly creating and sustaining the Spanish "Black Legend."

http://www.xxicentury.org/HCA/reform.html
Historical assessment of the Church's role in helping to establish and reform Spanish colonial policy; not limited to the New Laws and the abuses which prompted them.

The Age of Discovery and European Reactions to the New World

http://muweb.millersv.edu/~columbus
Extensive collection of indexed articles and issues pertaining to Columbus, the Age of Discovery, and both the short- and long-term impacts of Columbus's epic voyages on both Spain and the New World.

CHAPTER 17

East Asia in Transition, 1450–1700

The intellectual and religious developments beginning in the fourteenth century brought changes not only in the West but also in the East. Early European outreach to East Asia had a significant impact on the region and precipitated the beginning of the Enlightenment in East Asia. Although China, Japan, and Korea managed to keep their political unity while remaining isolated to the outside world, Western influence became almost irresistible. The guns, the cross, and the trade would eventually reshape the minds of East Asia and bring in a new era of change.

The fall of the Mongol Empire left a political vacuum that led to the restoration of Chinese imperial glory. China under the Ming Dynasty (1368–1644) regained its political centralization and resumed its commercial expansion. The traditional tribute system, designed to maintain China's political and economic superiority to its neighboring small states, was reorganized in the face of increasing Western commercial activities. In 1405, nearly 90 years before Christopher Columbus set off on his westward expedition to the "new world," China's Zheng He led the imperial treasure fleet of 62 ships through the southwestern Pacific and Indian Oceans to reach the east coast of Africa. However, such courageous voyages lasted for only 28 years, until 1433, when the Ming emperor called the missions off.

Japan, on the other hand, withdrew from its limited contact with the Europeans into isolation and remained that way until mid-nineteenth century. Both Japanese government and society became increasingly rigid under the rule of the shogun, especially during the Tokugawa period (1604–1868). On the Korean Peninsula, the Yi Dynasty (1392–1910) gave the Koreans over five centuries of peace and unity. Chinese patterns continued to affect Korea in a significant way.

The period between the fifteenth and eighteenth centuries was a time of recovery and consolidation for East Asia. Soon, the region would have to face the challenge from the West. Collision with European powers and different solutions to deal with them would lead to different paths toward modernization for the major countries in the region.

MATTEO RICCI'S JOURNALS

About the Document

Matteo Ricci was an Italian Jesuit missionary who went to China in 1583. He first learned to adapt to the Chinese way of life before attempting to convert the Chinese to Christianity. His modest manner amazed many Chinese, including the emperor. In 1601 Ricci was offered a position in the imperial court in charge of studies in mathematics and astronomy, as well as teaching Christianity to the Chinese elite class. Fluent in Chinese and well-versed in Confucian teaching, Ricci also composed a number of books in Chinese on various subjects. One of the most important was his *History of the Introduction of Christianity into China*. The imperial court was so impressed by his achievements that Ricci was awarded an honorable title as the Doctor from the Great West Ocean.

While in China, Ricci kept a journal reflecting on his experience and impression of the Chinese government and society.

*Image 17.1
Matteo Ricci and a
Chinese Convert to
Christianity*

The Document

We shall touch upon this subject only insofar as it has to do with the purpose of our narrative. It would require a number of chapters, if not of whole books, to treat this matter in full detail. . . . Chinese imperial power passes on from father to son, or to other royal kin, as does our own. Two or three of the more ancient kings are known to have bequeathed the throne to successors without royal relationship rather than to their sons, whom they judged to be unfitted to rule. More than once, however, it has happened that the people, growing weary of an inept ruler, have stripped him of his authority and replaced him with someone pre-eminent for character and courage whom they henceforth recognized as their legitimate King. It may be said in praise of the Chinese that ordinarily they would prefer to die an honorable death rather than swear allegiance to a usurping monarch. In fact, there is a proverb extant among their philosophers, which reads: "No woman is moral who has two husbands, nor any vassal faithful to two lords."

There are no ancient laws in China under which the republic is governed in perpetuum, such as our laws of the twelve tables and the Code of Caesar. Whoever succeeds in getting possession of the throne, regardless of his ancestry, makes new laws according to his own way of thinking. His successors on the throne are obliged to enforce the laws which he promulgated as founder of the dynasty, and these laws cannot be changed without good reason. . . .

The extent of their kingdom° is so vast, its borders so distant, and their utter lack of knowledge of a transmaritime world is so complete that the Chinese imagine the whole world as included in their kingdom. Even now, as from time beyond recording, they call their Emperor, Thiencu, the Son of Heaven, and because they worship Heaven as the Supreme Being, the Son of Heaven and the Son of God are one and the same. In ordinary speech, he is referred to as Hoamsi, meaning supreme ruler or monarch, while other and subordinate rulers are called by the much inferior title of Guam.

kingdom: Ricci often used the term kingdom instead of dynasty or empire to refer to China.

Only such as have earned a doctor's degree or that of licentiate are admitted to take part in the government of the kingdom, and due to the interest of the magistrates and of the King himself there is no lack of such candidates. Every public office is therefore fortified with and dependent upon the attested science, prudence, and diplomacy of the person assigned to it, whether he be taking office for the first time or is already experienced in the conduct of civil life. This integrity of life is prescribed by . . . law . . . , and for the most part it is lived up to, save in the case of such as are prone to violate the dictates of justice from human weakness and from lack of religious training among the gentiles. All magistrates, whether they belong to the military or to the civil congress, are called Quon-fu, meaning commander or president, though their honorary or unofficial title is Lau-ye or Lau-sie, signifying lord or father. The Portuguese call the Chinese magistrates, mandarins, probably from mandando, mando mandare, to order or command, and they are now generally known by this title in Europe.

Though we have already stated that the Chinese form of government is monarchical, it must be evident from what has been said, and it will be made clearer by what is to come, that it is to some extent an aristocracy. Although all legal statutes inaugurated by magistrates must be confirmed by the King in writing on the written petition presented to him, the King himself makes no final decision in important matters of state without consulting the magistrates or considering their advice. . . .

Tax returns, impost, and other tribute, which undoubtedly exceed a hundred and fifty million a year, as is commonly said, do not go into the Imperial Exchequer, nor can the King dispose of this income as he pleases. The silver, which is the common currency, is placed in the public treasury, and the returns paid in rice are placed in the warehouses belonging to the government. The generous allowance made for the support of the royal family and their relatives, for the palace eunuchs and the royal household, is drawn from this national treasury. In keeping with the regal splendor and dignity of the crown, these annuities are large, but each individual account is determined and regulated by law. Civil and military accounts and the expenses of all government departments are paid out of this national treasury, and the size of the national budget is far in excess of what Europeans might imagine. Public buildings, the palaces of the King and of his relations, the upkeep of city prisons and fortresses, and the renewal of all kinds of war supplies must be met by the national treasury, and in a kingdom of such vast dimensions the program of building and of restoration is continuous. One would scarcely believe that at times even these enormous revenues are not sufficient to meet the expenses. When this happens, new taxes are imposed to balance the national budget.

Relative to the magistrates in general, there are two distinct orders or grades. The first and superior order is made up of the magistrates who govern the various courts of the royal palace, which is considered to be a model for the rule of the entire realm. The second order includes all provincial magistrates or governors who rule a province or a city. For each of these orders of magistrates, there are five or six large books containing the governmental roster of the entire country. These books are for sale throughout the kingdom. They are being continually revised, and the revision, which is dated twice a month in the royal city of Pekin, is not very difficult because of the singular typographical arrangement in which they are printed. The entire contents of these books consist of nothing other than the current lists of the names, addresses, and grades of the court officers of the entire government, and the frequent revision is necessary if the roster is to be kept up to date. In addition to the daily changes, occasioned by deaths, demotions, and dismissals in such an incredibly long list of names, there are the frequent departures of some to visit their homes at stated periods. We shall say more later on of this last instance, which is occasioned by the custom requiring every magistrate to lay aside his official duties and return to his home for three full years, on the death of his father or his mother. One result of these numerous changes is that there are always a great many in the city of Pekin awaiting the good fortune of being appointed to fill the vacancies thus created.

Besides the regular magistrates there are in the royal palace various other organizations, instituted for particular purposes. The most exalted of these is what is known as the Han-Iin-yuen, made up of selected doctors of philosophy and chosen by examination. Members of this cabinet have nothing to do with public administration but outrank all public officials in dignity of office. Ambition for a place in this select body means no end of labor and of sacrifice. These are the King's secretaries, who do both his writing and his composing. They edit and compile the royal annals and publish the laws and statutes of the land. The tutors of kings and princes are chosen from their number. They are entirely devoted to study and there are grades within the cabinet which are determined by the publications of its members. Hence, they are honored with the highest dignity within the regal court, but not beyond it. . . .

The Chinese can distinguish between their magistrates by the parasols they use as protection against the sun when they go out in public. Some of these are blue and others yellow. Sometimes for effect they will have two or three of these sunshades, but only one if their rank does not permit of more. They may also be recognized by their mode of transportation in public. The lower ranks ride on horseback, the higher are carried about on the shoulders of their servants in gestatorial chairs. The number of carriers also has a significance of rank; some are allowed only four, others may have eight. There are other ways also of distinguishing the magistracy and the rank of dignity therein; by banners and pennants, chains and censer cups, and by the number of the guards who give orders to make way for the passage of the dignitary. The escort itself is held in such high esteem by the public that no one would question their orders. Even in a crowded city everyone gives way at the sound of their voices with a spontaneity that corresponds to the rank of the approaching celebrity.

Before closing this chapter on Chinese public administration, it would seem to be quite worthwhile recording a few more things in which this people differ from Europeans. To begin with, it seems to be quite remarkable when we stop to consider it, that in a kingdom of almost limitless expanse and innumerable population, and abounding in copious supplies of every description, though they have a well-equipped army and navy that could easily conquer the neighboring nations, neither the King nor his people ever think of waging a war of aggression. They are quite content with what they have and are not ambitious of conquest. In this respect they are much different from the people of Europe, who are frequently discontent with their own governments and covetous of what others enjoy. While the nations of the West seem to be entirely consumed with the idea of supreme domination, they cannot even preserve what their ancestors have bequeathed them, as the Chinese have done through a period of some thousand of years. . . .

Another remarkable fact and quite worthy of note as marking a difference from the West, is that the entire kingdom is administered by the Order of the Learned, commonly known as The Philosophers. The responsibility for orderly management of the entire realm is wholly and completely committed to their charge and care. The army, both officers and soldiers, hold them in high respect and show them the promptest obedience and deference, and not infrequently the military are disciplined by them as a schoolboy might be punished by his master. Policies of war are formulated and military questions are decided by the Philosophers only, and their advice and counsel has more weight with the King than that of the military leaders. In fact very few of these, and only on rare occasions, are admitted to war consultations. Hence it follows that those who aspire to be cultured frown upon war and would prefer the lowest rank in the philosophical order to the highest in the military, realizing that the Philosophers far excel military leaders in the good will and the respect of the people and in opportunities of acquiring wealth.

Analysis and Review Questions

Map 17.1
Trade Routes
to Asia

1. In your view, how well did Ricci understand Chinese traditions and society?
2. How does Ricci compare Chinese law with that from European tradition?
3. According to Ricci's account, what was the attitude of the Chinese magistrates to the Jesuits?
4. What was Ricci's description of the Chinese government?
5. Who might be Ricci's intended readers?

"CLOSED COUNTRY EDICT OF 1635" AND "EXCLUSION OF THE PORTUGUESE, 1639," BY IEYASU TOKUGAWA

About the Document

Ieyasu Tokugawa was granted the title of shogun in 1603 after defeating his rivals by using guns brought into Japan by the Europeans. His successors, however, began to fear that the growing trade with the West and influence of Christianity would directly challenge the Japanese value system. Below are two major shogun edicts intended to force foreign trade and missionaries out of Japan. Japan remained an isolated country for the next 200 years, until the Americans tried to open relations with Japan in 1853.

The Document

Closed Country Edict of 1635

1. Japanese ships are strictly forbidden to leave for foreign countries.

2. No Japanese is permitted to go abroad. If there is anyone who attempts to do so secretly, he must be executed. The ship so involved must be impounded and its owner arrested, and the matter must be reported to the higher authority.

3. If any Japanese returns from overseas after residing there, he must be put to death.

4. If there is any place where the teachings of padres° is practiced, the two of you must order a thorough investigation.

5. Any informer revealing the whereabouts of the followers of padres must be rewarded accordingly. If anyone reveals the whereabouts of a high ranking padre, he must be given one hundred pieces of silver. For those of lower ranks, depending on the deed, the reward must be set accordingly.

padres: Fathers (priests) of the Roman Catholic Church.

6. If a foreign ship has an objection [to the measures adopted] and it becomes necessary to report the matter to Edo,° you may ask the Omura° domain to provide ships to guard the foreign ship. . . .

7. If there are any Southern Barbarians° who propagate the teachings of padres, or otherwise commit crimes, they may be incarcerated in the prison. . . .

8. All incoming ships must be carefully searched for the followers of padres.

9. No single trading city shall be permitted to purchase all the merchandise brought by foreign ships.

10. Samurai are not permitted to purchase any goods originating from foreign ships directly from Chinese merchants in Nagasaki.

11. After a list of merchandise brought by foreign ships is sent to Edo, as before you may order that commercial dealings may take place without waiting for a reply from Edo.

12. After settling the price, all white yarns brought by foreign ships shall be allocated to the five trading cities° and other quarters as stipulated.

13. After settling the price of white yarns, other merchandise [brought by foreign ships] may be traded freely between the [licensed] dealers. However, in view of the fact that Chinese ships are small and cannot bring large consignments, you may issue orders of sale at your discretion. Additionally, payment for goods purchased must be made within twenty days after the price is set.

14. The date of departure homeward of foreign ships shall not be later than the twentieth day of the ninth month. Any ships arriving in Japan later than usual shall depart within fifty days of their arrival. As to the departure of Chinese ships, you may use your discretion to order their departure after the departure of the Portuguese galeota.°

15. The goods brought by foreign ships which remained unsold may not be deposited or accepted for deposit.

16. The arrival in Nagasaki of representatives of the five trading cities shall not be later than the fifth day of the seventh month. Anyone arriving later than that date shall lose the quota assigned to his city.

17. Ships arriving in Hirado° must sell their raw silk at the price set in Nagasaki, and are not permitted to engage in business transactions until after the price is established in Nagasaki.

You are hereby required to act in accordance with the provisions set above. It is so ordered.

*Image 17.2
A Japanese view
of European
Missionaries*

Exclusion of the Portuguese, 1639

1. The matter relating to the proscription of Christianity is known [to the Portuguese]. However, heretofore they have secretly transported those who are going to propagate that religion.

2. If those who believe in that religion band together in an attempt to do evil things, they must be subjected to punishment.

Edo: Old name of what today is Tokyo, before Meiji Reforms of 1868.
Omura: Area around Nagasaki.
Southern Barbarians: Westerners.
five trading cities: Foreigners could do business in Kyoto, Edo/Tokyo, Osaka, Sakai, and Nagasaki.
galeota: Portuguese ship.
Hirado: Island southwest of Nagasaki.

3. While those who believe in the preaching of padres are in hiding, there are incidents in which that country [Portugal] has sent gifts to them for their sustenance.

In view of the above, hereafter entry by the Portuguese galeota is forbidden. If they insist on coming [to Japan], the ships must be destroyed and anyone aboard those ships must be beheaded. We have received the above order and are thus transmitting it to you accordingly.

The above concerns our disposition with regard to the galeota.

Memorandum

With regard to those who believe in Christianity, you are aware that there is a proscription, and thus knowing, you are not permitted to let padres and those who believe in their preaching to come aboard your ships. If there is any violation, all of you who are aboard will be considered culpable. If there is anyone who hides the fact that he is a Christian and boards your ship, you may report it to us. A substantial reward will be given to you for this information.

This memorandum is to be given to those who come on Chinese ships. [A similar note to the Dutch ships.]

Analysis and Review Questions

1. What were the major restrictions imposed on the Japanese?
2. What were the major restrictions on foreign traders?
3. What was the primary purpose of the 1635 Edict?
4. What was the argument behind the shogun's decision of 1639 to expel the Christians?
5. How would these two edicts affect Japan's relations with the outside world?

Map 17.2
Voyages of
Zheng He

A MING NAVAL EXPEDITION

About the Document

Zheng He's daring adventures to explore the outside world came nearly 90 years earlier than Christopher Columbus's journey westward. Although the voyages did not last long, they proved to the Chinese, as well as the world, that China was able to carry out long-distance travel on the high seas.

Reading this stone tablet text commemorating the expeditions, it is not difficult to understand the pride of the Chinese in demonstrating their maritime power. One wonders what kind of naval power China would have become if the Ming emperor had not called off such voyages in 1433 and China had not lost its technological edge to the Europeans.

The Document

The Imperial Ming dynasty in unifying seas and continents . . . even goes beyond the Han and the Hang . . . the countries beyond the horizon and from the ends of the earth have all become subjects . . . Thus the barbarians from beyond the seas have come to audience bearing precious objects. . . . The Emperor has ordered us, Zheng He . . . to make manifest the transforming power of the Imperial virtue and to treat distant people with kindness. . . . We have seven times received the commission and ambassadors [and have visited] altogether more than thirty countries, large and small. We have traversed immense water spaces and have beheld huge waves like mountains rising sky high, and we have set eyes on barbarian regions far away hidden in a blue transparency of light vapors, while our sails loftily unfolded like clouds day and night controlled their course, traversing those savage waves as if we were treading a public thoroughfare. . . We have received the high favor of a gracious commission of our Sacred Lord, to carry to the distant barbarians the benefits of his auspicious example. . . . Therefore we have recorded the years and months of the voyages. [Here follows a detailed record of places visited and things done on each of the seven voyages.] We have anchored in this port awaiting a north wind to take the sea, and have thus recorded an inscription in stone . . . erected by the principal envoys, the Grand Eunuchs Cheng Ho and Wang Ching-hung and the assistant envoys.

Analysis and Review Questions

1. How did the Chinese view their overseas expeditions?
2. What was China's view of itself and the world?
3. What is the point of the description of the weather and waves on the high sea?
4. What role was played by the imperial power in China's overseas expeditions?
5. What might be the major contributions of these Chinese voyages to the world?

WEB LINKS

Selections from Longman World History—Primary Sources and Case Studies

http://longmanworldhistory.com
The following additional readings and case studies can be found on the Web Site.
Document 17.3A, European View of Asia
Case Study 17.1, A Chinese and a Japanese View of Europeans
Jesuits in China

*http://www.ibiblio.org/expo/vatican.exhibit/exhibit/
i-rome_to_china/Jesuits_in_China.html*

*http://www.ibiblio.org/expo/vatican.exhibit/exhibit/
i-rome_to_china/Rome_to_china.html*

http://mb-soft.com/believe/text/jesuit.htm

http://www.christianitytoday.com/ch/52h/52h024.html

Christians in Japan

http://www.baobab.or.jp/~stranger/mypage/chrinjap.htm
http://www.pnsnet.co.jp/users/cltembpt/cronology.html
http://satucket.com/lectionary/Japan_martyrs.htm
http://members.aol.com/DoJourney/Keikyo/

Zheng He's Voyage

http://www.chinapage.com/chengho.html
http://campus.northpark.edu/history/WebChron/World/Voyages.html
http://www.askasia.org/frclasrm/lessplan/l000069.htm
http://www.cronab.demon.co.uk/china.htm

CHAPTER **18**

Foreign Rulers in
South Asia, 1450–1750

Between 1450 and 1750 C.E., southern India was invaded and controlled by numerous foreign rulers. Many of these rulers, such as the Delhi Sultans and Babur, came from powerful entities within South Asia, but as these empires began to crumble, the English saw their opportunity to pick up the broken pieces for their own economic gain. With England's rise to power in South Asia came the influence of the Western world. As the fifteenth century dawned in South Asia, the Delhi Sultanate, a Muslim empire, had ruled northern India since 1192 C.E. Southern India was ruled mostly by local rulers and princes. On the horizon, though, were powerful foreign entities with an interest in India. The Delhi Sultans had come to India from Afghanistan, and the next invader came from there as well. In 1523 Babur invaded India, conquering Delhi and destroying the remnants of the Delhi Sultanate. Babur was the founder of the Mughal Empire, which ruled much of India until the early 1700s.

Around this time, after a century of increasing influence, the English became a dominant force in India. England's East India Company established commercial and financial monopolies, especially in the area of Bengal in eastern India. As it did so, it weakened the Mughal Empire. After the death of the Mughal emperor Aurangzeb in 1707, the empire was on the verge of collapse, and the English and the East India Company were there to pick up the pieces.

THE ENGLISH IN SOUTH ASIA AND THE INDIAN OCEAN

About the Document

Many European nations (especially Spain and Portugal) began overseas exploration and serious overseas trade during the sixteenth century. Preoccupied mainly by religious issues during the Reformation and Counter-Reformation, other nations, such as France, England, and later the Netherlands, followed suit only in the seventeenth century. Relatively poor trade connections in British and French America led these countries increasingly to seek commercial contacts in Asia.

European trade with Asia was nothing new, but it soon took on an unparalleled intensity. Nearly all of the aforementioned nations, except Spain, tried to increase their presence in India as well as in outer areas of the Indian Ocean such as Indonesia.

In 1614 King James I of England sent a diplomat, Sir Thomas Roe, to visit the Mughal emperor, Jahangir, and negotiate a trade treaty. The trade mission was successful, and the emperor wrote a letter, the first document here, to James afterward. A few years later, however, the English found things more difficult as they tried to encroach on Indonesia, already being plied by the Dutch. A French traveler recounts in the second document what happened between the Dutch and the English in 1617.

Map 18.1
The Delhi Sultanate
and Mughal India

The Document

Part One: Letter from Jahangir to James I of England

When your majesty shall open this letter let your royal heart be as fresh as a sweet garden. Let all people make reverence at your gate; let your throne be advanced higher; amongst the greatness of the kings of the prophet Jesus, let your Majesty be the greatest, and all monarchies derive their counsel and wisdom from your breast as from a fountain, that the law of the majesty of Jesus may revive and flourish under your protection.

The letter of love and friendship which you sent and the presents, tokens of your good affection toward me, I have received by the hands of your ambassador, Sir Thomas Roe (who well deserveth to be your trusted servant), delivered to me in an acceptable and happy hour; upon which mine eyes were so fixed that I could not easily remove them to any other object, and have accepted them with great joy and delight.

Upon which assurance of your royal love I have given my general command to all the kingdoms and ports of my dominions to receive all the merchants of the English nation as the subjects of my friend; that in what place soever they choose to live, they may have reception and residence to their own content and safety; and what goods soever they desire to sell or buy, they may have free liberty without any restraint; and at what port soever they shall arrive, that neither Portugal nor any other shall dare to molest their quiet; and in what city soever they shall have residence, I have commanded all my governors and captains to give them freedom answerable to their own desires; to sell, buy, and to transport into their country at their pleasure.

For confirmation of our love and friendship, I desire your Majesty to command your merchants to bring in their ships of all sorts of rarities and rich goods fit for my palace; and that you be pleased to send me your royal letters by every opportunity, that I may rejoice in your health and prosperous affairs; that our friendships may be interchanged and eternal.

Your Majesty is learned and quick-sighted as a prophet, and can conceive so much by few words that I need write no more.

The God of heaven give you and us increase of honor.

Part Two: Dutch Hostility toward English Merchants

[The original source refers to the Dutch as "Hollanders," but the more modern "Dutch" has been inserted in its place. A few other words have also been modernized.]

A relation of the Frenchmen which lately arrived into France in a ship of Dieppe out of the East Indies concerning the wrongs and abuses which the Dutch had lately done to the English there (1617):

Two English ships coming to Banda, in course of trade and traffic, the Dutch assaulted with certain of their ships, which English ships in their resistance and defense the said Dutch took, slew seven or eight of their men (whereof one was a chief factor), chained the captain, merchants, and mariners, and put the mariners in their galleys. All the munitions and victuals in the said English ships did the Dutch take out and carried the same ashore, challenged all to be theirs as their proper inheritance, and therefore will be lords of the same.

The Dutch likewise took an English ship going from Bantam (in Dutch Java°) to Jakarta, slew some of her men, wounded many more, chained the captain and mariners, and carried away the said ship at the stern of one of their ships into Bantam Road, and there anchored close by the admiral of the English in most despiteful and daring manner, making their vaunts that they were the chief people of all Europe; and to make a show of the same they advanced their own arms and colors, and under them placed the colors of England and France, and then shot at the said English and French colors in most contemptuous and disdainful manner.

At Bantam the English and Dutch had great disputes, insomuch as it was verily thought they would have fought together in the road, for the general of the Dutch had brought thither fourteen great ships, ready to fight, where the English had nine, which they fitted for defense; but they fought not, for the governor of Bantam forbad them to fight in his road, and threatened them that if they did fight contrary to his command he could cut the throats of all their men that he should find upon the land.

The 27th of November the Dutch declared war against all the English at the Mulluccoes, Banda, and Amboyna, threatening to make one and all prize and to put them to the edge of the sword; which proclamation of theirs they fixed upon the doors of their lodgings at Bantam, challenging all to be theirs as their proper inheritance.

Analysis and Review Questions

1. Are English merchants to be protected in any way in Jahangir's territory?
2. What restrictions are being placed on English merchants?
3. What prevented fighting between the English and Dutch at Bantam?
4. How did the Dutch offend the French?
5. From reading these two selections, why do you think the English gained a firm foothold in India, but failed to do so in Indonesia?

ABU TALEB ON THE WEST AND WESTERN INFLUENCE

About the Document

Muslims filled the top positions in much of India during the Mughal Dynasty. As European influence and trade increased, however, the Muslim empires and kingdoms weakened substantially. Upper-caste Hindus began to have their children

---

Java: Former Dutch colony, essentially today's Indonesia.

educated in Western schools, and, while relatively few Hindus had the chance to travel to Europe, many started to affect English ways and attitudes. The same cannot be said for Indian Muslims, who generally resisted Western influence on their lives and customs, but who were often more able to travel (unlike Hindus, they had no religious prohibitions against foreign travel).

One of the first educated Indians to travel to Europe was Abū Tāleb. Born in 1752, Abū Tāleb served the Mughal government for much of his early life, and, after retiring, spent three years in Europe. When he returned to Calcutta, he wrote *The Travels of Mirza Abū Tāleb Khan*. Written in Persian for his Muslim audience, the book illustrates Abū Tāleb's interest in English ways and life, but also displays the attitudes between the English and Indian Muslims.

The Document

Glory be to God, the Lord of all worlds, who has conferred innumerable blessings on mankind, and accomplished all the laudable desires of his creatures. Praise be also to the Chosen of Mankind [Muhammad], the traveler over the whole expanse of the heavens, and benedictions without end on his descendants and companions.

The wanderer over the face of the earth, Abū Tāleb, the son of Mohammed of Ispahan, begs leave to inform the curious in biography, that, owing to several adverse circumstances, finding it inconvenient to remain at home, he was compelled to undertake many tedious journeys, during which he associated with men of all nations and beheld various wonders, both by sea and by land.

It therefore occurred to him, that if he were to write all the circumstances of his journey through Europe, to describe the curiosities and wonders which he saw, and to give some account for the manner and customs of the various nations he visited, all of which are little known to Asiatics, it would afford a gratifying banquet to his countrymen.

He was also of opinion, that many of the customs, inventions, sciences, and ordinances of Europe, the good effects of which are apparent in those countries, might with great advantage be imitated by Mohammedans.

Impressed with these ideas, he, on his first setting out on his travels, commenced a journal, in which he daily inserted every event, and committed to writing such reflections as occurred to him at the moment: and on his return to Calcutta, in the year of the Hejira 1218 (A.D. 1803), having revised and abridged his notes, he arranged them in the present form.

[Here Abū Tāleb changes from the third to the first person, and laments:] I have named this work . . . "The Travels of Tāleb in the Regions of Europe"; but when I reflect on the want of energy and the indolent dispositions of my countrymen, and the many erroneous customs which exist in all Mohammedan countries and among all ranks of Mussulmans, I am fearful that my exertions will be thrown away. The great and the rich, intoxicated with pride and luxury, and puffed up with the vanity of their possessions, consider universal science as comprehended in the circle of their own scanty acquirements and limited knowledge; while the poor and common people, from the want of leisure, and overpowered by the difficulty of procuring a livelihood, have not time to attend to their personal concerns, much less to form desires for the acquirement of information on new discoveries and inventions; although such a passion has been implanted by nature in every human breast, as an honor and an ornament to the species. I therefore despair of their reaping any fruit from my labors, being convinced that they will consider this book of no greater value than the volumes of tales and romances which they peruse merely to pass away their

time, or are attracted thereto by the easiness of the style. It may consequently be concluded, that as they will find no pleasure in reading a work which contains a number of foreign names, treats on uncommon subjects, and alludes to other matters which cannot be understood at the first glance, but require a little time for consideration, they will, under pretense of zeal for their religion, entirely abstain and refrain from perusing it.

. . .

ODE TO LONDON

Henceforward we will devote our lives to London, and its heart-alluring Damsels:
Our hearts are satiated with viewing fields, gardens, rivers, and palaces.

We have no longing for the Toba, Sudreh, or other trees of Paradise:
We are content to rest under the shade of these terrestrial Cypresses.

If the Shaikh of Mecca is displeased at our conversion, who cares?
May the Temple which has conferred such blessings on us, and its Priests, flourish!

Fill the goblet with wine! If by this I am prevented from returning
To my old religion, I care not; nay, I am the better pleased.

If the prime of my life has been spent in the service of an Indian Cupid,
It matters not: I am now rewarded by the smiles of the British Fair.

Adorable creatures! Whose flowing tresses, whether of flaxen or of jetty hue,
Or auburn gay, delight my soul, and ravish all my senses!

Whose ruby lips would animate the torpid clay, or marble statue!
Had I a renewal of life, I would, with rapture, devote it to your service!

These wounds of Cupid, on your heart, Tāleba, are not accidental:
They were engendered by Nature, like the streaks on the leaf of a tulip.

. . .

The first and greatest defect I observed in the English is their want of faith in religion, and their great inclination to philosophy [atheism]. The effects of these principles, or rather want of principle, is very conspicuous in the lower orders of people, who are totally devoid of honesty. They are, indeed, cautious how they transgress against the laws, from fear of punishment; but whenever an opportunity offers of purloining any thing without the risk of detection, they never pass it by. They are also ever on the watch to appropriate to themselves the property of the rich, who, on this account, are obliged constantly to keep their doors shut, and never to permit an unknown person to enter them. At present, owing to the vigilance of the magistrates, the severity of the laws, and the honor of the superior classes of people, no very bad consequences are to be apprehended; but if ever such nefarious practices should become prevalent and should creep in among the higher classes, inevitable ruin must ensue.

The second defect most conspicuous in the English character is pride, or insolence. Puffed up with their power and good fortune for the last fifty years, they are not apprehensive of adversity, and take no pains to avert it. Thus, when the people of London, some time ago, assembled in mobs on account of the great increase of taxes and high price of provisions, and were nearly in a state of insurrection—although the magistrates, by their vigilance in watching them, and by causing parties of soldiers to patrole the streets day and night, to disperse all persons whom they saw assembling together, succeeded in quieting the disturbance—yet no pains were afterwards taken to eradicate the evil. Some of the men in power said it had been merely a plan of the artificers to obtain higher wages (an attempt frequently made by the English tradesmen); others were of opinion that no remedy could be applied; therefore no further notice was taken of the affair. All this, I say, betrays a blind confidence, which, instead of meeting the danger and endeavoring to prevent it, waits till the misfortune arrives, and then attempts to remedy it. Such was the case with the late king of France, who took no step to oppose the Revolution till it was too late. This self-confidence is to be found, more or less, in every Englishman; it however differs much from the pride of the Indians and Persians.

Their third defect is a passion for acquiring money and their attachment to worldly affairs. Although these bad qualities are not so reprehensible in them as in countries more subject to the vicissitudes of fortune, (because, in England, property is so well protected by the laws that every person reaps the fruits of his industry, and, in his old age, enjoys the earnings or economy of his youth,) yet sordid and illiberal habits are generally found to accompany avarice and parsimony, and, consequently, render the possessor of them contemptible; on the contrary, generosity, if it does not launch into prodigality, but is guided by the hand of prudence, will render a man respected and esteemed.

Analysis and Review Questions

1. In the first section of the excerpt, does Abū Tāleb think Muslims are going to take to Western learning? Explain.
2. Is the poem about London positive or negative? What makes you think so?
3. List two of the defects of the English pointed out by Abū Tāleb.
4. What is the overall consequence of the English arrogance toward social problems, according to the author?
5. What appears to you to be the biggest problem pointed out? Why?

Image 18.1 Akbar, Emperor of India

AKBAR AND THE JESUITS

About the Document

During the sixteenth through eighteenth centuries, many European countries were vying for trade and commercial arrangements in India and other parts of Asia. Some nations, primarily the dominant Catholic nations such as Spain, Portugal, and France, also brought a religious element to their contacts, sending missionaries and religious scholars to meet with their counterparts or rulers in Asia.

A group well-suited for missionary activity was one created specifically for that purpose: the Jesuit order. Founded in 1524 by St. Ignatius Loyola, the Jesuits were used during Europe's Counter-Reformation to "take back" areas that had become Protestant—for example, reclaiming Poland and parts of Germany for the Catholic Church. The Jesuits also spent considerable time in India, China, and Japan; they were welcomed there more for their secular learning than for their religious doctrines. French Jesuits spent years in India between the mid-1500s and 1600s, including time at the court of Akbar the Great, one of India's most noted rulers. One of the French Jesuits, Father Pierre du Jarric, around 1610 compiled an account of the fathers' exploits at the court of Akbar. Known as a tolerant ruler, Akbar presided over the Mughal Empire at its height. By his death in 1605, the Mughal Empire was well prepared for the future.

The Document

That we may the better understand the motives which led the Great Mogor to summon the Fathers of the Company from Goa,° we must bear in mind that the Viceroy in India of the Portuguese king, had, in the year 1578, sent as ambassador to his court a Portuguese gentleman named Antoine Cabral, who was accompanied by several others of the same nation. Whilst they were at his court, Akbar closely watched their behavior and manner of life, gaining thereby some idea of other adherents of the Christian religion, of which he had heard so much. He was very favourably impressed by what he saw of these persons; and showed himself so anxious to know something of the law they followed, that the ambassador did his best to explain to him its main principles, telling him also of the Fathers of the Company who were preaching it in India.

About the month of March in the year 1578, the good priest, whose name I have not discovered, reached Pateful, where the King then held his court, and was received with much kindness. It was not long before his Majesty told him the reason why he had sent for him, which was, he said, that he might clear his mind of certain doubts which prevented him from deciding whether it was better to follow the law of the Christians or the law of Mahomet.° The priest, accordingly, expounded to him the main principles of our faith, at the same time opening his eyes to the worthlessness of the law of Mahomet.

Akbar heard these things with evident gladness; and so strongly was he moved to abandon his faith that, one evening while conversing with his Caziques, or Mullas, as the priests of the Mahometan religion are called, he told them frankly that he had decided to follow the counsel of the good priest, and pray to God for light to see the truth, and the path to salvation.

A few days later, he asked the same priest to teach him to speak Portuguese; for he had a great desire (or so he said) to know that tongue, that he might the better understand his exposition of the Christian law. This the priest commenced to do with much care and zeal; and the first word that he taught the King was the sweet name of Jesus.

One evening the same priest was disputing with the Mullas in the royal ante-chamber, while the King sat listening in his private apartment. In the course of the dispute, the priest said that the law of Mahomet was a tissue of errors and lies. This so enraged the Mullas that they were on the point of laying violent hands on him when the King entered and restrained them, appeasing their anger by telling them that it was no unusual thing for one engaged in a disputation to hold his own views to be true, and those of his adversaries to be false.

While conversing with the King, the priest told him one day that there were in the town of Goa some very learned and holy Fathers, who had spread a knowledge of Jesus-Christ in many parts of India; and that if he would communicate his doubts to

Goa: The Portuguese-held port city in India.
Mahomet: Old European spelling of Mohammed, the founder of Islam.

them, he would learn from them, much better than from himself, all that he desired to know touching the Christian faith, in as much as they were much more learned in the holy scriptures.

[Another group of priests were sent to see Akbar.]

So great was the King's anxiety to see them that, during this period (as they subsequently learnt), he constantly calculated the number of days necessary for the completion of their journey, and repeatedly asked those about him when they would arrive. The moment he heard that they had come, he summoned them to his palace, where he received them with many marks of friendship, and entertained them in various ways until far into the night. Before they took their leave, a large quantity of gold and silver was brought to be presented to them. The Fathers thanked him very respectfully, but would not take any of the money, courteously excusing themselves on the ground of their calling. As for their livelihood, for which the King urged them to accept what he offered them, they said that it was sufficient happiness for them to enjoy his favour, and that they trusted to God to supply their daily needs. The King was much impressed by their refusal of the money, and for a long time could talk to his courtiers of nothing else.

Three or four days later, the Fathers again visited the King, who received them as cordially as on the first occasion. As he had asked to be shown the books of the law of the Creator (meaning thereby the holy Scriptures), the Fathers took with them and presented to him all the volumes of the Royal Bible, in four languages, sumptuously bound, and clasped with gold. The King received these holy books with great reverence; taking each into his hand one after the other and kissing it, after which he placed it on his head, which, amongst these people, signifies honour and respect. He acted thus in the presence of all his courtiers and captains, the greater part of whom were Mahometans.

Some time afterwards, he again sent for the Fathers, summoning at the same time his Mullas and Caziques, in order that they might dispute together in his presence, so that he might discover which were in truth the holy scriptures on which to place his faith. The Fathers clearly established the authenticity and truth of the scriptures contained in the Old and New Testaments, laying bare at the same time the falsehoods and fallacies with which the Koran is filled. This first dispute ended in the complete discomfiture of the Mullas and Caziques, who, unable to find any answer to the arguments of the Fathers, took refuge in silence.

Three days after the first dispute, another took place concerning the paradise which the Mahometan law promises to its followers. The Fathers assailed the infamous and carnal paradise of Mahomet with arguments so clear and convincing that the Mullas blushed for shame, not knowing what to say in reply. The King, seeing their perplexity, essayed to take up their cause; but he was as little able as they to disprove the incongruities that had been pointed out.

The Fathers now became anxious to ascertain what effect these disputes had had on the King, and whether the adoption of the Christian faith was a step that he was seriously deliberating. They accordingly made their way to the palace, the fact that they had not seen the King for some days affording a sufficient excuse for their visit. He received them with his accustomed courtesy and good-will. After some conversation on general subjects, the Fathers begged him to give them private audience; and when this was granted, Father Rodolfe Aquauiua, who was the superior of the others, thus addressed him—"Your Majesty wrote a letter to our R.P. Provincial demanding that some Fathers of the Company should be sent to you to expound the law of God.

We three have, accordingly, been sent; and we count it a peculiar happiness that God has led us to a Prince who is so powerful, and who desires so earnestly to know the divine law. This happiness was intensified when you made known to us that you had no other desire in the world but to discover and to embrace the true law. Our thoughts have been given day and night to this matter, and the means of attaining the end for which we have been sent here; and after earnest consideration, and continual prayers to God for guidance, it seems to us fitting that your Majesty should now, for the sake of your temporal and spiritual welfare, the preservation of your life, the increase of your dominions, the comfort of your conscience, and the salvation of your soul, set apart a time for hearing the interpretation of the divine law, and that, recognizing it to be true, and that there is no other which leads to salvation, your Majesty should adopt it as your own, and renounce that which is preached in all your kingdoms and provinces." In reply to these words, the King said that the matter was in the hands of God, who possessed the power to accomplish what they desired; and that, for his part, there was nothing in the world he desired more. By what he said, he gave them to understand that there were weighty reasons why he should not, at that juncture, declare himself a Christian.

Image 18.2
Portuguese Church
in Southern India

Analysis and Review Questions

1. Does Akbar appear to favor the priests or his own religious advisors? Explain.
2. Is the author favorably inclined towards Islam? Give evidence for your answer.
3. What is a Mulla?
4. Why didn't the priests accept gold or silver from Akbar?
5. Why do you think Akbar was not willing to convert to Christianity?

Map 18.2
The Maratha
Kingdom

AURANGZEB, MUGHAL RULER

About the Document

India's Mughal Empire was constantly trying to address the practical problems facing a minority Muslim population ruling over a much larger Hindu population. Some rulers, such as Akbar the Great (1556–1605), proved tolerant and accommodating to Hindus and other local religious groups. Akbar even attempted, unsuccessfully, to create a new religion that brought together elements from Islam, Hinduism, and Zoroastrianism, among others. Akbar's successors generally continued his tolerant policies.

There was, of course, another approach to the Mughal issue. Rather than accommodating Hindus, a ruler might oppress them to solve some of the problems of governance. A ruler who is remembered for doing so is Aurangzeb, who ruled from 1658–1707 and even executed his brother for being too tolerant of other faiths. In the early 1680s, an advisor of Aurangzeb, Baktha'war Khan, wrote a history of the world up through the time of Aurangzeb's reign. The following excerpt not only discusses the ruler's religious attitudes, it also addresses his personality and overall attitudes.

The Document

Be it known to the readers of this work that this humble slave of the Almighty is going to describe in a correct manner the excellent character, the worthy habits and the refined morals of this most virtuous monarch, Aurangzeb, according as he has witnessed them with his own eyes. The Emperor, a great worshiper of God by natural propensity, is remarkable for his rigid attachment to religion. . . . Having made his ablutions [ritual washings], he always occupies a great part of his time in adoration of the Deity, and says the usual prayers, first in the mosque and then at home, both in congregation and in private, with the most heartfelt devotion. He keeps the appointed fasts on Fridays and other sacred days, and he reads the Friday prayers in the mosque with the common people of the Muslim faith. He keeps vigils during the whole of the sacred nights, and with the light of the favor of God illumines the lamps of religion and prosperity. From his great piety, he passes whole nights in the mosque which is in his palace, and keeps company with men of devotion. In privacy he never sits on a throne. He gave away in alms before his accession a portion of his allowance of lawful food and clothing, and now devotes to the same purpose the income of a few villages in the district of Delhi, and the proceeds of two or three salt-producing tracts, which are appropriated to his private purse. . . . During the whole month of Ramadan he keeps fast, says the prayers appointed for that month, and reads the holy Qur'an in the assembly of religious and learned men, with whom he sits for that purpose during six, and sometimes nine hours of the night. During the last ten days of the month, he performs worship in the mosque, and although, on account of several obstacles, he is unable to proceed on a pilgrimage to Mecca, yet the care which he takes to promote facilities for pilgrims to that holy place may be considered equivalent to the pilgrimage.

Though he has collected at the foot of his throne those who inspire ravishment in joyous assemblies of pleasure, in the shape of singers who possess lovely voices and clever instrumental performers, and in the commencement of his reign sometimes used to hear them sing and play, and though he himself understands music well, yet now for several years past, on account of his great restraint and self-denial . . . he entirely abstains from this amusement. If any of the singers and musicians becomes ashamed of his calling, he makes an allowance for him or grants him land for his maintenance. . . .

In consideration of their rank and merit, he shows much honor and respect to the saints and learned men, and through his cordial and liberal exertions, the sublime doctrines of our pure religion have obtained such prevalence throughout the wide territories of Hindustan° as they never had in the reign of any former king.

Hindu writers have been entirely excluded from holding public offices, and all the worshiping places of the infidels [Hindus] and the great temples of these infamous people have been thrown down and destroyed in a manner which excites astonishment at the successful completion of so difficult a task. . . .

As it is a great object with this Emperor that all Muslims should follow the principles of the religion . . . and as there was no book which embodied them all, and as until many books had been collected and a man had obtained sufficient leisure, means and knowledge of theological subjects, he could not satisfy his inquiries on any disputed point, therefore His Majesty, the protector of the faith, determined that a body of eminently learned and able men of Hindustan should take up the volumi-

Hindustan: Old European name for India

nous and most trustworthy works which were collected in the royal library, and having made a digest of them, compose a book which might form a standard canon of the law, and afford to all an easy and available means of ascertaining the proper and authoritative interpretation. The chief conductor of this difficult undertaking was the most learned man of the time, Shaikh Nizam, and all the members of the society were very handsomely and liberally paid, so that up to the present time a sum of about two hundred thousand rupees has been expended in this valuable compilation, which contains more than one hundred thousand lines. When the work, with God's pleasure, is completed, it will be for all the world the standard exposition of the law. . . .

The Emperor is perfectly acquainted with the commentaries, traditions, and law. . . . One of the greatest excellences of this virtuous monarch is, that he has learned the Qur'an by heart. Though in his early youth he had committed to memory some chapters of that sacred book, yet he learned the whole by heart after ascending the throne. He took great pains and showed much perseverance in impressing it upon his mind. He writes in a very elegant hand, and has acquired perfection in this art. He has written two copies of the holy book with his own hand, and having finished and adorned them with ornaments and marginal lines, at the expense of seven thousand rupees, he sent them to the holy cities of Mecca and Medina . . . . He is a very elegant writer in prose, and has acquired proficiency in versification, but agreeably to the words of God, "Poets deal in falsehoods," he abstains from practicing it. He does not like to hear verses except those which contain a moral. "To please Almighty God he never turned his eye towards a flatterer, nor gave his ear to a poet."

The Emperor has given a very liberal education to his fortunate and noble children, who, by virtue of his attention and care, have reached to the summit of perfection, and made great advances in rectitude, devotion, and piety, and in learning the manners and customs of princes and great men. Through his instruction they have learned the Book of God by heart, obtained proficiency in the sciences and polite literature, writing the various hands, and in learning the Turkish and the Persian languages.

In like manner, the ladies of the household also, according to his orders, have learned the fundamental and necessary tenets of religion, and all devote their time to the adoration and worship of the Deity, to reading the sacred Qur'an, and performing virtuous and pious acts. The excellence of character and the purity of morals of this holy monarch are beyond all expression. As long as nature nourishes the tree of existence, and keeps the garden of the world fresh, may the plant of the prosperity of this preserver of the garden of dignity and honor continue fruitful!

Analysis and Review Questions

1. Why didn't Aurangzeb generally listen to poetry?
2. What was Aurangzeb's attitude toward Hinduism?
3. Does the author claim the king was dedicated to his religion? Explain.
4. What qualities does the author seem to respect in his ruler?
5. What do you think Aurangzeb's attitudes were toward what we might call "social welfare"?

WEB LINKS

http://longmanworldhistory.com
Document 18.5, St Francis Xavier, Jesuit in India
Case Study 18.1, Islamic Commentators in India
Case Study 18.2, Jesuits in India
Case Study 18.3, Two Very Different Mughal Emperors

http://www.freeindia.org
A massive site with large sections devoted to biographies of notable Indian gods, goddesses, and leaders. Search engine focusing on Indian Web sites is included as well.

http://www.123india.com
The site portrays itself as "India's Premier Portal" with good reason. Everything from current Indian news, online India chat, to Indian search engines can be found here.

http://www.museum.rbi.org.in/general.html
An online "monetary museum," this site shows currency from all periods of Indian history.

http://www.indianmuseum-calcutta.org
Exhibits, images, and other useful information from one of the world's oldest museums.

CHAPTER 19

African Kingdoms and Early European Contacts, 1450–1750

This chapter will examine primary documents that reflect the first extensive cultural interactions between African kingdoms and Europeans. As the Portuguese expanded their influence along the West African coastline, they engaged heavily in trade and sugar growing. They learned to interact with powerful African rulers who often dictated the terms of trade and, of course, controlled access to land.

For the most part, a special landlord-stranger relationship existed, marked by the need for reciprocity and accommodation to political, religious, ideological, economic, and social differences. The king of the Kongo hoped to consolidate his political control by promoting contacts with the Portuguese, who had weapons and mercenaries who could strengthen his army. Endemic warfare became a way of life in central Africa, as wars were encouraged to gain slaves. From the 1530s, São Thomé developed as a major transit point for captives being transported across the Atlantic to the new plantations in Brazil. With the increased demand for slaves, the São Thomé slavers evaded Portuguese royal control by establishing a slaving station at Luanda.

The Portuguese always took along missionaries who had a "civilizing" mission that was important in the minds of European monarchs. That mission was to convert Africans to Christianity in the hopes of building stronger ties with Europe. The king of the Kongo, Afonso I (1506–1543), became a Christian convert in 1506. Christianity was seen by some African kings as a tool to undermine the authority of local religious leaders. In the case of Ethiopian kings, Christianity was well established, and they resisted Portuguese efforts at reforming their traditional beliefs along Roman Catholic lines.

Image 19.1
Loango, the capital of the kingdom of the Kongo

"VOYAGE FROM LISBON TO THE ISLAND OF SÃO THOMÉ," BY AN ANONYMOUS PORTUGUESE PILOT, C. 1540

About the Document

Early descriptions of Portuguese travelers to West Africa are vital to our understanding of African life before the advent of colonial rule. These descriptions portray the nature of kingship, religion, social life, economic activity, and slavery in

Africa in the sixteenth century. This early account is particularly interesting because it describes the trade in gold and slaves in West Africa from someone other than an Arab traveler. It is well known that gold from West Africa was heavily traded in the trans-Saharan trade by Berber° merchants making their way to the major trading centers in North Africa and Egypt. This is perhaps one of the earliest accounts of gold being traded directly with Europeans along the Atlantic coast. Eventually this shift in trade routes would undermine the caravan traders in the north, as Europeans made direct contact with African merchants nearer the gold fields.

The Portuguese pilot is fascinated by the extent of the slave trade and the items that are given up in the trade, including cowrie shells, glass beads, coral, copper, brass items, and cotton cloth. Portuguese merchants and traders are also involved in the buying and selling of sugar grown on the islands off the west coast of Africa. Sugar was a lucrative trade item that was in high demand in Europe. It wasn't long after this time that Europeans began to set up sugar plantations in the New World.

The Document

The Ships which leave Lisbona to go to the island of São Thomé to load sugar, the wind they sail by to the Canarie islands, called by the ancients the Fortunate islands, the island of Palme, and the promontory called Capo di Boiador.

As your excellency knows, before I left Venetia, signor Hieronimo Gracastor ordered me, in his letters from Verona, to transcribe for him, as soon as I reached the Villa di Conde, from some notes which I had told your excellency I had with me, the whole of the voyage which we pilots made to the island of S. Thomé, when we went there to transport a cargo of sugar; together with all that happened during our voyage to this island, that seemed to him so wonderful and worthy of the study of a scholar. Your excellency also, on my departure, made the same request to me; and so, having arrived here, I began at once to write an account of the voyage in question, communicating also with some of my friends who took part in it. . . .

The various provinces of the West Coast of Africa, Guinea, the coast of Melegete [Malagueta], Benin, Manicongo; and the lords and kings of these lands; how the people worship their kings believing that they have descended from heaven; and of some of the ceremonies and customs of the kingdom of Benin on the death of the king.

To understand the negro traffic, one must know that over all the African coast facing west there are various countries and provinces, such as Guinea, the coast of Melegete, the kingdom of Benin, the kingdom of Manicõgo, six degrees from the equator and towards the south pole. There are many tribes and negro kings here, and also communities which are partly mohammedan and partly heathen. These are constantly making war among themselves. The kings are worshipped by their subjects, who believe that they come from heaven, and speak of them always with great reverence, at a distance and on bended knees. Great ceremony surrounds them, and many of these kings never allow themselves to be seen eating, so as not to destroy the belief

Berber: The people of northwest Africa.

of their subjects that they can live without food. They worship the sun, and believe that spirits are immortal, and that after death they go to the sun. Among others, there is in the kingdom of Benin an ancient custom, observed to the present day, that when the king dies, the people all assemble in a large field, in the centre of which is a very deep well, wider at the bottom than at the mouth. They cast the body of the dead king into this well, and all his friends and servants gather round, and those who are judged to have been most dear to and favoured by the king (this includes not a few, as all are anxious for the honour) voluntarily go down to keep him company. When they have done so, the people place a great stone over the mouth of the well, and remain by it day and night. . . .

The Negroes of Guinea are unmethodical even in their way of eating; they live long; certain superstitions among some of the negroes in this country; melegete spices; the tailed pepper; certain bushes with stems that have the flavour of ginger; soap made with oil of palms and with ashes.

The negroes of Guinea and Benin are very haphazard in their habits of eating. They have no set times for meals, and eat and drink four or five times a day, drinking water, or a wine which they distil from palms. They have no hair except for a few bristly strands on top of the head, and none grows; and the rest of the bodies are completely hairless. They live for the best part of 100 years, and are always vigorous, except at certain times of the year when they become very weak, as if they had fever. They are then bled, and recover, having a great deal of blood in their system. Some of the negroes in this country are so superstitious that they worship the first object they see on the day of recovery. . . .

Why the fathers and mothers of these negroes send their own children to be sold, and what they take in exchange; and how these slaves are taken to the island of San Jacobo, where they are sold in couples, that is, the same number of males and females; the coast of Mina, and why the catholic king has built a castle there.

All the coast, as far as the kingdom of Manicongo, is divided into two parts, which are leased every four or five years to whoever makes the best offer, that is, to be able to go to contract in those lands and ports, and those in this business are called contractors, though among us they would be known as *appaltadori*, and their deputies, and no others may approach and land on this shore, or even buy or sell. Great caravans of negroes come here, bringing gold and slaves for sale. Some of the slaves have been captured in battle, others are sent by their parents, who think they are doing their children the best service in the world by sending them to be sold in this way to other lands where there is an abundance of provisions. They are brought as naked as they are born, both males and females, except for a sheepskin cloth; and they have glass rosaries of various colours, and articles made of glass, copper, brass, and cotton cloths of different colours, and other similar things used throughout Ethiopia. These contractors take the slaves to the island of San Jacobo, where they are bought by merchant captains from various countries and provinces, chiefly from the Spanish Indies. These give their merchandise in exchange and always wish to have the same number of male and female slaves, because otherwise they do not get good service from them. During the voyage, they separate the men from the women, putting the men below the deck and the women above, where they cannot see when the men are given food; because otherwise the women would do nothing but look at them. Regarding these negroes, our king has had a castle built on the said coast, at

Mina, 6 degrees north of the equator, where none but his servants are allowed to live; and large numbers of negroes come to this place with grains of gold, which they have found in the river beds and sand, and bargain with these servants, taking various objects from them in exchange; principally glass necklaces or rosaries, and another kind made of a blue stone, not lapis lazuli, but another stone which our king causes to be brought from Manicõgo, where it is found. These rosaries are in the form of necklaces, and are called coral; and a quantity of gold is given in exchange for them, as they are greatly valued by all the negroes. They wear them round their necks as a charm against spirits, but some wear necklaces of glass, which are very similar, but which will not bear the heat of fire.

Description of the island of São Thomé, nowadays inhabited by many traders; the island called il Principe, the island of Anobon, and the city called Pouoasan.

The island of São Thomé, which was discovered 80 or 90 years ago by the sea-captains of our king, and which was unknown to the ancients, is round. It is 60 Italian miles in diameter, that is, one degree; and is situated under the line of the equator and half way between the north and south poles. The days and nights are of equal length, and one never sees the least difference, whether the sun is in cancer or capricorn. The Pole Star cannot be seen, but by turning a little one can see it; and the constellation called *il crusero* appears very far away. To the east of this island, 120 miles distant, there is a small island called Il Principe [O Principe]. This island is inhabited and cultivated at the present time, and the profits made from its sugar trade go to the king's eldest son; this is why it is called Il Principe. . . .

There is a bishop here, and the present one comes from Villa di Conde by order of the archbishop at the desire of the king. A corregedor° dispenses justice. There must be 600 to 700 families living here as well as many Portuguese, Castilian, French and Genoese merchants; and people of any nationality, who wish to settle here are welcome. They all have wives and children, and some of the children who are born there are as white as ours. It sometimes happens that, when the wife of a merchant dies, he takes a negress, and this is an accepted practice, as the negro population is both intelligent and rich; the children of such unions are brought up to our customs and way of dressing. Children born of these negresses are mischievous and difficult to manage, and are called *Mulati* [mulattoes].

Description of how the inhabitants of this island treat sugar; of the goods which the ships bring in exchange for sugar; of the fertility of the land and the way they cultivate sugar cane and trade it; of why the flesh of pigs in this land is so healthy and easy to digest.

The chief industry of the people is to make sugar, which they sell to the ships which come each year, bringing flour, Spanish wines, oil, cheese, and all kinds of leather for shoes, swords, glass vessels, rosaries, and shells, which in Italia are called *porcellette* [porcelains]—little white ones—which we call *buzios*, and which are used for money in Ethiopia. If the ships which bring these goods did not come, the white merchants would die, because they are not accustomed to negro food. All the population, therefore, buys negro slaves and their women from Guinea, Benin and Manicongo, and sets them to work on the land to grow and make sugar. There are rich men here, who have 150, 200 and even 300 negroes and negresses, who are obliged to work for their masters all the week, except on Saturdays, when they work on their own account. . . .

---

corregedor: Representative of the king.

Analysis and Review Questions

1. What can we deduce from this document about the relationship of African kings to their native subjects? What importance does this relationship have to early Portuguese travelers to West Africa?
2. How is the business of trade conducted within the Manicongo (Kongo) kingdom? What elements of capitalism are present in the indigenous system of land allocation?
3. Why do some African fathers and mothers send their own children into slavery? What items are taken in exchange for African slaves? Why do you suppose these items are acceptable as equal to a human life?
4. What is the value of gold in West African societies? What is the value of coral in the Manicongo (Kongo) kingdom? How do the Portuguese begin to tap into the thriving local economy of African kingdoms?
5. It is evident from this primary account that Europeans had a precarious existence in the early days of trade and exploration along the west coast of Africa. Since only men went to Africa to trade and grow sugar, what accommodations to African life did these Portuguese men have to deal with? What aspects of daily life were most life-threatening to Europeans? What might have been the importance of mulattoes to the Portuguese as they established long-term connections to African kingdoms and the trade that made their existence so viable?

Map19.1
(Interactive)
*African Empires in
the Western Sudan*

"A DEFENSE OF THE SLAVE TRADE," JULY 1740

About the Document

Justifying European involvement in the trans-Atlantic slave trade often involved the use of ideas that made the endeavor seem moral; it was considered part of the "white man's burden" to release Africans from a worse bondage at home. Merchants, in particular, felt the need for some justification for transporting and selling human cargo. In this document, an anonymous person writes about conditions along the Guinea Coast of West Africa and the cruel power of the local kings to control African slaves. The anonymous writer is responding to a letter published in the *Gentleman's Magazine* under the pseudonym Mercator Honestus, which argued against slavery and the slave trader.

It is well known that many of the great kingdoms of West Africa had dealt in a local slave trade for centuries. Slaves were used in agricultural production, in households, and as part of court life. These slaves were under varying degrees of bondage outside the realm of what we call "chattel slavery";° that is, under African customs, the condition of slavery was not hereditary and even

chattel slavery: Slavery based on the principle that men and women who are slaves enjoy no rights and can hold no property. In most cases, this type of slavery is hereditary, and humans are bought and sold as property by the owners. It was the prevalent form of slavery used by Europeans during the age of the Atlantic slave trade from the sixteenth to the eighteenth century.

slaves had some rights. What is interesting about this account is the heavy emphasis on Enlightenment° ideas such as the right of every human being to liberty and happiness. European merchants believed they were freeing Africans from an even worse fate, slavery without Western laws and Christianity.

The Document

Sir, The Guinea Trade, by the Mistake of some, or Misrepresentation of others, hath been charged with Inhumanity, and a Contradiction to good Morals. Such a Charge at a Time when private and publick Morals are laugh'd at, as the highest Folly, by a powerful Faction; and Self-interest set up as the only Criterion of true Wisdom, is certainly very uncourtly: But yet as I have a profound Regard for those superannuated Virtures; you will give me Leave to justify the African Trade, upon those Stale Principles, from the Imputations of "Mercator Honestus"; and shew him that there are People in some boasted Regions of Liberty, under a more wretched Slavery, than the Africans transplanted to our American Colonies.

The Inhabitants of Guinea are indeed in a most deplorable State of Slavery, under the arbitrary Powers of their Princes both as to Life and Property. In the several Subordinations to them, every great Man is absolute lord of his immediate Dependents. And lower still; every Master of a Family is Proprietor of his Wives, Children, and Servants; and may at his Pleasure consign them to Death, or a better Market. No doubt such a State is contrary to Nature and Reason, since every human Creature hath an absolute Right to Liberty. But are not all arbitrary Governments, as well in Europe, as Africa, equally repugnant to that great Law of Nature? And yet it is not in our Power to cure the universal Evil, and set all the Kingdoms of the Earth free from the Domination of Tyrants, whose long Possession, supported by standing Armies, and flagitious Ministers, renders the Thraldom without Remedy, while the People under it are by Custom satisfied with, or at least quiet under Bondage.

All that can be done in such a Case is, to communicate as much Liberty, and Happiness, as such circumstances will admit, and the People will consent to: And this is certainly by the Guinea Trade. For, by purchasing, or rather ransoming the Negroes from their national Tyrants, and transplanting them under the benign Influences of the Law, and Gospel, they are advanced to much greater Degrees of Felicity, tho' not to absolute Liberty.

That this is truly the Case cannot be doubted by any one acquainted with the Constitution of our Colonies, where the Negroes are governed by Laws, and suffer much less Punishment in Proportion to their Crimes, than the People in other Countries more refined in the Arts of Wickedness; and where Capital Punishment is inflicted only by the Civil Magistrates. . . .

Perhaps my Antagonist calls the Negroes Allowance of a Pint of Corn and an Herring, penurious, in Comparison of the full Meals of Gluttony: But if not let him compare that Allowance, to what the poor Labourer can purchase for Tenpence per Day to subsist himself and Family, and he will easily determine the American's Advantage. . . .

Nevertheless, Mercator will say, the Negroes are Slaves to their Proprietors: How Slaves? Nominally: Not really so much Slaves, as the Peasantry of all Nations is to Neces-

---

Enlightenment: The period in Europe when thinkers supported scientific advances and social scientific knowledge based on rational laws. Most important, the Enlightenment produced a set of basic principles about human affairs: human beings were good, could be educated, and were entitled to basic rights of life, liberty, and the pursuit of wealth. In sixteenth-century Europe, the enslavement of "barbarians" or nonbelievers was seen as positive—as a way to civilize others; however, during the Enlightenment, slavery came to be seen as backward and immoral. The slave trade in particular was criticized. It was the symbol of slavery's inhumanity and cruelty.

sity; not so much as those of Corruption, or Party Zeal; not in any Sense, such abject Slaves, as every vicious Man is to his own Appetites. Indeed there is this Difference between Britons, and the Slaves of all other Nations; that the latter are so by Birth, or tyrannical Necessity; the former can never be so, but by a wicked Choice, or execrable Venality. . . .

Analysis and Review Questions

1. What role do Enlightenment ideas play in justifying the trans–Atlantic slave trade? To what degree do you think English ideas on law, government, and justice contributed to merchant activity in the slave trade?
2. What was the author's attitude toward African indigenous slavery? Are there religious overtones to the passage? If so, describe and explain them.
3. What can we deduce from this document about the relationship between merchants and other elements of European society about the slave trade? Who might be particularly interested in the content and flavor of this publication?
4. What do the descriptions of African life along the west coast of Africa tell us about European perceptions of African slavery?
5. In addition to arguments based on moral principles, what other justifications *against* the slave trade might Mercator Honestus have used to criticize merchants involved in the traffic of human lives? Do you think these are valid claims? Why or why not?

Map 19.2
Africa 1500–1800

FRANCISCO ALVAREZ, "THE LAND OF PRESTER JOHN," C. 1540

About the Document

Ethiopia had long been the heart of Coptic° Christianity and was regarded as part of the ancient archdiocese of Alexandria. The Ethiopian Church developed its own individual characteristics. Ethiopians saw themselves as an outpost of Christianity—a sort of chosen people of God surrounded by pagans and Muslims. The Ethiopian kings built churches out of solid rock cut into mountains and caves. There is a total of 11 churches carved out near the capital, which was named Lalibela after the reign of Lalibela, who ruled between 1200 and 1250 C.E.

Conflict with the Muslim sultanates dominated life in the region. In 1526 a Muslim general named Ahmad ibn Ibrahim decided to wage a *jihad*, or holy war, against the Christian aristocracy. The Ethiopians kings sought Portuguese help in defeating Ahmad's army. The Portuguese responded by landing a small but well-equipped force in the north of the country. The combination of Portuguese and Ethiopians managed to save the Christian kingdom by inflicting a sharp defeat on the Muslim army in 1543. In the attached document, Father

Coptic: In Egypt, the bulk of Christians adopted a doctrine of Monophysitism which was unacceptable to the Roman Church. The Monophysites emphasized the divinity of Christ and denied that He could have been also human. In 451 C.E. the Roman Church declared this doctrine a "heresy," and many believers were expelled from the official Christian Church. Monophysite Christian missionaries pushed southward, carrying their distinctive doctrine and a strong monastic tradition into Nubia, Aksum, and Ethiopia.

Francisco Alvarez, chaplain to the first Portuguese embassy to Ethiopia, commented on life in sixteenth-century Ethiopia. Alvarez refers to the Ethiopian ruler as "Prester John," after a legendary priest-king of Ethiopia.

The Document

At a day's journey from this church of Imbra Christo are edifices, the like of which and so many, cannot, as it appears to me, be found in the world, and they are churches entirely excavated in the rock, very well hewn. The names of these churches are these: Emanuel, St. Saviour, St. Mary, Holy Cross, St. George, Golgotha, Bethlehem, Marcoreos, the Martyrs. The principal one is Lalibela. This Lalibela, they say, was a King in this same country for eighty years, and he was King before the one before mentioned who was named Abraham. This King ordered these edifices to be made. He does not lie in the church which bears his name, he lies in the church of Golgotha, which is the church of the fewest buildings here. It is in this manner: all excavated in the stone itself, a hundred and twenty spans in length, and seventy-two spans in width. The ceiling of this church rests on five supports, two on each side, and one in the centre, like fives of dice, and the ceiling or roof is all flat like the floor of the church, the sides also are worked in a fine fashion, also the windows, and the doors with all the tracery, which could be told, so that neither a jeweller in silver, nor a worker of wax in wax, could do more work. The tomb of this King is in the same manner as that of Santiago of Galicia, at Compostella, and it is in this manner: the gallery which goes round the church is like a cloister, and lower than the body of the church, and one goes down from the church to this gallery; there are three windows on each side, that is to say, at that height which the church is higher than the gallery, and as much as the body of the church extends, so much is excavated below, and to as much depth as there is height above the floor of the church. And if one looks through each of these windows which is opposite the sun, one sees the tomb at the right of the high altar. In the centre of the body of the church is the sign of a door like a trap door, it is covered up with a large stone, like an altar stone, fitting very exactly in that door. They say that this is the entrance to the lower chamber, and that no one enters there, nor does it appear that that stone or door can be raised. This stone has a hole in the centre which pierces it through, its size is three palms. All the pilgrims put their hands into this stone (which hardly find room), and say that many miracles are done here. On the left hand side, when one goes from the principal door before the principal chapel, there is a tomb cut in the same rock as the church, which they say is made after the manner of the sepulchre of Christ in Jerusalem. . . . This church and its chapels have their altars and canopies, with their supports, made of the rock itself, it also has a very great circuit cut out of the rock. The circuit is on the same level as the church itself, and is all square: all its walls are pierced with holes the size of the mouth of a barrel. All these holes are stopped up with small stones, and they say that they are tombs, and such they appear to be, because some have been stopped up since a long time, others recently. The entrance of this circuit is below the rock, at a great depth and measure of thirteen spans, all artificially excavated, or worked with the pick-axe, for here there is no digging, because the stone is hard, and for great walls like the Porto in Portugal.

The church of St. Saviour stands alone, cut out of a rock; it is very large. Its interior is two hundred spans in length, and a hundred and twenty in width. It has five naves, in each one seven square columns; the large one has four, and the walls of the church have as much. The columns are very well worked, with arches which hang down a span below the vaulted roof. The vaulted roofs are very well worked, and of great height, principally the centre one, which is very high. It is of a handsome height; most of the ends

Image 19.2
Solid Rock
Churches of
Lalibela, Ethiopia

are lower, all in proportion. . . . Above this church, where it should be roofed, there are on each side nine large arches, like cloisters, which descend from the top to the bottom, to the tombs along the sides, as in the other church. The entrance to this church is by a descent through the rock itself, eighty steps cut artificially in the stone, of a width that ten men can go side by side, and of the height of a lance or more. This entrance has four holes above, which give light to the passage above the edges. From this rock to the enclosure of the church is like a field; there are many houses, and they sow barley in it.

. . .

On the 4th day of the month of January Prester John° sent to tell us to order our tents, both that of the church and our own, to be taken from this place to a distance of about half a league, where they had made a large tank of water, in which they were to be baptized on the day of the Kings, because on that day it is their custom to be baptized every year, as that was the day on which Christ was baptized. We took thither a small tent for resting in and the church tent. The next day, which was the vigil of the day of the Kings, the Prester sent to call us, and we saw the enclosure where the tank was. The enclosure was a fence, and very large, in a plain. He sent to ask us if we intended to be baptized. I replied that it was not our custom to be baptized more than once, when we were little. Some said, principally the ambassador, that we would do what His Highness commanded. When they perceived that, they came back again with another message to me, asking what I said as to being baptized. I answered that I had been already baptized, and should not be so again. They still sent word that if we did not wish to be baptized in their tank, they would send us water to our tent. To this the ambassador replied that it should be as His Highness ordered. The Franks and our people had arranged to give a representation of the Kings, and they sent to tell him of it. A message came that it pleased him, and so they got ready for it, and they made it in the inclosure and plain close to the King's tent, which was pitched close to the tank. They gave the representation, and it was not esteemed, nor hardly looked at, and so it was a cold affair. Now that it was night they told us to go to our tent, which was not far off. In all this night till dawn a great number of priests never ceased chaunting over the said tank, saying that they were blessing the water, and about midnight, a little earlier or later, they began the baptism. They say, and I believe that such is the truth, that the first person baptized is the Prester, and after him the Abima, and after him the Queen, the wife of the Prester. They say that these three persons wear cloths over their nakedness, and that all the others were as their mothers bore them. When it was almost the hour of sunrise, and the baptism in fullest force, the Prester sent to call me to see the said baptism. I went and remained there till the hour of tierce, seeing how they were baptized; they placed me at one end of the tank, with my face towards Prester John, and they baptize in this manner.

. . .

In the tank stood the old priest, the master of the Prester, who was with me Christmas night, and he was naked as when his mother bore him (and quite dead of cold, because it was a very sharp frost), standing in the water up to his shoulders or

---

Prester John: A legendary East African priest-king who held many cities along the coast. The inhabitants of these cities were great merchants and owned big ships. The king was supposedly Christian, and many Portuguese accounts report looking for Prester John in order to forge an alliance against the Muslims along the Swahili coast. Father Francisco Alvarez called the ruler of Ethiopia in c. 1540 "Prester John," although that was not an accurate name. The title was obviously used to signify the special religious and political power of the kings in Ethiopia.

thereabouts, for so deep was the tank that those who were to be baptized entered by the steps, naked, with their backs to the Prester, and when they came out again they showed him their fronts, the women as well as the men. When they came to the said priest, he put his hands on their head, and put it three times under the water, saying in his language: "In name of the Father, of the Son, and of the Holy Spirit," he made the sign of the cross as a blessing, and they went away in peace. (The "I baptize thee," I heard him say it.) . . . After a great number of baptized persons had passed, he sent to call me to be near him; and so near that the Cabeata did not stir to hear what the Prester said, and to speak to the interpreter who was close to me: and he asked me what I thought of that office. I answered him that the things of God's service which were done in good faith and without evil deceit, and in His praise, were good, but such an office as this, there was none in our Church, rather it forbade us baptizing without necessity on that day, because on that day Christ was baptized, so that we should not think of saying of ourselves that we were baptized on the same day as Christ; also the Church does not order this sacrament to be given more than once. Afterwards he asked whether we had it written in books not to be baptized more than once. I replied, Yes, that we had. . . . Then they said to me that such was the truth, and so it was written in their books; but what were they to do with many who turned Moors and Jews after being Christians and then repented, and with others who did not believe well in baptism, what remedy would they have? I answered: For those who do not rightly believe, teaching and preaching would suffice for them, and if that did not profit, burn them as heretics. . . . And as to those who turned Moors or Jews, and afterwards of their own free will recognised their error, and asked for mercy, the *Abima* would absolve them, with penances salutary for their souls, if he had powers for this, if not, let them go to the Pope of Rome, in whom are all the powers. And those who did not repent, they might take them and burn them, for such is the use in Frankland and the Church of Rome. To this there came the reply, that all this seemed to him good, but that his grandfather had ordained this baptism by the counsel of great priests, in order that so many souls should not be lost, and that it had been the custom until now. . . . To this there came no answer except that I might go in peace to say mass. I said it was no longer time for saying mass, that midday was long passed. So I went to dine with our Portuguese and the Franks.

. . . This day, later in the afternoon, Prester John sent to call the ambassador and all his company. The baptism was already ended, and His Highness was still within his curtain where I left him. We entered there, and he at once asked the ambassador what he thought of it. He replied that it was very good, although we had not got such a custom. The water was then running into the tank, and he asked if there were here Portuguese who could swim. At once two jumped into the tank, and swam and dived as much as the tank allowed of. He enjoyed greatly, as he showed by his looks, seeing them swim and dive. After this he desired us to go outside and go to one end of the enclosure or circuit; and here he ordered a banquet to be made for us of bread and wine (according to their custom and the use of the country), and he desired us to raise our church tent and the tent we were lodging in, because he wished to return to his quarters, and that we should go in front of him because he was ordering his horsemen to skirmish in the manner in which they fight with the Moors in the field. So we went in front of him, looking at the said skirmish. They began, but soon there came such heavy rain that it did not allow them to carry out the skirmish which they had begun well.

Analysis and Review Questions

1. Father Francisco Alvarez wrote this vivid account of Abyssinia, or the "land of Prester John," so-called because of the legendary priest-king whose dominions were thought to be in Ethiopia. What indications are there that this kingdom in the Ethiopian highlands was extensive, wealthy, and powerful? Why the very detailed descriptions of the Lalibela churches?

2. Despite the fact that Arab conquests across northern Africa were very successful, there were islands of Christianity. The Egyptian Christian community, the Copts, maintained contact with Byzantium but later split away because of doctrinal and political reasons. The Ethiopian Church, too, developed along unique lines. What evidence does Father Alvarez provide that the Christian kings took their religious traditions very seriously?

3. What can we deduce from this document about the relationship between the Ethiopian Church and Rome? What are the Portuguese motives for accommodating the many differences in religious beliefs and customs?

4. Ideological, religious, political, and economic rivalries play themselves out along the coasts of the Red Sea and East Africa in the sixteenth century. Why do you suppose that the Portuguese were able to defeat the Muslims in nearly every instance?

5. According to the Ethiopian ruler, what is the purpose of annual baptisms? What is the role of the king in the religious ceremonies of his people? What seems to shock Father Alvarez most about the baptisms?

WEB LINKS

http://longmanworldhistory.com
Comparative Document 21.5, Imperialism and the White Man's Burden
The following additional readings and case studies can be found on the Web site.
Case Study 19.1, Portuguese Travelers in Africa
Case Study 19.2, "The White Man's Burden" across Two Centuries

http://vi.uh.edu/pages/mintz/primary.htm
A collection of excerpts from slave narratives.

http://www.law.umkc.edu/faculty/projects/ftrials/amistad/AMI_ACT.HTM
The career of the *Amistad*, a slave schooner that became the subject of a major motion picture on the trade.

http://docsouth.unc.edu/fpn/fpn.html
Narratives of slaves who lived in the American south.

http://www.bethel.edu/~letnie/AfricanChristianity/WesternNorthAfricaHomepage.html
A discussion on the history of Christianity in West Africa.

CHAPTER 20

The Middle East,
1450–1750

T his era was a vibrant and creative period for the still-expanding Islamic world. It was also a time of great urbanization. The city of Baghdad remained a major intellectual and religious center, and cities such as Cairo, Egypt, and Cordova, Spain, played important roles as well. Islam retained a firm footing in northern India and South Asia, as Muslim rulers there steadily expanded their control over parts of India.

However, the political unity of the Islamic empire had begun to decrease after the thirteenth century. The ruling Abbasid Dynasty was in decline, and separate Muslim states began to emerge. While religion was an important common denominator for these states, local differences became more pronounced. Indeed, even religion was not immune to local adaptation—variability in how Islam was practiced was noticeable in this period, especially in the Muslim areas of sub-Saharan Africa. By the eighteenth century, much of the Islamic world was in decline and about to confront a new period of European expansion.

Map 20.1
(Interactive)
The Middle East

MEHMED II

About the Document

As the ruling Abbasid Dynasty was declining in the late thirteenth century C.E., powerful local states emerged to take its place. One of these, the Ottoman Empire, was arguably the dominant Muslim state for the next 500 years. Centered in modern-day Turkey, the Ottoman Empire experienced its own period of vibrant cultural growth, but it is best remembered for its political and military complexity.

Writing in the fifteenth century, the Greek author Kritovoulos focused on one of the most important Ottoman emperors, Mehmed II, known as the "Conqueror." Mehmed II ruled from 1451–1481 and was responsible for conquering the last remnant of the old Byzantine Empire, the fortress city of Constantinople, in 1453. The following excerpt discusses the events before the takeover of the city and the actual attack, as well as what the emperor himself was like. Following this victory, the Muslim Ottomans would slowly push into southeastern Europe, forever changing the cultural and religious culture there.

The Document

16. It was the year [A.D. 1451] when the Sultan° Murad came to the end of his life, having lived a total of fifty-two years and having reigned thirty-one, a very good man in every way, high-minded, and also a very great general who had exhibited throughout his life many brave and wonderful deeds, as indeed these exploits show.

19. So when this Murad, of whom I spoke, died, his son Mehmed succeeded to the sultanate, he being the seventh Sultan and now in the twentieth year of his life. He was sent for from Asia, for it was there that he had his province which had been assigned him by his father.

20. Just at that period the Divine power sent many unusual, unexpected, and prodigious signs. These occurred both at the birth of this man and also at his entering on his rule as Sultan. For strange and exceptional earthquakes took place, and subterranean rumblings, also severe thunder and lightning from heaven, and whirlwinds and terrible storms, and an unusual light appeared in the sky, and many similar signs which the Divine power is accustomed to exhibit at the time of the greatest events and changes in the customary order.

21. The soothsayers,° sages and prophets and inspired persons foretold and foresaw many things that were to happen, and announced that the new Sultan would have every sort of good fortune and virtue, that his dominion would be very large in every way, and that he would surpass all the sultans before him in the very great abundance of his glory and wealth and power and accomplishments.

23. His physical powers helped him well. His energies were keen for everything, and the power of his spirit gave him ability to rule and to be kingly. To this end also his wisdom aided, as well as his fine knowledge of all the doings of the ancients. For he studied all the writings of the Arabs and Persians [Ottomans], and whatever works of the Greeks had been translated into the language of the Arabs and Persians—I refer particularly to the works of the Peripatetics and Stoics. So he used the most important philosophies of the teachers of the Arabs and Persians.

24. He did not postpone anything or put off any action, but immediately carried everything through. First he made a treaty with the Romans and the Emperor Constantine and after that, with Karaman, the ruler of Upper Phrygia and Cilicia, believing that for the present this move was beneficial to his affairs.

25. Then he gave himself to an examination of his whole realm. Using his judgment about the governorships of the nations under him, he deposed some of the governors and substituted others who he deemed to be superior to the former in strategy and knowledge and justice.

26. He also went over the registers and battle order of the troops, cavalry and infantry, which are paid from the royal treasuries.

27. In addition to this, he collected a supply of arms and arrows and other things needful and useful in preparation for war. Then he examined his family treasury, looking especially closely into its overseers. He carefully questioned the officials in charge of the annual taxes and obliged them to render accounts.

Sultan: Common Islamic title for "emperor" or "king."
soothsayer: Predictor.

28. And he discovered that much of the public and royal revenue was being badly spent and wasted to no good purpose, about one-third of the yearly revenues which were recovered for the royal treasury. So he set the keeping of this in good order. He greatly increased the annual revenue.

29. . . . Thus he prepared for greater things; and so everything contributed to the plan he had before him.

30. And this plan was: he meant to build a strong fortress on the Bosporus° on the European side, opposite to the Asiatic fortress on the other side; at the point where it is narrowest and swiftest, and so to control the straits by uniting both continents, Asia and Europe; and to cross there whenever he should choose, quite independently of any other individuals and with no least question that it was the Sultan himself who controlled the passage.

31. . . . Meanwhile the Emperor of the Romans [Byzantines] reigned securely in the City, always watching the times and the events, for the most part controlling the sea, making use of it sometimes to the advantage of his own nation, and injuring whom he pleased. In addition, the Italians, and especially the Venetians, in their quarrels with these others, often cruised in long triremes through the Bosporus and the Hellespont, preventing the crossing of these straits.

33. With this plan in mind, that winter he ordered all the materials to be prepared for building, namely, stone and timbers and iron and whatever else would be of use for this purpose.

34. The Emperor Constantine, on the other hand, and the men of the City, when they learned this, regarded it as terrible and as the beginning of great evils. Considering it a certain danger of enslavement—as indeed it was—they decided to fortify their town and to prepare the whole City. They were sorely troubled.

35. Hence he [Constantine] decided to send an embassy composed of his associates to try by any possible means to forestall this threat.

36. And they, when they arrived, used all sorts of arguments, citing the treaties and agreements. They told how, in all the previous treaties which had been drawn up and ratified, both with his forefathers and with his father, and indeed with him also, it was in every case promised that no one should build a fortress or anything else in this place. Furthermore it was specified that, if any such undertaking was begun, both sides would oppose this by every possible means. So the country had been saved from danger of this until now and was free. They said they would agree simply to the passing across of the Sultan's armies and other equipment from continent to continent, but they demanded that he should not in any way break the treaties, concluded but yesterday and the day before, for any trivial reason. For surely he did not wish to commit any injustice, as they certainly were not doing any injustice on their part.

37. The Sultan replied to them: "I have no intention to do you any injustice, O Romans, nor to do anything contrary to the agreements and treaties in this undertaking of mine, but only to protect my possessions while doing no injury to you. It is, however, just and right for each of us to guard and make sure of his own, not in the least injuring those with whom he has a treaty, and this is the desire of all. But, as you see, I rule over both Asia and Europe, continents separated from each other, and in each of these I have many opponents and enemies of my rule. . . . Besides, this place where I am now going to build a fortress is our own, being the place for crossing into our own territory,

Bosporus: The strait between the Byzantine Empire and the Ottoman Empire; today it separates European and Asian Turkey.

whether from Asia into Europe or from Europe into Asia. So you must not interfere too much. If you wish to enjoy peace, and if you have no intention on your part of preventing us from having this crossing-place, I on my part will neither break my pledges nor desire to do so, provided you will stay in your own place and not meddle at all in our affairs nor wish to be too prying."

38. With this reply, he dismissed the ambassadors. They on their return told everything to the Emperor Constantine and all the Romans [Byzantines]—the whole story and especially that it was not possible to prevent this undertaking entirely, either by argument or by persuasion, but only by resort to force, if indeed that were possible. And they, since they fully realized the exceeding gravity of the situation and that there was nothing they could do, kept an unwilling silence.

54. He also resolved to carry into execution immediately the plan which he had long since studied out and elaborated in his mind and toward which he had bent every purpose from the start, and to wait no longer nor delay. This plan was to make war against the Romans [Byzantines] and their Emperor Constantine and to besiege the city. For he thought . . . that if he could succeed in capturing it and becoming master of it, there was nothing to hinder him from sallying forth from it in a short time . . . and overrunning all and subduing them to himself. For this reason he could no longer be restrained at all.

234. So saying, he led them himself. And they, with a shout on the run and with a fearsome yell, went on ahead of the Sultan, pressing on up to the palisade. After a long and bitter struggle they hurled back the Romans from there and climbed by force up the palisade.° The dashed some of their foe down into the ditch between the great wall and the palisade, which was deep and hard to get out of, and they killed them there. The rest they drove back to the gate.

235. He had opened this gate in the great wall, so as to go easily over to the palisade. Now there was a great struggle there and great slaughter among those stationed there, for they were attacked by the heavy infantry and not a few others in irregular formation, who had been attracted from many points by the shouting. There the Emperor Constantine, with all who were with him, fell in gallant combat.

236. The heavy infantry were already streaming through the little gate into the City, and others had rushed in through the breach in the great wall. Then all the rest of the army, with a rush and a roar, poured in brilliantly and scattered; all over the City. And the Sultan stood before the great wall, where the standard also was and the ensigns, and watched the proceedings. The day was already breaking.

Analysis and Review Questions

1. Would you say that the author's account of Mehmed is generally positive or negative? Why?
2. Who were the soothsayers and sages?
3. Does Mehmed honor his treaties or not, according to the author?
4. How does the Byzantine emperor Constantine die?
5. Where was Mehmed when his father died?

---

palisade: A fence of stakes used for defense.

VENETIAN OBSERVATIONS ON THE OTTOMAN EMPIRE

About the Document

After Constantinople was conquered, the city was renamed Istanbul and was soon on its way back to the greatness it had enjoyed during the height of the Byzantine Empire. Indeed, just as the city had been the cultural, intellectual, and political heart for the Byzantines, so, too, would it be for the Ottoman Empire.

But, in many ways, the history of the Ottoman Empire was of a quick, decisive rise to power followed by a long, steady decline. Even by the seventeenth century, European observers, who admittedly tended to be biased against Muslim institutions anyway, were noticing signs of decay and weakness. One such individual was a Venetian ambassador to Istanbul, Gianfrancesco Morosini, who was in Turkey during the 1580s. His reports not only discuss the organization of the military and the government, but also provide a European view of the perceived strengths and weaknesses of the Turkish people. These and other dispatches also describe the Turkish capital.

Image 20.1
Mehmet II

The Document

They succeed to the throne without any kind of ceremony of election or coronation. According to Turkish law of succession, which resembles most countries' laws in this respect, the oldest son should succeed to the throne as soon as the father dies. But in fact, whichever of the sons can first enter the royal compound in Constantinople is called the sultan and is obeyed by the people and by the army. Since he has control of his father's treasure he can easily gain the favor of the janissaries and with their help control the rest of the army and the civilians.

Because this government is based on force, the brother who overcomes the others is considered the lord of all. The same obedience goes to a son who can succeed in overthrowing his father, a thing which bothers the Turks not at all. As a result, when his sons are old enough to bear arms, the sultan generally does not allow them near him, but sends them off to some administrative district where they must live under continual suspicion until their father's death. And just as the fathers do not trust their own sons, the sons do not trust their fathers and are always afraid of being put to death. This is the sad consequence of unbridled ambition and hunger for power—a miserable state of affairs where there is no love between father and sons, and much less between sons and father.

This lord has thirty-seven kingdoms covering enormous territory. His dominion extends to the three principal parts of the world, Africa, Asia, and Europe; and since these lands are joined and contiguous with each other, he can travel for a distance of eight thousand miles on a circuit through his empire and hardly need to set foot in another prince's territories.

The principal cities of the Turks are Constantinople, Adrianople,° and Bursa, the three royal residence places of the sultans. Buda is also impressive, as are the Asian cities—Cairo, Damascus, Aleppo, Bagdad and others—but none of these have the things which usually lend beauty to cities. Even Constantinople, the most important of them all, which is posted in the most beautiful and enchanting situation that can be imagined, still lacks those amenities that a great city should have, such as beautiful streets, great squares, and handsome palaces. Although Constantinople has many mosques, royal

Adrianople: Turkish city on the European side of the Bosporus.

palaces, inns, and public baths, the rest of the city is mazy and filthy; even these [public buildings], with their leaded domes studded with gilded bronze ornaments, only beautify the long-distance panorama of the city.

The security of the empire depends more than anything else on the large numbers of land and sea forces which the Turks keep continually under arms. These are what make them feared throughout the world.

The sultan always has about 280,000 well-paid men in his service. Of them about 80,000 are paid every three months out of his personal treasury. These include roughly 16,000 janissaries, who form the Grand Signor's advance guard; six legions, or about 12,000 cavalry called "spahi," who serve as his rear guard; and about 1,500 other defenders. . . . The other 200,000 cavalry . . . are not paid with money like the others, but are assigned landholdings [called timars].

The timariots are in no way inferior as fighting men to the soldiers paid every three months with cash, because the timars are inherited like the fiefs distributed by Christian rulers.

What about the fighting qualities of these widely feared Turkish soldiers? I can tell you the opinion I formed at Scutari, where I observed the armies of Ferrad Pasha and Osman Pasha (Ferrad's army was there for more than a month, and Osman's for a matter of weeks). I went over to Scutari several times to confer with the two pashas and also, unofficially, to look at the encampment, and I walked through the whole army and carefully observed every detail about the caliber of their men, their weapons, and the way they organize a bivouac site and fortify it. I think I can confidently offer this conclusion: they rely more on large numbers and obedience than they do on organization and courage.

Although witnesses who saw them in earlier times claim they are not as good as they used to be, it appears that the janissaries are still the best of the Turkish soldiers. They are well-made men, and they can handle their weapons—the arquebus, club, and scimitar—quite well. These men are accustomed to hardships, but they are only used in battle in times of dire necessity.

As for the cavalry, some are lightly armed with fairly weak lances, huge shields, and scimitars.

If I compare these men with Christian soldiers, such as those I saw in the wars in France or in the Christian King's conquest of Portugal, I would say they are much better than Christian soldiers in respect to obedience and discipline. However, in courage and enthusiasm, and in physical appearance and weapons, they are distinctly inferior.

The naval forces which the Great Turk uses to defend his empire are vast and second to none in the world. True, at present they do not have at hand all the armaments they would need to outfit the as yet uncompleted galleys, . . . But his resources are so great that if he wanted to he could quickly assemble what he needs; he has already begun to attend to this.

Analysis and Review Questions

1. From the document, how does it appear that a new king is selected in the Ottoman Empire?
2. Does the author consider Constantinople to be an attractive city?
3. What are the three principal Turkish cities?
4. How does the author evaluate the Ottoman army?
5. Would you consider this a positive or a negative account? Why?

THE DECLINE OF THE OTTOMANS

About the Document

Image 20.2
The Suleymaniye
Mosque

Istanbul, the former Constantinople, became a great cultural center under the Ottoman Turks. In the 200 years after its conquest in 1453, Istanbul took on an increasingly Islamic character, as society was irrevocably altered, buildings were modified, and architectural styles changed. Islam replaced Orthodox Christianity as the dominant faith.

However, despite the fact that the Ottoman Empire became powerful quickly, it had already started to decay by the seventeenth century. This fact was quickly noticed by European observers such as Gianfrancesco Morosini (see document 20.2) and Lorenzo Bernardo, both ambassadors from Venice to the Ottoman sultans in the late 1500s. While accounts of the decline may have been somewhat exaggerated by these European observers, Bernardo was also quick to praise the Turks for various accomplishments. In spite of any predictions about its collapse, the Ottoman Empire would exist until after 1918.

The Document

Three basic qualities have enabled the Turks to make such remarkable conquests, and rise to such importance in a brief period: religion, frugality, and obedience.

From the beginning it was religion that made them zealous, frugality that made them satisfied with little, and obedience that produced men ready for any dangerous campaign.

In former times, Serene Prince, all Turks held to a single religion, whose major belief is that it is "written" when and how a man will die, and that if he dies for his God and his faith he will go directly to Paradise. It is not surprising, then, that one reads in histories about Turks who vied for the chance to fill a ditch with their bodies, or made a human bridge for others to use crossing a river, going to their deaths without the slightest hesitation. But now the Turks have not a single religion, but three of them. The Persians are among the Turks like the [Protestant] heretics among us [Christians], because some of them hold the beliefs of Ali, and others those of Omar, both of whom were followers of Mohammed, but held different doctrines. Then there are the Arabs and Moors, who claim they alone preserve the true, uncorrupted religion and that the "Greek Turks" (as they call these in Constantinople) are bastard Turks with a corrupted religion, which they blame on their being mostly descended from Christian renegades who did not understand the Muslim religion.

As for frugality, which I said was the second of the three sources of the Turks' great power, this used to be one of their marked characteristics. At one time the Turks had no interest in fine foods or, if they were rich, in splendid decorations in their houses. Each was happy with bread and rice, and a carpet and a cushion; he showed his importance only by having many slaves and horses with which he could better serve his ruler. No wonder then that they could put up with the terrible effort and physical discomfort involved in conquering and ruling. What a shameful lesson to our own state, where we equate military glory with sumptuous banquets and our men want to live in their camps and ships as if they were back home at weddings and feasts!

But now that the Turks have conquered vast, rich lands they too have fallen victims to the corruption of wealth. They are beginning to appreciate fine foods and game, and most of them drink wine. They furnish their houses beautifully and wear clothes of gold and silver with costly linings. Briefly, then, they become fonder every day of luxury, comfort, and display.

Obedience was the third source of the great power of the Turkish empire. In the old days obedience made them united, union made them strong, and strength rendered their armies invincible. They are all slaves by nature, and the slaves of one single master; only from him can they hope to win power, honors, and wealth and only from him do they have to fear punishment and death. Why should it be surprising, then, that they used to compete with each other to perform stupendous feats in his presence? This is why it is said that the Turks' strict obedience to their master is the foundation of the empire's security and grandeur. But when the foundation weakens, when the brake is released, ruin could easily follow. The point is that with those other state-preserving qualities changing into state-corroding qualities, disobedience and disunion could be the agents which finally topple it.

This is all the more likely now that the chief officials have no other goal but to oppose each other bitterly. They have all the normal rivalries and ambitions of ministers of state, but they also have unusual opportunities for undercover competition with each other, because many of them have married daughters, sisters, and nieces of the Grand Signor. These women can speak with His Majesty whenever they want and they often sway him in favor of their husbands. This practice throws government affairs into confusion and is a real source of worry to the first vizier, who fears to take the smallest step without notifying the sultan.

Just as obedience to a prince creates a spirit of unity, so disobedience causes discord and strife. I have already said how much the pashas who are in office hate each other. In the same way, the *massuli* or dismissed pashas think of nothing but ruining the ones in office so they can return to their former posts.

The Grand Signor himself stirs up hatred and indignation among his subjects by making himself the heir of those who die rich, and grabbing their goods from their children. His avarice and penny-pinching are subjects for loud grumbling in every tavern and gathering place in the empire.

It seems reasonable to say that if the Ottoman Empire rose so remarkably fast in a short time because the Grand Sultan went on the major campaigns and because his men hoped and struggled for rewards, then its decline may now be under way. Sultan Selim, the father of the present Grand Signor, was the first to hold that a king or emperor's real satisfaction is not to be found in brave deeds on the field of glory but in peace and quiet, in gratifying all his physical senses, in enjoying the pleasures and comforts of the seraglios in the company of women and jesters, and treating himself to jewels, palaces, loggias, and every other human creation his heart desires. Sultan Murad has followed his father's example—in fact, he has gone further, because at least Sultan Selim occasionally left the seraglio and hunted as far away as Adrianople, but the present Grand Signor, as I said, hardly ever goes out.

My conclusion, distinguished gentlemen, is that the three basic qualities which made the Turks a great power—religion, frugality, and obedience—are vanishing. If this trend continues, and if the sultan's successors follow his example of remaining in the seraglios and letting others lead campaigns, then we can hope for the decline of the empire. Just as it rose to great strength very rapidly, it seems logical to expect it to decline very rapidly, in the same way that those plants which quickly mature and produce fruit are also quick to wither.

Even if the Turks have enormous armed forces, this does not mean their state will not decline. If armed might guaranteed that an empire would last forever, think how many examples one can find of powerful Greek and Roman empires, especially the Roman one (the world has never seen a mightier power), and yet it was totally ruined in little more than two hundred years. If having more money, more land, and more inhabitants always made one country more powerful than the others, the world would not have seen so many of those reversals in which countries with smaller but better armies wiped out larger ones. It is good government, not armies, that conserve an empire; fine laws and institutions have maintained our republic, with God's help, in a world where many states are more powerful.

This is a law of nature, that the same forces which caused a thing to grow must also keep it alive when mature. If the Turkish empire rose so high with the aid of the three qualities I have discussed, then when it lacks its wings it will surely fall.

Analysis and Review Questions

1. How well do Ottoman officials get along, according to the author?
2. What are the three "basic qualities [that] have enabled the Turks" to build their empire?
3. How did the Ottoman Empire rise so quickly to prominence, according to this excerpt?
4. Does the author make any evaluation of Ottoman military strength?
5. Is there anything positive pointed out in this excerpt?

WEB LINKS

http://longmanworldhistory.com
The following additional readings and case studies can be found on the Web site.
Case Study 20.1, The Ottoman Empire in the Late Sixteenth Century

http://ccat.sas.upenn.edu/~rs143/map.html
A Web page dedicated to maps relating to the history of Islam and the Ottoman Empire.

http://www.islamic.org
An all-inclusive Muslim-oriented site that includes the text of the Quran as well as excellent discussions on the history of Islam.

http://www.greece.org/projects/Romiosini/fall.html
A detailed account of the fall of Constantinople in 1453.

http://www.cyberiran.com
A complete site dealing with all manner of things Iranian, past and present.

PART III Comparative Case Study

BATTLEFIELDS TO COURTROOMS: CONFLICT AND AGENCY IN THE AMERICAS

Spaniards on both sides of the Atlantic contested issues of how to define, and subsequently treat, the Indians. To be sure, agendas varied considerably given the different circumstances and positions of the people acting within them. Even particular individuals might find their goals changing in a relatively short time. With the exception of the Indians' obvious religious differences, for example, Cortéz initially described the Tlaxcalans in terms that las Casas himself might have found agreeable. Yet the conquistadors, despite their earlier appraisals of the New World inhabitants, quickly reversed themselves and argued as to the Indians' barbarism, savagery, and need for instruction. Consider the circumstances Cortéz faced when writing his letter to Charles V, and consider as well the advantages he sought to gain through his carefully wrought depictions of the Tlaxcalans. The Spaniards' changing motivations and circumstances, however, were only part of the contested milieu. The Indians did not remain silent or passive. They also entered the debates, often through the less obvious means of the Spanish courts, acts that spoke highly of the Indians' level of civilization and political acumen. Over time, their "voice" helped to influence the king of Spain in his decision to implement the New Laws.

THE SECOND LETTER OF HERNAN CORTÉZ TO KING CHARLES V OF SPAIN (1519)

About the Document

In 1519 the Spanish attempted to expand their sphere of control in the New World. After several abortive and costly efforts to explore Mexico's Yucatán peninsula, the Spaniards embarked on an exploration of what is now central Mexico. Hernan Cortéz, who led the mission, kept King Charles V informed of events in the Americas through a series of five extensively detailed letters. Under constant pressure to justify both his own leadership and the expenses of conquest, Cortéz missed no opportunity to expound on either the riches of the New World or the willingness of many indigenous peoples to accept Spanish tutelage and rule. In the following excerpt, Cortéz relates his meeting with the Tlaxcalans, an indigenous civilization not fully under Aztec control. Despite Cortéz's ability to embellish and put a positive spin on the events taking place, on closer reading, his letter reveals many of the ambiguities he experienced in attempting to understand the Tlaxcalans and their motives.

The Document

When we had rested somewhat, I went out one night, after inspecting the first watch, with a hundred foot soldiers, our Indian allies and the horsemen; and one league from the camp five of the horses fell and would go no further, so I sent them back. And although all those who were with me in my company urged me to return, for it was an evil omen, I continued on my way secure in the belief that God is more powerful than Nature. Before it was dawn I attacked two towns, where I killed many people, but I did not burn the houses lest the fires should alert the other towns nearby. At dawn I came upon another large town containing, according to an inspection I had made, more than twenty thousand houses. As I took them by surprise, they rushed out unarmed, and the women and children ran naked through the streets, and I began to do them some harm. When they saw that they could not resist, several men of rank of the town came to me and begged me to do them no more harm, for they wished to be Your Highness's vassals and my allies. They now saw that they were wrong in not having been willing to assist me; from thenceforth I would see how they would do all that I, in Your Majesty's name, commanded them to do, and they would be Your faithful vassals. Then, later, more than four thousand came to me in peace and led me outside to a spring and fed me very well.

And so I left them pacified and returned to our camp where I found that those who had remained behind were very afraid that some danger had befallen me because of the omen they had seen in the return of the horses the night before. But after they heard of the victory which God had been pleased to give us, and how we had pacified those villages, there was great rejoicing, for I assure Your Majesty that there was amongst us not one who was not very much afraid, seeing how deep into this country we were and among so many hostile people and so entirely without hope of help from anywhere. Indeed, I heard it whispered, and almost spoken out loud, that I was a Pedro Carbonero to have led them into this place from which they could never escape. And, moreover, standing where I could not be seen, I heard certain companions in a hut say that if I was crazy enough to go where I could not return, they were not, and that they were going to return to the sea, and if I wished to come with them, all well and good, but if not, they would abandon me. Many times I was asked to turn back, and I encouraged them by reminding them that they were Your Highness's vassals and that never at any time had Spaniards been found wanting, and that we were in a position to win for Your Majesty the greatest dominions and kingdoms in the world. Moreover, as Christians we were obliged to wage war against the enemies of our Faith; and thereby we would win glory in the next world, and, in this, greater honor and renown than any generation before our time. They should observe that God was on our side, and to Him nothing is impossible, for, as they saw, we had won so many victories in which so many of the enemy had died, and none of us. I told them other things which occurred to me of this nature, with which, and Your Highness's Royal favor, they were much encouraged and determined to follow my intentions and to do what I wished, which was to complete the enterprise I had begun.

On the following day at ten o'clock, Sintengal, the captain general of this province, came to see me, together with some fifty men of rank, and he begged me on his own behalf, and on behalf of Magiscasin, who is the most important person in the entire province, and on behalf of many other lords, to admit them to Your Highness's Royal service and to my friendship, and to forgive them their past errors, for they did not know who we were. They had tried with all their forces both by day and by night to avoid being subject to anyone, for this province never had been, nor had they ever had an over-all ruler. For they had lived in freedom and independence from time immemorial and had always defended themselves against the great power of Mutezuma and against his ancestors, who had subjugated all those lands but had never been able to reduce them to servitude, although they were surrounded on all sides and had not place by which to leave their land. They ate no salt because there was none in their land; neither could they go and buy it elsewhere, nor did they wear cotton because it did not grow there on account of the cold; and they were lacking in many other things through being so enclosed.

All of which they suffered willingly in return for being free and subject to no one, and with me they had wished to do the same; to which end, as they said, they had used all their strength but saw clearly that neither it nor their cunning had been of any use. They would rather be Your Highness's vassals than see their houses destroyed and their women and children killed. I replied that they should recognize they were to blame for the harm they had received, for I had come to their land thinking that I came to a land of friends because the men of Cempoal had assured me that it was so. I had sent my messengers on ahead to tell them that I was coming and that I wished to be their friend. But without reply they had attacked me on the road while I was unprepared and had killed two horses and wounded others. And after they had fought me, they sent messengers to tell me that it had been done without their consent by certain communities who were responsible; but they were not involved and had now rebuked those others for it and desired my friendship. I had believed them and had told them that I was pleased and would come on the following day and go among them as I would among friends. And again they had attacked me on the road and had fought all day until nightfall. And I reminded them of everything else that they had done against me and many other things which in order not to tire Your Highness I will omit. Finally, they offered themselves as vassals in the Royal service of Your Majesty and offered their persons and fortunes and so they have remained until today and will, I think, always remain so for what reason Your Majesty will see hereafter.

Analysis and Review Questions

1. What problems does Cortéz experience with his own men?
2. What greater reasons or purposes does Cortéz offer as justification for his actions and those of his fellow conquistadors?
3. What reasons do the Tlaxcalans (through their representatives Sintengal and Magiscasin) give for wishing to support the Spaniards?
4. Were the Tlaxcalans sincere in their arguments, or were they simply trying to minimize the consequences of the earlier conflicts they lost? Is there evidence of other motives or perhaps of conflicting agendas within the Tlaxcalan ranks?
5. How would you characterize Cortéz's assessment of the Tlaxcalans' hospitality and sincerity of motive? What reasons might he have for providing an assessment perhaps more positive than events suggested?

THE NEW LAWS OF THE INDIES FOR THE GOOD TREATMENT AND PRESERVATION OF THE INDIANS (1542)

About the Document

In 1542 Spain's King Charles V instituted a sweeping administrative reform of his New World colonies. Designed to ensure fairer treatment for the Indians while weakening his more ambitious Spanish subjects, the New Laws sparked serious resentment and led to several rebellions against Crown rule. The oft-cited phrase "I obey but I cannot comply" is said to have originated when Spanish bureaucrats were unable to enforce the king's new legislation. Charles V subsequently suspended several of the New Laws—most notably those concerning the enslavement of Indians—until he could consolidate his power enough to guarantee their enforcement.

Despite the level of attention that the treatment of Indians received in the reforms, the New Laws dealt as much with issues of how the Spanish monarchy might extend and consolidate its power over its own peoples as they did with issues of how to treat new subjects. Like the Romans before them, and the globe-spanning empires to follow, the Spanish monarchs found that the challenges of empire often diminished the rewards of empire.

The Spanish arrival in the Americas arguably posed as many challenges for the Iberian monarchy and its peoples as it did for their New World counterparts. In a very short time span, Spain grew from a loose confederation of kingdoms into a global empire. Even as Christopher Columbus was embarking on his epic voyage to the West, King Ferdinand and Queen Isabella were struggling to consolidate their power over the Iberian peninsula. The more than 700-year effort to repel the Moorish invasion from North Africa had just ended in 1492, and the monarchs faced considerable obstacles. On the one hand, they had to contend with the question of how to assimilate peoples that geography, culture, and religion (the Moors, for instance, were Muslims) long had distanced from one another. On the other hand, and in the absence of a clearly defined common enemy, they had to find a means of maintaining and strengthening their hold over the sizeable population of nobles (*hidalgos*) who earlier had offered them their loyalty in exchange for the possibilities of material gain. With the fighting over, the monarchs could no longer offer the longstanding incentives of land, honor, and treasure as a means of reigning in the nobility. Ferdinand and Isabella sat atop a veritable powder keg.

Columbus's arrival in the New World drew Spain's internal conflicts and challenges into the global arena where distance made them even more problematic. Spanish encounters with indigenous civilizations, for example, exacerbated the issue of how successfully to assimilate different peoples and cultures under the rubric of a single empire or identity. While the discovery of new lands provided much needed incentives for hidalgos and, at least temporarily, a means by which the monarchy could continue to direct and control their impulses, the two often were at odds. Ferdinand and Isabella sought to find in the Indians loyal and obedient subjects. The hidalgos, by contrast, sought to find uncivilized barbarians whom they could then rob, plunder, and enslave. By the time that Cortéz and Pizarro began their conquests of Mexico and Peru, Spanish priests and missionaries already were complaining to the Crown of the conquistadors' abuses of the native populations.

Realizing that their control over affairs in the New World and over their Spanish subjects depended on their ability to both administer the Indian populations and continue to provide material incentives to the hidalgos, Ferdinand and Isabella instituted the practice of the encomienda.° Not to be confused with a land grant—since, after all, there was still considerable debate over whether the Indians were civilized enough to possess their own lands—the encomienda entrusted the indigenous inhabitants of a particular area or region to a hidalgo for the duration of his life. In exchange for administering, protecting, and Christianizing the inhabitants entrusted to him, the *encomendero* was entitled to some of their labor. The institution was, in sum, a short-term means of establishing control over the Americas and pacifying the Spaniards until an effective bureaucracy could be established in the New World.

Affairs went from bad to worse almost immediately. The encomienda often proved little more than a pretext for enslaving, robbing, and otherwise abusing the Indians. In their search for wealth, the encomenderos frequently placed their own material interests above the spiritual interests of the people they were entrusted with Christianizing. Consequently, rifts in the Spanish community occurred as settlers squared off against missionaries and priests. In the Yucatán region of Mexico the struggles grew especially bitter. Franciscan missionaries contended, for example, that Spanish abuses had led entire villages of Mayan Indians to revert to idolatry and human sacrifice. Worse, in the eyes of many members of the Spanish religious community, was the fact that encomiendas were becoming hereditary in practice.

By the 1530s, Spain's King Charles V recognized the severity of the crisis he faced. While engaged with conflicts in Europe, he had lost control of his new colonies. Nowhere was this more evident than in relation to the treatment of the Indians. Despite a 1537 papal bull declaring the Indians to be human beings, complete with souls and reason, and despite the protestations of Bishop Bartolomé de las Casas, Spanish settlers continued to enslave and wage war on the indigenous peoples in their care. The hidalgos demonstrated repeatedly their reluctance to obey any orders, whether from Church or King, that might conflict with their aims. Corruption and conflicts of interest virtually ensured that a fair administration of the new lands and their peoples would not be possible so long as the hidalgos were entrusted with such responsibilities. King Charles V subsequently focused his attentions on the enforcement of his rule. The 1542 New Laws of the Indies were the king's response to affairs in the Americas.

encomienda: This was the practice of entrusting the care of a specific indigenous population to a hidalgo. In exchange for Christianizing and protecting them, the hidalgo had the right to some of their labor.

The Document

Whereas one of the most important things in which the Audiencias° are to serve us is in taking very especial care of the good treatment of the Indians and preservation of them, We command that the said Audiencias enquire continually into the excesses and ill treatment which are or shall be done to them by governors or private persons; and how the ordinances and instructions which have been given to them, and are made for the good treatment of the said Indians have been observed. And if there had been any excesses, on the part of the said Governors, or should any be committed hereafter, to take care that such excesses are properly corrected, chastizing the guilty parties with all rigour conformably to justice. The Audiencias must not allow that in the suits between Indians, or with them, there be ordinary proceedings at law, nor dilatory expedients, as is wont to happen through the malice of some advocates and solicitors, but that they be determined summarily, observing their usages and customs, unless they be manifestly unjust; and that the said Audiencias take care that this be so observed by the other, inferior judges.

Item, We ordain and command that from hence forward for no cause of war nor any other whatsoever, though it be under title of rebellion, nor by ransom nor in other manner can an Indian be made a slave, and we will that they be treated as our vassals of the Crown of Castile° since such they are.

No person can make use of the Indians by way of Naboria or Tapia or in any other manner against their will.

As we have ordered provision to be made that from henceforward the Indians in no way be made slaves, including those who until now have been enslaved against all reason and right and contrary to the provisions and instructions thereupon, We ordain and command that the Audiencias having first summoned the parties to their presence, without any further judicial form, but in a summary way, so that the truth may be ascertained, speedily set the said Indians at liberty unless the persons who hold them for slaves show title why they should hold and possess them legitimately. And in order that in default of persons to solicit the aforesaid, the Indians may not remain in slavery unjustly, We command that the Audiencias appoint persons who may pursue this cause for the Indians and be paid out of the Exchequer fines, provided they be men of trust and diligence.

Also, we command that with regard to the lading of the said Indians the Audiencias take especial care that they be not laden, or in case that in some parts this cannot be avoided that it be in such a manner that no risk of life, health and preservation of the said Indians may ensue from an immoderate burthen; and that against their own will and without their being paid, in no case be it permitted that they be laden, punishing very severely him who shall act contrary to this. In this there is to be no remission out of respect to any person.

Because report has been made to us that owing to the pearl fisheries not having been conducted in a proper manner deaths of many Indians and Negroes have ensued, We command that no free Indian be taken to the said fishery under pain of death, and that the bishop and the judge who shall be at Veneçuela direct what shall seem to them most fit for the preservation of the slaves working in the said fishery, both Indians and Negroes, and that the deaths may cease. If, however, it should appear to them that the

Audiencias: Spanish courts of justice established in the colonies to which, theoretically, both Spaniards and Indians had recourse.
Castile: Castile was the name of the Iberian kingdom in which the Spanish monarchy was housed. It was also the birthplace of Queen Isabella and a powerful kingdom at the time of her marriage to Ferdinand of Aragon.

risk of death cannot be avoided by the said Indians and Negroes, let the fishery of the said pearls cease, since we value much more highly (as is right) the preservation of their lives than the gain which may come to us from the pearls.

Whereas in consequence of the allotments of Indians made to the Viceroys,° Governors, and their lieutenants, to our officials, and prelates, monasteries, hospitals, houses of religion and mints, offices of our Hazienda° and treasury thereof, and other persons favoured by reason of their offices, disorders have occurred in the treatment of the said Indians, it is our will, and we command that forthwith there be placed under our Royal Crown all the Indians whom they hold and possess by any title and cause whatever, whoever the said parties are, or may be, whether Viceroys, Governors, or their lieutenants, or any of our officers, as well of Justice as of our Hazienda, prelates, houses of religion, or of our Hazienda, hospitals, confraternities, or other similar institutions, although the Indians may not have been allotted to them by reason of the said offices; and although such functionaries or governors may say that they wish to resign the offices or governments and keep the Indians, let this not avail them nor be an excuse for them not to fulfill what we command.

Moreover, We command that from all those persons who hold Indians without proper title, having entered into possession of them by their own authority, such Indians be taken away and be placed under our Royal Crown.

And because we are informed that other persons, although possessing a sufficient title, have had an excessive number of Indians allotted to them, We order that the Audiencias, each in its jurisdiction diligently inform themselves of this, and with all speed, and reduce the allotments made to the said persons to a fair and moderate quantity, and then place the rest under our Royal Crown notwithstanding any appeal or application which may be interposed by such persons: and send us a report with all speed of what the said Audiencias have thus done, that we may know how our command is fulfilled. And in New Spain let it be especially provided as to the Indians held by Joan Infante, Diego de Ordas, the Maestro Roa, Francisco Vasquez de Coronado, Francisco Maldondo, Bernardino Vazquez de Tapia, Joan Xaramillo, Martin Vazquez, Gil Goncales de Venavides, and many other persons who are said to hold Indians in very excessive quantity, according to the report made to us. And, whereas we are informed that there are some persons in the said New Spain who are of the original Conquistadores and have no repartimiento° of Indians, We ordain that the President and Auditors of the said New Spain do inform themselves if there be any persons of this kind, and if any, to give them out of the tribute which the Indians thus taken away have to pay, what to them may seem fit for the moderate support and honourable maintenance of the said original Conquistadores who had no Indians allotted to them.

So also, the said Audiencias are to inform themselves how the Indians have been treated by the persons who have held them in encomienda, and if it be clear that in justice they ought to be deprived of the said Indians for their excesses and the ill-usage to which they have subjected them, We ordain that they take away and place such Indians under our Royal Crown. And in Peru, besides the aforesaid, let the Viceroy and Audiencia inform themselves of the excesses committed during the occurrences between

Viceroys: Situated atop the colonial bureaucracy, viceroys were royal bureaucrats who served as the king's New World proxies. Though subordinate to the king himself, the great distances between Spain and the colonies often necessitated that the viceroys act independently and without outside council.
Hazienda: The Hacienda was the Spanish equivalent of a Department of the Interior.
repartimiento: Forced labor draft in which up to one-seventh of a given indigenous population could be drafted to labor for a set amount of time on a plantation, in the mines, etc.

Governors Pizarro and Almagro in order to report to us thereon, and from the principal persons whom they find notoriously blameable in those feuds they then take away the Indians they have, and place them under our Royal Crown.

Moreover, we ordain and command that from hence forward no Viceroy, Governor, Audiencia, discoverer, or any other person have power to allot Indians in encomienda by new provision, or by means of resignation, donation, sale, or any other form or manner, neither by vacancy nor inheritance, but that the person dying who held the said Indians, they revert to our Royal Crown. And let the Audiencias take care to inform themselves then particularly of the person who died, of his quality, his merits and services, of how he treated the said Indians whom he held, if he left wife and children or what other heirs, and send us a report thereof together with the condition of the Indians and of the land, in order that we may give directions to provide what may be best for our service, and may do such favour as may seem suitable to the wife and children of the defunct. If in the meantime it should appear to the Audiencia that there is a necessity to provide some support for such wife and children, they can do it out of the tribute which the said Indians will have to pay, or allowing them a moderate pension, if the said Indians are under our Crown, as aforesaid.

Analysis and Review Questions

1. To what extent do you think Cortéz's descriptions of the Tlaxcalans make a strong case for the Indians' level of civilization and autonomy being sufficiently high so as to dictate against enslaving them?
2. In less than 25 years, Spaniards and Indians transferred their conflicts from the battlefield to the courtrooms *(audiencias)*. To what extent did this mark a transformation from Indian to Spanish rule? What might be the long-term significance of the Indians' utilization of the Spanish courts?
3. Cortéz cited the Spaniards' religious imperative in conquering the Aztecs. From your reading of the New Laws and the abuses they sought to end, do you think the Indians' Christianization remained a priority for Spanish settlers?
4. In comparing the two documents, to what extent do you believe that the Spanish abuses were part of a longer tradition of struggle and contest that preceded the Spaniards' arrival?

Credits

12 From *Readings in Ancient History: From Gilgamesh to Diocletion*, ed. Nels Bailkey. Copyright © 1976 by Houghton Mifflin Company.

16 Reprinted by permission of Princeton University Press from *Ancient Near Eastern Texts Relating to the Old Testament*, ed. James B. Pritchard. Copyright © 1950, 1955, 1969, renewed 1978 by Princeton University Press.

17 "The Instruction of Ptah-hotep," from *Readings in Ancient History: From Gilgamesh to Diocletion*, ed. Nels Bailkey (Lexington, MA: D. C. Heath, 1976), 39-43.

19 Reprinted by permission of Princeton University Press from *Ancient Near Eastern Texts Relating to the Old Testament*, ed. James B. Pritchard. Copyright © 1950, 1955, 1969, renewed 1978 by Princeton University Press.

21 Reprinted by permission of Princeton University Press from *Ancient Near Eastern Texts Relating to the Old Testament*, ed. James B. Pritchard. Copyright © 1950, 1955, 1969, renewed 1978 by Princeton University Press.

22 "The Majesty of Darius the Great: A Persian Royal Inscription," from *Civilization: Past & Present*, 9th ed., ed. Palmira Brummett, et al. (Longman, 2000), 47.

25 Reprinted with the permission of the publisher from *Sources of Indian Tradition*, ed. Theodore de Bary. © 1958 Columbia University Press.

26 From *The Law of Manu*, by Manu, in *The Sacred Books of the East*, vol. XXV, ed. F. Max Muller, (Oxford, UK: Clarendon Press, 1886), 12-14, 24.

28 Reprinted by permission from *The Principal Upanishads*, ed., trans. S. Radhakrishnan (HarperCollins Publishers Ltd.).

30 Reprinted with the permission of the publisher from *Sources of Indian Tradition*, ed. Theodore de Bary. © 1958 Columbia University Press.

31 Reprinted with the permission of the publisher from *Sources of Indian Tradition*, ed. Theodore de Bary. © 1958 Columbia University Press.

32 *Buddhism in Translations: Passages from the Buddhist Sacred Books*, by Henry Clarke Warren (Harvard Univ. Press, 1953), 368-374.

35 Reprinted with the permission of the publisher from *Sources of Indian Tradition*, ed. Theodore de Bary. © 1958 Columbia University Press.

39 From *The Law of Manu*, by Manu, in *The Sacred Books of the East*, vol. XXV, ed. F. Max Muller (Oxford, UK: Clarendon Press, 1886), 195-97.

40 Reprinted by permission of the Feminist Press at the City University of New York (www.feministpress.org) from *Women Writing in India: 600 B.C. to the Present*, vol. 1. Copyright © 1991 by Susie Tharu and K. Lalita.

43 *Confucian Analects, the Great Learning, and the Doctrine of the Mean*, in *Chinese Classics Series of the Clarendon Press*, vol. 1, trans. James Legge (Oxford, U.K.: Clarendon Press, 1893).

46 From *The Sacred Books of the East*, vol. 39, ed. F. Max Muller, passim.

48 Reprinted by permission from *The Complete Works of Han Fei Tzu*, vol. 1, trans. W. L. Liano (1939).

51 "Sima Qian on Qin Shihuang," from *Records of the Historian*, trans. Yang Hsien-yi, Gladys Yang (1979). Reprinted by permission of Foreign Languages Press.

54 "Li Si and the Legalist Policies of Qin Shihuang," from *Records of the Historian*, trans. Yang Hsien-yi, Gladys Yang (1979). Reprinted by permission of Foreign Languages Press.

58 Reprinted by permission from *Greek Lyric Poetry*, trans. Willis Barnstone (Bantam Books, 1967).

61 "The Earth Mother: A Homeric Hymn," trans. P. B. Shelley, from *Hesiod: The Homeric Hymns and Homerica*, trans. H. G. Evelyn-White.

63 Reproduced by permission of Penguin Books from *The Politics by Aristotle*, trans. T. A. Sinclair, rev. Trevor J. Saunders (Penguin Classics, rev. ed., 1981). Translation copyright © the Estate of T. A. Sinclair, 1962; revised translation copyright © Trevor J. Saunders, 1981.

65 From *Thucydides, Peloponnesian War*, trans. Richard Crawley (London: J.M. Dent, 1903), vol. 1, 120-128; vol. II, 59-67; language modernized.

68 Plutarch, *Plutarch's Lives*, trans. Bernadette Perrin, vol. 1 (Harvard Univ. Press, 1914), 219, 221, 223, 225, 227, 229, 231, 233, 241, 245, 247, 249, 257, 259, 279, 283, 289.

70 *Plutarch's Lives*, vol. 7 (1908), 225, 231, 233, 235, 241, 243, 245, 289, 291, 339, 340, 355, 359, 361, 399, 401.

76 *The Lives of the Twelve Caesars*, trans. Alexander Thomson (London: George Bell & Sons, 1909), 87-92, 96-97, 115-16, 129-30, 145-46.

80 Scripture quotations used by permission from the *New American Standard Bible*. Copyright © 1960, 1962, 1963, 1968, 1971, 1972, 1973, 1975, 1977, and 1995 by The Lockman Foundation (www.gospelcom.net/lockman).

83 "Aelius Aristides, Oration on the Pax Romana," from *A History of Rome*, by Moses Hadas (1956). Reprinted by permission.

85 Excerpts reprinted by permission from "The Governance of God," in *The Writings of Salvian, the Presbyter*, trans. J.F. O'Sullivan (Catholic University of America Press, 1962).

87 Reprinted by permission of Oxford University Press from *The Institutes of Gaius*, by Francis de Zulueta, 23-27, 1946-53.

89 *The Theodosian Code and Novels and the Sirmondian Constitutions*, trans. Clyde Pharr (Princeton, NJ: Princeton University Press, 1952).

93 Reprinted by permission of HarperCollins from *The Koran Interpreted*, trans. A.J. Arberry (HarperCollins). Text © A.J. Arberry, 1981.

98 *A Mirror for Princes*, by Kai Ka'us Ibn Iskander, trans. Reuben Levy (London: The Cresset Press, 1951), 45-48.

100 Reprinted with the permission of the publisher from Usamah Ibn-Munqidh, *An Arab-Syrian Gentleman and Warrior in the Period of the Crusades*, trans. Philip K. Hitti. © 2000 Columbia University Press.

102 Reprinted with permission of St. Martin's Press from: *Rubaiyat Omar Khayya*, trans. Edward FitzGerald. Copyright © 1983 by St. Martin's Press.

108 Reprinted by permission from *Classical India*, ed. William H. McNeill, Jean W. Sadler (1969).

111 Selections from Machiavelli, *The Prince*, trans., ed. David Wootton. Copyright © 1995 by Hackett Publishing Company. Reprinted by permission of Hackett Publishing Company. All rights reserved.

117 Reprinted by permission of Archabbey Press from *The Rule by Saint Benedict of Nursia*, trans. Dom Justin McCann (1950).

121 Reprinted by permission of the publisher from David Herlihy, *The History of Feudalism* (Amherst, NY: Humanity Books, copyright 1970) 177-183.

125 Reprinted by permission from *The Alexiad of the Princess Anna Comnena*, trans. Elizabeth A. S. Dawes (Routledge & K. Paul, 1967), 33-34, 248-50.

129 Reprinted by permission from Eusebius, *Life of Constantine*, trans. Colm Luibhèid, I. 26-31.

131 "The Russian Primary Chronicle," Samuel H. Cross, *Harvard Studies and Notes in Philology and Literature*, vol. 12 (London: Oxford University Press, 1930), 197-201, 204-5, 210-11, 213.

135 Reprinted with the permission of the publisher from *Anthology of Old Russian Literature*, ed. Ad. Stender-Petersen in collaboration with Stefan Congrat-Butlar. © 1954 Columbia University Press.

139 "Filofei's Concept of the Third Rome,'" trans. Basil Dmytryshyn, from *Medieval Russia: A Source Book, 850-1700*, ed. Basil Dmytryshyn (Gulf Breeze, FL: Academic International Press, 2000), 259-61. Reprinted by permission.

143 Reprinted by permission of Pearson Education Limited from *Sundiata: An Epic of Old Mali*, by D.T. Niane, trans. G.D. Pickett (Pearson Education Limited). © Longman Group Limited, 1965.

147 Leo Africanus, *The History and Description of Africa and of the Notable Things Therein Contained* (London: Hakluyt Society, 1896), 819-25.

151 Barbosa, *Description of Coasts of East Africa and Malabar in the Beginning of the 16th Century* (London: Hakluyt Society, 1866), 4-15.

158 Reprinted with the permission of Simon & Schuster and the Balkin Agency from *Popol Vuh*, by Dennis Tedlock. Copyright © 1985, 1996 by Dennis Tedlock.

162 "I Say This," from *Fifteen Poets of the Aztec World*, by Miguel Leon-Portilla. © 1992 University of Oklahoma Press. Reprinted by permission.

163 Reprinted with the permission of Stanford University Press (www.sup.org) from *Cantares Mexicanos*, trans. John Bierhorst (1985). Copyright © 1985 by the Board of Trustees of the Leland Stanford Jr. University.

165 "The Midwife Addresses the Woman Who Has Died in Childbirth," from the *Nahuatl*, trans. John Bierhorst (1994). Reprinted with permission.

170 *Alberuni's India*, ed. Edward C. Sachau (Delhi: S. Chand and Co., 1964), 17-20, 22-25.

172 "The Ideal Monarch," by Vidyapati Ratnakaravarni, trans. C.H. Prahlada Rao. Reprinted by permission.

173 Reprinted by permission of HarperCollins Publishers, Ltd., and UNESCO from *Love Songs of Vidyapati*, trans. Debra Bhattacharya (HarperCollins).

176 Reprinted by permission from *Travels in Asia and Africa 1325–1354*, trans. H.A.R. Gibb, Augustus M. Kelly (1969).

178 Reprinted by permission from *The Wonder That Was India*, by A. L. Basham (Macmillan, 1954).

182 "Drinking Alone," by Li Po, trans. Joseph J. Lee, Irving Yucheng Lo, from *Sunflower Splendor: Three Thousand Years of Chinese Poetry*, ed. Wu-Chi Liu, Irving Yucheng Lo. © 1975 by Wu-Chi Liu and Irving Yucheng Lo. Reprinted by permission of Irving Yucheng Lo.

183 "Farewell of an Old Man," by Tu Fu, trans. Irving Yucheng Lo, Ronald C. Miao, from *Sunflower Splendor: Three Thousand Years of Chinese Poetry*, ed. Wu-Chi Liu, Irving Yucheng Lo. © 1975 by Wu-Chi Liu and Irving Yucheng Lo. Reprinted by permission of Irving Yucheng Lo.

184 *Diaries of Court Ladies of Old Japan*, trans. Annie Shepley Omori, Kochi Doi (Boston: Houghton Mifflin, 1920), 71-73, 86-87, 89-90, 130-34.

188 *The Travels of Marco Polo*, trans. W. Marsden (1818); rendered into modern English by A. J. Andrea.

191 Reproduced by permission of the University of Pennsylvania Press from *The Chronicle of Fulcher of Chartres*, trans. Martha Evelyn McGinty. Copyright © 1941 University of Pennsylvania Press.

196 Reprinted by permission from *The Song of Roland*, by Dorothy Sayers (Penguin, 1957).

200 Reprinted from *Luther's Works*, vol. 51, ed. John W. Doberstein. Copyright © 1959 Fortress Press. Used by permission of Augsburg Fortress.

205 Reprinted by permission of Oxford University Press from *Documents of the Christian Church*, 3rd ed., ed. Henry Bettenson, 364-67.

207 Reprinted from *The Political Works of James I* (1616), intro. Charles Howard McIlwain (Cambridge, MA.: Harvard University Press, 1918), 53-70.

212 *A King's Lessons in Statecraft: Louis XIV: Letters to His Heirs with Introduction and Notes,* by Jean Longnon, trans. Herbert Wilson (Port Washington, NY: Kennikat Press, 1970), 39-40, 48-51.

217 Reprinted with the permission of The Johns Hopkins University Press from *On the Revolutions: Nicholas Copernicus Complete Works*, by Nicholas Copernicus, ed. Jerzy Dobrzycki, commentary by Edward Rosen, 3–5. © 1978 The Johns Hopkins University Press.

219 *An Ambassador's Report on The Ottoman Empire*, 1555, from *The Life and Letters of Ogier Ghiselin de Busbecq*, ed. C.T. Forster, F. H. B. Daniell, vol. I (London: C. K. Paul and Co., 1881).

221 Excerpted from *A Source Book for Russian History*, ed. G. Vernadsky, R. T. Fisher, Jr. Copyright © 1972 by Yale University Press. Reprinted by permission.

223 Reprinted with permission of Cambridge University Press from *On the Corruption of Morals in Russia*, by Prince M. M. Shcherbatov, ed., trans. A. Lentin. Copyright © 1969 by Cambridge University Press.

229 From *The Bernal Diaz Chronicles*, trans. Albert Idell. Copyright © 1956 by Albert Idell. Used by permission of Doubleday, a division of Random House.

229 Reprinted by permission of Beacon Press, Boston, from *The Broken Spears*, by Miguel Leon-Portilla. © 1962, 1990 by Miguel Leon-Portilla. Expanded and updated edition © 1992 by Miguel Leon-Portilla.

232 Reprinted by permission from *In Defense of the Indians*, by Bartolome de las Casas, ed., trans. Stafford Poole (Northern Illinois University Press, 1974).

234 Margaret Sayers Peden's translation of *La Respuesta a Sor Filotea*, the first translation of the work into the English language, was originally commissioned by a small independent New England press, Lime Rock Press, of Salisbury, CT. It appeared in 1982 in a limited edition entitled *A Woman of Genius: The Intellectual Autobiography of Sor Juana Inèz de la Cruz*, with photographs by Gabriel North Seymour. Copyright © 1982 by Lime Rock Press, Inc. Reprinted with permission.

239 From *China in the Sixteenth Century*, by Matthew Ricci, trans. Louis J. Gallagher, S.J. Copyright 1942, 1953, renewed 1970 by Louis J. Gallagher, S.J.

242 Reprinted by permission from *Japan: A Documentary History*, trans., ed. David John Lu (Armonk, NY: M. E. Sharpe, 1997).

244 *East Asia: A New History*, 2nd ed., by Rhoads Murphey (Longman, 2001), 127.

248 *Readings in European History*, vol. II, ed. James Harvey Robinson (Boston: Ginn and Co. 1906), 333-35.

250 Reprinted with the permission of the publisher from *Sources of Indian Tradition*, ed. Theodore de Bary. © 1958 Columbia University Press.

253 *Akbar and the Jesuits*, trans., with introduction and notes by C.H. Payne (New York & London: Harper & Brothers, 1926), 211-13.

256 *The History of India as Told by Its Own Historians*, 8 vols., ed. Henry M. Elliot, John Dowson (London: Truebner, 1867-1877), vol. 7, 157-62.

260 "Description of a Voyage from Lisbon to the Island of Sao Thomë," from *Europeans in West Africa 1540-1560*, ed. John William Blake. Reprinted by permission of The Hakluyt Society.

264 From "A Defense of the African Slave Trade, 1740," *London Magazine*, 9 (1740), 493-94, in Elizabeth Donnan, *Documents Illustrative of the History of the Slave Trade to America* (Washington, DC: Carnegie Institution, 1930), II, 469-70.

266 From Father Francisco Alvarez, *Narrative of the Portuguese Embassy to Abyssinia During the Years 1520–1527*, trans., ed. Lord Stanley of Alderley (London: Hakluyt Society, 1881), 122-26, 240-45.

271 Reprinted by permission of Princeton University Press from *The History of Mehmed the Conqueror*, by Charles T. Riggs. Copyright © 1954, renewed 1984 by Princeton University Press.

274 Reprinted by permission of HarperCollins Publishers from *The Pursuit of Power: Venetian Ambassador's Reports*, by James C. Davis, ed., trans.,127-29, 131-34. English translation copyright © 1970 by James C. Davis.

276 Reprinted by permission of HarperCollins Publishers from *The Pursuit of Power: Venetian Ambassador's Reports* by James C. Davis, ed., trans., 156-57, 159-60, 162-66. English translation copyright © 1970 by James C. Davis.

280 Reprinted by permission of Yale University Press (www.yale.edu/yup) from *Hernan Cortez: Letters from Mexico*, ed. Anthony Pagden. © 1986 Yale University Press.

284 *King Charles V. The New Laws of the Indies for the Good Treatment and Preservation of the Indians* (New York: AMS Press, 1971), xii-xix, 542-43.